The Book of Earth

Also by Steven Forrest

The Inner Sky

The Changing Sky

The Night Speaks

The Book of Pluto

Measuring the Night (with Jeffrey Wolf Green)

Measuring the Night Vol. 2 (with Jeffrey Wolf Green)

Stalking Anubis

Skymates (with Jodie Forrest)

Skymates II (with Jodie Forrest)

Yesterday's Sky

The Book of the Moon

The Book of Neptune

The Book of Fire

The Book of Earth

Making It Real

by Steven Forrest

Seven Paws Press, Inc.
Borrego Springs, CA

Published in 2019 by Seven Paws Press, Inc.
PO Box 82
Borrego Springs, CA 92004
www.sevenpaws.com

Copyright © 2019 by Steven Forrest

All rights reserved. No part of this publication may be reproduced or
transmitted in any form or by any means, electronic or mechanical,
including mimeographing, recording, taping, scanning, via Internet
download, or by any information storage and retrieval systems, without
permission in writing from Seven Paws Press, Inc.
Reviewers may quote brief passages.

ISBN 978-1-939510-04-4

Cover art by Diren Yardimli

Printed in the United States of America
LCCN 2019950659

ACKNOWLEDGMENTS

Deep gratitude to my friend, student, and benefactor, Rafael Nasser, both for writing the Foreword to this volume of my Elements series and for his financial support. He bought me the precious time I needed in order to write this book. Thank you, Rafi.

Once again, my gratitude to my manager, web-wizard, and friend, Tony Howard. He has built the digital bridge that connects my work to the wider world. Without him, I would still be singing in a canyon that refused to echo.

Even though this book was truly *written* rather than simply transcribed from talks, it was an enormous help to be able to refer to a transcript of my original "Earth" program, offered back in May, 2016, at my bi-annual Apprenticeship Program meeting in Alpine, California. For the painstaking, tedious work of producing that transcript, I thank my student, JoAnn Anderson. My gratitude also to my editor Shelley Madsen for skillfully removing grammatical egg from my face before anyone could see it.

A profound thank you to the people who have run my various Apprenticeship Programs around the world over the years. The workload is enormous and I wouldn't have had the patience to do it myself. Here are their names in lights, in no particular order. In southern California, Ingrid Coffin and her team at the Blue Sky Ranch Fellowship, with special thanks there to Cristina Smith, Jonathan Sacks, Paula Wansley, and Carey Nash. In China, Felicia Jiang and David Railey, along with the amazing No-Door team. In North Carolina, Kathy Hallen and her able assistants, Carol McLauren and Tricia Mickleberry. In Nelson Bay, Australia, and various places around Europe, the indomitable Mercurial Connections team, Lisa Jones and Christine Murfitt. Finally, in northern California, I thank Joyce Van Horn, Kathy Jacobson, and Deni Mateer. My Apprenticeship Programs have come and gone, as have the people who have made them possible. Thanks, *emeritus*, to Karen Davis, Vinessa Nevala, Barbara King, and the late David Friedman.

Finally my gratitude to the following people who were actively engaged with me in various ways during the writing process: Scott Ainslie, Virginia Bell, Cheryl Benedict, Gail Boulton, Catie Cadge, Matt Cohen, Chip Conley, Cui "Chloe" Ying—my intrepid Chinese translator, Carol Czeczot, Rona Elliot and Roger Brossy, Michael Faith, Hadley Fitzgerald, Rishi Giovanni Gatti, Robert and Diana Griffin, the Grossenbacher clan: John, Tracy, and Ryan, Susie Latimer Hodge, Sylvia Hsiao, Barış İlhan, Bill Janis, Kelly Jean, Robert A. Johnson, Mark Jones, Kathy King, Peter and Ingrid Kondos, Lisa Kostova, Kate and Alex Laird, Jackie Larsen, Rick Levine, Elizabeth Long, Ralph MacIntyre, Barbara Matson, Mary Ann McGuire, Kym and Scott McNabb, Cristin McVey, Randy Meeks, Linnea Mirron and Ricky Williams, Dominic Miller, Jim Mullaney, Brian O'Flynn, Annette O'Neill, Marie O'Neill, Nina Ortega and Miguel Bracho, Carol Peebles, Jeff Parrett, Joey Paynter, Steven Poster and Susan Williams, Aminah Raheem and Fritz Smith, Claire Rauwel, Dusty Recor and "Indian Joe" Stewart, Ray Ristorcelli, Evelyn Roberts, Paige Ruane and Jack McDonald, Fran Slavich, Sting and Trudie Sumner-Styler, Tem Tarriktar, Kay Taylor, Elaine and Mark Thomas, Julia Trawick, Jaan Uhelszki, Dick and Artemisa Walker, and Helen Zou.

And thanks to my life-partner Michelle Kondos for her love, her innate sanity, and for helping me feel younger than cold mathematics might suggest—not to mention for filling our home with luminous oil paintings worthy of the finest art museums in the world.

TABLE OF CONTENTS

PART THREE: VENUS, MERCURY, AND SATURN THROUGH THE TWELVE SIGNS AND HOUSES

PART FOUR: SEEING POSSIBLE FUTURES

For embodying every perfection of his six planets in Virgo and for
a decade and a half of competent support and wise counsel,
I gratefully dedicate this book to my friend and manager, Tony Howard.

FOREWORD

When Steven Forrest invited me to write the foreword to *The Book of Earth*, I drew a blank. How do I honor a man whose brilliance shaped my mind so profoundly and whose astrological fingerprints scatter across so many of my life-defining decisions? As I contemplated this question one evening, gazing over the illustration of Dante Alighieri's depiction of the highest heaven—*The Empyrean*—that hangs in my home, an answer came to me.

As most of us know, Dante is the author of *The Divine Comedy*, a 14th Century allegorical journey that tracks the metaphysical journey of the protagonist, also named Dante. He is a middle-aged man who is lost and yearning for higher meaning. He meets a guide who agrees to accompany him on a journey to the topmost realm of creation. When they finally reach the highest heaven, Dante perceives a radiance of divine light surrounded by concentric circles of angels and exalted spirits blissfully immersed in a state of perfect peace.

I was lost in this image, blurry-eyed, with recollections of Steven streaming through the river of my mind, when a vision emerged. Dante's mandala of light morphed into a luminous astrological wheel and, I saw, Steve's face aglow contemplating the radiant symbols as angelic intuitions resonated through the shimmering glyphs.

The vision lingered, and as I reflected on its significance, I realized that every astrological reading I have had from Steven over the past three decades radiated a similar aura of higher wisdom. In Steve's hands, a birth chart becomes a magical tool that opens up a circle of sacred space and sacred time. Inside that circle, profound changes take place. As he begins a reading, the room seems to fill with benevolent energy. I feel safe. My ego dissolves, my mind expands. As I become receptive to his artfully-crafted imagery and words, my tectonic plates shift.

I can't prove that Steven's astrology is rooted to a higher sphere of knowledge, but it sure feels that way.

Comedy, in the literary sense of the word, refers to a story that begins badly and ends well. That is in distinction to *tragedy* which is the opposite: it begins well and ends poorly. The kinds of astrological readings I had experienced prior to meeting Steve were usually "tragic" narratives. They were dominated by references to an onslaught of impersonal planetary forces sweeping me involuntarily like driftwood tossed by the high seas.

Steven's readings were different. His interpretation of the symbols veered into "comedy"—again, in the literary sense of that word. Under his guidance, any astrological dynamic, no matter how challenging, becomes an opportunity to transform the present moment into a meaningful choice. The premise underlying each interpretative step of his work is that a life that aligns consciously with the birthchart symbolism is filled with meaning and purpose, despite any scars and bruises the journey might entail.

Those bruises and scars don't disappear. Fundamental to Steven's astrological worldview is the notion that the unresolved traumas of previous lifetimes set up the learning experiences for this one. Your birth chart, in other words, is an *effect* that derives from *causes* that predate your birth. Steven's readings thus stretch beyond the here-and-now. His vision of the way astrology works extends deeply into metaphysical territory. A reading transports us back to circumstances that defined us—and wounded us—in a previous lifetime. In this lifetime, we are ready to heal them. Whether you really were a nihilistic pickpocket in ancient Baghdad or a defenseless monk who perished in a Viking raid is besides the point. Steven's astrology is symbolic, not literal. His stories are *truthful*, rather than "factual," as he always says loudly and clearly. Their purpose is to heal the psyche and orient the soul towards meaningful action, not to clutter the head with more information. Steven does not predict events: he describes archetypal attitudes that underlie the synchronicities that shape our present destinies.

As I meditated further on my vision, I realized that Steven's and Dante's work share the same deep structure. Dante's journey begins with a vertiginous descent through the ten circles of the Inferno, where he encounters beings burning and freezing—we might say, "burning and freezing in the karmic results of their disastrous responses to previous transits and progressions." The Inferno is populated by souls who intentionally transgressed relative to the expression of the planetary forces and archetypes. In his allegorical journey, Dante encounters "Venusian types" who indulged in flighty pleasures of the flesh, "Solar" maniacs who abused power in the pursuit of self aggrandizement—and worst of all, backstabbing "Plutonian" malefactors who justly spend eternity in the fetid company of the Big Bad Dude that rules the sulfuric netherworld.

Steven always acknowledges the potentially-tragic power of "the shadow." He does not shy away from exposing the dismal moral chasms and evolutionary dead-ends that are scattered across anyone's birth chart. But whereas astrologers often divide the pantheon of symbols into "good ones" and "bad ones," Steven considers each symbol to be potentially benevolent or malevolent—with mindful choice as the force that tilts the scales one way or the other.

More than once, I stood on the edge of making a very bad choice, and unwittingly inching myself toward one of Dante's infernal pits. More than once, I was saved by the wisdom underlying Steven's astrological counsel. On those occasions when I crossed the line into shadow territory, I was often able to backtrack before it was too late—again, thanks to Steven's admonitions echoing inside my head.

After their journey through the Inferno, Dante and his guide make their way back up to the surface, muddling up the footpath to Purgatory. Here they encounter mediocre souls that didn't do anything so terrible. They simply never lived up to their potential. In his work, Steven seems to recognize a similar footpath. His readings always warn against becoming the underachieving "couch potato" spending precious days glued to the television set. Or the procrastinating "closet artist" who creates a thousand clever excuses to avoid creating any real work.

Those are the kinds of souls who crowd Dante's vision of Purgatory—the could-have-beens who never were, the folks who never seriously considered their inner lives.

Over twenty years ago, my college roommate, Jon, had a reading with Steven. When I mentioned being invited to write this Foreword, he said, "Say hi to Steve! He probably doesn't remember me, but let him know that his reading changed my life!" Having polled a sizable sampling of friends who have had readings with Steven, I can attest to his ability to inspire them all to live lives which aimed beyond "Purgatory."

Back to Dante's narrative—and the map it supplies for Steven's work. At the summit of Purgatory, Dante and his guide reach *Earthly Paradise*, a.k.a the Garden of Eden. It is a pretty realm, but it is inhabited by well-intentioned, ignorant souls. Things kind of look good here—after all, innocence is inherently unblemished. But innocence is not quite the same as purity. It lacks inner striving and evolutionary drive. A shallow life governed by cosmetic values does not feed a soul the kind of experiences it needs for its evolution. Benign, superficial souls are not transgressors like those in Inferno, nor are they like the existential escape-artists populating Purgatory, but they lack the mark of inspired destiny.

If you're embodied but cannot yet "walk on water," chances are that you are here on earth to learn something. Steven's work assured me that I can evolve beyond any limiting perspective that might define my current condition, no matter how inured I am to the circumstances. If I am a shiny 60 watt bulb, I can become a brilliant 100 watt bulb. The evolutionary nature of Steven's astrology implies that even those of us leading copacetic lives in an idyllic "Garden of Eden" can do even better. If you play his readings backwards, you'll hear him whisper, "Don't settle for Paradise when you can ascend to Heaven."

The next leg of Dante's journey lofts him skyward towards the Heavens where he visits the planetary spheres in ascending order, starting with the Moon, and proceeding to Mercury, then Venus, Sun, Mars, Jupiter, Saturn, the Fixed Stars, and beyond. Heaven is populated by souls who honored their innate sense of purpose and fulfilled their destiny. In Steven's lingo, those are the souls who chose the high road, at least more often than not.

On the Moon, Dante encounters the *inconstant* folk who started, but never finished their serious soul work. On Mars, Dante encounters "holy warriors" who consciously and intentionally sacrificed their lives fighting for a noble cause. On Jupiter, he encounters powerful souls who devoted their lives to the pursuit of noble justice.

On each planetary sphere, in other words, Dante encounter souls whose biographies reflect the highest virtues of that planet.

A defining mark of Steven's style of astrology is his exquisite ability to discern the themes that stand out in a birth chart. My own chart is eminently Mercurial—and when Steve reads for me, I feel as though I'm being addressed by archetypal god himself. Steven has mastered the ability to shape a reading in language, imagery, and stories imbued with the very qualities he seeks to awaken and inspire in the soul of the client. This, to me, is one heavenly aspect of Steven's work. Maybe you need permission from the cosmos to pursue rugged adventure, stoic mysticism—or to just allow yourself to be hugged. Maybe you've been waiting lifetimes to own that experience.

For me personally, Steven's most liberating words were, "Your soul is here to explore consciousness itself." That one sentence totally diverted my life path. At some point in a Steven Forrest reading, the sky will part, a ray of light will flood the room and Steve will deliver the perfect sentence, sending your soul straight to heaven.

Back to Dante. Beyond the Fixed Stars abides the *Empyrean*—the abode of God. This is the image that hangs on my wall, the one I was contemplating that evening when inspiration struck me about how I was going to write this foreword. Here, Dante beholds divinity and attains the Beatific Vision of the ineffable goodness of God. Taking a step back, he attempts to capture his experience in words. Still shimmering in the afterglow, he struggles and ultimately likens the Empyrean to an enormous blooming rose of unblemished perfection, surrounded by "petals" who are exalted souls and angels fluttering like bees, carrying the ambrosia of Grace.

I gazed at the wall-hanging, eyes soft and unfocused, and a new vision emerged. I saw the bright face of Steven Forrest wedged between a pair of angel wings. He was flashing a sagacious smile, and I could almost swear that he nodded and winked. I blinked and Steve was gone.

Encountering Steven's work at a young age was a blessing. As a twenty-three year old, green-eared Virgo who knew little about astrology, I signed up for a reading. Back then he lived in North Carolina and a reading cost $135 and it took only three weeks to receive it. I recall slipping the tape-cassette into the player and clicking Play. Steve's voice is not your everyday voice. He entranced me. His evocative imagery captured my attention and the door of my imagination swung wide open. All of this happened three sentences into the reading—and from that point on, the *shakti*-field only got stronger. Steve created a symphony of meaning that resonated across the entire spectrum of my being. He gonged my soul. Steve's timeless words reverberate even now as I write these words.

My natal reading inspired me so deeply that I became a student. I bought every Steven Forrest recording and read every word he wrote. Eventually I became an apprentice and attended his workshops. I learned to translate a bramble of ink blots into a meaningful and inspiring tapestry of meaning. Best of all, I was able to make a difference in the lives of others by sharing astrological insights. Someone offers you a fancy watch as a gift, and you say thank you. What do you say to someone who offers you a taste of Heaven? The appropriate response is hands in prayer position and a bow of reverence.

When Steven announced that he was planning a legacy project that consisted of four books, each devoted to one of the four elements, I banged the table and yelped in gladness. I felt compelled to support this initiative as a token of appreciation. In return, he unexpectedly offered me to write the Foreword to *The Book of Earth*. *The Book of Fire* had already been spoken for, and since my birth chart abounds in Earth and lacks Fire, becoming involved with this project made a lot of synchronistic sense.

The Book of Earth, like all of Steven's other books is destined to become a classic. It is saturated with wisdom and insight. It will refine your understanding of astrology and yourself, whoever you are, whenever you read it. Steven speaks the language of timeless archetypes and reveals deep and unwavering human truths that will remain relevant into the far-flung future. I imagine astrologers in the year 2500 exploring the millennial astrological classics and encountering the work of Maestro Forrest. Perhaps a few of those astrologer-explorers may even read these words.

And if you do, I'm directing this Foreword to you . . .

Should you stumble upon this book, know that the man who wrote *The Book of Earth* is no ordinary astrologer. He imbued his teachings with impeccable heart and unrivaled clarity. His insights will gong your soul. And as you immerse your consciousness in his work and lose yourself in its depths, perhaps you too will glimpse Divinity winking at you through his words.

Keep his work alive, humanity still needs it.

—Rafael Nasser
Author, *Under One Sky*

1

MAKING IT REAL

Spirit and Flesh—an ancient marriage or an ancient argument? The first premise, that it is an ancient marriage, is beyond debate. Just look in the mirror. There's your evidence. Something deep and luminous inside of you is beholding that reflection, and it's contemplating it through the eyes of a primate.

Spirit and skin are indubitably married—and reflecting on the prospect of their inevitable, eventual divorce is a famously productive meditation.

What about spirit's *argument* with the flesh? That's an ancient notion too, and it's uniquely human—cats and walruses do not seem to be bothered by it. We see the anti-flesh argument in many aspects of life and culture, but it has often been formally institutionalized in religious doctrine. So many of the world's holy books have taught that the body—and, really, the entire physical world—is the mortal enemy of spirit.

More about that venomous lie in a moment, but fear not: in *The Book of Earth* we will come down on the opposite side of that debate. We will see "the flesh"—and "flesh" is central to any human understanding of the Earth element—simply as the place where spirit potentially comes into actual manifestation.

In the New Testament of the Bible, in the fifth chapter of *Galatians*, St. Paul tells us, "For the desires of the flesh are against the Spirit, and the desires of the Spirit are against the flesh."

That's a pretty clear message not to trust your body . . . but not so fast—before we bash the Bible or fall on our knees before it, here's the 14th verse of the Gospel of *John*: "And the Word became flesh and dwelt among us, full of grace and truth."

So, according to Paul, spirit and flesh are irreconcilable antagonists, while according to John, spirit can actually become flesh and remain pure and unsullied.

Hey, Bible, which side of this argument are you on?

I did a lot of academic Bible study many years ago when I got my Bachelor's degree in Religion at the University of North Carolina. And I do mean "academic"—this was a non-sectarian education, not preparation for the Ministry or anything like that. After that college experience, I came away with the realization that, on many subjects, the Bible does not speak with one single voice. It was written over a millennium or two by a lot of different people representing a lot of different cultures and traditions. The marriage of spirit and flesh is a very tricky theological subject. Basically, the Bible is a compendium of all the arguments.

The religions of the East show a similar ambivalence about spirit and flesh. The body is seen with a mixture of revulsion (it is a trap for the soul) and glory (it is a possible vehicle of liberation.) Take the traditional Buddhist meditation practice called *paikkula-manasikara*, usually translated to mean "reflections on repulsiveness." You focus on thirty-one body parts, one at a time, reflecting on a feast of graphic adjectives regarding their "impurities"—body hair, tendons, bone marrow, kidneys, large intestines, small intestines, and so on. There's another practice, from the *Satipatthana Sutta*. This one is really not for the faint-hearted. If a monk sees the corpse of someone who has been dead for two or three days—swollen, blue and festering—he should think: *My own body is of the same nature; such it will become, and will not escape it . . .*

Neither of these practices are indicated for anyone with body-image issues.

And yet, paradoxically, out of that same Asian cultural soil, sprung the great tradition of yoga, so popular in the West now—and clearly a celebration of the physical body as a pathway to higher states of consciousness. Many of you readers have walked that path and have direct knowledge of its validity.

There, in the East, we find that same spirit-flesh ambivalence—very much like what we saw in the Bible.

Speaking of yoga, how many practitioners are doing their *asanas* there in class because of their zeal for spiritual evolution versus the number who are there in pursuit of a cute butt?

But, wait a minute here, Steve—where do you get the idea that there is some kind of natural opposition between the desire for enlightenment and the desire for a cute butt? Might they actually not be opposites at all?

How can I plead? Guilty!—and I am hoping for the jury's mercy on the basis of the fact that I grew up in churches, then moved on to Buddhism.

Unless you are sitting in a pew in a conservative church reading this book of heresies, St. Paul's words—*for the desires of the flesh are against the Spirit, and the desires of the Spirit are against the flesh*—probably ring false for you today. In contemporary society, we tend to *celebrate* the flesh. We, in fact, think of little else. Beautiful bodies are everywhere, at least in the media, driving everyone a little crazy with desire and comparison.

Opposites spark each other, eternally: along with the pervasive worship of beautiful bodies, we see the inevitable counter-current of *body-shaming*. It is everywhere too, and not just in the form of bullying. Every time you see one of those "beautiful bodies" on a billboard or in an advertisement, doesn't the message include a nasty little subliminal message about your own shape?

Pick one: a cute butt or enlightenment. Many people today are going to have give that choice some lengthy thought.

How many of us are content with our bodies? Not many! A *Psychology Today* study from the late 1990s found these results—which, I suspect, would be even more dispiriting were the study to be repeated today.

Fifty-six percent of women say they are dissatisfied with their overall appearance. Their self-disparagement is specifically directed toward their abdomens (71 percent), body weight (66 percent), hips (60 percent), and muscle tone (58 percent). Men show escalating dissatisfaction with their abdomens (63 percent), weight (52 percent), muscle tone (45 percent), overall appearance (43 percent), and chest (38 percent).

Several lines back, I quoted the Buddhist practice of *paikkula-mana-sikara*, where we are taught to sequentially shame thirty-one of our body parts. (And I know "sequential shaming" is not the term the guru would use, but that would be the result, at least for many people.) I chose that particular practice as an illustration partly for its very obscurity—to almost all of us, criticizing our bodies, limb by limb, organ by organ, seems alien and weird. And yet, as you read the *Psychology Today* results I just quoted, can you see how many modern humans are busily engaged with their own version of *exactly the same practice?* Every day, they silently chant their mantra: "my butt is too big, I'm too soft in the middle, I suffer from thunder thighs, I'm a 98-pound weakling, my eyes are beady, I need a nose job, my sagging this, my sagging that, I hate my body, my body is not good enough . . ."

It is a short walk from there to, *"I am trapped in the flesh . . ."* We might as well be 11th century Benedictine flagellants "mortifying the flesh . . ."

Even today, *Paikkula-Manasikara* 'R' Us.

The point is that even though the argument—or alleged argument—between spirit and flesh sounds antiquarian when we use Bible verses to illustrate it, the debate is alive and well today—and perhaps more poisonous than ever. Even today, the denial and shaming of this face of the Earth element is the source of a tremendous amount of suffering in the world. And as we will soon see, the issue goes far, far beyond questions about our relationships with our physical bodies. Those body-questions illustrate the problem nicely though, so let me take them a little bit further.

Once, as a young astrologer in my early thirties, a woman had made an appointment to see me for a reading. Through mutual friends, I had learned that she had once been featured as a centerfold model in *Playboy* magazine. True to form, when I set up her chart in advance of our appointment, she had Venus conjunct her Ascendant in Pisces—she had to be a goddess, right?

Truth is, I was scared to see her—afraid that I would make a fool of myself by staring at her chest or asking her to marry me or something equally inept and goofy. When she knocked on the door, I was shocked by how normal she looked. I never saw her centerfold photo, but if I did, my guess is that I would not have recognized her in it. She was just a human being, attractive, but not supernaturally so.

The point is that these people whom we set up as physical ideals and against which we are supposed to judge our Earth-selves *do not actually exist at all*. They are idealized products of lighting, airbrushing, and Photoshop.

Strange as this might sound, *those images actually come from a higher realm*—they are archetypal ideals, in other words. Getting ahead of myself here, that does not mean that they are false—only that they originate in the pure domains of Fire, Air and Water, not in the grounded, warts-and-all, domain of Earth.

We can visualize them, but we can't really see them walking down the street.

I've never met film star Michelle Pfeiffer, but I am not alone in thinking that she is one of the most physically beautiful human beings who ever lived. I actually think I would like her personally too—and not so much for her physical charms as for this quote from a 1990 *People* magazine interview with her. "You know, I look like a duck. I just do . . . I should have played *Howard the Duck*."

Pfeiffer is a Taurus with a Virgo Moon—an Earth child, for sure. And, at least in her own mind, even she herself has not reached that fabled golden city of perfection . . .

And with that comment, we approach the heart of the matter we are exploring in this book:

The work of the Earth Family is the endless, impossible, noble, inescapable task of trying to bring that golden city down to earth—which is to say, making it real.

NOTHING IS EVER GOOD ENOUGH

We hear those words and they sound like whining. And I suppose they often are. They could easily emanate from the mouth of a complaining, chronically dissatisfied man or woman, moaning about some petty existential frustration—a delayed flight, for example, or an imperfect *soufflé*—while bloating the complaint into a dark cosmology in which he or she is always singled out by a demonic god for particular vexation.

And yet there is an absolutely fundamental truth about human existence built into those hard words. Indeed, nothing is "ever good enough." We earth-monkeys had better get used to it.

Here is an illustration of what I mean:

Back in the summer of 1981, on the strength of a sample chapter, an outline, and a nice Jupiter transit, I got the contract to write *The Inner Sky* for Bantam Books. I was thirty-two years old, and hungry, and the deal was about as welcome as the first sip of beer after a hard day's work in July. As early discussions about the direction of the book unfolded, I was told in no uncertain terms that I should minimize my use of the word "soul" in the manuscript—that "modern readers would be put off by such churchy words." (Thomas Moore's #1 New York Times bestseller, *The Care of the Soul*, was still a decade in the future at this point.) I mostly complied. I completed the book within the linguistic parameters my editor required. The book was published and it did well.

I am still proud of *The Inner Sky*, but it was not exactly the book I wanted to write. Left to my own devices, it would have been more unabashedly metaphysical.

At this point, I am honestly not sure whether that would have made it a better book or not. Over the years, I have learned to appreciate skillful editorial suggestions. But my point is that the *idea* of *The Inner Sky* and the *actual reality* of its printed incarnation were not the same. The book fell short of the particular version of "good enough" that I had in my mind.

They say that "a camel is a horse designed by a committee."

Well, everything is.

As ideals strive to become realities—as, in other words, *the higher realms strive to express themselves through the Earth element*—they always meet resistance. They encounter obstacles, people with opposing ideas, budgetary constraints, enemies, and practical limitations. They are compelled to make deals—or to die of their own intransigent idealism.

Compromise is no one's favorite word, and yet without it, nothing ever happens.

Welcome to the planet Earth.

PERFECT IS THE ENEMY OF GOOD ENOUGH

I first heard that line from a software developer. I wasn't sure if he was a fountain of practical wisdom, or a slippery guy trying to evade responsibility for a buggy computer program.

In his defense, it is fair to say that trying to make anything "perfect" can lead us down an endless road in which nothing is ever completed. Actually to do anything real in this world involves the distinctly Earth Family process of climbing down from the ivory tower and dirtying our hands. We must accept imperfection as a fundamental feature of the material world. And as they say in aviation, "any landing you can walk away from is a good landing."

But do you really want your airline pilot thinking that way?
There's that ambiguity again.

At first hearing, I thought that "perfect is the enemy of good enough" was some kind of modern Silicon Valley proverb. Turns out, Google tells me that it's an old Italian saying from not later than the 18th century, and probably much earlier—*Le meglio è l'inimico del bene*. Human beings, I suspect, have faced this very real—and very Earth-sign—dilemma since the beginning of time. It's not an easy one to work out. Dogmatic idealists inevitably crash and burn. In 1968, the Rolling Stones sang, "Hey, think the time is right for a palace revolution, but where I live the game to play is compromise solution." They were whining—but ask anyone: half a century later, "compromise solution" is still the game to play if you want to get anything done in politics.

And elsewhere.

This coin has two sides. What I've written so far is the grown-up, eat-your-spinach, side of the Earth sign argument. "Perfect" doesn't ever happen, so get used to it. Get real. Make your best deal. Quit your whining. We might even call this "Flesh's" side of the argument—or the World's side.

Here's Spirit's side:

At some point, you have got to make your stand. At some point, you need to just take your best shot. Compromise can go too far; you can give up too much, make so many deals that somewhere along the way, your soul got lost. You need a dream—but then you face the Earth sign challenge: you have got to make the dream real, working on one hand, with the street-realities of the world, and on the other hand, *with not losing sight of the essence of what you are living for.*

Some things cannot be compromised, ever.

There is nothing emptier or more futile than a life lived without a dream or a vision. But there is nothing sadder than a dream that didn't . . . hmmmm . . . I almost wrote "have the courage to make its stand." But "courage" is really more of a Fire sign issue. Here, in the realm of Earth, let me say it with more realism and less bombast. There is nothing sadder than a dream that didn't *negotiate* effectively, fiercely—and even cunningly, if necessary—with that old demon we call "reality."

As you will see in the pages that follow, the three Earth signs and their associated planets and astrological houses provide the map for those delicate, morally treacherous, negotiations. Your life depends on getting them right.

Before we get there, let me take a quick loop through exactly where this chapter began.

SPIRIT, FLESH, AND ASTROLOGY

Spirit and Flesh—an ancient marriage or an ancient argument? And how does astrology itself fit into that debate? Modern psychological astrology often operates as does modern psychology—without any overt spiritual basis at all.

As if sanity were even possible without a spiritual life of some sort.

As if being "real" and being "spiritual" were opposites.

As if we were not luminous beings in a dreamlike universe on an incredible, incomprehensible journey.

That's my sermon. I'll spare you the rest of it. If you're interested, check out *The Book of Neptune.* I assume the pulpit at greater length there.

For most of its long history, astrology has always been embedded in larger metaphysical contexts. In my opinion, that approach is healthier than the alternative—but of course the health of the metaphysical contexts themselves bears mightily upon the issue. Earlier in this chapter, we saw evidence of the ambiguity in Eastern and Western spiritual traditions toward the relationship of spirit and flesh—or, to put it more broadly, the relationship between idealism and manifestation. That same ambiguity runs through astrological traditions as well.

As we saw a few pages ago, generally the major religious traditions of the world reflect a deep suspicion regarding the flesh, "this world," and the tempting perils of incarnation. To understand the mysteries of the Earth element, we must part that veil. *We must see this imperfect world as a manifestation of something higher.*

Regarding the three Earth signs, astrologers have not always succeeded in doing that any more than have the theologians.

I step out on thin ice here. I want to quote a Boston astrologer, now deceased. I want to do so critically, but without dishonoring her. She was a Leo, born in 1903, on the cusp of the Age of Aquarius. Her name was Isabel M. Hickey. She wrote the seminal *Astrology: A Cosmic Science.* She did much to bring spiritual perspectives back into then-contemporary astrological practice. For that work I am grateful. To some extent, I am standing on her shoulders—and by that, I am humbled. She was also friends with my own soul-mother and my first true spiritual teacher, Marian Starnes, to whose memory I dedicated *The Book of Fire.*

So I tread carefully here, knowing that Isabel Hickey's vision was shaped by the times in which she lived, as my own vision certainly is. Yours too.

Quoting from *Astrology: A Cosmic Science:*

Earth signs are physical and have to do with purely material affairs. They are the practical and stolid signs that represent the earthly field in which the personality is planted. The keynote for the earth signs is 'practicality.'

. . . If there are many planets in Earth signs the person puts too much emphasis on material things and he has to attain a truer sense of values.

Much astrology prior to recent times is far too rigid for my tastes. In broad terms, Hickey very obviously illustrates that limitation here. The old astrologers typically put people in neat little boxes labeled "your fate" or "your nature."

The problem with that way of thinking is that people actually do sometimes grow and change; I celebrate that. That is ultimately why I call the work I do "evolutionary astrology"—simply because it is about helping people to evolve.

That said, Isabel M. Hickey rightly nails what I would call the *shadow* of the Earth Family—people born under its influence can indeed get so caught up in the "fuss" of life that they foolishly miss any larger point to it all, or any meaning in it.

But that is just the dark side of the picture. While it is healthy to keep one eye on it, still something fundamental is missing in what Hickey writes. The Earth signs represent a sacred, spiritual path, every bit as holy as the paths of Fire, Air, and Water. *Earth is about making spirit visible.* It is about bringing ideals and visions "down to earth." It is about making them real.

Do you have many planets in Earth signs? You have come to this planet *actually to do something.* You have a task. We might call it your mission. And, unlike a monk meditating in a cave, if you succeed, there will be visible evidence of your success.

Perspective: let's honor all the mystics who lived and died in those caves, doing purely inner work. Let's honor the poets whose poems were never spoken, the composers whose music was never heard, the novelists whose work never saw the printed page. Inner accomplishments, invisible to this world, live on in the transcendent realms.

But if you are "earthy," that kind of ghostly invisibility is not your path. Your spiritual playground—or schoolhouse—in this incarnation lies in rearranging the atoms and molecules of this imperfect world. You are here to leave a mark. There is no need for grandiosity—your mark can be humble, even mostly unnoticed by the world at large. No problem—so long as you have taken an inner vision and made it real. You actually wrote the book, even if it didn't get published. You raised a sane family, warts and all, and you still love each other after all these years. You won't lie on your death-bed thinking, "I missed my shot"—even if you failed, you at least know that you *took* the shot.

A dear friend of mine is a big fan of the wonderful Russell Crowe film, *Gladiator.* She must have had a past life in the Roman Empire. She's got the movie poster on her wall. On it are the words, *What We Do in Life Echoes in Eternity.*

That's the Earth-path, in eight muscular words. Following that path will take everything you've got—and it will give imperfect expression to a part of what you actually, transcendently, are. And "imperfect" is good enough. It is difficult, like climbing a mountain. But how can you find a mountain worthy of that extravagant expenditure of energy, discipline and commitment?

What if you were to climb the wrong mountain? The Earth symbolism in your birthchart answers those questions quite definitively.

Read on. It's time to name your mountain, to learn how to find it inside yourself, and to pick up the mountaineering skills you are going to need to reach the summit.

2

THE GRAND SCHEME

Meet the Earth Family's Holy Trinity: Taurus the Bull. Virgo the Virgin. Capricorn the Sea-Goat. Each of these metaphors comes pre-loaded with confusion. To understand, there are veils we must part . . .

* The first one is a creature regarding which the Spanish custom of the bullfight has hopelessly confounded our understanding. We often now think of bulls as fire-breathing carnivores hell-bent on mayhem. In understanding Taurus, it is helpful to recall that bulls are male cows, fairly placid creatures until you start sticking them with *banderillas*.

* The second—the Virgin—is an anachronism nowadays: as a culture, few of us any longer have a reflexively positive attitude toward simple sexual inexperience, as if we automatically "lost virtue" the first time we ever loved someone with our bodies.

* And finally: a Sea-Goat? Half fish and half mountain goat? To say the least, that is a very queer piece of biological engineering.

Some serious decoding obviously lies ahead for us. As we will see, each of these mysterious faces of the Earth element represents a critical ingredient in the process of *sacred manifestation,* which is the essence of our subject in this book..

The Book of Earth is not only about Taurus, Virgo and Capricorn—it is also about the trio of planets that rule those signs: Venus, Mercury, and

Saturn, respectively. As we will see, those three bodies just carry different expressions of essentially the same energies that we see in the signs they rule.

And then there are the three "Earth" houses—although for fear of total confusion, astrologers generally do not usually use that term. These are houses two, six, and ten—resonating of course with Taurus being the second sign of the Zodiac, Virgo the sixth, and Capricorn the tenth.

The Earth Family is thus composed of *nine members*: a trio of signs, a trio of planets, and a trio of houses. Each one is distinct, just as are the members of your own blood-family. But, like your family, we might recognize a certain crook of the nose or spacing of the eyes that marks you as "a Kelly" or a "Sanchez." Again like a family—or at least like any functional one—each of these symbols is appreciated for possessing certain areas of necessary skill or expertise, areas where other family members might be deficient. We shouldn't trust spacey Tracy with figuring out the taxes—that's Hayley's bailiwick.

But Tracy sure can cook.

Actually to succeed in *doing what you have truly been born to do* . . . (that is to say, to manifest it, to make it real, with no excuses) . . . you need all nine of these family members. Each one needs to pull its own weight, with each one operating in its own recognized area of expertise. Together, these nine symbols can potentially become an efficient team—an interdependent whole—capable of accomplishing . . . well, *anything* . . .

. . . but "anything" is too vague a word for our individual human purposes. Life is not long enough for any of us to do everything. That practical attitude—an acknowledgment of reality and its inherent limitations, along with keeping one eye on life's brevity—is in the very bone marrow of all nine Earth symbols. They focus. They set priorities. They make the tough choices. They drive hard bargains. They commit to excellence on a particular path—and in so doing, they turn their backs on other paths, even if those other paths are worthy ones.

Illustration: let's say you want to do a good job of being married. Here's an Earth-sign tip: choose a partner—and don't forget that you are married to him or her no matter how worthy, spiritual, sexy, and compatible someone else might seem.

Illustration: How do you get to Carnegie Hall from here? *Practice, practice, practice* . . .

Easy?

Well, easy to *understand* . . . but maybe not so easy, actually to do.

And "actually doing it" is what the Earth family is all about.

STEVE'S VERY EARTH-SIGN DILEMMA

Signs, planets, and houses interlock. They depend on each other. If one fails, all of them suffer. If one excels, all of them are uplifted. But they are different beasts. Crystalline clarity in astrological analysis depends upon keeping their differences straight.

And now a word from our sponsors . . .

Please buy *The Book of Fire*. And, once they are written, please buy *The Book of Air* and *The Book of Water* too. My cats need cat food. My mortgage broker is counting on you. But more seriously, this series of four books is really one single work spread over four volumes. I am really trying to accomplish two things at once: I want each book to stand alone as a complete work, and I also want to present an integrated, evolutionary approach to the entire basic vocabulary of astrology.

Trying to cover both of these bases leads inevitably to some repetition—for example,I will introduce the idea of astrological aspects in each volume. At the same time, I don't want the books to become annoyingly repetitive. Resolving that dilemma entails my making a lot of "Earthy" judgment calls about what to repeat and what to leave out.

My immediate intention here over the next few pages is to clarify the distinctions among signs, planets, and houses. But I already did that once, back in chapter two of *The Book of Fire*, "Astrology's Holy Trinity: Signs, Planets, and Houses."

What should I do? I could copy/paste that whole chapter here . . . but many of you have already read it in the earlier volume . . . should I make you buy the same thing twice, in other words?

Not fair!

But somewhere there is a pecunious Taurus with no Fire planets at all and who therefore didn't want to waste money buying *The Book of Fire*. Should I leave that person to wobble, twist, and gyre in the winds of his self-imposed ignorance? Should I leave him not understanding that signs, planets and houses are *not* interchangeable?

That is not right either.

Damned if I do, and damned if I don't, in other words—which is not the most original dilemma in the world. Those words are familiar to us all because the *situation itself* is so familiar. We have all been there, dealing with that very Earth-sign imbroglio: *compromise.*

Normally I would not burden a book with these kinds of ruminations. As the author, it's my job to cut to the chase. But here I couldn't resist some "thinking out loud" *because these kinds of impossible questions in an imperfect world are the very essence of the Earth Family.* My dilemma illustrates exactly the kinds of issues with which we will be wrestling throughout this book.

So, cutting (finally) to the chase, here's what I'm going to do: I will *make a deal.* I will write a few brief, telegraphic paragraphs about how to distinguish signs from houses, and how planets fit into the big picture. Then I will tell everyone to look to *The Book of Fire* if they want a deeper understanding of the issue, along with some further practical illustrations.

I will do something similar later in this volume when we get to the chapter regarding astrological aspects—which again are covered in more detail in the first volume of this series.

My problems are compounded though. There's more compromise ahead. Planet-wise, in *The Book of Fire* we dived deeply into Mars, the Sun, and Jupiter. Here, in *The Book of Earth*, we similarly get to know Venus, Mercury, and Saturn. No repetition, no problem—not yet. But in *The Book of Air*, Mercury and Venus will again appear. What should I do? Leave them out or repeat them?

For the sake of completeness and easy reference, I will repeat the "cookbook" (sign by sign, house by house) thumbnail descriptions from this Earth volume in that later Air volume. Similarly, Mars and Jupiter will make a second appearance in *The Book of Water.*

The Air sign Aquarius must of course figure in *The Book of Air.* Experience compels me to accept the dual rulership of that sign, however, so I will introduce the planet Uranus in that third volume of this series—but I will also repeat the Saturn "cookbook" sections you will soon be reading in these pages. Saturn rules Aquarius as well as Capricorn—something modern astrologers forget only to their peril.

I will face similar conundrums with Pluto and Neptune, and I will handle them in the same way.

And so, in Earth-fashion, we muddle onward in this imperfect physical realm, making our best deals, doing our best.

The controversial Buddhist teacher, Chogyam Trungpa Rinpoche, was once asked what he thought of this world—*Samsara*, as its called in the Tibetan cosmology. He gave a very Earth-sign response. He simply said, "It's workable."

Fittingly, Chogyam Trungpa had planets in all three of the Earth signs.

KEEPING SIGNS, PLANETS AND HOUSES STRAIGHT

We are our signs and we do our houses. Signs represent values, motivations, attitudes, and psychological agendas, while houses represent areas of life where we make concrete decisions and deal with circumstances as they present themselves. Houses are where we face the concrete effects of synchronicity, in other words.

Suzy has been married seven times and she's thinking about marriage number eight. *Is she an introvert or an extrovert?* You can't answer that question. That's because I gave you *house* information, then asked you a *sign* question. I told you about her circumstances, then asked you about her nature.

John is a studious, bookish sort of person who avoids chit-chat, but enjoys a long, deep conversation with an intellectual equal. *Do you think he should move to Panama?* Again we hit a brick wall. You can't answer a house question based on sign information.

When we think about the astrology of romantic relationships, we might hear a line such as this: "one of them is a Gemini and the other one is a Pisces, so I don't know . . ."

I wouldn't jinx anyone's intimate life with that kind of mechanical astrology, but Gemini and Pisces are square to each other and there will definitely need to be some "meeting in the middle" if these two lovebirds are going to stay in the same nest. Putting their energies together will generate a certain amount of "thinking vs. feeling" friction.

But how often have you heard this line? *"One of them has the Sun in the third house and the other one has the Sun in the twelfth . . ."*

Never, right? That configuration might actually raise some legitimate astrological questions too—but we all know that love is really more about how two "energy bodies" get along than it is about more circumstantial questions.

That's sign stuff, not house material.

What about planets? They are the basic components of the psyche, sort of similar to the way "ego, id and superego" work together in the psychoanalytic model. We all for example have some *need to connect with other human beings*—an affiliative drive. In astrology, we label that drive "Venus." But your Venus and my Venus are probably very different. Maybe I love meeting new people, while you prefer a few familiar friends. Maybe I am naturally "the marrying type," while you are happier with more independence. The nature of the basic affiliative drive is quite variable from person to person, depending on what values motivate it (*that is to say, the sign Venus occupies*) and its natural style of behavioral expression, not to mention the synchronistic components of "fate" or circumstance—as revealed by Venus's *house* position.

Throw in some knowledge of astrological aspects, plus the lunar nodes, and these last four hundred words really represent the practical essence of our craft. The combo platter of a planet in a sign and a house is the essential quantum of astrological analysis.

* The first step toward astrological mastery lies in learning to understand any such triad as one integrated psychic reality.
* The second step lies in putting ten or so of them together in one coherent, interactive package.

It might take you a few years to accomplish that. So does medical school. So does learning how to write a good novel. So does reaping the fruits of following any worthy spiritual path.

THE GRAND SCHEME

There are only nine words in the Earth Family vocabulary: that might trick us into thinking that it is an easy language to learn. Most of us can pick up nine words in a foreign language if we have a two-week vacation somewhere. The trouble is, astrological "words" are very different from English words—or French or Chinese ones. Their range of possible meanings is far vaster. Words always divide the universe into little boxes, each with a label. Scissors. Car. Genius. Moron. Astrology has far fewer words—so if we are going to use it to describe the universe, each "box" has to be a whole lot bigger.

What does Taurus mean? Well, for starters, bulls, literally . . . and cows too, of course. And nature in general. And music. And massage. And money—which quickly devolves into food and shelter, not to mention bills and banking and credit cards. Trees are on the list, along with comfy quilts and cuddling up with your sweetheart . . .

I could fill the rest of these pages with "what Taurus means" and I might still not have gotten to page 4267, where we begin the "Taurus psychology" section.

So: there are just nine words to learn, but they are really big words.

Before we are done, we will make a serious attempt to at least scratch the surface of each of these symbols. That's about as far as we will be able to delve within the space limits of any book of reasonable length. In fact, wrestling with that reality is what led me to realize that it would take me four volumes rather than one to cover the astrological Elements in anything approaching the depth they deserve.

In the next chapter, we will begin by exploring "The Taurus Clan" in detail. That will mean not only taking a deep look at the sign Taurus, but also a journey into the heart of Venus and the second house. In chapters four and five, we will do the same for Virgo and Capricorn.

When it comes to details, you will soon be drinking from the proverbial fire hose.

But before we get there, let's sit on the mountaintop and take in the view. We got a taste of the broad meaning of the whole Earth Family in the opening chapter: *all the challenges and joys of making something real or of turning a vision into reality.*

Our next step is a pivotal one: it is to realize that *underlying the triad of the three Earth signs, there is an interlocking, interdependent structure. A grand scheme.* If you can grasp it, most of the rest of the details emerge in logical fashion.

The general custom in astrological discourse is to acknowledge that the three Earth signs are bound together by a shared quality of "practicality"—then to launch into a fragmented recitation of personality traits associated separately with each one of them. It's a short step from there to shopping mall astrology, where "all the Tauruses live for their dinners, while Virgos excel at putting everything in alphabetical order for people who are more interesting than themselves. Meanwhile all Capricorns look plausible in business suits, but you wouldn't want to go to bed with one."

Hippocrates and Plato would cringe.

My aim in the next few paragraphs is to present as simply as I can the grand underlying scheme that binds Taurus, Virgo and Capricorn together in one unified, interdependent whole. Each one of them, as we will see, plays a critical—but very distinct—role in the Earthy process of turning visions into reality.

By the way, to keep all of this as clear as I possibly can, in what I am about to explore with you, I will avoid all references to planets and houses, and just stick to the three Earth signs themselves. As the book unfolds, you will see that those planets and houses have actually left their invisible fingerprints in all the words that follow.

* There are four *Cardinal* signs in astrology. Their job is to trigger things—to light the fuse, to make a beginning.
* There are four *Fixed* signs, whose job is to follow through, to sustain things, to hold their ground in the face of distorting pressures and challenges.
* Finally there are four *Mutable* signs. Their job is to adjust things to fit evolving circumstances—and, sometimes, to accept that ultimate adjustment: that it is a good day to die.

We begin our exploration of Earth's grand scheme with the sparkplug—the Cardinal expression of Earth energy: Capricorn the Sea-Goat.

Cardinality starts things, so that is where I will start too.

CAPRICORN

As we pointed out earlier, an actual Sea-Goat would be a very strange piece of biological engineering. Half fish and half goat: kind of a hopeless case—but not in the world of symbolism, where Capricorn represents *mastery*. That symbolic creature can "climb the highest mountain and swim the widest sea." Capricorn is about really sinking your teeth into something. It is about keeping your eye on the prize. It is about relentless, sustained self-discipline. It is about buying the famous "pearl of great price" for which we must be willing to sacrifice everything else. In a nutshell, Capricorn is about accomplishing your *Great Work*, whatever that term might mean for you. It could be something professional—but just as easily it could be learning to play Chopin *etudes* on the grand piano. Or raising a sane child. Or writing a novel.

Once Capricornian focus and discipline have "acquired a target," there is no stopping them.

But what if they have chosen the wrong target? Then Capricorn is an unguided missile. Gangster Al Capone was a Capricorn. So was disgraced U.S. president Richard Nixon. Without sane inspiration and a true fire in the belly, Capricorn becomes a malevolent machine.

TAURUS

Choosing the right target—that is where Taurus comes into the picture. Taurus is the Bull—but I prefer to describe it more simply and generally: Taurus the *Animal*. And we humans are animals too, of course—which means that we are born endowed with a formidable set of instincts: *things that we know without knowing how we know them.* Some of them are universal, such as caution around heights, fire, and rushing water. Other instincts are more personal—and closer to the heart of the point we are exploring here.

Illustration: if you are bonded in life with another human being, how did you choose that person? Logic? Of course not—reason may have been involved, but in the end, *love is a choice that the heart has to make.* By instinct, in other words. Ditto for whatever faith, goals, or values give personal meaning to your life—by what method did you discover them? Rational analysis? Again, I doubt it. *"Something inside you told you"* to explore Buddhism, or to grow roses, or to play the violin or to volunteer at the hospice.

None of these are logical processes. That is the point. They all lie in the realm of the *instinctual*—that orientation to life which arises naturally in the human heart. And such know-it-in-your-bones instinct is the essence of Taurus, the sign of our attunement to the inner animal.

There is a craft to letting ourselves be in touch with those instincts. There is an art to listening to message in the marrow of your bones. Not everyone is good at it—that is why people sometimes choose the wrong mate or the wrong profession.

Or the wrong mountain to climb . . .

See the interdependent connection of these Taurean "animal instinct" with the mighty engines of Capricorn? The Sea-Goat is a wonder when it comes to climbing mountains, but it depends on Taurus—the instinctual wisdom of the wise inner animal—to identify the right peak to scale. Without that connection to something ancient, primeval, and wise inside of us—something that transcends reason and logic—mere Capricorn is only a lost soul with a full schedule.

VIRGO

Let's say you have chosen your mountain correctly. Your better angels approve. Your heart has a good feeling about the whole thing.

So far, so good. Taurus: *check.*

You commit to actually climbing. You make a plan. You buy your mountaineering shoes and your airline tickets and off you go. You are really going to do it.

Capricorn: *check.*

(The "mountain" can of course be any Great Work that is worthy of you, but let's stick with the literal mountain metaphor for a while.)

Let's say that the mountain you have chosen to climb is Denali, the highest peak in North America at 20,310 feet—or 6190 meters, if you prefer to take your freezing to death, your dying by misadventure, or your expiration by asphyxiation and altitude sickness in the metric system.

Yikes, climbing Denali! Really? Are you completely nuts?

Climbing that mountain is a noble and very Capricornian goal—and let's say that your inner Taurus has actually prompted the decision, so you are grounded that way too. Good news: you have the seal of approval from your better angels.

But how do you actually, successfully get to the top of Denali?

To accomplish that, you need practical know-how. You need tools: ropes and crampons and a ice-ax—and the knowledge of how to use them. You will need snow goggles and probably an oxygen tank. You should probably write your Will too.

Above all, you need *instruction.* You need a *teacher* or *teachers*—people who have climbed mountains themselves and thus can *mentor* you in the learning process.

There is a long tradition of humans climbing mountains. There is a *lineage* of mountaineers, in other words. Take your rightful place in that lineage—and start where you belong, which is as a student.

Every word you have just read is right in the cross hairs of the sign Virgo.

Without Virgo skill, Capricorn falls off the mountain.

Without Virgo skill, Taurus never gets out of bed.

WHAT IF I HAVE NOTHING IN ONE OF THE EARTH SIGNS?

No planets in (pick one) Taurus, Virgo, or Capricorn? Does that mean you lack one of these three absolute essentials for actually getting things done in this world? No worry! That is where the houses and planets come into play—something we will be exploring in more detail later on. Briefly, you might have nothing in Capricorn—but you surely have Saturn somewhere in your chart. Saturn will help fill the Capricorn void. Furthermore, unless we are looking at Capricorn as an intercepted sign—that is to say, completely swallowed up by a particularly wide house—then the Sea-Goat makes an appearance by setting the tone of the house on whose cusp it appears.

Then there is of course a tenth house in your chart, which carries into the behavioral realm some of those "Capricornian" themes and possibilities.

Bottom line, *we all need all three of these primal Earth energies, but there is more than one way to get them.*

HYPOSYMBOLOSIS

Hypothermia means you lack heat. Well, humans shall not live by heat alone. We need symbols too.

That could be a long essay, but I will spare you. Here is the short version: behind the enormous complexities of life, there are basic patterns and structures—*archetypes*, in other words. Sometimes looking at any complex human situation through the lens of an archetype offers us a kind of clarity and understanding that might otherwise get lost in all the fuss, shuffle, and sidetracks.

That is the good news about symbols.

The bad news is that life is not actually symbolism—symbolism just illuminates life, helps to explain it, and offers some navigational tips.

Maybe you are a Saturn type—born, for example, with the Sun in Capricorn conjunct Saturn. Fair enough. But how would you feel if your partner explained your every move— your every foible, victory, every failure—as "typical of all you Saturn types?" Wouldn't that begin to cloy after a while? You would feel as if your unique humanity were being dismissed.

This is often why people "don't like astrology." Who wants to be "explained" so glibly, shallowly, and in so few words? You're a person, not a symbol. Saturn symbolism may help us to understand you. But we need to recognize that, while archetypes are complex, human beings are vastly more so. Each one of us is a compound of many archetypes. And so is every situation you will ever face in life.

We need to commute between two poles in our thinking here. We might call the poles spirit and flesh—or the world of astrological symbolism and the world of everyday life.

Just as daily life can become too complicated, symbolism can become too simple. Symbols cast light on the most complex situations—yet where we actually live and love and quiver in our boots is in the realm of the living. Like moths in October, we need to stay close enough to the flame to avoid freezing, while remaining far enough from it that we do not burn our wings.

The practical point of these ruminations is that what I have written here in this "grand scheme" section veers strongly in the direction of pure abstraction. These words represent my best understanding of the integrated, underlying, interdependent reality of the Earth Family.

And it is fairly simple; it only took me 1500 words or so to express it.

In case you would prefer it even more simply, here is the whole system reduced to just thirty words: *Taurean gut instincts choose the goal, Virgoan skills support the process of becoming the person who can attain the goal, while Capricornian focus, discipline, and relentlessness actually reach the goal.*

But wait a minute . . . didn't I say earlier that Taurus represents cows? Why is there nothing about cows in those thirty words?

It's a fair question, so let me answer it. Those thirty words are pretty close to pure spirit. To learn about Taurus and cows, we would have to swing the pendulum a lot closer to the realm of flesh. In doing that, we will need more than thirty words—and more than fifteen hundred words too.

In the next three chapters, that is exactly what we will do. We now move into the technical material. We will look penetratingly at all nine words in the Earth vocabulary, starting with Taurus and its ruling planet and associated house. In chapter four, we will do the same for Virgo, Mercury, and the sixth house. Chapter five will bring us to a long look at Capricorn, Saturn, and the tenth house.

It will be complicated. To be skilled at the craft of astrology, we need to become fluent in describing that complexity. And yet those thirty words I wrote are about as close to the Holy of Holies as I can take us.

I am a Capricorn myself, so I've got to be mindful about a tendency to be too controlling. Let me risk it—and please forgive me if I overstep: this might be an excellent time to read those thirty words again.

PART ONE

THE THREE EARTH CLANS

3

THE TAURUS CLAN: VENUS, THE SECOND HOUSE, AND THE SIGN OF THE BULL

L et's meet Taurus in detail, cows, bulls, and all.

What we explore in this chapter actually ranges beyond the sign itself. We also need to contemplate the mysteries of Venus, the planet which rules Taurus—and we all know that trying to figure out ways of the "goddess of love" has felled more trees for paper pulp than any other subject in the history of the world.

Also on the docket is the second house—the house of money, among many other things. Money—there's another subject that has unleashed a flood of ink over the centuries.

Love and money. Do I have everyone's attention? For all of us, these are compelling subjects, fraught with confusion, promising joy, sometimes delivering it—and sometimes leaving us broken-hearted, pitiful, and empty.

Love: whose life has never been shattered by falling in love with the wrong person? Who among us has not confused sex and love? Who has not experienced the soul-draining pain of loneliness, either within a relationship or without one?

Money: who has not at times been tempted to abandon a meaningful path in life for the sake of "security?" And that's just simple security—food on the table and a roof over your head. We aren't even talking about a greedy obsession with amassing wealth. But greed and materialism sometimes take their toll as well, turning human beings into monsters. As Bono and the boys in U2 put it, "You can't get enough of what you don't really need."

Love and money: welcome to the Taurus clan and the pressing questions it raises for our souls.

Among mainstream astrologers, Venus is often referred to as "the lesser benefic." *What have they been smoking?* This planet, along with its sign and natural house, can get us into trouble twice as fast as Pluto. Don't take it from me. Just look in the mirror of your own intimate history and you will probably see what I mean.

How can we navigate this seductive, treacherous terrain without degrading ourselves? None of us want to wind up as characters in sad Country & Western tunes. And none of us want to be poor—nor to wind up like that skinflint Jacob Marley in *A Christmas Carol,* having sacrificed our souls for money. There is only way to avoid those miserable fates: you have got to "get right" with the Taurus.

Listen carefully, and your chart will tell you how.

The path of grace and wisdom begins with understanding . . .

THE SIGN TAURUS

Often when I'm teaching a class about the twelve signs of the zodiac, I find I get a lot of questions about Taurus. People seem to have a hard time understanding it. Perhaps it's my own fault as a teacher. My lunar North node lies there, so even for me the sign remains something of a mystery. Still, I think the problem is more fundamental than my own blindness. In a nutshell, *I think that the problem is not that Taurus is too complicated; rather that it is too simple.*

People who are drawn to astrology are generally intelligent. They are oriented to the complexities of psychological thinking. Inevitably, they—myself included—tend to become attached to those complexities. Confronted with genuine simplicity, we "psychological types" often find ourselves scratching our heads, studying it in a spirit of frustration—frustrated by being unable to detect the complexity we "know must be hiding in there somewhere . . ."

The joke is on us. Taurus really is that simple. In fact, I would like to label it *the wisdom of simplicity*. That, at least, is the spiritual goal the sign represents.

The young disciple approaches the wise old Zen master. "What is the secret of your enlightenment? And the Zen master replies, "When I am tired I sleep, when I am hungry I eat."

Again the disciple approaches the master, this time saying, "You are old and enlightened and I am young and a fool. Help me by telling me what you were doing when you were my age. That way I will at least know that I am on the right path."

The master responds, "I chopped wood and I carried water."

The disciple says, "But that is what you do now."

The master says, "Yes."

The first story illustrates the wisdom of just being natural—a kind of "animal" simplicity. Eating when we are hungry, sleeping when we are tired. The second story is a deeper one, although it is cut from the same Taurean cloth. Can we imagine an enlightenment that *changes nothing at all,* at least on the surface? What is going on in the *consciousness* of that Zen master as he "chops wood and carries water?" Letting life be what it is, without embellishment or unnecessary complication is a fine art.

Here is another way to express it: what is the difference between you eating a potato and an enlightened being eating a potato? It's the same behavior, but presumably a different experience. If we could understand that difference, we would understand the essence of the evolutionary goal epitomized by the sign Taurus.

Again we encounter our enigmatic term: *wise simplicity.*

Remember what we learned in the previous chapter: Taurus is your *inner animal.* It is about instinct. It is about the part of you that, *if you let yourself simply be,* is automatically in alignment with natural law, without making any effort to understand it or analyze it. Taurus is about the wisdom of refraining from over-thinking and over-complicating everything. It is about how *not* to tie yourself in mental knots. It is about peace and calm and naturalness and silence. It is about the wisdom of your body. It is about all the things you know in your bones.

TIRED OF BEING SINGLE?

Back when I was in my early thirties, I had a sagacious friend, a novelist, perhaps a decade older than myself. She was a Jewish woman who wonderfully embodied the "chicken soup" wisdom for which Jewish people are often celebrated. At that time, I was contemplating marriage—but like anyone with a brain in his head, I had my doubts about it as well. Discussing my dilemma on the phone with my friend one day, I heard myself telling her that *one reason I was thinking about getting married was that I was tired of being single.* (Those courtship dramas were getting exhausting!) But I also felt that my being "tired of being single" was not a particularly good reason to get married.

My friend's response was absolutely brilliant—and utterly Taurean. Without missing a beat, she said, *"Tired of being single? That sounds like a good reason to get married."*

Everything Scorpionic in me thought she was joking. "My God," said my Scorpio south node, "don't you have any appreciation for the complexity of life? Can't you see the enormity of the existential questions that I am facing here?"

And yet, Taurus-fashion, my friend reminded me that behind all life's complexities, there often lie some pretty simple realities. For example, when it comes to human sexuality, there are just three items on the menu: marriage, celibacy, and dating for the rest of your life.

Take your pick.

I got married and it lasted for almost thirty years.

AN OLD MAN WALKING

Picture an old man walking down a dirt road. One of his feet is labeled *wisdom.* The other foot is labeled *peace.* He gets his wisdom foot forward. If he wants to keep walking, he needs to plant that foot and advance his peace foot. Then *vice versa.* There is a rhythm to his steps: first wisdom, then peace, then wisdom . . .

Everyone is in favor of wisdom, at least in principle. But people do not exactly flock to it. The reason is easy to understand. Getting your wisdom foot forward can be a painful process. It often makes you miserable at first. Cherished illusions are shattered. Embarrassing passion plays are staged, with you playing a leading role. Losses arise. Dramas unfold.

Get a group of ten people together and ask them about experiences that have made them wiser. Guaranteed, you will hear at least eight sad stories. We might hear: my divorce made me wiser. Bankruptcy made me wiser. My father's death made me wiser. Losing my job made me wiser. Betrayal made me wiser. Failure made me wiser.

Wisdom is a good thing, but the process of acquiring is often stressful. The question Taurus raises, is *how can we recover from that process?* After any harsh experience, you really need to get your peace foot forward.

That's what Taurus is all about.

Illustration: a couple has a big fight one Tuesday evening. They love each other, but something messy and unresolved has been festering between them. He says the wrong thing; she overreacts to it. Soon it is World War Three.

Two hours later, they have worked through it. They both agree that while the fight was awful and exhausting, they are glad to have "talked about everything." They're glad they have cleared the air, doing the necessary maintenance on their marriage.

They got their wisdom foot forward, the poor things.

The next night, the couple decides to avoid any heavy subjects, to rent a funny movie, maybe get a pizza. That is a good idea too—it is now time for them to get their peace foot forward. If you have had a growth experience in your relationship on Tuesday, the last thing you need is another growth experience on Wednesday. How much "wisdom" can you take in a given week?

There's some chicken soup wisdom . . .

Here is the same story, told another way. After two years of intense psychotherapy, the client walks into the therapist's office and says, "I think I'm done." And the therapist agrees.

Is this person now "perfectly sane?" I doubt it, that being an exceedingly rare condition. But is there such a thing as "being done with therapy" anyway? You've spent two brave years getting your wisdom foot forward.

Maybe now it is time to just live—to stop second-guessing everything that you do or feel.

Time to get your peace foot forward—your Taurus foot, that is.

I am using this "peace foot, wisdom foot" imagery in order to help us understand the essence of Taurus—but actually it helps us to understand the polarity of Taurus/ Scorpio. As I am sure many of you have figured out—and as we will explore in deep detail in *The Book of Water*— Scorpio is your wisdom foot.

But if you are carrying a lot of Taurus energy in this lifetime, here is the most fundamental truth that evolutionary astrology reveals about the purpose of your incarnation: *you are here to calm down.* You are here to sleep when you are tired and eat when you are hungry.

You are here trying to get your peace-foot forward.

WHAT MAKES EVOLUTIONARY ASTROLOGY DIFFERENT

Those statements, by the way, immediately direct our attention to the heart of evolutionary astrology and what makes it so distinct from every other branch of our field.

Any astrologer will purport to tell you *what it means* that you have the Sun in Taurus. Evolutionary astrologers take it one step further: they tell you *why* your Sun is in Taurus. Our reasoning is built on one inescapable observation—that you have been a Taurus ever since the day you were born. Therefore any reason that you are a Taurus must predate your birth.

So who were you before you were born?

The question is obviously a very slippery one—one that brings us inevitably into metaphysical territory. I use the language of reincarnation here myself. I believe in it and it works well for me, although you may prefer a different framework of understanding. An actual past-life story for a Taurean-influenced person can take many possible forms, but one observation cannot be avoided: if you are trying to "get your peace foot forward" in this lifetime, it follows that in a previous lifetime, you must have "gotten your wisdom foot forward." *Something shook you,* in other words. In a prior lifetime—one whose karma has now ripened—something hurt you. Whatever that trauma was, if you are carrying a lot of Taurus energy in your chart, you are currently in recovery from it.

The detailed methodology of karmic analysis is not the subject of this book. If you are drawn to that kind of inquiry, have a look at my book *Yesterday's Sky: Astrology and Reincarnation.* That will get you started. Understanding your karmic background is absolutely central to the larger logic of evolutionary astrological analysis. But so is a grasp of all the basic astrological building blocks: signs, planets, houses, aspects, and the rest. That's what these four Elements volumes are about.

Bottom line: Taurus planets in your chart? The universe is inviting you to calm down.

You probably don't appear that way to other people. The standard-issue description of Taurus makes it sound as if the sign were pretty mellow already. What those descriptions miss is that the cultivation of "mellowness" is an evolutionary method. As a Taurus-type, the universe has given you the "starter kit." Use it! Listen to that inner animal. Try to be like the Zen master: eat when you are hungry and sleep when you are tired. Cultivate wise simplicity. Above all, think twice before complicating your life unnecessarily.

Your soul could use some chicken soup.

YOUR FAVORITE ANIMAL

For reasons we noted in the previous chapter, the Spanish *corrida de toros* has made the Bull a problematic symbol in modern astrology. We easily forget that bulls are male cows, and that they are generally peaceful creatures unless you poke them with pointy sticks.

To avoid the potential quagmires that bullfights have created, with my Taurus-influenced clients I generally take the thinking up one order of magnitude. Instead of talking about bulls, I talk about animals in general— and specifically about our own animal-natures. One of my favorite ways of getting to the heart of all that is to inquire about my clients' favorite animals.

Sometimes people have to think back to their childhoods in order to answer that one. Kids seem universally to go through a developmental stage where they've identified with horses or eagles or bears. A few generations back, a gentleman by the name of Walt Disney made a few dollars by promoting a connection between kids and mice.

Another way to get at the animal connection is to ask people about their *totem animal.* Some people think that way, while others will give you a blank look.

Either way, this animal-as-metaphor path bring us directly to the Taurean realm.

YOUR NATURAL HABITAT

Animals are happiest—and calmest—in their natural habitats. Deep down, that must be true for humans as well. But at this point in our cultural evolution, how can we even define a natural habitat for *homo sapiens?* We can live anywhere—in crowded cities, in space, under the sea.

Once we have established the identity of the Taurean person's "favorite animal," we take the next step: *to suggest that he or she spend time in the environment with which we naturally associate that animal.* We recognize that time spent there will have a calming, soothing, centering, healing effect—and thus accelerate the calming, centering process which propels Taurean evolution.

If someone, for example, claims the deer as their totem, I might suggest time in the forest—we know that deer favor a woodland habitat. The client who claims the eagle or the hawk would lead me to suggest high country—places with soaring mountain views, where we can look down on the world. The dolphin promises spiritual benefits from the seaside or the open water. The bat or the owl from exposure to darkness and night.

Underlying all of this is a profound psychic reality: as "innocent" and "childlike" as the notion seems, simply following in the paw-prints of one's favorite animal is a healing path. Again, it is easy here to detect the "wise simplicity" that is the keynote of Taurus: "Forget psychoanalysis, you don't need another insight—just go to the beach."

I would encourage you to get creative with this approach. First, with these totem animals, there is no limit—a person can have several such favorite beasties. Each one will offer a helpful message; each will suggest a healing, comforting habitat.

One client of mine, for example, chose the bear. After a bit of back-and-forth, here is where that bear led us. Free-associating, we realized that bears hibernate. That's not a practical option for a human being, especially one with bills to pay—but it led us directly to the idea of him needing more sleep!

And that very creature-comfort suggestion led to the life-changing dreams that came with that sleep . . .

Never have I heard anyone chose for their totem animal the Norway rat or the cockroach. These are creatures that have made their homes in the urban environment. I have some hope for someone someday choosing a squirrel or a pigeon, but neither of them have ever come up either. This leads us to another core observation: *Taurus loves nature.* Time spent quietly in nature is a fundamental evolutionary strategy for this sign. Sometimes the wisest move a Taurus can make is to find a rock in the forest or the desert and just sit on it for a while.

Two scenarios to take us deeper:

Number One: You win a contest in your local grocery store. The prize is a gala, all-expense-paid, week in Paris, complete with tickets to the ballet, sightseeing, five nights in a *fin du siècle* hotel, fancy dinners . . .

How do you feel when you get back home?

The trip was fun, but you are exhausted. Your nervous system is fried. You feel like you "need a vacation from your vacation." You went; it was a good experience. But it wasn't very Taurean. You are now starving for some Taurus. How good does your familiar bed feel to you when you crawl into it again?

Number Two: A friend offers you a week's use of her cabin in the mountains. She warns you that there is nothing to do—and no cell phone coverage or Internet access. You go. For the first couple of days, you are bored out of your skull, walking from room to room, wondering why you are even there. About day three, you get into the groove, waking up with sunrise, enjoying the fading light of evening. By day four, you've made friends with a certain chipmunk. By day five, you've gone as long as ten minutes without a worry or even a thought in your head.

Welcome to Taurus.

Is a cabin in the mountains better than a week in Paris? The point is more subtle—if you are trying to support your Taurean planets, nature and silence will help you more effectively than urban buzz.

What if destiny carries you to a city? No worry, that is not a disaster or any kind of spiritual failure—but if you have any Taurus planets, it would do you good to at least have some green plants in the apartment, a pet if possible, and above all to get out of town from time to time.

Remember, in our Grand Scheme, everything began with that Taurean attunement to your animal wisdom. That is where the inspiration—we might call it the divine guidance—arises. That is what reveals your path, what names your mountain. Everything we have been exploring here about Taurus—and everything we will explore later about Venus and the second house—boils down to "yoga" for finding that peaceful point of intuitive clarity.

Before you can know which mountain to climb, you need to quiet yourself enough to hear your animal-voice. Otherwise you will find yourself atop a mountain that is not yours, having successfully lived a life that has nothing to do with who you are.

VANAJA

Years ago I had a friend named Vanaja. She grew up in India, a member of the high *Brahmin* caste. She was getting her doctorate in astrophysics at North Carolina State University while I was establishing my astrological practice in the nearby town of Chapel Hill. Vanaja was very formal and traditional. She always wore a *sari* and I never saw her without the spot of a *vibhuti* between her eyebrows. I never touched her even though I would have liked to—you just do not touch a Brahmin.

No surprise: her Capricorn Moon was very obvious in her demeanor, as was the great power of her natal Saturn.

Once I took Vanaja to hear a spiritual teacher of mine. On the way home, she said words I will never forget. I asked her what she thought of the teacher. She responded that, while she liked everything the teacher said, that *"she did not have the silence in her."*

I am not sure that comment was fair to the teacher, but it was such a brilliant— and such a very Indian— insight that I have been thinking about it ever since. Vanaja's words sunk into me like a stone. *To find the silence in us*—that is pure Taurus.

The latest *guru-du-jour* in Los Angeles— who gets a thousand dollars a head for a weekend workshop and packs the audience even at that rate—

may indeed say brilliant and useful things. A parrot can be trained to say brilliant and useful things. *But has he or she found the silence?*

To me, that seems like perhaps the ultimate spiritual test.

How can we know if someone has found that silence? In response to that obvious question, I want to take you directly to the very heart of Taurus: I want to say, *just look.* Just feel. Forget your complexity. Forget analysis. *Just look* at that person and ask yourself, does he have the silence in him? Has she found the silence?

Trust your instincts.

If you resonate with what I am talking about, you have found the part of your consciousness that we call Taurus. You have learned to hear the voice of the Wise Animal.

Listen to that voice, trust it—and you will never make another serious spiritual mistake in your life.

That is how precious it is.

TAURUS AS THE SIGN OF SILENCE— AND MUSIC

A hot-dog guitar player who has carefully mastered all his cool moves in front of a mirror might dazzle a gullible audience—but the other musicians are probably rolling their eyes. When musicians compliment each other, you are more likely to hear expressions such as these. "I love how you listen . . ."

It's a bit of a paradox, but music springs from silence. And Taurus is, above all, the sign of silence. For that reason, for anyone with planets in Taurus, music itself can be a spiritual path.

Must you be a Taurus to be a musician? That would be plainly wrong. Fine musicians have arisen in every sign of the Zodiac. With that said, it is helpful to remember that Venus, the ruler of Taurus, is indeed the goddess of the arts. It is fair to say that artists in general tend to have prominent Venusian energy—and being "a Taurus" is one way to embody that astrological inclination.

As we have seen, in order to be in touch with that core of instinctual and intuitive self-knowledge that tells you which mountain is the one that you are supposed to climb, you need to cultivate inner silence. Music is just one way of accomplishing that. That is because when you are listening to music—really truly listening—your inner silence is what is doing the hearing.

That method is probably even more effective if you are actually *playing* music yourself—even if it's just you singing badly in the shower.

How else can we cultivate this sacred silence? We've already looked at some other methods and there are more to come. Venus will offer some guidance of its own in a little while. A right response to the biographical terrain of the second house is critical too.

But finding that silence is not easy. That chattering voice in your head—when was the last time it simply shut up for two minutes? Here are six practical suggestions:

* Time spent in nature is helpful, especially in the kind of habitats toward which your inner animal is attracted.
* The same is true for time spent with animals—remember you and that chipmunk up there in that mountain cabin. Hang out with a cat or a dog or a horse.
* Being mindful of your body and its messages—eating when you are hungry, sleeping when you are tired.
* Touching and being touched.
* Yoga. Massage. Dance.
* Singing in the shower. Losing yourself in the magical rhythm of a drum circle.

All of these help.

PEACE AND QUIET

"Peace and quiet"—we use those words together so much that the phrase has become like one of those compound German words—*der peaceunt-quiet*, or something like that. And that synthesis is natural since peace and quiet go together. Everyone knows that it is harder to find peace in a noisy place—and also that if you manage to find some quiet time, there is a good chance that some degree of peace will follow.

For all of us, peace and quiet are welcome sometimes. But our deeper point here is that out of that silence, a very specific kind of wisdom can spring: *a sense of where you need to go in life*. It is not a logical process. It may not even be a reasonable one. But that guidance is right and true, and it is your path—or your mountain to climb, as we are expressing it here in these pages. *Ultimately, all of the truly pivotal decisions in life have to be made that way, at least if we are going to make them wisely and correctly.* Call it following your heart, or your guts, or the voice of the marrow of your bones. Whatever you call it, you have got to hear it or you are eyeless in a field of rattlesnakes.

And that primal Taurean place in you speaks with a very quiet voice, in a language older than all the languages of this world—the language ravens hear, and wolves, and whales . . . along with the wisest, happiest members of a certain species of clothes-wearing, cell-phone-carrying, articulate primate.

CELEBRATING VENUS

The goddess of love. The goddess of the arts and of beauty. The goddess of peace. All of these faces of Venus are relevant to our investigation of the Earth element, and of the Taurus Clan in particular. (Later, in *The Book of Air*, we will reflect on the more Libran dimensions of the planet. Here, we'll be a bit more "earthy.")

With Venus, everyone naturally wants to cut to the chase and talk about love, but let's start with peace instead. Peace is the root of everything we need to grasp here in the context of the planet's Taurean connection. As you will soon see, our meditation on peace leads quickly to art, beauty—and, eventually, to love.

While Taurus is about getting "your peace foot forward," here is how Venus gets tied into the picture. It is the part of your consciousness that is in charge of helping you *return to equilibrium* after stress or a shock.

Illustration: maybe you get some brutally bad news out of the blue. A friend *reminds you to breathe.* And it helps. Remembering to breathe—that's a Venus function. (Please also notice, by the way, that we are already talking about love—while disoriented by that shock, you needed a friend to remind you of something as basic as breathing.)

I once shared life with a very fine three-legged, one-eared, stray cat named Vincent—hence, Seven Paws Press, by the way. He was an outdoor cat a lot of the time, and even after his amputation, he just was not going to accept becoming housebound. Once I saw him barely escape the slavering jaws of three feral dogs. With his three legs, he made it up a tree in the knick of time.

Five minutes later he was lying in a patch of sun, as calm as a pond at dawn, having a kitty-bath.

Now, If three *velociraptors* chased me up a tree and I escaped them by inches, I would be so PTSD that I would need six months of therapy before I could even take a breath.

Not Vincent the cat! There he was, lying in the sun, as serene as a Buddha. If he could have spoken, he would have said, "Hey, it's over. That was then, this is now. No worry. You humans worry too much."

Sometimes I wish I were an animal.

But I actually am, and so are you. Our problem is that we tend to forget that. Hardwired into our heads and hearts is a kind of innate wisdom about how to live in the present moment, to let the past be the past, and to return to peace.

How exactly can you best reclaim that balance? A big part of your particular answer is encoded in your natal Venus. What house is it in? What sign? What aspects does it make? Those are the clues. Peace is the prize you win for following them.

We will explore all of that, sign by sign and house by house, in Part Three of this book.

For now, our task is simply to understand Venus itself.

(Some astrologers, by the way, would have probably written that last sentence as "Venus *herself*." Not me! I'm male, but take a look—I have Venus right there in my chart, in Sagittarius and in the first house. If any sexist astrologer wants to rob me of it, he or she is going to get a taste of my Mars. The period of history where it was appropriate to assign gender to planets is over, and good riddance. Every human needs all of them in order to be complete.)

WALKING IN BEAUTY

The Navajo people—or *Diné*, as they prefer to be called—have a particularly lovely way of expressing all of this. They speak of a state of balance called *hózhó*—a Venusian state where we are right with the world, in right relationship with all its creatures visible and invisible, and in right relationship with the community and with our own souls.

If there were any doubt about the roots of *hóhzó* being Venusian, the most common Navajo blessing should dispel them: *Walk in Beauty.*

Michelle and I have been fortunate enough to spend Time in the traditional Navajo lands—Monument Valley, Canyon du Chelly, and so forth. Just recalling the simple memory of those beautiful places has sometimes pulled me back from the brink of committing murder as I, for one example, suffered the indignities of modern air travel. Like you, I "walk in beauty" a lot better if I have actually *seen* some beauty.

Next time you are bent out of shape about something, try this little Venusian experiment, or some variation on it. First, really get into your rage or resentment or self-pity, or whatever is your most characteristic *klesha.* Then play Beethoven's 9th Symphony nice and loud. Watch what happens. The part of you that is attached to your lack-of-*hóhzó* will put up a good fight against Ludvig's spell. You will not want to let the music beguile you—but after a while, it almost surely will win.

Study your own mind as this is happening. *The part of you that is fighting against your rage and resentment is Venus.* It calls you to calmer waters. It helps you get over things.

So here is one core Venusian principle: *peace arises as we immerse ourselves in art and beauty.* What kinds of art and beauty are most effective? The answer is connected to the specific nature of your Venus in terms of its sign, house, and aspects. Beethoven might not work for you. Canyon du Chelly might not do the trick. But *something* will—whether it is the beauty that other humans create, or that you create yourself, or the purely Taurean beauty of nature itself.

Unless your life is absolutely free of stress or adversity, a time will come when you need those Venusian skills. Those *velociraptors* are everywhere. After we deal with them, we need to deal with the psycho-spiritual consequences of our having encountered them. You cannot live long in this wild world without contracting at least a small dose of Post Traumatic Stress Disorder.

A right relationship with Venus is what gets you through it.

LOVE AND THE SENSE OF SMELL

Here is a true story—a sad one, but it teaches us almost everything we need to know about the intimate, interpersonal side of Venus. A dear friend of mine was a very accomplished woman in many ways—warm, wise, magnetic, professionally well-loved and well-established, intelligent, with an active spiritual life and practice. And quite beautiful on the outside as well.

In love, we naturally seek an equal partner. Paradoxically, she was so wonderful in so many ways that she suffered a lot from loneliness. That sounds strange, but the bottom line was that she couldn't find *someone worthy of her*—and I hasten to say that this is my language and my interpretation. She was far too humble ever to express her dilemma that way.

But that, in my estimation, was its exact nature.

Then she met a man. I am tempted to say that he looked perfect for her "on paper"—but "on paper" makes it sound as if the opposite were true. It wasn't—he was indeed quite a fine fellow, and very much my friend's equal in all of those categories. On the surface, they looked like a good match.

A few weeks down the road of their courtship, she came to my office to speak with me. She went on about her long history of loneliness and how splendid this gentleman was in every category. Then with a look on her face so stricken that I remember it vividly to this day, she said, *"But Steve, he just doesn't smell right."*

She immediately launched into a defense of his personal hygiene. We were close enough that I could say, "Shut up, Jane. I know what you mean."

(I am making up her name, but not the story.)

Let me take the tale a little further. "Jane" didn't listen to her nose—which is of course a reference to her animal instincts—a reference in this case to the Taurean dimensions of Venus. She and this fellow struggled for three or four years to make a misbegotten, unnatural, anti-instinctual relationship work. Neither one of them ever behaved in awful ways—they were not of that nature—but they damaged each other terribly with the sheer frustration, heartbreak, and emptiness of trying to make a silk purse out of a sow's ear.

If only she had trusted her Taurean nose . . .

Many of you have probably already hit upon the idea of *pheromones*—those chemical signals many animals, ourselves included, release in order to transmit scent messages, often of a sexual nature, to other members of their own species. In this body-mind-spirit universe we inhabit, I am sure that pheromones were part of Jane's little drama.

I would also use this story I am telling as Exhibit A in making my case that humans are fully capable of ignoring and overriding pheromonal messages—to our peril.

Pheromones aside, I am not going to reduce Jane's "sense of smell" to mere biochemistry. That would be like believing one of those magazine articles that reduce human love to enzymes, hormones, and brain biology—not to deny those physical realities, but only to reserve a little space in the equations for something less material, more magical, something emanating more from the spiritual realm than the physical one.

Jane's "sense of smell"—the Taurean instincts she chose to ignore, at least for a while—can be understood as the result of three million years or so of human evolution. If we trust our noses, we can be the beneficiaries of quite a lot of sexual trial and error on the parts of our ancestors.

How complicated is love? How hard is it to find someone with whom you can actually live? These are not strictly modern problems. Humans have been trying to make what we call "love" work for a very long time. Those who succeeded probably had more babies—or to put it more precisely, did a better job of keeping those babies alive. Gradually, over millennia, our "noses" improved.

You meet someone. He or she seems kind of cute and interesting. What else do you know? Very little. You touch; one thing leads to the next. *Given the impossibly multidimensional complexities involved in the happy marriage of two human psyches, what are the odds against you getting it right?*

This could quickly get depressing!

But there is no need for despair. First, we can take comfort in the fact that people often *do* get it right. We can see that. There are many happy couples in the world.

How do they accomplish it? The human intellect boggles at the complications of intimacy—and those complications are further vexed by a zillion unknowns and unknowables . . . who will this person become in five years? Who will you become?

And yet, there are those successes.

How? *The nose knows!* It sounds so simple-minded to say it that way, but it is the truth. *If we can only part the veil of intellect, trusting our instincts instead of a dating service, we can plug into a three-million-year-old mate-selecting computer.*

Again, exactly how?

Well, that is what we have been exploring for many pages now. At the risk of being repetitive, let me point telegraphically to what we have already learned about following the high path of the Taurus Clan . . .

THE SIX TAURUS CLAN DISCIPLINES

* First, you need to find that great silence inside yourself. That is fundamental. You have got to be quiet to hear that ancient voice.
* Second, you need to spend time in your "natural habitat." There is a good chance that place is somewhere in the natural world rather than in the noise and chaos of urban life. You don't need to "move" there. You just need to spend time there, soaking up the silence.
* Third, listening to music might help to shut you up. And if you are on a conscious spiritual path, *mantra* or chant can do the same thing.
* Fourth, develop a friendly dialog with your own body. Learn to listen to its messages. Eat and sleep when it prompts you. Recognize your need to touch and be touched. Cuddle up with a friend.
* Fifth, honor your animal companions. They have something important to teach you. You may be better at conjugating English verbs or solving mathematical problems, but even your cat or dog is better than you are at staying in touch with the instinctual side of life. And animals living in nature are even wiser than Felix or Fido. Hang with them if you can.
* Sixth, immerse your five senses in aesthetic rapture whenever the opportunity arises. Walk in beauty. Stop and smell the roses, literally.

Practice those six disciplines, and without even thinking about it, you are cultivating an ability to recognize true love when it hits you over the head—and to sort it out from love's dead-end streets. You can also find little pockets of peace in this crazy world—and that's true for everyone, but it is even more critical for you if you have some serious Taurean energy in your birthchart.

Above all, it is down this good Taurean road that something wise and ancient inside of you points to a very special "mountain"—a mountain that is worthy of you. A mountain that represents the Great Work of your life.

To climb it, you must first recognize it.

And to recognize it, you need to find *the silence in you.*

HUITLACOCHE

Here is a standard joke about Taurus among astrologers: what's the first thought in a Taurus's mind when confronted with any unfamiliar object?

Answer: *I wonder if I could eat that . . .*

It's a good giggle, and like a lot of humor it is very loosely based on a gross exaggeration of an observed reality: Taurus people enjoy the pleasures of the flesh 0.000097% more than the rest of us. Taurus is, after all, the sign of the inner animal—and if you have a cat or a dog, you know their attitude when dinner is an hour late.

Not to kill the joke, but let's take it one step deeper. "I wonder if I could eat that" might sound like mere teasing, but it is actually a profoundly practical question. Food equals survival, and there is no more practical question in this world than how to stay alive.

In Mexico, I've enjoyed a delicacy called *huitlacoche*—English translation: *corn smut.* Google it if you have a strong stomach. A photo alone might put you off your dinner. It's an ugly-looking, grayish fungus that grows on corn. It looks exactly like something you might find on corn cobs you'd forgotten and abandoned in the *Gulag Archipelago* in the back of your refrigerator eight months ago.

Who could have possibly come up with the idea that *huitlacoche* might actually taste good, let alone not kill you?

Here's my best guess: a very, very hungry Taurus.

And that starving Taurean stayed alive when others died of famine, all because she or he asked that deeply practical question, *I wonder if I could eat that . . .*

That little tale echoes some of what we have learned about instinct. Watch where else it carries us.

THE SECOND HOUSE

Let's pivot from Taurus to its corresponding behavioral expression in the realm of the astrological houses. As Taurus is the second sign of the Zodiac, it has a natural resonance with the second house.

Ask almost any astrologer the meaning of the second house and you will hear one word: *money*. And it is true: planets in the second house reveal much about your attitude toward money as well as the sources of income in your life, and your possible financial blind spots. That is completely valid, proven astrological practice, and it is important to know about it.

But when I teach about the second house, I bring up the subject of money, then I immediately pivot to what seems like a rhetorical question: "money—*why is that stuff so popular?*"

Inevitably, there are giggles. The answer seems obvious, but let's spell it out: money buys food and shelter, and there can be no question about why they are "popular." Money buys survival.

Money of course buys more than food and shelter. Once you have those bases covered, worlds of joy opens up: Status! Toys! Sexual partners! Adventures! Comforts!

And a universe of complications.

(Note how we have gone from the motivational, attitudinal realm of the sign Taurus into the practical, behavioral house realm of the second house. We have gone from "being in touch with the inner animal" to figuring out what he or she is going to eat tonight. There's our underlying sign-house distinction in action—and a passing reference to *huitlacoche.)*

THE PEACE CONNECTION

Remember that from the evolutionary perspective, both Taurus and Venus are about aspirations and pathways toward inner peace. As befits the very down-to-earth nature of all of the Taurus Clan symbols, we can see exactly that same theme continuing in very straightforward fashion in the second house.

Let's say it very simply at first: *poverty is stressful.* It is hard to relax if you have nothing to eat. It is hard to relax if you do not have the money to pay the rent or the mortgage.

I am sorely tempted to add the word, "duh . . ."

With planets in the second house, one of your soul's basic behavioral intentions in living life in this modern world is to establish *a right relationship with money*. Realistically, you can't relax unless you do that.

That's where the questions become slippery. How much money is enough? And have you paid too high a spiritual price for your financial solvency? There are many ways to make money—which one is right for you? What about when financial calamity strikes—how much of that drama do you let into your heart? Clearly paying it no attention is not a workable answer . . . on the other hand, is losing your home truly the end of the world? Do you want to give that much power over your soul to a piece of architecture—or to some digits on a computer screen?

At what level of prosperity do you become "perfectly secure" in this world?

That last question is actually an easy one—there is no such level. Here is a basic insight into the true source of your worldly security: *the second house resources that support your inner peace are not limited to your bank account.*

We'll get there in a moment.

Money-wise, the second house casts two shadows: *too much thinking about money and too little.* In terms of peace and wellbeing, somebody making $50,000 a year and living a $45,000 lifestyle is way ahead of the person making a million bucks a year while trying to live a $1.2 million lifestyle.

That is part of what we mean by a "right relationship with money."

There is another very practical thread we need to follow. Planets connected with the second house give us a sense of where your money is likely to originate. Here, technically, we are not only talking about planets that happen to lie in your second house, but also about the position of the planet that rules the sign on the second house cusp—if that second house ruler happens to be in the ninth house, for example, there may be income from foreign connections, religion, or education.

I do not want to get bogged down in those details at this point. Remember—in Part Three of this book we will break much of this down planet by planet, sign by sign.

Let's go one inch further on this financial thread before we leave the realm of money behind us. While some degree of financial security, predictability and stability are obviously connected with maintaining "a peaceful, easy feeling," a right relationship with money must include some attention to the *ethics of how we are earning it*. How would you like to make a million dollars a year as a *Mafia* hit-man? Or a child pornographer or a sex trafficker? Those are hyperbolic examples, but they do make the point. People make a lot of money hurting other people, but I doubt many of them sleep peacefully at night—and that is not just a convenient proverbial saying here: sleeping peacefully at night is close to the heart of the evolutionary intention of the Taurus Clan.

"Don't be evil" is one way to say it—simple, but it needs to be said.

Here is the next step and it is not quite so blunt: there are harmless, blameless ways to be financially stable—but perhaps they are not connected positively to your highest path. Maybe, for example, you have Mercury in the second house. Maybe you are a retail clerk or a typist. There is no shame in either of those professions—but think how happy you would be teaching other people something that you actually believed in and which excited you . . . there's one higher expression of that Mercury.

BEYOND MONEY

That the second house is about money and the things it buys is solid, practical astrology. *But there was a time before money.* Our paleolithic grandparents had second houses too. What could the second house have meant to them, long before bills and coins—and long before astrology as we understand it existed? Food and shelter—yes indeed. But here is a more primal way of saying it, as relevant to modern urbanites as it was to cave-people: the second house represents *the material basis of survival.*

How would you feel if you had no food? How would you feel if the temperatures were headed down below freezing tonight and you had no roof over your head and no coat to wear?

Scared, of course. Or insecure. "Insecure" is a good word, but it sounds too psychological. In such a case, your "feelings of insecurity" would arise because you *actually were* insecure, objectively.

In such a situation, you need a meal and a coat, not psychotherapy.

And with that simple realization, we enter another dimension of the second house—one that is often far more relevant in the modern counseling room, now that most of us can count on dinner being on the table.

In the second house, we are dealing with the question of *self-confidence*—which is the polar opposite of "insecurity." In this house, we wrestle with the basis of our *sense of legitimacy* in this world. We are dealing with the question of our *primal animal dignity,* and how to support, develop, and sustain it.

Some of that success comes from attitude and psychological change—but a lot of it arises from far more concrete realities.

DO YOU HAVE WHAT IT TAKES?

Maybe you are a golfer with upwardly-mobile social aspirations and not much imagination. You would love to be a member of the most prestigious country club in your local bailiwick. You inquire about the annual dues. The answer is $100,000. You can't afford that. You literally "don't have what it takes."

How do you feel about the situation? You are not going to starve or freeze to death because you aren't welcome in that club. You aren't exactly scared—that is not the right word. But you probably feel *diminished* somehow. Rejected. Unworthy. Resentful—or its kissing cousin: *ashamed.*

(Note how we are teetering here, on the brink that separates the practical from the psychological. Welcome to the second house.)

Maybe you are madly attracted to someone. Cupid's arrows have pierced your heart. You make overtures, and the resultant shocked and dismayed look in your *enamorata's* eyes seems to be saying, "Are you, like, *kidding . . .?*"

What is the implication? Simple: he or she is saying that you don't "have what it takes." Forget about ever sharing a bed with me.

That scenario is not about money—at least, we hope not. Perhaps that situation is about your perceived level of physical attractiveness—and one's self-evaluation in that area is often a very charged second house focus. Am I pretty? Is my nose too big?

But let's quickly add the grown-up perspective: the issue that disqualifies you as a potential lover in our example might be about your intelligence, your personality, your level of spiritual evolution—at least as those qualities are evaluated by the object of your desire.

Turn these two sad tales around. That golfer goes out and makes some serious money. He joins the country club, finds himself welcomed there, "raised to peerage" with the other millionaires. How does he feel now? Vindicated. Successful. On top of the world. He has *proven himself to himself* through that accomplishment.

After that romantic rejection, our protagonist is motivated to become more attractive: she changes her hairstyle—not a deep statement, but not totally irrelevant either. (Remember, Taurus is practical.) Maybe he tones his body at the gym. Maybe she learns to listen better. Maybe he takes up meditation. "Attractiveness" is a complex subject, so there are many things we could say here. Bottom line, he or she acquires more of "whatever it takes." And his or her intimate fortunes improve—and with them, self-confidence.

Positively, the action of the second house again lies in *proving one's self to one's self.* We start out with an insecurity—*and the key is to realize that the insecurity, while it has a very real basis, is addressable.* We can improve. We can work on ourselves. *We can strengthen the objective basis of our self-confidence.* That utterly practical, concrete work has profound psychological implications.

THE HEART OF THE SECOND HOUSE

Here, just to be as clear as I possibly can, is the step-by-step essence of how I go about interpreting any planet in the second house.

1. Realize that you were not *born* with enough skill and confidence regarding that particular planetary function to do what you came to Earth to do.

2. Emphasize that the situation is not as dire as it sounds—you were also born with the ability to *develop* that skill and confidence.

3. That planet must *prove itself to itself.* It badly needs a victory in the real world. Groundless self-congratulation and feel-good "paperback self-help" attitudes are not sufficient.

4. Confidence arises from the hard work of *developing proper and necessary resources.* Those resources take many practical possible forms: skills, certifications, tools, allies . . . maybe even money.

5.   Accept that there is a driven, even uncomfortable, feeling in the second house, even when we get it right. It is hungry and aspirational right to the end.

6.   As these evolutionary developments advance, you are likely to find that motivations and concerns specifically around money fade into the background. They seem to "take care of themselves" as you focus on larger issues more central to your life's actual purpose.

And with that, we have completed our broad survey of the Taurus Clan. We are not done with it though—in Part Three, we will break it down sign by sign and house by house. Right now though, we are concerned only with the big picture.

4

THE VIRGO CLAN: MERCURY, THE SIXTH HOUSE, AND THE SIGN OF THE MAIDEN

Poor Virgo! When it comes to astrological humor, this sign was born with a bull's eye on its forehead. It is constantly lampooned for its alleged fussiness and nitpicking. Ask anyone: even Virgo's socks are stored in alphabetical order . . . or so they say. Further slanders: Virgo is good at handling matters too trivial for the other eleven signs. Virgo, the "natural born servant," is bound by destiny to count beans for people more interesting, memorable and sexy than himself or herself.

It's all hogwash.

Read a few more pages and watch me make the case that Virgo is the most exciting sign of the Zodiac. That statement may be a bit hyped, but it's good medicine against all the undeserved calumny.

Truth is, all twelve signs are pretty exciting, once you understand them.

VIRGINITY

Some of Virgo's public relations problem stems from the word itself. We hear "Virgo" and we think "virgin," with all its unfashionable connotations of sexual prudery.

Sometimes when I'm entertaining people a lot younger than myself, I feign a creaky, old man's voice, point my finger at them accusingly, and announce, *"I remember virginity . . ."*

And I actually do.

Even when I was young, its importance—especially in a female—was rapidly fading. But back then those judgments and prohibitions were still a cultural reality in many circles. A young woman who "had lost her virtue" was seen as damaged goods when it came to marriage—at least by my grandparents' generation.

Those days are gone, praise God. Most of us have come to realize that our sexual experiences—and by that I mean our experiences of coupling love, not just literal sexual intercourse—typically make us *more* virtuous, not less. We *learn* from love, and the deepest lessons it teaches seem to arise when we love with the body, as well as with the mind and the soul. Loving with the body doesn't leave much room for hiding.

So: goodbye to the sacred cult of sexual inexperience, and good riddance.

The world turns: what was once a source of pride is now often a source of shame and mockery. And that change in our collective attitude toward sexual inexperience has completely upended our understanding of the sign Virgo—and probably helps to explain why Virgo is the brunt of so many jokes. There is still a whiff of nervousness in the air.

Truly to grasp the heart of this sign, we need to put sexuality aside and look at the *underlying structure* implicit in all that I have just said about virginity. Try this statement: *God creates us all as pure as the driven snow, then we come to the earth and screw it up.*

The indelicate term "screw" is essential to my meaning here. The cult of virginity may be finished, but we still unconsciously use the same judgmental terminology—that "sex" reduces "virtue." If something is "screwed"— and to keep my PG Rating intact I am avoiding the obvious reference to the infamous f-bomb—we know that it is in a "fallen" condition.

"The mechanic tells me that my transmission is royally screwed . . ." Could anyone mistake the meaning of that sentence?

That insight leads us to the underlying structure, which is the very essence of Virgo: *the comparison of the ideal and the actual,* the comparison of what *could be* and what *actually is,* the Divine Plan versus the human reality.

And in every case, the actual human reality falls short of that higher ground.

That critical sense of discrimination—*what could be versus what is*— is the fundamental template of perception that underlies, enlivens, and motivates any Virgo planet.

THIS ROOM'S A MESS

You walk into your bedroom. Your first thought: "This room looks like the bottom of a bird cage." Entropy has taken its toll. That is an experience to which I am sure we can all relate, Virgos or not.

What is the underlying structure of that perception? *Here is the room as it should be; here is the room as it actually is.* That is pure Virgo.

What do you do about the situation? Maybe you close the door and walk away. Or maybe you pick up the room, get out the vacuum cleaner . . . wash the windows, get rid of the clothes you don't wear anymore, wash the drapes, detail the baseboards, buy a new sofa, consult an interior designer . . .

When does it stop? And no matter what the answer is, the room is still not perfect. That's because perfection is an ever-receding goal. Perfect is the enemy of good enough. Like the north star, perfection orients us, but we never expect actually to arrive there.

HOW VIRGO WORKS IN AN ASTROLOGICAL CHART

Let's say your natal Sun lies in Virgo. Start with the question, what does the Sun represent? What exactly is being *conditioned* by Virgo? We could write a book about the Sun, but let's reduce it to one quintessential term: the Sun is your *self-image.* If the Sun is in Virgo, then let me give you *Genesis I* in the formation of your self-image: *here is what I should be. On the other hand, here is what I actually am.*

How do you react to that perception? At the high end of the spectrum, you react by becoming *hungry to improve*. You want to reach your potential, to become what you are capable of becoming. You want to "clean up the room," in other words.

At the low end of the spectrum, you "close the door and walk away." You give up on yourself. You define yourself as a failure or a hopeless case.

You are still a Virgo, however—that critical energy doesn't just go away. Instead it niggles at you. You beat yourself up. You sabotage yourself. You act out your shame.

In keeping perspective here, we need to remember that perfection is inherently unreachable. Nobody actually ever gets there. Perfection is an incredibly harsh standard. In working with Virgo energy, it is essential to judge ourselves only by the standard of the *intensity of our effort*. If we start judging ourselves against the standard of perfection itself, we always fall short. And shame, self-sabotage, and failure to invest in ourselves are the consequences.

Learning to love yourself—that phrase, of course, sounds like a platitude—something to be found written amongst the pastel butterflies and roses on a tacky coffee mug.

And yet learning to love yourself is the life-blood of any higher expression of Virgo.

If you are carrying a lot of Virgo energy, you have come here to learn *radical self-acceptance*—but you are attempting that feat in the most difficult context imaginable: that of a very honest mind. You will see yourself clearly, illuminated by the unforgiving light of perfection . . . you will see yourself "warts and all."

WHY ARE WE ALL HERE IN THE FIRST PLACE?

That is obviously life's single most persistent philosophical question. What is the purpose of our existence? Humans have come up with a lot of answers over the years, many in the category of religious teachings. In Asia, we might hear that we are on earth to struggle toward Enlightenment. A Christian might say that we are "working out our Salvation." Psychologists might speak of self-actualization—or simply of sanity and its close cousin, happiness.

There is a lot of diversity of opinion, but underlying all of it is a kind of unity. All the answers are about personal growth, one way or another. It is always about motion toward some ideal.

The language may vary, but in other words all of the answers boil down to 100% pure, quintessential Virgo: here is what I am and there is what I need to become.

Effort. Hunger. Drive. Divine discontent.

These are the engines that drive growth.

And rapid growth is exactly what Virgo is all about, at least when it is on track. At least when it has not derailed itself with self-criticism.

THE MOST EXCITING SIGN OF THE ZODIAC

Earlier I said that we would make a case for Virgo being the most exciting sign of the Zodiac. We are there.

We are all here on earth to grow, and there is no more efficient mechanism for that growth than Virgo. With planets in Virgo, you are burning evolutionary rocket fuel. In principle, your level of drive—of divine discontent—is such that you will not waste a moment of this precious human incarnation. You will goad yourself, press yourself, and never rest on your laurels.

You don't need anyone else to give you a pain in the ass, in other words. You can do that all by yourself.

FLYING CARPETS

Legend has it that rug-weavers in ancient Persia would always make sure that there was at least one error in their intricate geometric designs. Once, with a Virgo client, I came up with what I thought was a pretty good metaphor. I pictured him visiting a museum where there was a display of such carpets—a dozen large ones hanging on the walls. Fancifully, I described him walking into that salon and instantly pointing to the upper left-hand corner of one particular giant carpet, saying, "Look! There's the mistake!"

The client appeared slightly shocked. He said, "How did you know about that? That's in my chart?"

He had actually had that precise experience a few weeks earlier.

Consider again the underlying template of perception in that story: here is the actual carpet. Here, in my imagination, is the perfect one. Blink, blink, blink, back and forth—and in ten seconds the error jumps out.

And he was right.

There is no such thing as a perfect Persian carpet.

Now let's switch a couple of parameters and tell the same story over again. If, instead of looking at Persian carpets hanging on a museum wall, our Virgo was looking at *you,* comparing his perceptions of the reality of what you actually are with the potential reality of what you could be . . . well, blink, blink, blink . . . and out comes a detailed catalog of all your failures, shortcomings, and areas requiring improvement.

How do you feel about receiving that catalog?

Ask any astrologer. Virgos are critical. And therefore probably over-represented in the population of victims of intimate homicide.

This tendency toward niggling may not be observable in every single Virgo case—but that critical function is really just another way of talking about the comparison of the ideal and the actual, and so it is present in some form in every Virgo planet.

For most of us, it is not a comfortable experience to be on the receiving end of it.

And here is the irony: if we squawk, we are likely to see a stricken, bewildered look on our Virgo partner's face, followed by the faint protest, *"I was only trying to help . . ."*

And he or she would pass the lie detector test on that one.

If there is any comfort in all this, here it is: those Virgo people are treating you in exactly the same way that they are treating themselves.

WHERE WE NOW ARE ON THE MAP OF THE WORLD

All of this gives us a good start on understanding the energy, psychic function and evolutionary purpose of the astrological sign Virgo. It also gives us a glimpse at Virgo's dark side, which boils down to a tendency toward excessive criticism, both of the self and of other people, places, and things. But that is not all bad news: self-criticism in particular—an ability to see ourselves clearly and without any delusions of grandeur—plays an essential role in the Earth-sign process of "making it real"—of reaching toward our true potential. And in this case, what we are making real is our vision for who and what we could eventually become, if we get "everything right."

Later on, in Part Three, we will wrestle with each planet individually as it is conditioned by each of the three Earth signs. How, for example, is Venus in Virgo different from Mars or Jupiter in Virgo, and so on? But first, we need to look at a second dimension of Virgo—one that will seem very different, even unrelated, to what we have seen so far, at least until we really delve into it. Then we will see that there are two sides of the Virgo coin—and like any coin in your pocket, there is no way to take away either side and still have any coin left at all.

THE SERVANT AND THE CRAFTSPERSON

Virgo is often conventionally called the *servant*. The word is useful and we're going to keep it—but it comes packaged with a big problem. Unfortunately, the term "servant" can imply a lowly or servile condition, as if all the Virgo people were born to wash out the toilets at the local No Tell Motel. God bless all of the people doing that kind of work, but it would be misleading to imagine that Virgo must always operate in that kind of subordinate context. So I keep the traditional Virgo word, servant, but I add a second word to balance it. That word is *craftsperson*.

Now, a craftsperson has certain skills and is honored and valued for them. He or she experiences dignity and some degree of social status as a result of simply being *good at something* which other people appreciate. Thus, the craftsperson *serves* the community. He or she is indeed a "servant"—but now when we use the word, there is no implication of low status. In fact, quite the opposite.

Virgo represents a fundamental human urge: we all want to be seen as *competent*. This "craft" can take many forms. The basket weaver has a craft—but so do the brain surgeon and the pilot of a Boeing 787. *In each case, the outward manifestation of the skill triggers an inward condition of dignity and self-respect.*

And that is our critical link.

You may recall from a few paragraphs ago the nature of the Virgo shadow: self-doubt and self-criticism. The dignity and self-respect that arise as we exercise skill in the world— especially skill that other people appreciate and deem useful—are effective remedies for those shadow pieces.

A few lines back, I wrote that there were two sides to the Virgo coin, and that initially they would seem unrelated. They are, on one hand, the *generation of self-love* in the context of an honest mind, and on the other hand, *finding one's right work*. Now we can see their interdependency: the "evolutionary rocket fuel" which Virgo is burning is simply too dangerous to use unless it is balanced by actually being good at something that makes a difference in the lives of other people.

AN EGYPTIAN MOMENT

My dear friend, Ingrid Coffin, who has faithfully run my southern California teaching program for two decades, once shared a beautiful prayer with me. She tells me that it has roots in ancient Egypt, back in the time of the pharaohs. If you have any planets in Virgo, these words should resonate deeply in your soul.

God grant that today I do work that matters.

That is all. So simple, and so luminous.

What is work that matters? The answer could take myriad forms, but they all hold one thread in common. For work to "matter," it must have a positive impact on someone else's life. I am thinking of the airline pilot who gets you safely across the ocean through turbulent skies. I am thinking of the brain surgeon who saves the life of someone you love.

And, with equal respect, I am honoring the person who washes the toilets at the motel.

Skill in service of other beings—that is a core motivation in the sign Virgo. To help you along with this, if you are born with Virgo energies, the universe has made you a promise: the ability to develop some such a skill is innate to you. Your job is to find it and to polish it.

Astrology can help. As we decode the messages of any planets you might have in Virgo—or in the sixth house, but we will get to that soon— we find clues as to where those skills might lie. The key is that once you have "work that matters" in place in your life, you have a bulwark strong enough to preserve your dignity as you peer into the painfully honest mirror of self-reflection that we call Virgo.

One more point, and it is also pivotal: when we speak of "work that matters," we are not necessarily speaking narrowly of a career for which you are paid. That "professional" category of experience can certainly be part of this Virgo evolutionary process, but let's not limit our imaginations. Doing a good job of raising a family is "work that matters," even though no one pays you to do it. Playing music in a weekend bar-band that gives people joy and release is work that matters. Certainly anything for which we volunteer in our communities matters—teaching kids to read, helping out at a hospice.

What "matters" is skillful service and the dignity that comes from a job well done. Money is not the point.

LINEAGE

As synchronicity would have it, in about two weeks I will attend a memorial service for a man who was a dear friend of mine. I mentioned him earlier in this volume. His name was Robert A. Johnson. He wrote a number of books on Jungian psychology, and sold over a million of them. Around the time I was born, he had followed his "slender threads" and was actually in Europe studying directly under Carl Gustav Jung himself. When I was a young astrologer, I read all of Robert's books. He shaped my practice in significant ways.

The story of how I met Robert Johnson is long, convoluted, and full of synchronicities. I will not clutter these pages with it. Suffice to say it had that quality of miraculous improbability that often characterizes meetings triggered by the sort of karma that links souls together across the abyss of time.

In common with most astrologers whose work has a psychological tone, I owe a great debt to Carl Jung. Since I was young, I have been studying his work. But after befriending Robert, I felt that I understood Jung's work far more deeply. It is important to point out that Robert was not my teacher at any formal level. I never studied with him, at least not officially. Here is the best way I know to say it: Robert had *received an energetic transmission* directly from Carl Jung, and through some ancient, mysterious mechanism, he passed that energetic transmission along to me.

I suspect that if we could interview Carl Gustav Jung, he could tell us about human beings from whom he himself received such energetic transmissions. Great souls are born and die—but before they die, they often pass on a flame. The word for this precious miracle is *lineage*. We do not hear the word very often in modern society. That is a loss, but it does not diminish the reality and the power of the phenomenon.

The astrological symbol for participation in such a lineage is Virgo. Later in this chapter we will learn that the sixth house refers to the actual biographical behavior of such sacred participation.

Long before I met Robert A. Johnson, I had been blessed by transformative meetings with other mentors. This is an astrology book, not my autobiography, so I will not fill these pages with my personal story. Suffice to say that I have Saturn in Virgo tightly conjunct my midheaven, which directly links my *career* (Midheaven; tenth house) to the Virgo idea of *lineage*.

Without my teachers, I could not have become the astrologer I have become. How can I ever pay them back for this extraordinary gift? The answer is actually easy—I pay them back by *keeping the flame burning after they're gone*—and by passing it on so it continues to burn after I myself am gone.

I opened this chapter with a reference to how Virgo often does not get much respect, at least in pop-astrology circles. I promised that I would make a case that Virgo is in fact the most exciting sign of the Zodiac. My first argument for that excitement was a reference to the burning evolutionary drive inherent in this sign. Now I make my second argument: *lineage is the life-giving spiritual oxygen in the bloodstream of the human race.* To participate in lineage is one of the most exciting avenues in life that I can imagine.

Remember our Virgo prayer: "God grant that today I do work that matters." Developing such skills requires an abundance of the obvious virtues: study, effort, and self-discipline. But the magic bullet that puts us over the top in that search for our right work lies in *encounters with our mentors.* That is a critical—and often ignored—piece of the Virgo puzzle.

We can go further: your contract with the universe assures us that *those mentors are actually there to be found.* The laws of synchronicity promise that if you do not find them, they will find you. Your task is to recognize them and to submit to them. We might reflexively say that such surrender requires some degree of "ego transcendence" on your part. True enough—but with Virgo, we stand that notion on its head. The real question is not narrowly about humility. It is the question of *whether you love and value yourself enough* to seek these mentors in the first place—or whether you will sabotage yourself by turning away from their gift?

MERCURY RULES VIRGO—AND GEMINI TOO

Almost everyone who studies astrology quickly grasps the natural association of Mercury and Gemini—to put it simply, the planet of the mouth has a natural rapport with the sign of the mouth. Any questions? But when I teach about rulership, I often see a lot of head scratching about Mercury's connection with Virgo.

In the next book of the series, *The Book of Air*, we will delve into the vigorous interaction of Mercury with Gemini. Here in *The Book of Earth*, we naturally focus our attention on the planet's particular symbiosis with Virgo.

A big piece of the Mercury-Virgo connection derives directly from what we just learned about the connection between Virgo and mentoring in the last few paragraphs. In Virgo, we see the human urge to participate in lineage. *In other words, we see the ancient archetypal marriage of teacher and student.*

And there it is, right before our eyes: could there possibly be a more "Mercurial" image than teacher and student doing their age-old minuet?

If we watch the process with patience, we can learn something deeper: we witness *the transformation of a student into a teacher.*

Students. Teachers. The transmission of ideas. Language. Learning. Striving to understand. Burning the midnight oil. Reading. Concentration. The wrinkled brow as we push the far limits of our intellectual powers. It would be nearly impossible to miss the Mercury signature in all of those words—and every one of them has a Virgo signature as well.

Once we grasp the mentor-mentee dimensions of Virgo, its natural link with Mercury leaps forward.

QUESTIONING AUTHORITY

Getting precisely one full book ahead of myself here, let me say that Gemini is very much about *questions*. It is about a willingness to question our own assumptions, to doubt everything—including our teachers. In *The*

Book of Air, we will have some fun exploring the rebel joys of that equally sacred Mercurial process: questioning.

Here, as we contemplate the specifically Virgoan dimensions of Mercury, the planet takes on a far more humble—and far more grounded—face. We submit modestly and gratefully to those who already possess the knowledge to which we aspire.

In a nutshell, the risk entailed by the particularly Geminian face of Mercury is that we spend a lot of time "re-inventing the wheel." In the Virgo face of Mercury, we save a lot of time and move forward with more efficiency by realizing that the wheel has already been invented. All we have to do is to look it up in the Encyclopedia—or sit at the feet of the genius who already did the work.

Let me make this come alive for you in a concrete way with a practical example:

Since you are reading this book, I suspect that you have wrestled with the problem of there being so many different systems of house division in astrology: Placidus, Koch, Porphyry, Whole Sign, Equal, and so on. It is totally confusing to the beginner—and more advanced astrologers would do well to hang onto a little of that confusion themselves!

Personally, I use the Placidus system. In my hands it is the house system that seems to produce the most precise, consistent, and helpful results. But I would never waste a moment arguing with an astrologer who uses a different system. In one of the best lines I have heard in my entire astrological career, the great astrologer Robert Hand was asked which house system was the best. He responded with a question: *which is truer, French or German?*

If people speak a different language than my own, I do not immediately assume that they are lying.

And yet here's my Virgo/Mercury point: in my apprenticeship programs, I am a total tyrant. I insist that we all use Placidus houses. The reason is that these are *apprenticeship programs*—not general introductions to all the varieties of astrological practice. I am not teaching my students "how to do astrology"—as if there were only one way to learn it. What I am teaching them is "how Steven Forrest does astrology." In my heart, this does not come out of a place of arrogance or any sense of superiority. Instead, it is simply a pure expression of Virgo: I am trying to pass on a specific flame that has burned very well for me, in the hopes that it will burn well for my students too.

From time to time in my apprenticeship programs, I tell the students that I celebrate their ultimate individuation. Little birds fly from the nest eventually and find their own lives. That is worth celebrating. I am not exactly trying to clone myself, at least that is not the ultimate goal—but that "cloning" is unabashedly a practical Earth-sign step along the way.

In essence, here is what I am saying to my students: humble yourselves; learn what I know. Then take it and run with it in directions I can only imagine. The teacher who must constantly maintain a role of superiority relative to the students has failed as a teacher, in my opinion.

Still, an equal but opposite mistake is available to all teachers as well: the teacher who abdicates from passing on the teachings he or she has received has also failed the students—and failed his or her own teachers as well.

This point is fundamental to the sacred contract of lineage—and while Virgo and the sixth house represents lineage, without the teaching and learning function of Mercury the process could not exist.

MERCURY, VIRGO AND CRITICAL THINKING

A young woman in one of my classes had her name pulled from our famous Sorting Hat. That meant that I would do an analysis of her birth chart as a demonstration for the class. She showed great potential as a creative, innovative astrologer.

To strengthen this point about the whole *gestalt* of mentoring, I shared a fantasy with the class. I imagined this young woman much later in her life, perhaps in her sixties, long after I am dead and gone. I imagined her having published a breakthrough astrological book. In my fantasy, she was being interviewed. The interviewer said, "I understand that many years ago you studied under the late Steven Forrest . . ."

And she, with obvious diplomacy, ambivalence, and hesitation, responded, "Well, I was perhaps somewhat *influenced* by Steven Forrest . . ."

Everyone in the class laughed of course. It was as if I was joking about her inability to honor the "enormous, incalculable intellectual debt that she owed me." But that was not what I actually meant at all. What I meant was that she had taken everything I taught her and wrestled with it, keeping that which was good and true—only she took it all further, down good roads that had never crossed my mind.

Furthermore, in comparing my teaching to the realities she had actually experienced, she criticized my work—probably correctly.

In thinking critically about it, she improved it.

The flame itself is more important than the egos of those who briefly carry it. Bless the ones who do carry it and preserve it—and twice bless the ones who add something to it and make it burn more brightly in healing service to this dark world.

BOILING IT DOWN TO THE BONES

Remember scanning those Persian carpets for the single mistake? Comparing the perfect with the actual, back and forth, blink, blink, blink? This is very much the Virgo face of Mercury. It represents intellectual rigor, sustained feats of concentration, mental self-discipline, and hard, critical questions. But its foundation lies in learning—in receiving existing, hard-won bodies of knowledge, and honoring the flame.

Here, by way of summary, is the formula for the particularly Virgoan face of Mercury:

* First, it burns the midnight oil. It humbles itself before the existing knowledge and those teachers who embody it.
* Second, it thanks those teachers and honors that knowledge by seeing that it does not die, but instead is passed onward into the future.
* And thirdly, it adds to the treasure of that knowledge by thinking critically about it, improving it, and further purifying it.

MERCURY AS A UNIVERSAL ARCHETYPE

In the foregoing paragraphs, in pursuit of our larger goal of understanding the Earth family in astrology, I have been attempting to illuminate the particular connection between Mercury and Virgo. As promised, in *The Book of Air* we will look at a very different face of the planet via its rulership of Gemini. In Part Three of this volume, we go through Mercury in each of the twelve signs and twelve houses. In doing that, we will stretch beyond some of what I've written here. We will move into realms of Mercurial expression which are not so strictly channeled down Virgo avenues.

To lay the groundwork for those later sections of the book, let's briefly explore Mercury in broader, less Virgoan, fashion.

Ask any astrologer what Mercury means and you will soon hear words such as "communication" or "language" or "media." *Data in and data out*—that's Mercury. It is indeed about speaking—hence the idea that Mercury people have a tendency to chatter. The word "chatter" might be uncharitable, but there is sometimes an observed truth in it.

Mercury is every bit as much about *listening* as it is about speaking. Listening is a form of *perception*—and that is perhaps the most fundamental Mercury word of them all. Mercury represents how we *perceive* the world. The sign in which it lies reveals what values, interests, and assumptions underlie—and bias—our perceptions.

Here a few quick illustrations. In very simple terms, if your Mercury lies in Aries, the sign of the warrior, you are inclined to perceive the world through the lens of *competition*. If your Mercury is conditioned by Libra, your perceptions are conditioned by questions of *taste* and *aesthetic sensitivity*, along with attention to interpersonal dynamics. You expect paradoxes. Mercury in Pisces? The *mystical* mind. Mercury in Capricorn? A *disciplined* mind, oriented toward great efforts. Mercury in Scorpio? A *psychologically penetrating*, even suspicious, mind.

These are thumbnail sketches of complex ideas. We will go more deeply into all of them in Part Three, the "cookbook" section. For now it is enough to remember that Mercury has many faces, not only that of Virgo.

WHAT ABOUT THE SIXTH HOUSE?

Astrologers often conflate signs and houses, as if they were the same thing. It is easy to understand how they make that mistake. There are indeed strong parallels between signs and their corresponding houses. We will see that phenomenon very clearly as we talk about the sixth house and the sign Virgo, which is of course the sixth sign of the zodiac. I delved more deeply into the differences between signs and houses in *The Book of Fire*, as well as briefly touching on the question earlier in these pages, so I will not repeat all of that here. Bottom line, some of the language we use in describing Virgo we will also used in describing the sixth house.

Still, keeping one eye on the sign-house distinction often resolves interpretive conundrums, and unfailingly adds reliability and precision to our interpretations. That is why, when we get to Part Three, there will be no section heading, *If Your Mercury Is in Virgo or the Sixth House*. To me, that is just sloppy astrology.

THE HOUSE OF SERVANTS

Open almost any astrology book and turn to the chapter about the sixth house. You will see it described as the *house of servants*. You will read that it is associated with *duties* and *responsibilities*. You will learn that it is connected to daily *routines*—brushing your hair, visiting the dentist, getting out of bed on cue when the alarm clock demands it.

Basically it is as if everything *necessary but boring* in life was given to the sixth house. Thus, if you want to fill seats at an astrology conference, you would do well to choose a different topic. No one is very excited about having to get out of bed in the morning and go to work. No one is excited about grocery shopping or paying the monthly bills.

As we will see, all of those points are in fact quite relevant to the realities of the sixth house. None of the foregoing ideas are wrong. The problem is not what is written about the sixth house; the problem is what is left out.

We will get back to brushing your hair, visiting the dentist, and getting out of bed to go to work.

But let's start with the heart of the matter.

AUNTS AND UNCLES

Aunts and uncles in relation to their nieces and nephews—historically, those relationships figured prominently in everyday life as well as in the astrology of the sixth house. Nowadays those kinship connections do not loom as large as they once did, at least for most of us. It is common today for people to live far from their blood relatives. The importance of those relationships has been diluted. But historically, the relationship between an aunt and her niece or an uncle and his nephew was very often quite significant. It was a relationship of *mentoring*.

And with that word, we enter familiar Virgo territory.

Let's quickly add a modern variant: *"You have got to meet my uncle Jack . . he's not really my uncle but . . ."* We all know what that phrase means:

Uncle Jack is not actually the brother of my father or my mother—but he is a trusted older man who took a special interest in me, who helped me grow up, and whom I love and appreciate.

The sixth house mentoring relationship, in other words, does not any longer depend upon genetic ties. In the old days, before the Industrial Revolution broke up clans and dispersed families across the country—back when your aunts and uncles were your neighbors too—back then, I suspect the sixth house had a very active, literal connection with these kinds of family ties. While that is far less true today, the institution of mentoring—and the psychological necessity for it—has not gone away. It has only changed in form.

Our mentors are still there, in other words—it is just that nowadays they are often not our actual relatives.

Sixteen-year-old Joanne approaches her beloved Aunt Sue. She opens the conversation with an ancient ritual phrase—one which immediately binds Aunt Sue to absolute confidentiality. Joanne says, *"Promise you won't tell my mother, but . . ."*

Notice something unsettling: an older woman has just agreed to collude with a younger one in deceiving the younger one's mother. Furthermore, the older woman has agreed without even yet knowing the nature of the collusion. She will keep the secret.

Sounds bad, right?

And yet I suspect the words made you smile. Your sixth house recognizes and appreciates these kinds of relationships, and instinctively understands the rules that govern them.

Once young Joanne utters that ritual phrase, it would require extraordinary and extreme circumstances for Aunt Sue to rat out Joanne to her mom. Again, the point is that *we all understand this.* That is because we are in the presence of an ancient, sacred archetype—one symbolized by the sixth house.

Aunt Sue nods her head. She is now bound to confidentiality. Joanne continues, *"Jason and I did it."*

A young woman has embarked upon the stormy seas of human sexuality. Isn't it wonderful, isn't it fundamentally healthy, that she has an older woman who loves her *and who is not her mother* in whom she can confide and from whom she can seek guidance?

No one grows up right without mentoring. I have mentioned that this dimension of the sixth house is often ignored in astrological practice. Much of that ignorance derives from a very simple source: the rest of society is also rather ignorant about the importance of the mentoring relationship. Astrologers always reflect their societies and their own upbringing.

One disastrous side effect of that particular ignorance is that today we ask far too much of parents. They are asked to carry a burden—the burden of raising a sane child—that used to be carried far more jointly. The proverb, "it takes a village to raise a child," is deeply relevant here. And it is all about the sixth house.

One further step: a fine predictor that you will become an excellent aunt is that *you had one yourself.* A fine predictor that you will become an excellent uncle is, again, that you had one.

Thus, once more, we are looking at the word lineage: something precious is passed on down the line. A flame is kept burning even after the hearts that carried it for a while have stopped beating.

Look at you, reading this book: you are carrying a flame too.

A HEARTBREAKING
CONTEMPORARY FOOTNOTE

Mom's best friend has always had a special affection for little Debbie. They simply liked each other right from the beginning. As the years go by, Debbie gradually becomes Deborah—but her warm relationship with the older woman—her "aunt" Christine—deepens and continues. Throughout Deborah's teenage years, the two of them often go shopping together or have lunch and a long, intimate conversation.

Perhaps one day, Deborah said those fateful words about "Jason"— and her "Aunt Christine" was there for her throughout that passage, never breathing a word to Debbie's mom.

Anyone with a heart who hears of such a bond between an older woman and a younger one immediately feels its sweetness. The "aunt" and the "niece" have enhanced each other's lives. The world is a better place for it. Deborah will grow up saner and happier as a result of this mentoring she has received.

Everyone knows that; no one questions it. Everyone celebrates it.

Compare all that with the following scenario: *an older man, not a member of the family, has taken a strong personal interest in a young boy . . .*

Uh oh, right?

Unless you are blessed with an absolute immunity to the toxicity of modern culture, immediately suspicion arises about the older man's motives. Could he be a pedophile?

The woman-girl mentoring relationship is still greeted with delight and respect, while the man-boy relationship tends to be viewed with considerably more caution. The effect is that such relationships are discouraged, sometimes subtly, sometimes aggressively. Their frequency, privacy, and intensity are inhibited. We are in the realm of tribal taboo.

A few paragraphs ago, I made the comment that no one grows up right without mentoring. Being human is very difficult—but humans have been working on it for a long time. We have cultural traditions that are not instinctual structures, but instead behaviors, values, and attitudes which must be learned from someone who already embodies them—someone who presumably learned them a while back from someone else. They are passed down the generations.

Lineage, in other words.

None of us can figure all this "human" stuff out all by ourselves. It must be transmitted, in one-to-one relationships, from older people to younger people.

This transmission is undervalued and mostly unremarked in modern culture—but with females it is at least still mostly supported. With males, on the other hand, due to toxic—and hopefully transitory—conditions in the *zeitgeist*, these mentoring relationships have been significantly shattered.

If I am right when I say that no one grows up right without proper mentoring, then all this would predict an epidemic of *particularly masculine madness* poisoning society. We are seeing the results in all those boys who grew up without guidance or role models—guidance from men who were not their fathers.

I am tempted to simply say, any questions? The results of the situation are painfully obvious.

Boys need time spent in the company of men, away from women—just as girls need the company of women, away from men. Lacking that sixth house guidance, we foolishly expect boys left on their own to figure out graceful and appropriate ways to handle surges of Mars energy—translation: the energies of sex and violence—energies that are so powerful in their psyches that it is probably fair to say no woman can understand them in the same way.

I am aware that my last line could get me in trouble in some circles. My only defense is to add that no man, in my opinion, can really understand childbirth or the depth of a mother's bond with a baby—or what it must feel like to have basic biological processes so magically synchronized with the phases of the Moon.

All that female experience must be amazing, but I would be the first to admit that I am not in a very good position to understand it.

RECOGNIZING YOUR MENTORS

Maybe you have Pluto in your sixth house. Then your mentors—people without whom you cannot fully become who you need to become—are Plutonian. You can recognize them by their intensity. You will have the sense that these are people to whom you can say anything, however extreme it might be, and that they will not be frightened or judgmental.

Maybe Neptune is in your sixth house. Then the mentors you need will help you stabilize your own psychic sensitivities. When they were younger, someone helped them learn to live comfortably with the same challenge. Now they want to pass the teaching along to you, at least by example.

Maybe Mercury is in your sixth house—look for articulate people who can express themselves fluently. Maybe they are writers or teachers.

Venus? Your mentors may be artists. At the very least, they are human beings with a lot of "people skills."

You get the idea: any planet in your sixth house helps you to recognize your mentors. Technically, it is also helpful to pay attention to the sign on the cusp of the sixth house, along with the position of the planet that rules that sign.

There is another level to all of this—implicit in the previous statement is the assumption that you *need mentoring* in those kinds of areas. Thus while those planets represent skills you need to develop, they also represent *the kinds of people who will help you develop them.*

At this point, we only need to understand the principle—that the sixth house is about mentoring, and that any planet in that house spotlights the nature of your mentors.

Later, in Part Three, we will consider in some depth the individual meaning of each planet when it finds itself in this house.

THE SIXTH HOUSE AND MONDAY MORNING

Monday morning has a shady reputation. The weekend is now officially deader than a doornail; it's time to face the music: drag your poor carcass out of bed and go to work. You need to steel yourself to face your responsibilities. Duty calls. Quit your whining too: if it were fun, they wouldn't have to pay you to do it. And while you are at it, cheer up—Friday is only five days away.

Note how my language here does more than summarize the collective attitude toward Monday morning. It also embodies much of the conventional astrological understanding of the sixth house.

But is it possible to not hate Mondays? Does that violate some elemental law of the universe? Those questions can potentially lift us up out of the sixth house funk.

I will readily admit that after a hard week of astrological client work, I am eager for the weekend. But I can also honestly say that I am grateful for this work I do. It pays me a lot more than money. I am rarely so fully alive as when I am sitting with an intelligent, engaged client, swept along by energies greater than myself, doing an astrological reading. In anticipation of such a session, I often feel some degree of dread—I know it will take everything I've got to do a good job. But once we have dived into the process, I am happy and energized.

Even on Monday.

I do not mean to fuss about myself. I am just pointing out that "not hating Mondays" is not some exotic concept out of a fairy tale. I am saying that it is potentially a reality—that, simply said, *there are many people in the world blessed with work that they enjoy.*

Remember our ancient Egyptian Virgo prayer? *God grant that today I do work that matters.* That is a sixth house prayer too. The difference is that while Virgo simply represents the *urge to exercise those meaningful skills* of craft and service, the sixth house begins to focus our attention on their *ex-*

act natures. It actually describes the work that will "matter" for you—work that just might put a better complexion on Monday morning.

WAIT A MINUTE ...
WHAT ABOUT THE TENTH HOUSE?

Ask any astrologer about the symbolism of career in the birthchart and your attention is far more likely to be directed to the tenth house than to the sixth. Never fear, we will meet the tenth house in a big way in the next chapter. As we will see, calling the tenth the "house of career" is quite correct. But astrologers often underestimate the relevance of the sixth house to questions of work and profession. It is a big part of the picture too.

In a nutshell, the tenth house is connected to how you are *perceived socially* as a result of the work you do, while the sixth house has a lot more to do with the practical "craft" realities that you actually face on Monday morning.

Let's say that you are a successful novelist. That is a career which plays very well at cocktail parties. Should someone ask you "what you do," your answer immediately confers upon you a certain status. In most circles, in other words, it is considered "cool" to be a professional novelist.

All that is a very tenth house perspective.

But if you are a novelist, here is the reality you actually face on Monday morning—that is to say, the reality of your sixth house. You have probably overdosed on coffee. Your hair has not been brushed. You are wearing an old T-shirt touting a band that last toured in 1987. You are gnashing your teeth trying to iron out a plot-mistake you made six chapters ago without having to rewrite the entire book.

Call the men in the funny white suits. You look like a mad person. You feel like one too.

So much for the "romance" of being a novelist.

The tenth house is what you look like, how you are seen and interpreted by the community. The sixth house is the work itself.

I love murder mysteries. One of my favorite authors in that genre was a man named Robert B. Parker. He wrote a brilliant series of best-selling novels that featured a hard-boiled, two-fisted, private detective named Spenser. The tales were spiced in a more contemporary way by the presence of Spenser's mostly-faithful lover and foil, psychiatrist Susan Silverman, along with his enigmatic—and very urbane—black sidekick, Hawk. Just to give you a feeling for Hawk, he once uttered the immortal line, "I asked for champagne, but they brought me Korbel."

Parker died at age 77 on January 18, 2010, while sitting at his desk in Massachusetts. When his heart stopped, he was in mid-sentence, working on another novel.

He was a Virgo. He died doing work he loved.

Talk about excellent karma.

FINDING WORK, FINDING MENTORS

Earlier I celebrated my friendship with Robert A. Johnson, the Jungian writer and analyst. I had already been doing astrology for a long time when we met, but he gave my work a boost to a new level.

As a young man, I met the great spiritual teacher, Ram Dass—my band was opening for him, and we had a brief chance to chat. Transmission? I think so—and at a critical age. Meeting Ram Dass was directly relevant to the subsequent tone of my astrological work.

Khenpo Karthar, Rinpoche, once touched his forehead to mine—and my understanding of Buddhism was mysteriously boosted.

On September 9, 1995, I shook hands with master guitarist, Eric Clapton—and couldn't wait to run home and play my guitar. I think his handshake actually helped my playing.

Crazy? I know it sounds that way, but I don't think so.

I could go on and on. Probably, if you think about, so could you. Lineage is a reality. Everyone has a sixth house, and even if you were not born with any planets there, planets will certainly trigger it via transits, progressions, or solar arcs.

The enigmas posed by the transcendent riddles of lineage may baffle us. They may lie outside our present cultural description of how reality works.

But they are universal nonetheless.

Do remember that the gifts our mentors pass on to us are not limited to areas we might label "work" or "career." They range far more widely than that, embracing any area of human life where skills that are not simply instinctual might arise. Outside of professional categories, our mentors help us spiritually. They demonstrate skills that help us to maintain our relationships in sane and realistic ways. They help us creatively, even if we never make a penny with our creativity.

Perhaps above all, they help us find the skills in ourselves that lead us to our right work—and the dignity that goes along with finding it. They help us find that Holy Grail of the sixth house: work that matters.

HEALTH

Physical health has long been connected to the sixth house. In the old astrology books, it was often called the house of illness. About the time the language of the weather report turned from "partly cloudy" to "partly sunny," the sixth house switched from illness to health. And of course they are different sides of the same coin.

In a spirit of honesty and transparency, the first thing I want to say is that the astrology of health and illness is an area about which I simply do not know very much. In the spirit of Hippocrates, I have tended to follow his famous dictum, "First Do No Harm." I have been afraid, in other words, that in my ignorance, I might offer a client damaging medical advice.

Better to simply keep my mouth shut.

I am mostly going to follow that path here. I do not have much to say about the sixth house and medical diagnosis. If you want to pursue it, I can recommend Noel Tyl's 1998 book, *Astrological Timing of Critical Illness*. Another excellent one is *A Handbook of Medical Astrology* by Jane Ridder-Patrick.

Let me make two simple and reliable points however. They both revolve around the interactive trinity of body, mind, and spirit. Both assume that keeping mind and spirit healthy can only be good for your physical body. Most physicians acknowledge the powerful role of attitude in maintaining our resistance to disease and in supporting our recuperative powers.

* The first point is that finding right work and thus enhancing our sense of meaning in life has got to be good for your health.
* The second is that the sixth house is very much about habits, routines, and the kinds of responsibilities we accept in life. An uplifting weekend workshop about physical vitality is not going to do you nearly as much good in the long run as a commitment to eating plenty of organic vegetables, exercising, and avoiding toxins.

By consciously choosing healthy sixth house habits, you strengthen your health.

Signs and planets do correlate with specific organs and processes in the physical body. Traditionally, finding those signs and planets in your sixth house would indicate areas of medical vulnerability.

Again, I have not worked in any depth with those ideas. Rather than risk doing you any harm, I will just encourage you to consult the works of proficient medical astrologers.

One more point—as we have seen, any planet in your sixth house is connected to your mentors, to those whom you yourself might mentor, and to your right service in this world. My feeling is that in responding well and consciously to that evolutionary path, you also enhance your physical health. And conversely, any failure to rise to those potentials increases your medical vulnerabilities.

There are many rewards for getting the sixth house right. Among other things, it gives you a reason to live.

And doesn't that sound healthy?

5

THE CAPRICORN CLAN: SATURN, THE TENTH HOUSE, AND THE SIGN OF THE SEA-GOAT

If anyone ever needed proof that the mysterious origins of astrology must lie in the northern hemisphere, he or she would need look no further than the sign Capricorn. When the Sun enters Capricorn, winter begins—at least up here, north of the equator. The symbolic match is pure perfection. As we will soon see, winter provides a flawless metaphor for the nature of the Zodiac's tenth sign. Both Capricorn and winter represent challenge and difficulty; both require enormous patience and commitment; both focus our attention on the practical fundamentals of survival.

Our ancestors could not have missed the connection.

What about all the solar Capricorns born in Australia, Chile, or South Africa? The fit between Capricorn and winter is so perfect that the question is legitimate and natural. When I was a young astrologer, ready and eager to challenge everything I had been taught, I entertained the idea that there might be a reversal of the polarity of the signs in the southern hemisphere—that Australian Capricorns, for example, would actually behave like Cancers.

But they don't. They are as Capricornian as their northern sisters and brothers. Like many a reasonable hypothesis, this "reversal" notion foundered on the rocky shore of fact and observation.

A person conditioned by modern ways of thinking would then conclude that the equation of Capricorn and winter was "a happy accident"—sort of a lucky clue for our astrological ancestors. That interpretation works, but personally, I am more inclined to think of it as evidence of the benign intelligence of the universe guiding us. There is good reason to consider this more metaphysical version of things. Mars did not have to be the orange-red of dried blood, nor did Venus have to be a beautiful jewel in the twilight sky. Mercury didn't have to be quick nor Saturn slow. Those observations, and many others, have led me to have great faith in the existence of some higher intelligence shepherding us toward increasing levels of self-awareness. The universe was not trying to make astrology more difficult or more obscure than it had to be. Instead, it laid out a trail of breadcrumbs for us to follow.

And winter is indeed difficult—and all of the virtues we must muster in order to survive it are the virtues of Capricorn, no matter which hemisphere we call home.

A SHORTAGE OF BEANS

Let's imagine that you are stranded in a rustic lakeside cabin deep in the Yukon Territory. Even worse, it's early January—and freezing cold. The seaplane that is going to rescue you cannot arrive until the ice that covers the lake has melted. Without water to land on, the pilot can only wait.

You are going to be there in that cabin for a while, in other words. Your food supply is meager: four cartons of baked beans, twenty-four cans to the carton. You have to make those beans last until you are rescued—but of course you don't know exactly when that will happen. Maybe you'll get lucky and the spring melt might come early. Or it could be a month late. You had better be on the safe side. You do the math, and you do it conservatively. The end of May is five months from now, which means about 150 days. And you have ninety-six cans of beans. You're going to have to tighten your belt—that, or you can eat like a king for a couple of months, then starve to death. It's your call.

Winter is not mean; winter just doesn't care.

No matter what sign of the Zodiac you were born under, this little anecdote puts you solidly in tune with the Capricorn archetype. It is about the *survival of the fittest*— we just have to be very careful about how we understand that famous phrase. The "fittest" are not necessarily the biggest or the most aggressive; the fittest are the ones who look at reality with a cold, clear eye, and adapt most effectively to its requirements.

Capricorn "does the math"—whether it's about beans, money, or the quest for love.

ANOTHER FROZEN LAKE

You have managed to get yourself lost on a winter hike through a snowy forest. It is late in the afternoon. Night will soon fall. The temperatures are already below freezing. The situation is getting scary.

You stumble onto the shore of a frozen lake. It is about half a mile wide. On the other side, across the ice, you can see the inviting lights of a village. You wonder . . . *is the ice thick enough to bear my weight?* If so, I could just stroll right across the lake and be warm and safe in ten minutes.

Walking around the lake through the snow, on the other hand—well, you have no clear idea exactly how long that might take.

You spy a rock the size of a basketball. As a way of testing the situation, you roll it out onto the ice. The ice cracks, but just a little bit. The stone does not fall through.

The results are uncertain . . .

Maybe you decide to take the risk and walk across the lake. Maybe you arrive on the far shore, safe and sound, congratulating yourself for having made a smart choice.

The reality is entirely different: *you actually made an incredibly stupid choice and you got lucky.*

Ask any Capricorn: in winter, sooner or later, that attitude will kill you.

When I tell that story to my Capricorn clients, it becomes something like a Zen *koan*. Here's the grand finale: I say to them, *you have come here to the planet Earth in order to learn how to walk around the lake.*

There is, in Capricorn, a certain element of "cash and carry" karma: if you have signed the Capricorn contract, you simply cannot get away with much in this life. If you cut corners, the corners will cut you. Three

Capricorns come to mind as illustrations, two of whom I've already mentioned earlier in the book. Richard Nixon thought he could get away with "Watergate." He didn't. Al Capone, the famous mobster, got away with murder—but he was busted for "tax evasion."

And Janis Joplin thought she could shoot heroin and live to tell about it.

A VERY WEIRD PIECE OF BIOLOGICAL ENGINEERING

Half fish, half goat. That is Capricorn. As we commented a few chapters back, such a creature would not have much practical hope of survival in this world. But in the world of symbolism, it is formidable. The Sea-Goat represents absolute mastery of the material plane. It can climb the highest mountain, swim the widest ocean, dive to the bottom of the deepest sea. Nothing can stop it. Once Capricorn sets an intention, it either fulfills it or dies in the process of trying.

Here is a standard-issue litany of astrological keywords for Capricorn: *self-discipline, practicality, patience, reason, determination, relentlessness, resolution, focus, single-mindedness, forbearance, longsuffering, stoicism, resourcefulness, logic, abhorrence of waste, self-sacrifice, maturity, sobriety . . .*

It sounds like Capricorn is a real party animal, right?

Those keywords are all accurate and useful, but something has been lost, both from our understanding of Capricorn and from history.

CAN CAPRICORN BE CAPRICIOUS?

Before we consign Capricorn to the bin labeled "practical but not exactly date-bait," let's throw one more word on the pile: *capricious.* The Oxford English Dictionary defines it as, "Given to sudden and unaccountable changes of mood or behaviour." And that description of course bears very little resemblance to the "Sun Sign" Capricorn of twenty-first century pop astrology.

Etymologically, the word "capricious" appears obviously to be related to Capricorn. Some scholars differ, thinking that it is connected to another word, one for the humble hedgehog. Still, most academics see "capricious" connected with the Latin word for goat, *capra.*

I am going with the goat rather than the hedgehog, and not just because I am biased. If you have ever watched goats in action, you can see that they are indeed "capricious" creatures. They frolic and play and excel at getting into mischief.

A hedgehog, on the other hand, basically lies there.

I am not a mythologist, but without digging too deeply, further evidence is available. The Greek god, Pan, was famous for frolicking carnally with the nymphs. He is always represented with classic Capricornian signatures: the hindquarters, legs, and horns of a goat.

And Pan was indeed the ultimate party animal.

What about Dionysus, the "god of wine?" Like Pan, he too had a rather orgiastic reputation. His birth is generally represented as occurring around Christmas—thus another historical link between Capricorn and the wild side of life.

So what is going on here? Did we lose something barbarous and ancient when we dressed poor Capricorn as a conservative banker and hung him out to dry?

There are deep waters here, and we must fathom them if we are going to understand Capricorn as it actually is, and must be.

STAYING ALIVE

There is a poem by William Butler Yeats with an utterly Capricornian title: *The Fascination of What's Difficult.* Just five words, but they epitomize the essence of this sign of the Zodiac. The metaphor of climbing the highest mountain or swimming the widest ocean—difficult things—pervades everything about it. This is the sign of *Great Works.* Every monumental act of human doggedness and persistence reflects a strand of Capricornian DNA. As Thomas Edison said, "genius is one percent inspiration and 99% perspiration."

Capricorn is the perspiration part.

The connection with "capricious?" All that relentless effort gets tiring after a while. Capricorn needs a break—but its tendency toward one-pointed focus can blind it to its own human needs. *Thus, the tension between the requirements of monumental effort, on one hand, and the reality of human limitations on the other can lead to a train wreck.* Maybe we see simple exhaustion or burn-out. Maybe we see stress-related collapse.

Or maybe that old mythological "goat-god" just grabs the steering wheel, cancels all the obligations, and goes hunting for wine and nymphs.

TIME OUT FOR MOTHER MOON

It is helpful to remember that Capricorn opposes Cancer, the sign ruled by the Moon. And the Moon is always about *self-care*. The point is not that Capricorn is *opposed* to self-care. The point is that Capricorn keeps its eye on the prize, and those qualities of focus, commitment, and self-discipline can effectively run counter to self-care.

   * Engaged with any project, for example, Capricorn is the part of you—and we all have some of it in us—that might forget to eat.
   * It is the part of you that might disregard signals of the body telling you that you have reached a point of exhaustion.
   * Capricorn is the part of you which, when faced with the kind of errors that arise from exhaustion, does not choose to sleep, but rather re-doubles its efforts.

In all of this, we are beginning to contemplate Capricorn's shadow territory. Every sign of the Zodiac comes with blind spots. Here we encounter some of the ones associated with Capricorn. All of them stem from either misguided or excessive self-discipline.

Here is another verse of that poem by William Butler Yeats.

The fascination of what's difficult
Has dried the sap out of my veins, and rent
Spontaneous joy and natural content
Out of my heart.

It is through Yeats' lens that we begin to understand the relationship between Capricorn and the word capricious. There are two sides to this coin, a bright one and a dark one. Over the next several pages, we will come to understand their implications more deeply, but let me state them simply here:

The bright side of the coin is the recognition that handling Capricorn energy skillfully and mindfully requires accepting that the human psychic organism—not to mention the physical organism—needs a break from time to time. That break might boil down to simply getting some sleep, but often it means something broader. The word *recreation* comes to mind.

In a nutshell, Capricorn cannot survive its own monumental focus and determination without some balance in its life. Its evolutionary intention must include that provision or collapse awaits.

"Collapse" brings us to the dark side of the coin. Literal physical collapse based upon exhaustion is one possibility.

But there are other kinds of collapse.

Capricorn can lose its 1% of inspiration, and become merely mechanical, going through the motions of its many duties, grimly checking them off the list, sleeping briefly, and facing them in renewed fashion the next morning. At some point down that road, something breaks. Repressed hunger, repressed humanity, and repressed need can rise up fiercely out of the psychic depths and grab the helm.

Everything else being equal, we can think of Capricorn as a sign that is *inherently moral.* It wants to *do the right thing*, in other words. For the Sea-Goat, *integrity counts.* However, if the breaking point creeps up on the unwitting Capricorn, moral collapse can ensue. Here we see a more cautionary reading of Pan or Dionysus, along with the dark side of the word "capricious." When this primal wildness rises up in rebellion from the psychic depths, it can be destructive, barbarous, and unthinking.

These two sides of the coin—the necessity of self-monitoring, recreation, and self-care, and the terrible dangers of ignoring them—are absolutely fundamental to our understanding of the Capricorn clan. We see them in the sign, which is our immediate subject here. We will also see their fingerprints the tenth house and in the planet Saturn that rules them both.

REMEMBERING CAPRICORN'S PLACE IN THE EARTH FAMILY TRINITY

One of life's great ironies is the way we sweat our tiny decisions and often make our big ones whimsically. Maybe you need to buy a new laptop computer. Night after night, you peruse the Internet, reading reviews of various models, weighing their features, searching for the best price. You are careful; you do not want to buy the wrong machine. The decision is worth some effort. An error could cost you money and frustration.

Meanwhile, you see a movie and it triggers in you a decision to move to Arizona. Or maybe you meet someone and a few weeks later you are engaged to be married.

We can laugh at ourselves for this apparent irony, but I actually think we need to celebrate it. *I believe that all of the truly important decisions in life have to be made whimsically*—or to say it more precisely, they have to be made by the heart. The heart is simply better suited to the job.

That probably sounds a little too good to be true, but let me try to prove it to you.

Your intellect can stay on top of most of the variables connected with buying that new laptop. The decision is complex—but it is child's play compared to a decision about where to spend your life or with whom you might choose to spend it. With the latter kinds of decisions, there are just too many variables and too many unknown quantities for mere intellect to have a prayer of navigating them successfully.

Icing the cake is the fact that, unlike buying the computer, these are decisions of the heart. We cannot ignore their emotional components and still get them right. Who, faced with the prospect of choosing a life partner, would prefer to leave the final decision up to Match.com? The voice of the heart, for all its potential blind spots, still must have the final vote.

This insight brings us right back to Capricorn's natural place in the interdependent Earth Family trinity. As we saw earlier in this book, Taurus is the sign connected with our animal instincts. Taurus tells us whether "Arizona" *smells right*—or if Aubrey "smells better" to us than Sinclair. That Taurean part of us partakes of an ancient heritage of monkey-wisdom, something honed and purified over countless millennia—something intimately connected with the parts of our psyches that we call heart or soul. Like the proverbial iceberg, 90% of you is invisible, under the waves. Over the centuries, that primeval part of you has gone by other names as well: instinct, the unconscious mind, "feelings in your bones."

Whatever we name it, much of the secret of happiness in life derives from learning to trust it.

With its single-mindedness, propensity for logical strategy, and self-discipline, the Sea-Goat can climb any mountain—including the wrong one. Capricorn is powerful beyond measure, but it can also be an unguided missile. On what mountain should Capricorn unleash its formidable energies? What mountain is worthy of it? If you are a Capricorn, here's the question with which you must wrestle: of all the mountains in the world, which one is actually mine to climb?

Your intellect and your reason cannot answer those questions. It is your guts—or your soul—that must answer them. In other words, *Capricorn's reason must be guided by Taurus's nose.* This is their interdependency.

And of course, as we learned earlier, Virgo comes into play here as well, providing the skills to make it happen—but I don't want to muddy the water by repeating all that here.

William Butler Yeats warned us all about how succumbing to "the fascination of what's difficult" can "dry the sap out of our veins, and rend spontaneous joy and natural content out of our hearts." That is the Capricorn shadow and if you were born with any planets in that sign, you must be wary of it.

The problem, however, cannot be reduced to the idea of simply "working too hard." This sign is indeed all about working very hard; that is not the issue. The issue lies squarely in the question of determining at *exactly what* you were born to choose as your work. Get that part right, and the effort will give you energy rather than subtracting energy from you.

And that determination must be made by your Taurean "sense of smell" rather than by any kind of calculation. Your heart must have the final vote; otherwise, Capricorn simply exhausts itself for no ultimate purpose or reason.

RESISTING TEMPTATION

As I sit here at my desk writing these words, I am full of gratitude for the chance to work on a book. It is Friday, the day I have set aside each week for the sake of this Elements project. And I really love to write—in principle, at least.

In reality, I must struggle to concentrate. When distractions arise, my "official position" is that I resent them. Reality is more complex—there is *part of me that relishes any excuse to get a break from the relentless, exhausting level of concentration that goes into writing a book.* I need to resist the temptation to go for a stroll in my garden or go to look over Michelle's shoulder as she paints at her easel. My poor cats could use a pat or a scritch—what kind of cat-friend am I that I so callously ignore them? I could easily waste an hour answering trivial emails or reading the latest news out of Belarus or Namibia. The list goes on.

Let me quote another line from William Butler Yeats: *"All things can tempt me from this craft of verse."* He and I are in the same boat. Maybe you are too. We all hear the Siren song of laziness—anything to get us off the hook of trying to do our level best.

It is tempting to say that, if there is any hope of my ever finishing this book, I must resist all such temptations. There is some truth in those words—and yet, if I were to become utterly impervious to all such temptations, that level of focus might lead to another kind of disaster. Were I to go down that cold-heartedly relentless road, after a while I might become dangerously and unwittingly "capricious."

I might explode, in other words.

Resisting temptation is an essential component of Capricorn fulfilling its "eye on the prize" intentions. That part is obvious.

Equally necessary is judiciously *succumbing to temptation* from time to time, lest all of that effort "dries the sap out of its veins," leaving the Sea-Goat subject to physical or moral collapse.

With planets in Capricorn, that is the tightrope you must walk. That is your balancing act.

CAPRICORN THE CONTROL FREAK

Popular astrological literature is full of references to Capricorn offering people free, if unsolicited, breathing lessons. All Capricorns, even females, have an alleged tendency to "mansplain"—at least according to those conventional pop-astrology sources. Reading on, we learn that at the slightest provocation, Capricorn types launch into lecture mode, belaboring the obvious, correcting the errors they perceive in their hapless captive audience.

In my experience, most astrological clichés—*all the Geminis talk too much, all the Pisceans have lost their car keys*—are actually worth knowing. The same is true for the idea that Capricorn is a *control freak*. It is just that in order to make proper use of these clichés, we must always remember to file them under "S" for "Shadow." As silly as most of them sound—and as incorrect as they often are in individual cases—they do crystallize the dark side of each sign.

At its best, Capricorn is not about controlling other people. It is about *controlling itself.* Failing that, it can quickly succumb to attempting to control everyone else.

Let's say it a little more deeply. At its best, Capricorn *resists temptation*—something no one enjoys doing, not even Capricorn. In any healthy response to Capricorn, our ultimate, highest intentions have dominion over appetite, fear, and all other needs or desires. That is how the Sea-Goat maintains focus and gets to the mountaintop.

Staying focused and resisting distraction are forms of self-control.

Here is the key: the energy that can potentially allow Capricorn to succeed in that self-mastery can be easily misdirected. If we have become mechanical, *if we have chosen our mountain without questioning whether it smells right,* then eventually a certain instability enters the system. We have already listed some of those "capricious" risks.

To our cautions around the word "capricious," we must now add one more: *the tendency to project our personal need for control onto everyone except for the one person who actually needs it.*

And that is the person you see when you look into the mirror.

THE ELDER

One rather universal perspective on the planet Saturn among astrologers is its connection with *old age.* We will explore that idea more deeply in the next section of this chapter. I mention it now because, since Saturn rules Capricorn, that same energy pervades the sign as well as the planet.

Sitting with Capricorn clients, I often fantasize about a time when they were five years old. I imagine them standing in the presence of two wise elders. After a while the young Capricorn wanders off. One of the elders turns to the other and says, "She is going to make a terrific old lady."

The other Elder laughs and says, "Every time I see her, I think the same thing."

Sitting with the client, the next thing I do is to criticize those two elders for being fortune-tellers. I point out that what they are actually seeing in the little girl is the *seed* of a terrific old lady. Perhaps there is telltale gleam of mischievous wisdom in her eyes. *Certain kinds of experience, over many decades, could potentially turn that seed into something truly precious, but that is the only guarantee.* That little girl has some lessons ahead of her—lessons that can potentially forge that gleam in her eye into true wisdom.

In this little anecdote, we understand something fundamental about the evolutionary intention of Capricorn. It is the aim of *becoming an elder.* And that does not mean simply getting old—many people get old without becoming elders.

    * If I had to define the term "elder," here is how I would do it: an elder is an older person surrounded by younger ones *who want to be there.*

    * Someone who is merely old may indeed be surrounded by young people—but only because they feel they *have* to be there.

Everything else being equal, Capricorn energy ages well. Still, we must be careful—if you are a Capricorn, you can indeed do great things even when you are young. You can even be an "elder" at a tender age, if only in the sense that your peers turn to you when they are lost or need guidance and insight. There are Capricorn "elders" in third grade playgrounds all around the world. You recognize them by their *gravitas,* and by that "gleam of mischievous wisdom in their eyes."

SOLITUDE

Archetypally, Capricorn is often related to the archetype of the Hermit. Since Saturn is the traditional Lord of Solitude, you can readily feel the signature of Saturn's rulership in that dimension of the Sea-Goat. And indeed a common characteristic of people with strong Capricorn influences in their natal charts is simply that they *need a lot of time alone.*

Still, calling them introverts is not always accurate. The same can be said for assuming that Capricorn people are antisocial or misanthropic. None of those statements are reliably true. Given enough time alone to charge his or her batteries, a Capricorn person can be lively, engaged company.

But if you want to drive Capricorns crazy, send them to cocktail parties that last forever.

Some of this self-sufficient quality derives from the Sea-Goat's single-minded focus on Great Works. Why waste time on idle chit-chat when you are only halfway up the mountain and you have just gotten a terrific idea for where to put your foot next?

Some of that need for solitude runs deeper, into a primeval and ultimately unfathomable vein of Capricornian mystery. Here's how to keep perspective: why do Librans have such a hunger for aesthetic experience? Why do Geminis starve without conversation and fresh ideas? Why are Scorpios energized and uplifted by conversations which many of us would find emotionally draining?

Capricorn's need for solitude is cut from the same cloth—something so innate to the sign that wondering about it is like wondering why the universe exists at all.

Much of what we have learned in the last few pages about Capricorn casts light on Saturn as well. But, as always, there are differences of nuance and function between a sign and a planet.

Let's make friends with the so-called Greater Malefic.

THE PLANET THAT GIVES US THE ABILITY TO DO WHAT WE DO NOT FEEL LIKE DOING

With those baleful words setting the tone for my discussion of Saturn, you might feel a temptation to quickly skip a few pages ahead. You might immediately sense why so many of the astrologers of yore viewed this planet as the worst of the lot: the infamous Greater Malefic. Who wants to do what he or she doesn't feel like doing?

Nobody!

As we will soon see, behind its grim mask Saturn's reality includes a smiling, even joyful, face. True to the nature of Saturn however, we will have to work for a while before we get a taste of that joy.

At the risk of pontificating, let me begin by pointing out that only ever doing "exactly what we felt like doing" is a famous formula for catastrophe. Who, for example, has ever *felt like* resisting temptation? And yet if we have no such ability to resist, what will happen to us? The world is crammed full of ice cream, easy money, shopping opportunities, whiskey, and beguiling strangers . . .

Just thinking about it all gives me palpitations—and, praise God, it gives me some degree of cautious hesitation too.

That wise, self-preserving *hesitation to "just say yes"* is pure Saturn.

When was the last time you were simply in the mood to clean the house? When was the last time nothing would please you more than a visit to the dentist— or the proctologist? Have you ever experienced an irresistible whimsy to do your tax returns? How's about cleaning out all of the science projects that have been growing in the back of your refrigerator?

Nobody in the history of the world has ever had the slightest desire to do any of those things. Worse, most of us have known people who decided to "trust their feelings" in these regards and simply ignore those necessities. Most of them wound up as human shipwrecks—with half of them knocking on our doors to borrow money or to sneak them across the state line before the sheriff arrived with the warrant.

Our exploration of Saturn will get darker before it gets lighter. But I promise: it will get lighter.

Maybe you have a dear friend who just lost her teenager in a terrible automobile accident. How do you feel as you contemplate knocking on her door to console her? How do you feel talking to your mother or your father when they have just learned about a life-ending medical diagnosis? Or your dear friend whose life-work has come to nothing?

We all know the emotions we feel about facing those kinds of dispiriting situations. We all feel the same way. When they come along, we pray for the strength to "do what we do not feel like doing." We want to do the right thing. We pray that we do not shame ourselves as adult men and women. We pray that we do not fail ourselves.

Whether we know it or not, we are then praying to the ancient god, Saturn.

Saturn governs *right action*. Saturn is the energy that allows us to live in moral, ethical ways. Saturn is the part of you that keeps your promises. Saturn is the part of you that kept your zipper up when it needed to be up. Your Saturn has often pushed away the second bowl of ice cream and said no to the third margarita.

Saturn is, in other words, a planet without which we could have no basis for dignity or self-respect at all.

Virtue has a stark beauty all its own. We admire moral strength. We admire *character*. These are Saturn qualities. It is natural that we take pride in them.

But a few lines ago, I promised something different from pride. I promised joy. We are moving in that direction, trust me. Here's a start in that direction, even though it might initially appear inauspicious . . .

CLEANING THE HOUSE

Unless you are rich enough to have servants, here is a scene from your life. It is time for a major house cleaning. We used housecleaning as an example earlier in thinking about Virgo, and we need to second look at it now as we contemplate Saturn and Capricorn.

You have made a list of all the looming tasks you face: washing the floors, washing the windows, vacuuming all of the dark corners. Not a single dust-willy is going to be safe around you.

You dread it, of course. But you are resigned: today is the day. You get out the vacuum cleaner and you dive into the project, probably feeling a lot of rapport with Christ Crucified.

Four hours later, you have finally come to the end of your list. Because you were so focussed and engaged, the time actually went by quickly, even though you would never say that you were exactly "enjoying yourself."

You sit down on your sofa, admiring your handiwork.

And almost guaranteed within two minutes you are on your feet again. You have remembered one more thing that needs to be done . . .

Now, there is always an infinitely long list of "one more thing(s)" that needs to be done. Everyone knows that. A house is never perfectly clean. Why can't you just sit there, relax, and bask in the glory of your (adequately) shining home?

This is an utterly Saturnian moment. The strangest thing about it is that discussing our true subjective experience here is slightly taboo, or at least unusual. If I were to say that "there is part of us all that loves to clean the house," most people would laugh at me. And yet, as we sit there on the sofa, there is something inside us that *misses the structure, focus, and absolute engagement that characterized our last four hours of housework.*

We miss that Saturnian single-mindedness.

There is solace and aliveness in hard work, even though people do not generally talk about it that way. Without it, life's uncertainties and petty anxieties rise up again to assail us. Turning around the words of *Amazing Grace,* "we once were found, but now are lost . . ."

I think there's still some dust on those upper mouldings . . .

WASTING AWAY AGAIN IN MARGARITAVILLE

Your great aunt Minnie dies and leaves you $238 billion with only one string attached: you must move into her 12,000 square foot condominium in the Caribbean and from that moment on you must walk in her footsteps, living the life of an indolent aristocrat. All you have to do—and all you are allowed to do—is to put your feet up, run the servants ragged, and gaze over the palm trees out to sea, sipping a drink.

For most of us, there are days when such a prospect might have a certain appeal. But Saturn is the part of you that understands how miserable you would soon be in that scenario. "Wasting away in Margaritaville" that way is like the famous Chinese water torture. At first, it might not seem so bad, but drop by drop, you realize what is happening to your soul.

We are all conditioned to think of weekends as good, while Mondays are the heart of darkness. But the psychological reality is more complex. Again, even though there is a pervasive cultural taboo against talking about it, many of us have experienced aimless, soul-sucking weekends—and getting back to work on Monday actually feels pretty good.

Obviously, the opposite is true quite a lot! But that is not the point. *The point is that some degree of work, challenge, and structure are a critical ingredient in maintaining human happiness.*

And it would be difficult to imagine a more Saturnian insight.

Each planet represents a particular set of needs. To experience basic well-being, all of those needs must be met, at least to some degree. Something inside us all *wants* to work, wants to be *good at something*, wants to be respected—and thus to have a good reason to respect ourselves. Something inside us all wants to get our teeth into life, and to "just do something."

That something is called Saturn, Capricorn's cousin. For your joy to be complete, its needs must be met too. Without it, your life would feel pointless.

Because it would be.

DEPRESSION

Astrologers commonly relate Saturn to depression. That is a slippery truth. While there is reality to it, we must always remember that depression—like all pathological states—only arises when we have made a suboptimal response to some planetary configuration—and that insight really applies to *any* planetary configuration, not just to Saturn.

Turn it around, and that same astrological configuration can supply the *antidote* to the depression—simple: get the planet right and you'll be happy, get it wrong and you'll be sad.

If I were to write that "Venus is the planet of depression," most astrologers would doubt me. Venus represents the drive to connect and to establish intimacy. So what happens if that need is thwarted? *You are lonely.* And being lonely is depressing.

What's the cure? Venus again. Sometimes it is as simple as calling a friend.

With Saturn in particular, there are three unique and particular sources of possible depression:
  * One, which we have already explored extensively, is to exhaust ourselves climbing the wrong mountain for the wrong reasons.
  * Another is to have nothing in our lives that we can sink our teeth into, nothing really to live for—to "waste away in Margaritaville." Meaningful work, meaningful responsibilities—these are powerful antidepressants.
  * The third is to remain caught in a life and a set of responsibilities which we have outgrown—staying "in high school" forever. Let's call it "failure to mature."

BLOCKAGE

"Where Saturn lies in your chart, you were born with a blockage." That depressingly old-school sentence, while it might not sound very encouraging, is actually the beginning of wisdom when it comes to an evolutionary understanding of the planet. *The key is to realize that your inborn blockage is just the first link in a long chain of higher possibilities*, a chain which culminates in a kind of ultimate liberation. Thus, thinking of Saturn as "the planet of blockages," while accurate, can also be misleading and unnecessarily glum. Where astrologers get into trouble is when they forget the rest of the links in the chain.

In the next few lines, I want to outline the basic developmental structure of an evolutionary response to Saturn. My hope is to make its bones crystal-clear, then to add some flesh and complexity to them later on.

Where Saturn lies in your natal chart . . .

* You were born with a blockage. In its essence, the blockage is nearly always some kind of *fear*.
* One dimension of the Great Work of your life lies in breaking through that blockage.
* The first step in accomplishing that Great Work lies in taking responsibility for the blockage—that means, recognizing it and admitting its existence.
* Breaking the blockage requires commitment, self-discipline, and sustained effort over time
* At the end of the process, you may not be "old"—but you will have achieved a new level of maturity, along with self-respect and a renewed, updated basis for happiness. Whatever your age, you will qualify as "an Elder," and people will react to you accordingly.

SATURN SQUARE VENUS

Let's clarify those steps with a concrete example: a natal square between Saturn and Venus. For the sake of clarity, let's keep it simple. We will leave out the signs and houses, and just look at the core planetary issues.

Our first question is, *why* were you born with Saturn square your Venus—or more broadly, why were you born with the birthchart you have? As we have seen earlier, that is the question that separates evolutionary astrology from all other systems. We assume that everything in your chart is purposeful. It arises in response to *evolutionary necessity*—which is to say that its roots lie buried in the karmic past.

Wherever your Saturn is located, we assume that it reflects *unresolved issues around some hardship, fearful circumstance, failure, or limitation you experienced in a prior lifetime*. Almost certainly, you do not remember it. Yet, without any consciousness of its source, *you are filled with fear that it will happen again*.

This Saturn phenomenon is always connected to the notion of "once burned, twice smart." We are not, in other words, simply talking about cowardice or a bad attitude on your part. *We are talking about an actual trauma which occurred before you took birth in your present form.* Because it happened once, you are naturally afraid that it could happen again.

There is nothing crazy about that at all.

Saturn square Venus? *Were you bereaved or betrayed in a previous life?* Did it hit you so hard that even now, perhaps centuries later, you are still guarded about trusting anyone?

There is another possibility: does your blockage manifest as that classic karmic signature: *repetition.* Do you have a tendency to choose people whom you will again lose, one way or another? Do you choose people who will fail you?

In any case, whatever the origin of your blockage, you have come to a point in your evolutionary journey where your intention is to no longer be limited by it. That work—and it will be demanding—is fundamental to the contract you signed with your first breath.

Success is not guaranteed; all that is guaranteed is that success is possible.

Let the great god Saturn speak: *effort will be rewarded, while laziness will lead to experience that might be perceived as punishment.* In actuality, that "punishment" is simply a deadening, unconscious continuation of our slavery to the blockage.

There is a great soul-victory in even recognizing the *existence* of the issue. Many do not achieve that victory, instead imagining themselves to be victims of bad luck or of other people's malfeasance, never realizing their own complicity in the continuation of the blockage.

A great swath of depressing astrological writing about "unlucky" Saturn derives from that precise error.

No single insight—and certainly no weekend workshop—will resolve a Saturn blockage. They might help, but with Saturn we are always in it for the long haul. Once we have recognized the nature of our inborn blockage and taken personal responsibility for it, we are talking about *sustained effort* over years of time. We are talking about burning bridges behind you. We are talking about irreversible lifestyle changes.

I am reminded of Chief Joseph of the Nez Perce people saying, "From where the Sun now stands, I will fight no more forever." It is only that kind of resolve that cures Saturnian issues.

With the Saturn-Venus square, everything starts with choosing *trustworthy people* as friends and partners—people who will typically show strong Saturn or Capricorn signatures in their charts. With their help—and with time—gradually the heart heals.

Almost fifty years ago, I helped a young woman named Carol kick a heroin habit. We both understood the fact that quitting was up to her. I could help her in my way, but only if she truly wanted to be helped. I still feel a strong surge of emotion when I remember her knocking on my door one summer morning. Without preamble, she looked me squarely in the eye and simply said, *"I flushed everything down the toilet."*

Out of context, that line is not exactly William Shakespeare. To me, it is among the most heroic words I have ever heard from another human being.

Through an agony of focus and self-discipline, she made it. That is Saturn, at its best.

This planet is "the Greater Malefic?"

Give me a break.

FLYING AA . . .

Over the years, I have had many clients who were members of the fellowship called Alcoholics Anonymous. By definition, these people are profoundly committed to their spiritual growth—"Spirit or spirits," they say. They support each other in their daily quest for sobriety.

Word quickly gets around about how helpful astrology can be in any healing process. That is how so many members of AA found their way to my door.

In AA, there are as many individual stories as there are dried-out alcoholics. Some of them "hit bottom"—that is, they found themselves in the gutter or in bed with a stranger. Or in jail. Each one of them made a commitment to stop drinking, "one day at a time," hopefully for the rest of their lives.

I have great respect for such souls. They are often among the most truly spiritual people I have ever met. The successful ones are masters of

Saturn. Having hit bottom, they have been humbled. Generally speaking, they have been refreshingly free of the displays of arrogance and self-importance that I have often encountered in other spiritual circles. Each member of the AA fellowship has faced something terrifying in themselves; each one of them has achieved an estimable victory.

Each one has illustrated the highest expression of Saturn.

The "twelfth step" in AA involves making a commitment to helping anyone else who has faced similar difficulties in his or her life. As a result, some members of the fellowship become "sponsors," offering individual help, support, and counsel to newer members.

Here is a Saturn line I used a couple of pages ago: *at the end of the process, you may not be old, but you will have achieved elderhood.*

These AA sponsors may not be old in years—but they are certainly elders in every functional sense of the word.

They illustrate the bright culmination of Saturn's evolutionary process.

THE TENTH HOUSE

Many astrologers make the assumption that all Capricorn-inflected people are career-oriented. This is not a reliable statement at all. The mistake derives from that pervasive error we explored earlier: the conflation of signs and houses. I will spare you my usual rant; you have already seen it a time or two. Suffice to say that while the tenth house is indeed related to career, the sign Capricorn bears a much more tangential relationship to it. Capricorn, as we have seen, only represents an *impulse toward Great Works*, that is all—a "fascination with what's difficult."

Those Capricornian Great Works can take many forms. Raising a sane, happy family is a Great Work—and deserves to be honored as an honorable expression of Capricornian energy. Building yourself a log cabin in the north woods would qualify. So would learning to be a fine guitarist, even if you never made any money with the instrument. Enduring seven years of intensive Jungian analysis is a Great Work, as is doing a week-long silent meditation retreat.

The list is long. All of these actions are lofty expressions of the energy of Capricorn, even though none of them will make you any money at all.

Not so the tenth house. There is indeed money to be made there—although let us immediately affirm that money is not really the point. When society gives you money, it is typically *expressing gratitude for a job you have done well.* Words such as work, career, and ambition are often associated with the tenth house. Those are all accurate; I have no problem with expressing the meaning of the tenth house that way, unless it constricts our imaginations to the point that we miss a far more global perspective.

There is one word, however, which I vastly prefer, one that brings us face to face with that more global perspective. That word is *mission.*

The tenth house is the house of your mission in the world.

Another useful word with the tenth house is *community.* It is here in this part of the chart, that individuals relate to the wider social world—the world of "community," a *world that begins where our personal relationships end,* and which extends indefinitely from there out to the far horizons of society.

To some of the medieval astrologers, the tenth house was the house of *honor.* It is important to note here that the word "honor" had nothing to do with character, ethics, or morality. It was purely about status.

Supplicant client in the days of yore: "Am I in good odor with the Duke of Chesterfield?"

Wise old astrologer: "Ah . . . let us consider the condition of your tenth house."

Here is the modern translation. Go to any contemporary cocktail party and try to count quietly to a thousand without hearing someone utter the following inquiry of a stranger: *"By the way, what do you do?"*

"Do" here is an obvious reference to one's professional status.

There is a stealth element to the cocktail party inquiry as well—once we have an answer, we can, for example, estimate the other person's income. More broadly, we have a sense of their position on the hierarchical totem pole of human society.

You may not care about any of that social game-playing yourself—but others care about all of it as they decide where to place *you* in their mental files. Your experience in the world will be at least somewhat impacted by their view of you. The ways that doors open and close in our faces is always related to our perceived status.

All of this is tenth house territory. As you are seeing, the word "career" is relevant, but so are words like *status* and *reputation.* Go from being married to being single—and watch how people's attitude towards you changes in the blink of an eye. Have your first child. Buy a fancy house—or move to a smaller one. It is all tenth house territory. One quick definition of the tenth house is that it reflects *the way we look to people who barely know us at all.*

Humans have always lived in societies. Advantages, vexations, alliances, enemies, mating opportunities, comforts, competition, rivalries, victories, defeats, and the crushing tyranny of custom—all are derived from society.

And all are reflected in the tenth house.

Calling it the house of career is kind of like saying Beethoven played the piano.

MISSION

As I wrote a few moments ago, "mission" is my favorite word in describing the tenth house. I like the term for a lot of reasons, but foremost it is because it implies some kind of *cooperative, meaningful relationship with our community.* Hopefully, we are offering something to the village, something it needs and values—and, almost incidentally, for which it will offer us some recompense. We get paid for it, in other words.

"Career" is far from a dirty word, but if we are not careful, it can imply the urge to *get ahead* in some fundamentally narrow or selfish way. That orientation really misses the point of the tenth house. We cannot grasp it fully without some reference to more altruistic motivations. Before we float off into the clouds with that lofty notion, here is a fine curse I have developed for my worst enemies:

May you have a job that pays you only money.

Talk about a truly diabolical malediction! No matter how much money we are talking about, such an empty job would gradually drain all the heart and soul from our lives.

What then must a job pay *beyond money?*

There are many answers, but they all boil down to one idea: *meaning.* And for work to be meaningful, it must *meet some need* out there in the world. It must trigger some reaction of appreciation in the minds of people who do not know us deeply or personally—and probably trigger respect for us as well.

Such a job must *offer a gift to our community.* We ourselves must become that gift. The honest automobile mechanic is doing it. So is the school teacher. So is the jazz musician who lifts our souls.

NOTHING IN THE TENTH HOUSE?

We live in a culture that often evaluates people by their professional status. "I am the C.E.O. of a Fortune 500 company" typically triggers a more impressed reaction than "I am a stay-at-home mom."

This is unfair and damaging to many people, but it is the way of the world.

The simplest way to get into this subject is to consider a situation where a person has no planets in the tenth house. I would not leap from that astrological observation to the conclusion that therefore he or she has "no mission in the world."

But that is a possibility. *There are profound purposes in life that have nothing to do with a pubic mission.*

I do not want to get bogged down in lengthy technicalities at this point. We will save those for later. Suffice to say that as we saw in the previous chapter, the sixth house overlaps considerably with the tenth house. Planets in the sixth house can also be understood to indicate a mission, and to help clarify its nature. Seeing planets in the sixth house, but none in the tenth, should still lead an astrologer to speak in terms of work and mission.

Going a little bit further, everyone has a *sign on the midheaven*—that is, on the cusp of the tenth house. That sign also gives some information about our natural purpose in the community.

Even more telling is the position of the planet that rules that midheaven sign.

Here is the drum I really want to beat: *while everyone has a purpose in life, that purpose does not always necessarily involve impacting the lives of people whom you do not know personally.* It is not always "a job," in other words.

That simple insight can be extraordinarily liberating for anyone who has been conditioned by the narrowly "career-centric" values of our culture and who simultaneously lacks these kinds of mission indicators in his or her natal chart. Simply said, if your chart fits that description, your evolutionary work in this lifetime lies elsewhere. Your chart will point you in the right direction.

Here's to all the yogis meditating in Himalayan caves. Here's to all the poets living in countries where all the poets are starving. Here's to those stay-at-home moms nurturing the souls of their kids—any one of whom could be the next Shakespeare, Martin Luther King, or Claude Monet.

Society often does not honor these people. My hope is that a new generation of astrologers can take up some of that slack.

PLANETS IN THE TENTH HOUSE DO ONE THING QUITE POORLY . . .

With any planet in the tenth house, we can confidently state that your soul has reached a point in its evolutionary journey where you are ready to *bear fruit in your village*. You are ready to have an impact upon the *myths and the symbols by which your community knows itself*. And your "community" might be the south side of the little town in Iowa—or it might be the collective culture of the planet earth.

In either case, you have something important to do—*but that is true of each and every one of us*. We *all* have something important to do. That is why we are here. The unique point about you, assuming mission-symbolism in your chart, is that if you get your mission right, it will help other people too.

So what exactly is your mission? That is obviously the million-dollar question.

Answering it is something that planets in the tenth house can only do in a limited way. The reason is logically inescapable: there are currently about ten things that we call planets—although the word "planet" has become somewhat elastic nowadays. And there are 1.79 *bazillion* things you might possibly do in the world. Do the math: *each planet lies at the head of an incredibly long list of possibilities*. At best, they only offer impressionistic clues about the concrete reality of your mission.

Maybe you have Mercury in the tenth house. That implies that your mission probably has something to do with *communication*. But what if Mercury is in Libra versus Sagittarius or Scorpio? The sign will condition the nature of Mercury's expression, and thus focus the tenth house message, making it somewhat clearer—but the point is, it is still very broad.

By the time we are done with this Elements series, we will have explored "cookbook" interpretations of the role each planet plays when it lies in the tenth house. In Part Three of this present volume, we will look at Venus, Mercury, and Saturn in that tenth house "mission" context. All of that will bring helpful focus to the question of the exact nature of your mission.

But we will still be faced with the basic dilemma: *the number of possible "jobs" available to us vastly exceeds the number of possible astrological configurations.*

Once again, planets in the tenth house are not useless in defining the nature of our mission. But logic dictates that their efficacy is limited.

BUT THESE PLANETS DO ANOTHER THING VERY WELL . . .

When we look at "mission" from the evolutionary perspective, suddenly any planet in the tenth house blossoms into the most prescient and sagacious career counselor unimaginable. The core concept is quite straightforward: any planet in the tenth house represents *a function in your psyche which you must develop to a profound degree if your mission is going to find you.*

The idea of your mission "finding you" rather than the other way around might seem naive or fanciful, at least in the usual "careerist" framework. But we have already critiqued that framework, at least in so far as attempting to unravel the mysteries of the tenth house goes. Remember: the heart of our deeper understanding of the tenth house is that there is a *natural synergy between you and the community.* Any planet there is trying to express itself, trying to hold up its end of the synergistic contract. The word "mission" itself implies that interdependency.

As the Hindus say, "When the flower opens, you do not need to look for bees."

Your job, in other words, is only to get your flower open. The universe, God, synchronicity—whatever you want to call it—will do the rest.

The very idea of a planet *developing over time* is the essence of evolutionary astrology. Going from a weak response to a planet to a higher response is the purpose of life. Sinners evolving into saints is an obvious expression of this principle in action, but most of the time we don't need to be so black and white about it.

Let me illustrate this idea of evolutionary development with a little tenth house tale.

A GIRL WAS BORN WITH MERCURY IN HER TENTH HOUSE . . .

When she was young, she was in nursery school. Perhaps she stood out as a child who developed speech a little sooner than the other kids. That's a pubic (tenth house) expression of Mercury. She is off to a good start.

We tune in a few years later, and she is doing well in high school. She has a bit of a reputation as "a smart kid." Upon graduation, she is the valedictorian of her class. Standing behind that podium, she is the embodiment of Mercury.

She goes to college, majoring in education. Mercury again.

When she graduates, she gets a job as a kindergarten teacher. The work is meaningful to her; she enjoys it. But gradually she finds herself hungry to work with older children.

Four years later, we tune in and she is teaching English in an honors class at a high school.

A few years of that, and she begins to long for something more. She begins taking night classes, aiming toward a distant goal: getting her PhD in English literature.

Eventually she completes her doctorate. She is now an associate professor in a university. She is teaching in the English Department, with a focus on creative writing. Soon she is on a tenure track.

While she is teaching creative writing, in her spare time she begins work on her own novel. Her academic schedule is demanding, but she sticks with the project, promising herself that she will write at least one page every day.

The novel sells. It receives positive reviews. Her status as a professor of creative writing has received a boost. Based on that success, she moves to a more prestigious university. Soon she is granted tenure there too.

Meanwhile she begins work on a second novel. That one also sells well, and her third one does even better.

Perhaps she is in her fifties by now. After some soul struggle, she makes the difficult decision to resign from her professorship in order to devote herself full-time to her career as a novelist.

By the time she passes from this world, she has written a dozen novels which, together, have touched the souls of millions of people.

There is the story. Note that at each stage of it *she is doing fine.* We honor her Mercury path as the most precocious child in her nursery school. We honor her memory as one of the great voices of her generation.

And we honor each step in between.

Her tale illustrates an ascending, evolutionary path through the potentialities of Mercury in the tenth house. The process of getting her flower open unfolded over her entire span of years. At each stage, she followed Robert A. Johnson's *"slender threads"*—those signs and omens that can potentially guide all of us, sometimes arising in the circumstances of the world, sometimes arising as the inner promptings of our souls manifest through dreams, meditations, and intuitions.

That is how it works when we have a mission. Those "slender threads" lead us onward; all we need to supply is energy and faith.

As you read through the four volumes that will eventually constitute this series, we will see how each planet in the tenth house can be parsed out as we just did with Mercury. If a planet lies there in your chart, that is the path that is calling you.

That is the ever-rising road of your mission in this world.

6

THE HANDOUT

The material upon which *The Book of Earth* is based originated in a four-day seminar which I offered in my astrological apprenticeship program. That particular meeting happened in Alpine, California, in May 2016. Those programs are in a classroom format; I present the material, and after a while, we cut to the chase and draw the names of a few class members out of a hat. We use their charts to demonstrate and test the principles that I have taught.

To supplement the oral material, I always provide the class with a short handout. Usually it is just a single page. There is no way to squeeze the entire contents of such a class onto a sheet of paper, so the handout is intended only as an aid to memory, nothing more. My hope is that in later reviewing it, my students will remember some of the deeper perspectives we explored in class—deeper perspectives such as what you have been reading for the past five chapters.

I am including the text of that Earth Family handout here, along with some explanation, in hopes that it will speed your own learning as well.

MAKING IT REAL:
EXPLORING THE EARTH FAMILY

Everybody has a "self-improvement" plan—at least for others. We all know what's wrong with everything—men, women, the government, the world, the medical system, the food supply. The sheer inertia of collective stupidity is appalling. "Just put me in charge for a month or two and we'll soon see a better world . . ."

Ask any teenager. Or any barstool philosopher.

But Platonic ideals famously have a hard time getting translated into concrete solutions. Something is always lost in translation. The devil is in the details. Chaos theory—and Murphy's Law—rule the grown-up, three-dimensional, social world. Unintended consequences abound and they ramify like viruses. The battle plan lasts until the first shot is fired.

Simply dealing with reality—and thus turning visions into some semblance of fact and accomplishment—is the task of the Earth family— Taurus, Virgo, and Capricorn, along with their associated houses, and the planets that rule them. These symbols correlate with everything that supports the ever-compromised, always imperfect *magic of actual manifestation* in our lives.

Taurus and Venus
To Grasp the Heart that Sustains the Matter . . .

Antagonists: Over-thinking. That which would complicate you or twist you into knots.

Key Concepts: Trusting your instincts. The wisdom of simplicity. Things your body knows. Trusting your nose. Finding the silence within yourself. The truth that resides in beauty. Listening to music. The need for touch. "It's in his (or her) kiss." The wise old Navajo grandfather or grandmother. "Chicken soup" wisdom. Returning to nature. Tactile perception. Animal companions. The notes you don't play. Mind-numbing, stubborn conservatism. "Blink"—the curious prescience of first impressions.

Virgo and Mercury
To Bravely See What Is Wrong With Everything, Including Yourself . . .

Antagonists: Talent wasted; dithering; self-sabotage. That which undercuts your self-confidence.

Key Concepts: Tense comparison of the Ideal and the Actual. Analysis. Precision and competence. The drive to improve. Divine Discontent. Polished skills. The urge to be of use to others. "God grant that today I do work that matters." Learning; mentoring—and being mentored.

Keeping your eyes on the prize. Language. Memory. "Perfect is the enemy of good enough."

Capricorn and Saturn
To Never, Ever Give Up . . .
Antagonists: Inertia; crippling caution. Harnessing one's self to external or unworthy goals and standards. Climbing the wrong mountain. *Key Concepts:* Self-discipline. Sustained effort. Great works. The fascination of what's difficult. "Because it was there." Patience. Being a self-starter. Focus on results. "Slow and steady wins the race." Dignity based on actual accomplishment. Morals. The value of Integrity. Focus. Tolerance for solitude. The Elder; the Wizard. Capriciousness as self-care; capriciousness as self-destruction and a symptom of exhaustion. Moral collapse.

ONE HUNDRED THIRTY-NINE WORDS TO SAY IT ALL

In quick summary of what we have explored so far, we have the three Earth families:

* *Taurus and Venus,* whose fundamental purpose lies in keeping us calm, silent, and natural enough that we can hear the voices of our own hearts and our own bodies. They help us "walk in beauty"— which is to say, in full instinctual attunement to the right underlying values that can guide us home.

* *Virgo and Mercury,* where we learn to be sufficiently skillful, competent and informed to successfully transmute our visions into reality. Here we cultivate the humility and constructive self-criticism needed for practical evolution. We attract mentors, and later, if we are successful, apprentices.

* *Capricorn and Saturn,* where we take aim at the Great Work, our passions and efforts guided by sound Taurean instincts and our methods supported by Virgoan skills. Thus inspired and equipped, we joyfully succumb to the "fascination of what's difficult," with relentless focus and self-discipline.

THE ANTAGONISTS

Antagonists arise for each of these positive energies. These are the catabolic and entropic energies of the mind which oppose our evolution. They are the Shadow, the ancient enemy. They are actually an unconscious part of our own psyches, which means they have access to our full intelligence and our capacity for cunning, and they turn them against us. That is why medieval monks cringing in their monastic cells called them demons. In a way, that is a natural method for thinking about these antagonists. They do sometimes "grab the steering wheel" of your life as if they were malicious independent entities.

     * The antagonist that arises to battle our healthy response to Taurus and Venus is simply *disquiet*. When you are trying to juggle seventeen balls all at once, with your phone ringing and your email pinging and someone knocking on the door, it is tough to hear the still small voice within. Noise, chaos and over-extension nourish this terrible antagonist. So does running on too little sleep. Ditto for unnatural food. And super-ditto for going too long without any human touch.

     * The antagonists to Virgo and Mercury are, ultimately, self-doubt, self-sabotage, and shame. Perfection is an unreachable standard; judging ourselves by it is always fatal. If we succumb to these antagonists, the Shadow manifests in a multiplicity of ways, all with the same fundamental DNA. We cripple ourselves with endless preparation, never actually doing anything. We enslave ourselves to demanding, but meaningless, work and responsibilities. And we project our own self-doubt onto other people in the form of niggling, unending litanies of criticism.

     * For Capricorn and Saturn, the antagonist is time-serving martyrdom for the sake of something that does not really matter. The formidable capacity for self-discipline, seriousness, and sustained focus that characterizes these symbols must ultimately be rooted in whimsy. That word might sound strange, but it refers to the way the soul actually communicates with the conscious mind—and in this branch of the Earth Family, in the final analysis, everything depends on the Taurean heart calling the shots. Otherwise Capricorn

and Saturn descend into mere mechanism, leading eventually and inevitably to depression and breakdown.

THE QUOTATIONS

For each branch of the Earth Family, I have supplied a quotation. Choosing them was a classic illustration of the Saturn-function in action—it was really hard, and at the same time a lot of fun.

For Taurus, I've chosen one simple line from a poem I love so much that I have actually quoted it in two of my books—Ezra Pound's Canto 120:

Do not move. Let the wind speak. That is paradise.

Pound's line is a lovely reminder of all the deep things we simply know in our bones if we seek quiet, inside and out, especially when sitting in the embrace of nature.

For Virgo, I have used a line about life on the highway from comedian George Carlin:

Everyone in front of you is a moron and everyone behind you is a maniac.

Like all good comedy, there is more than laughter going on here. I have often thanked Carlin for this memorable line when I am behind the wheel in heavy traffic myself. There are times when his words seem uncannily relevant to the realities I am experiencing with other drivers. Then I realize that the joke is on me. In projecting this criticism onto the blank canvas of the universe, I am in the grips of the almighty human ego, thinking that I am the center of everything—and suffering all the more for it.

For Capricorn, I've gone to musician and master lyricist, Bruce Springsteen.

In his anthemic evocation of the dead-end realities of working class life, *The River*, he sings . . .

Is a dream a lie if it don't come true, or is it something worse?

His words are "... something worse that brings me down to the river," to be precise—but I decided to cut the line off with "worse" because that way it fits Capricorn like a bolt fits a nut. With healthy Capricorn, we must always start with the dream—with Taurean soul-instinct, so to speak. That dream is nothing less than the inner call of spirit, beckoning us to some Great Work. Our purpose in life is to "make it true," which is to say, to make real, to make it actually happen. If we hear that call, and then ignore it, and thus fail to make the effort to do what we were born to do . . . well, it is indeed ominously "something worse."

PART TWO

MASTERING THE ALCHEMICAL MARRIAGE OF SIGN, HOUSE, AND PLANET

The word Archetype has an impressive ring to it, as if it were something we might contemplate for a decade in a cave or a monastery. Still, it helps us keep perspective if we remember that no human being is ever truly an archetype—each one of us is in fact vastly more complex than that. The reason is that everyone of us is composed of an ironical, ambiguous synthesis of all of the astrological archetypes at once. What varies—and what makes us different from each other—is simply their mixture.

Furthermore, an archetype such as Mercury or Saturn never exists alone, in and of itself, at least not in the human world. Each of them draws their character from a sign and a house.

Learning to place the members of the Earth Family in their astrological context is the essence of the next couple of chapters. Here we learn how to put it all together.

Master what we have explored so far, and you are a philosopher. Master what follows, and you are well on your way to becoming a working astrologer.

7

SYNTHESIS I: PUTTING AN EARTH PLANET IN A SIGN

Astrologers speak glibly of Mercury as if it were part of a secret code we had cracked. And we are right—at least in part. Cracking the soul-code of the heavens is indeed one of humanity's most brilliant accomplishments. But Mercury's actual meaning is so fluid, so potentially variable, that claiming we know anything at all about it verges on pure hubris.

Here, at the human, experiential level, is the face of reality: Mercury in Scorpio in the third house squared by Jupiter. Or Mercury in Libra in the tenth. Or Mercury in Pisces trine Venus.

It is these triads of planet, sign, and house, flavored by aspects, that are the fundamental quantum units of astrological reality. That is how we actually experience the human face of the planets. It is those triads that we must understand if we are to give—or receive—helpful astrological counsel.

And even with the same planet at the center, they differ from each other profoundly.

HOW SIGNS INTERACT WITH PLANETS

The best way I know to understand the meaning of the twelve astrological signs is to think of them as *motivational agendas*—goals and values—which animate our behavior.

Illustration: There's a big, loud party tonight. You'll have a chance to meet dozens of cool people you have never met before. Aren't you excited? Get out your dancing shoes.

Well, if you are an introvert, you probably blanched as you read those words. If you are an extrovert, the prospect of meeting those strangers probably had a certain allure.

Introversion is not a psychiatric disorder. Extroversion is not inherently virtuous. Likewise, *vice versa.* They are just different ways of being human. Different values. Different motivational agendas. As such, they reflect the nature of the astrological signs. Some are introverted while some are extroverted.

Everything else being equal, if you put Mercury in Libra, the Libran agenda of *making human connections* animates a person's Mercurial *curiosity.* Put Mercury in Capricorn, and Mercury's cognitive agenda is motivated by the Sea-goat's eye-on-the-prize attitude.

Quickly, with Mercury in Capricorn rather than Libra, "wasting time" meeting random strangers "for no practical reason at all" loses its appeal.

It is essential to avoid value judgments here. Beyond the core principles of natural law—don't kill, don't steal, protect the children—there are countless perfectly fine ways of being human. Each sign is ultimately a legitimate evolutionary path, and in each one there are instinctual values that arise to support it.

One essential quality in the professional astrologer is the ability to avoid projecting his or her values onto other people—to meet them where they are, as that mystery is revealed in their birth charts.

Back to Mercury . . .

What is the right *cognitive style* for you? How can you *best learn*? What are your most *productive interests*? What is your optimal *relationship with language*?

Mercury itself cannot answer any of those questions. Mercury *is* those questions—all of them. What answers them is the sign in which Mercury finds itself.

We think similarly with Venus and Saturn—and really with all the rest of the planets. We cannot understand their actual manifest natures unless we place them in the motivational context of a particular sign.

With Venus, what values must be optimized in a relationship that is truly good for you? What qualities characterize your *natural mate*—and, by the way, is it even helpful for you to think about having a natural mate? What about your tastes and relationship to the world of aesthetic choices? How can you best find peace?

For answers to those questions, again look to the sign Venus occupies.

Saturn works the same way—certain particular values naturally animate your ability to recognize the exact nature of the Great Work that is worthy, fruitful, and appropriate for you. How can you best simply "make meaningful things happen" in your life? What qualities must you cultivate in order to develop self-respect and true maturity?

In a nutshell, the twelve signs of the Zodiac are what make the planets human, giving them character, engaging them with life's possibilities—and life's hard choices. Otherwise they remain in the abstract, Platonic realm we call the Heavens.

A MAP FOR THE NEXT FEW MINUTES OF YOUR LIFE

In this chapter, my plan is to explore in some depth a single example of each one of our Earth planets as they are conditioned by having their presence in a particular sign. In doing that, I am hoping to give you a feeling for how the planet-sign synthesis works in practice.

In chapter eight, we will do the same for a planet in each of the houses.

My hope is that some of the deeper interpretive processes we consider in this present chapter will breathe life into those short thumbnail descriptions.

Learning to "think astrologically" is always the truest goal. While "cookbook" paragraphs can be helpful, if you are not careful they can also make you look like the kid on your neighborhood who never got rid of the training wheels on his bicycle.

A few lines ago I wrote that it is the triads of planet, sign, and house, flavored by aspects, that are the fundamental quantum units of astrological reality. Here, in this chapter, we are only concerned with how signs fit into the picture. As I mentioned, the next chapter brings us to the twelve astrological houses in the same way.

Adding aspects to the mix is essential as well—Mercury in Virgo *squared by Neptune* is not your grandmother's Mercury in Virgo—especially if hers were conjunct Saturn. Unlike her, your Mercury might have lost the car keys again, even though it can write poetry that puts tears in everyone's eyes.

Meanwhile, grandma balances her checkbook to the penny, but she tends to take your poetic metaphors a little bit too literally.

There are so many possible aspectual combinations that all I can do is to help you figure them out for yourself. We will have a look at how aspects fill out the picture in chapter fifteen.

For now, let's roll the dice and come up with three random planet-sign combinations. Let's watch Venus, Mercury, and Saturn as they each dance with an individual sign. We will start with Venus in Capricorn—but our real aim here is not so much to understand that particular combination as to grasp the basic strategy for seeing how a sign shapes the agenda of a planet.

VENUS IN CAPRICORN

The Sea-goat loves getting to the peak of the mountain. It is hungry to set out across the wide ocean, bound for the farthest shore. Earlier in the book, we invoked "the fascination of what's difficult" as a way of understanding Capricorn.

So what happens when focused, serious values such as those animate one's intimate, Venusian choices?

There is not one single answer that fits everyone. As always with astrology, each symbol represents a wide spectrum of possibilities, ranging from self-destruction to enlightenment. And each planet-sign-house triad interacts with the rest of the chart, typically in paradoxical ways. But we have to start somewhere, and a planet in a sign is always part of the foundation.

Might a person with Venus in Capricorn be drawn to *difficult relationships*?

Or, to put it more directly, relationships with difficult people? Yes indeed—that pattern would certainly be consistent with this combination of astrological energies, although there are other possibilities.

Complicating the picture even further, we recognize that Capricorn also carries a capacity for *stoic endurance*. In other words, having chosen an "impossible" or "difficult" relationship, such a person might also display a misguided capacity to hang in there, dining on thin, cold soup as the anniversaries creep by.

Obviously with those words we are not talking about "the higher ground." Such self-imposed martyrdom reflects only one possible face of this sign-planet combination—one of its Shadow-faces.

Remember: Capricorn, at its best, is hungry for a Great Work. Winning the "Who Suffered the Longest" prize doesn't qualify. It may be work, but it's not great.

Here is what wins the evolutionary Olympic gold with Venus in this sign: *a long-running relationship in which both people have worked on themselves and on their partnership—one in which after many years, they are proud of the treasure they have created together.* They have been honest and faithful; they have kept their promises as best they could; insofar as it is humanly possible, they made reality resemble their ideals. They can sincerely say that, "we have grown up together"—even if they first met when they were fifty years old.

With Venus in Capricorn, the values and attitudes that underlie such a marriage of souls are the ones that work best for you. But it takes two to tango—the partner you choose had better share those values with you too, or it will not work.

That last point is actually one of the most compelling mysteries of Venus: your Venus says something about you—but it also says something about your natural partner. Since we are talking about love, the two perspectives—yours and that of your partner—cannot be separated. Your natural partner may not be "a Capricorn," but he or she had better reflect some of those kinds of values and virtues. Likely, in looking at that person's chart, we will see some literal Capricorn influences or perhaps a strongly-placed Saturn.

Let's go a little further.

Capricorn is ruled by Saturn, the Lord of Solitude. On the face of it, that does not sound like the most copacetic environment for the goddess of love. No worry: with Venus in Capricorn, you simply *need more time alone* than most people, time apart from your partner. There is nothing loveless about that at all. All sophisticated lovers understand the aphrodisiacal qualities of simply missing each other. It is the best antidote in the world for taking each other for granted.

Once again, this statement about you is simultaneously a statement about your natural partner: it follows that he or she must "have a life;" that is to say, to be engaged with projects and endeavors that do not require your presence.

Corollary: *if you have Venus in Capricorn, clinging, dependent people need not apply.*

Now that we have mentioned solitude, let's take a look at another Shadow side of this configuration: *self-imposed loneliness.* Break-ups are hell; everyone knows that. And the leading cause of break-ups is, without a doubt, falling in love in the first place. Capricorn knows "not to walk out on the thin ice" of that frozen lake we talked about a couple of chapters ago. *So why fall in love at all?* Solitude can be a form of self-protection.

Here's a slight variation on that same theme: waiting for a relationship that is so perfect that there is no way it could possibly fail.

That is of course a very long wait indeed.

Underlying all of these observations about Venus in Capricorn is our fundamental insight about planets in signs: it is the sign that gives the planet its tone. Venus has twelve faces. Each planet opens up a set of questions—in the case of Venus, the question of human intimacy. Then the sign supplies the values that help us navigate soulfully and wisely through the questions.

The planet may be the boat—but the sign is the compass that guides it across the fog-bound seas of life.

MERCURY IN PISCES

Conventional astrologers view this combination as inherently unfortunate. The reason is that Mercury rules Virgo, which is opposite Pisces. When the planet is in Pisces, it is as far from home as it could be, faced with a strange and unnatural habitat. In technical terms, when Mercury is in Pisces, it is said to be in *"detriment."*

I tend not to use the term myself. No one can hear it without thinking of it as a problem. In reality, it is just another path—another way of being human. Overriding that gloomy language is one absolute bedrock principle of evolutionary astrology: *everything in your chart is perfect.* Everything reflects a potentially positive evolutionary intention and a method for fulfilling it. Nothing astrological is automatically bad—or automatically good, for that matter. Questions of consciousness, mindfulness, and self-awareness rule over everything.

Still, the tension between the nature of Mercury and the nature of Pisces is real enough. The old astrologers were onto something. We just have to recognize that the differences between Mercury and Pisces can operate in creative ways. Mercury likes logic and precision, while Pisces prefers dreams and poetry. Mercury appreciates the reliable rules that govern our three dimensional, time-bound world. Pisces gets a good laugh out of them.

Ask Pisces—Mercury thinks too much.

Ask Mercury—Pisces could use a little bit of lead in its shoes.

All of that is true. It explains why the old astrologers thought this sign-planet combination was troublesome. And, in practical terms, if you have Mercury in Pisces, you should probably balance your checkbook—twice. Someone else should figure out your taxes. And you do yourself real kindness by making sure that there is a special, reliable place in your house for the scissors, the tape, and the band aids.

But there is potential gold in this planet-sign combination as well. Let's find it.

In Pisces, we see a mystical motivational agenda. We see a hunger to explore the vast and wondrous realms of consciousness itself. This includes spiritual perspectives—but Pisces also makes equally vivid reference to the inner life in general: imagination, creativity, dreams, and visionary inspiration.

What happens if our Mercurial intelligence and curiosity are animated by such an imaginative, visionary agenda?

This question does not seem weird or unnatural—and it leads us directly to the higher ground represented by this planetary combination. We can imagine such a person avidly studying metaphysics. We might see an interest in parapsychology—ghosts, ESP, reincarnation memories. He or she has the makings of a fine hypnotist or meditation teacher. Everything else being equal, we are looking at a powerful creative drive. Might this person *write* (Mercury) *fantasy* (Pisces)? Might he or she be a filmmaker? People born with Mercury in Pisces can *hear* (Mercury) the music of the spheres when no one else can hear anything at all—and then translate what they have heard directly onto a piano.

Defining intelligence is a notoriously impossible task. What score would Vincent van Gogh have achieved on a standard IQ test? And yet who would argue that he was not a genius?

Astrologers who dismiss Mercury in Pisces would probably dismiss the intelligence of Vincent van Gogh as well.

(Actually, I bet that they would not make that mistake—I just wish that they would update their astrological vocabulary by applying the same broad values to Mercury in Pisces.)

With this configuration, *the mind is bombarded by perceptions whose origins lie outside the boundaries of reality as it is conventionally defined.* Life will abound with garden-variety psychic events: dreaming of a long-lost friend, and then finding that person contacting you on Facebook two days later. Knowing—for no obvious logical reason at all—that the man with whom your best friend is about to have her first date will soon be her husband.

As we contemplate these kinds of uncanny and inexplicable experiences, they point to the existence of a far more multidimensional reality then the one we learned about in high school science class. That larger reality is the realm of Pisces. We will explore it in deep detail at the end of the series, in *The Book of Water.* For now, it is enough to realize that with Mercury in Pisces, the mind is suffused with perceptions which have their origin in that far more primal framework.

Only a fool—or a pedantic, nineteenth century logician—would define those perceptions as a problem.

Speech is a Mercury function. And with Mercury in Pisces, everything else being equal, one's speech tends to be full of imagery and metaphor. Poetry, genuine insight, and a humorously warm-hearted sense of life's various absurdities abound.

With the deeper layers of consciousness so close to the surface of the mind, there is often a *free-associative* quality to the speech. While that can enhance creativity, it can also potentially be hard to follow. As we slip down towards Shadow land, we can find the person with Mercury in Pisces whose meandering speech is simply very difficult to understand. Such people presumably understand the point they are trying to make; the question is whether anyone else is making the same intuitive leaps through logical hyperspace. Who can follow them?

We can honor the potentially positive dimensions of this configuration. But, being mindful of its liabilities, we might also suggest the usefulness of making an outline before making a speech.

Creating lists of practical things that really need to be remembered can be very helpful.

Perhaps above all, someone with Mercury in Pisces might benefit from paying attention to the subtle cues that other people offer when there are becoming lost or confused in their attempt to follow his or her point: glazed eyes, bewildered glances at one another, and barely-suppressed yawns.

Note that in all of the foregoing cautionary points, we are not dismissing Mercury in Pisces as an unfortunate configuration. Instead, we are honestly reflecting on its potential liabilities, while conjuring up corrective measures to counter them. And all the while we are celebrating the gifts of imagination, creativity, and sensitivity which are part of the package.

SATURN IN LIBRA

Having the Lord of Solitude in a sign as relationship-oriented as Libra sounds as if it were another situation of "detriment." Technically, it is not; in fact, to the astrologers who use such language, Saturn is actually said to be "exalted" in this sign. I am not even going to go there, except to repeat that there is something sacred and honorable about each one of the 144 sign-house combinations.

Saturn, as we have seen, always wants to get its teeth into something. It likes a challenge; it is fascinated with everything that is difficult. It is looking for a Great Work—an endeavor worthy of its capacity for relentless self-discipline and its ability to keep an eye constantly on the prize.

What does Libra seek? What is the Libran motivational agenda?

In *The Book of Air*, we will explore those questions in detail. Suffice here to say that the ultimate goal of Libra is *serenity of spirit*. In a word, *balance*. In an effort to reach that higher ground, Libra benefits enormously from immersing its senses in beauty and aesthetic rapture. It also benefits from meaningful, harmonious intimacy—marriage of course, but also friendship. Both of those activities calm the soul.

Earlier in this chapter, we considered Venus in Capricorn. Here, we are in similar territory. Libra is ruled by Venus and Capricorn is ruled by Saturn, so we might expect to use interchangeable language in describing both configurations. And indeed, if we wind up saying some of the same things about each of them, no worry: that does not indicate that we are making a mistake. There are indeed many parallels between the two configurations. They are, after all, composed of very similar energies: solitude and love.

There is a reason I've chosen to look at Saturn in Libra in the same chapter where we just considered Venus in Capricorn. Along with our basic aim of deepening our understanding of how signs interact with planets, we can now get some practical experience in another area: parsing out the differences between similar astrological configurations.

Venus in Capricorn and Saturn in Libra are not exactly the same—but they resemble each other about as much as do non-identical twins.

And non-identical twins are different people.

Focusing on Venus . . .
With Venus, human relationships are always on center stage. In contemplating a person's "relationship to relationship," start with Venus, not with Libra. A prominent Venus marks a person as one for whom the catalytic impact of other souls consistently plays a pivotal biographical role.

Having a single planet in Libra does not do that. It is just not "as loud in the mix"—not the main spice in the stew. Perspective: that is one important difference between the two configurations. The planet is the actual drive; a sign only conditions it.

Focusing on Saturn . . .
Saturn correlates with self-sufficiency and the human need for solitude. Right away, we recognize its tension with the relational dimensions of Libra; Saturn somewhat weakens them—while potentially underscoring other aspects of Libra, as we will see. That is another important difference. While Venus puts relationships on center stage, Saturn puts a blockage—and the Great Work of getting past it—there.

Always start with the basic meaning of the planet, in other words, then flavor it and give it motivational tone with the sign.

Since we are talking about Libra, we know that Saturn's underlying agenda will *include* a motivation to establish helpful relationships. We just have to remember that there are going to be other elements in the final equations. Let's start there, with relationship—and skate that thin line that keeps us from the error of equating this structure with Venus in Capricorn.

Saturn wants a Great Work and Libra wants, among other things, meaningful human connections. As with Venus in Capricorn, we see a motivation to *improve* our primary emotional bonds and a willingness to *devote energy* to the process. As with Venus in Capricorn, a good metaphor for soul-victory here is a *long marriage* or profound, decades-long *friendships* that fill both people with a mixture of joy and dignity. They treasure each other—but they are also proud of their accomplishment in staying together through life's endless changes..

Again, let's keep perspective by remembering that Saturn in Libra has other kinds of Great Works in mind as well—we will get to them momentarily.

* For someone with Saturn in Libra to have not experienced such intimate bonds in this life would be sad.
* For someone with Venus in Capricorn, it would be difficult to shake the sense that it was some kind of fundamental spiritual failure.

Again, just as we saw with Venus in Capricorn, there is a specific Shadow dimension to this Saturn-Libra configuration: the *longsuffering, stoic endurance of empty relationships.* "Too much Saturn, not enough true Libra" would be the proper diagnosis in that case. Where Saturn lies, we can be very hard on ourselves. We can live on stale bread and tepid water. Rather than succumbing to the Libran hunger for human warmth, we might foolishly push it aside in the holy name of morality, maturity, or propriety.

The prize we win for that accomplishment?

Loneliness.

The tightrope we walk as we contemplate Saturn in Libra lies in giving intimate human connections real priority, while not falling into the trap of becoming so beguiled by romance and sexuality that we forget one simple fact: *there is a lot more to Libra than partnerships.*

Libra correlates with the human motivation to experience beauty, whether it is the beauty of the natural world or the beauty that people themselves create, which is to say the *arts.*

Might the Saturn Great Work in this case be one's development as an artist? That is certainly one possibility. With Saturn in Libra, those aesthetic values underlie Saturn's characteristic self-discipline and long-term focus. They give flavor to the Saturnian fascination with what's difficult—and carry us *beyond the realm of intimacy into the realm of creativity, the cultivation of taste, and cultural sophistication.*

Aesthetics and disciplined effort: does this sign-planet synthesis mean that people with Saturn in Libra tend to be artistic? In my experience, individual by individual, while that is worth saying, it is not a particularly reliable prediction. I suspect that there is a disproportionate demographic pulse of artists born with this configuration, but nothing "we can take to the bank" in individual cases.

Artistry, astrologically, requires more than a planet in Libra. Generally speaking, Venus must be strongly placed as well. Very typically, there is a planet or two in the self-expressive the fifth house—see *The Book of Fire* for a fuller discussion of that connection.

Aesthetics and disciplined effort—yes, but let's tweak Saturn's side of the Libran equation a bit by linking aesthetics and another classic Saturnian theme: *maturation.*

A quick personal example: I grew up on rock 'n roll. I still like it. But as I have aged, I have come to appreciate jazz more deeply. Have my aesthetics matured?

Here's another angle on "maturation"—in this case, one that can unfold in months instead of decades: think of your favorite musical recording. Maybe you enjoyed it the first time you heard it—but probably not like it moves you today. *With time, your appreciation of the artist's work has become more profound.* Your relationship with the artwork has matured—deliciously.

With music, there is always a learning curve. The more we listen, the more sophisticated our taste becomes.

We can of course say exactly the same thing for the rest of the arts: literature, painting, film, poetry, architecture, whatever.

The list goes on, but the principle is the same: *sustained Saturnian focus, motivated by Libran hunger for aesthetic experience, leads to an ever more sophisticated level of taste and appreciation.*

One purpose of Saturn in Libra? The refinement of one's capacity for aesthetic experience. Okay—but while no one would be likely to argue against respecting such refinement, at first glance it might not seem to be such a pressing spiritual goal.

That quibble leads us to the next step, which is actually the heart of the matter.

Put the refinement of your capacity for aesthetic experience on the back burner for a moment.

At the beginning of this section, we spoke of Libra as the sign of *peace, serenity,* and *balance*. Unlike developing more sophisticated musical tastes, almost anyone would agree that those virtues are inseparable from real spiritual accomplishment. If you are born with this configuration, we could say that you are trying to learn the *practical discipline of serenity* in this lifetime.

So why don't you . . .

CALM DOWN IMMEDIATELY!

If you were in a panic and I were to order you immediately, under the pain of death, to calm down, I doubt that my order would be very successful. Your levels of stress and fear would only increase. The "discipline of serenity" does not derive from commands, not coming from others nor coming from ourselves. It derives from certain skills. There are *methods* we can use to calm ourselves.

And Saturn—the most practical of all the planets—loves methods.

If you are in a panic and I really want to help you, I might suggest that you simply take a breath and let it out. That out-breath is famously tranquilizing. It will not solve your problems, but it will begin the process of chipping them away.

Being mindful of one's breath is a straightforward example of a sure-fire Saturn-in-Libra method. *Mindful breathing is one of the effective disciplines of serenity.* It is one step on the path to this particular Great Work.

If I personally have had a hard day, listening to music calms me down. I just have to remember to do it. So does going for a walk in the beautiful desert that surrounds my home. These aesthetic experiences help me relieve tension.

Remember how we put the refinement of our capacity for aesthetic experience on the back burner a few paragraphs ago? Let's bring it back to center stage. We learned that the appreciation of beauty can be cultivated. The more you develop your taste, the more profound is the impact of beauty on your consciousness. Here's the proof of that point, which you can evaluate for yourself: the beloved musical recording that you have heard a thousand times—that is what you play when you really need a boost. You may not be the musician who created the work—but you have done the work of entraining your consciousness to a source of peace and restoration.

Here we see the deeper reason behind the importance of a Libran Saturn being immersed in beauty: the outer harmonies of perception quickly translate into an inner harmony of spirit. As our tastes mature and deepen, the healing effect of art and beauty becomes increasingly pronounced. This sophisticated cultivation of aesthetic experience thus emerges as a skillful, direct means for achieving that high Libran aim: serenity.

And it has nothing to do with relationships.

BACK TO LOVE

Before we leave our meditation upon Saturn in Libra, let's return to the question of human intimacy. As ever, in talking about Libra, we cannot ignore it. We just have to avoid being totally hypnotized by it.

Hopefully, what we have just explored has clarified how Saturn in Libra differs in tone from Venus in Capricorn, without our falling into the trap of creating any undue polarity between them.

If, in other words, you are slightly confused about their distinction, you are probably right on target.

When someone we love has experienced a terrible blow, we have an instinct to reach out to them—literally to extend our arms toward them and offer an embrace. Why does a simple hug help us so much when we are hurting? That is an Earth-sign mystery that lies deep in the animal-wisdom of the sign Taurus, as we explored back in chapter three.

Maybe we do not need to understand it; perhaps all we need is to remember, both to offer a hug and to ask for one.

There are hugs and there are hugs. The kind embrace of a stranger can be meaningful, but a hug from someone with whom you have done the Great Work of building trust and affection over time typically helps a lot more.

TURBULENCE

Once, a few years ago, I was in the last row on a jet flying from Beijing to Los Angeles. We hit a lot of turbulence right after take-off—and of course the back of the plane got the worst of it. It was not "a Libra moment."

Sitting next to me was a rather formal Chinese woman in her fifties. I would not have been surprised to learn that she was a solar Capricorn. In truth, our aeronautical situation was not particularly dire, but this poor woman was clearly terrified. I suspect she had not had much experience with flying. After asking me a few nervous questions about what was happening, she turned to me and compulsively hugged me.

It was a primal, animal response to her fear.

I held her in my arms for five or ten minutes. Eventually the flight stabilized. She did not have much English, nor do I have any Chinese. But there was an ancient, inarticulate—and slightly awkward—connection between us for the next twelve hours as we headed through calmer air across the Pacific Ocean.

I actually treasure that experience, and I feel confident that I helped this woman through a difficult time. That feels good.

But in terms of its comforting value when I'm feeling slammed, there is no embrace as magical as the embrace of my dearest friends or, even better, my partner, Michelle.

Hugs—especially from people whom we have loved, tried-and-true, for many years—are one of life's ultimate *disciplines of serenity*. With Saturn in Libra, cultivating such bonds serves the evolutionary intentions of your soul splendidly.

Later in Part Three of this book, we will explore Venus, Mercury, and Saturn in each one of the twelve signs. Our language in that section will be more telegraphic, the presentation more formulaic. Hopefully, the deeper meditations about the resonance between a sign and a planet that we have explored in this chapter will carry over into those thumbnail sketches, and help you find the soul between the lines.

8

SYNTHESIS II: PUTTING AN EARTH PLANET IN A HOUSE

The twelve astrological houses—the power of our craft is cut in half if we don't use them, and yet there is no area of modern astrological practice that is more fraught with controversy.

From the moment the first glimmer of astrological thought dawned on some primal human somewhere in Africa countless millennia ago, it surely seemed self-evident that being born at sunrise was a different kettle of fish than being born at midnight.

Who could doubt that?

In that moment, the astrological houses were born. They relate the big cosmic framework of the solar system to two more immediately pressing realities:

* *The time of day*
* *The ground upon which you happen to be standing.*

Time of day: is the Sun overhead? Is it setting in the west? And where is the Moon? Has it risen yet? Let's say you wanted to point your finger at the planet Venus. In what direction would you point right now? There will be a different answer a little later in the day. Maybe Venus is below the horizon, not yet visible. Maybe in an hour, it will rise.

These questions, which existed long before the invention of clocks, are essentially *questions about time.* Humanity invented the astrological houses as a way of answering those questions.

The ground upon which you happen to be standing: this house question is slightly more subtle, but equally relevant and not hard to understand. A baby is born at dawn in California. Astrologically, her Sun is conjunct the Ascendant—that is what being born at dawn means.

Imagine that right at the instant of her birth, you took off flying eastward in a supersonic jet, heading straight for the heart of the rising Sun. As you zoomed east at Mach 3, heading around the curve of the Earth, the Sun would seem to rise dramatically fast. (Remember: 6:00 am in California is 9:00 am in New York.)

Another way to say it is that a baby born in New York *at exactly the same moment* would have the Sun much higher in the sky—perhaps in her eleventh house rather than conjunct the Ascendant.

The bottom line is that the astrological houses relate a chart both to space and to time. And everyone agrees, that is important information.

Then the fun begins. There are dozens of different house systems. Most of them, but not all, are built around knowing the exact degree of which sign happened to be rising at the instant of the birth—the astrological Ascendant. Inseparable from that idea is a specific degree that would be on the Midheaven. Once we have the Ascendant and the Midheaven established, we automatically know the degree of the Descendent and the Astrological Nadir: they are in the same degrees, but in opposite signs.

So: dawn and sunset, high noon and midnight—in the vast majority of systems of house division, these *Four Angles* are the skeleton upon which everything else hangs.

To me, that makes a lot of intuitive sense. The horizon and the meridian represent concrete, visible daily realities.

But where do we place the intervening house cusps? Unlike dawn and sunset, high noon and midnight, they are just points floating arbitrarily in space. And thus we have the Tower of Babel in contemporary astrological practice, with Koch houses, Porphyry houses, Meridian houses, Morinus houses, Alcabitius houses—and heavily-armed advocates for each one parading menacingly at every astrological conference around the world.

As I mentioned earlier, I use Placidus houses. Many astrologers whose work I respect, and who help their clients effectively, use other systems.

My best advice is to choose a house system and stick with it. Decide which language you want to speak. I think that at some deep level, you make a pact with the universe that way. You have agreed upon the protocols within which the universe will communicate with you.

This is one of the great mysteries of the art of divination.

WHAT ABOUT WHOLE SIGN HOUSES?

With the resurgence of ancient forms of astrology, there has been a great revival of interest in *whole sign houses*. In this system, which dates back to the Hellenistic traditions a couple of centuries before the birth of Christ, if Gemini were rising when you were born, anything in Gemini is taken to be in your first house. Cancer comes after Gemini, so anything in Cancer is in your second house, and so on around the circle.

Why not? I respect the Hellenistic tradition even though it is very different from the system in which I practice.

Similarly, I am not going to be foolish enough to argue with a Vedic astrologer that he or she is using the wrong zodiac, even though I have a very hard time wrapping my head around the idea that in that system, I become a Sagittarian with a Pisces Moon.

I feel that we are deep in the mysteries of the divine mind with these kinds of questions. To be dogmatic about them is, to me, approximately as half-witted as my offering Jesus, Buddha, or Mohammed some helpful tips on their meditation practices. I am happy to bow before the unfathomable mysteries of the universe, and to respect people to whom it has given different messages than the ones it has given me.

End of sermon.

Still, about those whole sign houses, I do have one more comment to make, and it is a rather obvious one: two millennia ago, *there were no clocks.* Telling time was an approximate affair based on where the Sun or the stars were in the sky. I do not want to belabor this point, but here is a quick quote from Wikipedia:

The first mechanical clocks, employing the verge escapement mechanism with a foliot or balance wheel timekeeper, were invented in Europe at around the start of the 14th century, and became the standard timekeeping device until the pendulum clock was invented in 1656.

The bottom line here is that the *possibility* of reliably and consistently determining an accurately-timed Ascendant or Midheaven is a relatively recent historical development.

In my style of astrology, I need to know a person's time of birth within a few minutes. Without that vital information, I do not feel it would even be ethical for me to attempt to present an interpretation.

In a way, this is a weakness in the system I use and teach. For me, errors in the time of birth are catastrophic—and they do happen sometimes.

Hats off to our astrological ancestors. Without access to accurate timekeeping technologies, they developed an elaborate and effective work-around in the form of whole sign houses. Certainly, they were vulnerable to errors around the charts of people who were born when the signs on the horizon were changing. I feel confident that an ancient Greek baby born with the ascendant at 29° 45' of Scorpio was probably mistakenly labeled as having Sagittarius rising from time to time.

The good news was that astrology, both then and now, simply works. As that baby grew into adulthood, his or her behavior would quickly reveal the error.

So God bless us all—but when it comes to astrological houses, the language I speak is Placidus.

PUTTING EARTH-FAMILY PLANETS IN HOUSES

How do Venus, Mercury, and Saturn manifest behaviorally in the twelve houses? In Part Three, we will go through each one of them, house by house, providing thirty-six paragraphs of formulaic guidance—and hopefully a solid launching pad for deeper, more integrative interpretations that you will make yourself.

Here, in the rest of this chapter, I want to do for houses what I attempted to do for signs in the previous chapter. I want to roll the Astro-Dice in my head, put each one of these planets in a specific house, and dive into a deeper analysis. As with signs, my aim is to illustrate a *style of thinking* which can be applied to any combination of any planet in any house.

Hopefully reading this chapter will save you from the astrological dead-end of just parroting stock paragraphs and keywords. Interpretively, those stock paragraphs and keywords are a good beginning, but they should never become the end point in your work. Down that road, you might as well be a microchip.

VENUS IN THE SECOND HOUSE

Most commonly called the house of money, the meaning of the second house ranges over a much more multidimensional psychic terrain. But it is indeed about money—and all the things money can buy, starting with food and shelter. One helpful phrase is to think of the second house as representing *the material basis of survival.* Those words bring us face-to-face with the raw heart of the matter.

The next step is an easy one: imagine that you have no food, no shelter. How do you feel? In a word, *insecure.* That is a second house word too.

In the modern world, the term "insecurity" rings a psychological bell. We will get there, looking into the correlation between *psychological insecurity* and the second house—but let's not forget its roots in practical, Taurean, energy: lacking the material basis of survival triggers feelings of insecurity in us that have nothing to do with psychological issues. Without food and shelter you would indeed be in an objectively precarious position.

And what is the cure for that?

Easy: find some food, find some shelter.

One helpful skill in working with second house energy lies in doing our best to not over-complicate it. Very often, simple, objective efforts yield far more healing results here than the generation of elaborate theoretical insights.

The starting point for any planet in the second house can be understood as an innate feeling of insecurity or self-doubt. The evolutionary path that rises out of that starting point lies in initially recognizing the feelings of insecurity, then seeking *resources* which effectively ameliorate those concerns, thereby gradually *proving ourselves to ourselves.*

Let's put all that on the back burner for a moment and turn our attention to Venus. Then we will put the planet in the second house and see how it goes about gaining confidence.

I want to begin our Venusian explorations with one of the most slippery, perilous words in the English language: *attractiveness.* It says something profound about our society that when we hear that word, most of us immediately think in terms of *physical* attractiveness. And yet—at least once we are out of high school—as we contemplate the possibility of intimacy with another person, his or her physical attractiveness is only one element in a far more complex calculation.

A physically beautiful person with an annoying personality quickly loses luster.

If we are contemplating a serious relationship with someone, many considerations loom at least as large as the shape of flesh, face, and bones. Unless we are truly crazy, we also factor in that person's spiritual accomplishment, moral character, intelligence, humor, shared values, and financial solvency, for a few examples.

On the down side, what reduces a person's perceived attractiveness? What about unresolved familial baggage, flagrant materialism, a history of failed relationships, psychotic madness, ill health, a crushing load of debt, and so on?

We might think of an "attractiveness quotient" as a way of pulling together this ball of threads. There is nothing objective at all about this idea; it is not rocket science. Naturally, people's tastes and values vary. But here is a fairly reliable, if somewhat cloudy bottom line: *successful relationships tend to form between people with similar attractiveness quotients.*

And the more mature we become, the less simple physical beauty dominates these calculations.

Now we light the fuse: let's place Venus actively in this second house evolutionary, existential and psychological context.

Our self-perceived attractiveness quotient now lies in an astrological framework that initially implies a degree of insecurity or self-doubt. We can improve, but as ever, we have to start where we actually find ourselves.

SWIMMING POOLS

When I am sitting with a client with Venus in the second house, here is a metaphor I often use to good effect.

Let's say that you are ten feet deep—that is the deep end of the pool, for sure.

Let's say you fall in love with someone who is seven feet deep. That is not shallow water—but three feet of you is out of that person's reach, eternally unfathomable.

Now we add the critical second house ingredient: *even though you are ten feet deep, you were born believing that you are only seven feet deep . . .*

And that explains everything.

You have underestimated your "attractiveness" in the deepest, most fundamental sense of the word.

Systematically, at least until evolution unfolds, you are doomed to be attracted to people who virtually by definition can only leave you feeling lonely and unfulfilled.

What is the cure? At the deepest level, it lies in *learning to love yourself.* That sounds like a cliché, but it really is the heart of the matter. Meditate on yourself as "a catch"—as someone who is desirable, someone whom a wonderful person would treasure as a friend or a partner.

As we have seen, with the second house we cannot ignore "chicken soup" perspectives. They are an essential piece of the puzzle. So, in practical terms, how might people actually go about proving their attractiveness to themselves? What behaviors might we suggest?

Here is a method: *to try reaching out as equals to people whom they might initially think of as being out of reach.* If you are the one with Venus in the second house, you will probably be surprised at their receptivity. And that feedback is a powerful remedy for your initial tendency to underestimate yourself.

Note here how an *intentional behavior change* (house activity) is what triggers inward evolution. That is the way it is with houses. They are something that you *do.* If *insight* drives the signs, then it is *behavior* that drives the houses. "Fake it 'til you make it" has some relevance here—which is to say, actual action and experience have a triggering impact upon one's inner state.

Here are some other Venus-in-the-second methods: change your hairstyle, buy more flattering clothing. These simple outward behaviors, when working synergistically with the inward developments we have been describing, can have a powerful healing effect, both on your attitude about yourself and on the way you are perceived.

Those new clothes will cost you some money. If you told me that you could not afford them, I would have to take that possibility seriously—but I would also wonder if you were falling into a classic second house trap: wrapping self-punishment in a cloak of conveniently-imagined "financial limitations."

The Holy Grail with Venus in the second house lies in becoming worthy in your own mind of the kind of partners or soul-friends who are actually worthy of you. To accomplish that, you will need to walk your talk—that is to say, make some positive changes in the *actions* that define your life: that is the domain of the astrological houses. Act as if you loved yourself, and others will follow suit.

MERCURY IN THE ELEVENTH HOUSE

Back in chapter five, there is a section with the heading, "A Girl Was Born with Mercury in Her Tenth House . . ." For the sake of variety, I am going to take us down a different road here, but as you contemplate how Mercury interacts with house symbolism, that section is worth a second look.

Classically, the eleventh house is the house of friends. That is quite accurate, so long as we define that ever-ambivalent word, "friends," in a very inclusive way. For your closest friends, the symbolism of your *seventh* house is much more relevant. The eleventh house resonates more with that *sea of familiar faces* that surrounds you. It reflects your *crowd* or your *tribe*. If you are involved with organizations of any sort, or any teams, your eleventh house will cast light on their natures, as well as upon the role you play in those contexts. Its meaning, in other words, is *social* rather than intimate.

Once we understand that, calling the eleventh house the house of friends works perfectly well.

There is another level of meaning, however, to the eleventh house—one that I have come to consider even more central to the symbolism. This is the house of the *future*, at least as we aspire to create it. It is about our goals and our strategies for reaching them. It is about intentional development over time. It is about *setting priorities.*

Here is how these two threads of symbolism—friends and the future—come together. *If you want to become a musician, hang out with musicians.* If you want to become a dentist, connect with dentists—or at least with people who share that same ambition. Many of us with spiritual interests have found help, encouragement, and support in various spiritual fellowships: the congregation, the *sangha*, the meditation group or the yoga class.

"House of friends" is a venerable term. I do not want to start a crusade to change it. But for me, I prefer to think of the eleventh as the house of *helpful alliances*.

A moment's reflection on this perspective reveals our most fundamental insight: *the goal must come first.* Only when we have defined it can there be an organizing principle in our selection of social relationships. Otherwise there is no underlying unifying principle in these relationships.

It follows that the dark side of the eleventh house lies in *fragmented, purposeless, social over-extension.*

To the Romans, Mercury was the messenger of the gods. Its nature is bound to language. With Mercury in the eleventh house, your developmental goal over time is easily summarized: *your aim is to find your voice.* The process will take time. It requires long-term commitment. And pivotally, it requires "a little help from your friends."

If you want to become a writer, hang out with writers.

Other ambitions are worthy of Mercury in the eleventh house too, but let's start with the idea of writing. That is certainly one face of Mercury.

Many authors have benefitted from membership in writers' groups, where people offer helpful critiques of each other's efforts. Even writers who believe that "the pot boils best with the lid on" sooner or later must face an editor or an audience—that, or they will never have the experience of their voices actually being heard.

Writing is only one possibility here. There are other ways to "find our voice." If you want to become a teacher, hang out with teachers. If you want to become a documentarian, hang out with other filmmakers. Want to act? Study theater.

Humans have been telling stories to each other ever since our ancestors first sat around a campfire in the Olduvai Gorge. One of your main evolutionary intentions with Mercury in the eleventh house is to become part of that endless conversation.

I want to express respect for anyone who, for example, has ever written a novel—even if it has never been published. The "failed novel" is still a spiritual success. But that statement is more in the spirit of Saturn than Mercury. With Mercury in the eleventh house—the house of other people—there is a public, community, dimension to the symbolism. For you truly fulfill your soul's intention here, *the village must hear your voice.* That is what completes the circle. The unpublished novel is actually a failure here.

Often planets in the eleventh house develop dramatically over time. They are not necessarily weak when we are young, but they do gather momentum, confidence, and individuality as years go by. The only proviso I would add to that comment is that it is only true if we actually make the effort. Nothing spiritual grows automatically. A common trope in literary book reviews nicely captures this point in the context of Mercury in the eleventh house: *"In this, her seventh novel, Smith appears to have finally found her voice."*

We understand exactly what the reviewer means. A person who has already written six novels is obviously not weak in the Mercury department. But from the reviewer's perspective, her earlier work was derivative—we could easily trace her influences. But now, with her seventh book, "Smith" has found her vision. She is now writing in a way that no one before her has written.

Maybe she is sixty years old—and the victory she has just attained has been worth fifty years of effort.

Let us take one moment to contemplate the bottom of the garbage can. What does this configuration look like if we get it wrong? The energy of Mercury in the eleventh house cannot simply go away. If we do not manifested well, we will surely manifest it poorly.

* As time goes by, we might, for example, become a terrible chatterbox, boring the pants off anyone who has the misfortune to encounter us.
* Simple nervousness is likely to increase—a quality that is often evident in people who speak compulsively.
* Socially we will become scattered, surrounded by people who are similarly scattered.

* Dark Mercury correlates with silliness and immaturity—words which in this sad expression of the configuration will characterize not only ourselves, but also the sea of faces around us.

* Our life will embody endless distraction. Our epitaph might be, "All tactics, but no strategy."

As always, it is more fruitful to start the long journey towards the higher ground. Write a page a day in your journal. Read. Improve your vocabulary. Speak up in front of people when you have a chance. That will set your foot on the right path.

SATURN IN THE FIFTH HOUSE

A quick rundown of the keywords usually associated with the fifth house makes it sound like paradise, at least for a hedonist. Essentially everything we do for pleasure is linked to it. Famously, it is the house of *love affairs*. It has a powerful and authentic association with *creativity* and with *performance* on stage. It is about *parties*. It is about *shopping*. It is about *drinking*—both too much and just enough. It is about *flamboyance* and "living large."

Frank Sinatra had his Jupiter there, along with his Pisces Moon conjunct the fifth cusp. You could hardly find a better illustration of the spirit of this house than "old blue eyes" himself.

Probably the most common name for the fifth house, however, is the *house of children*. And it objectively relates literally to children—but even there, if we look just a little bit deeper at the way kids behave, we are right back to that hedonist's paradise. Children, unless they are terribly damaged, *love to play*.

And play itself is fundamental to the fifth house, and to joy itself.

So far, I have been recounting the astrologically-standard perspective on the fifth house. This is what I learned about it when I was a young astrologer—although back then descriptions of this house were often laced with moral cautions against the temptations of debauchery and excess.

Fair enough—the tragic, brilliant Welsh poet, Dylan Thomas, had Venus in Sagittarius in the fifth house. There's his magnificent creativity, but also his downfall. He died horribly, in the grips of alcohol-related *dele-*

rium tremens, before he was forty. His wife, Caitlin, described him in his last hours as "possessed of 10,000 raving demons."

That bleak dimension of the fifth house provides a key to a far deeper—and a more compassionate—understanding of the symbolism. Why would anyone destroy themselves with alcohol or drugs? It is a well-trodden path, and well-mapped; there are ultimately no surprises on it.

It is tempting to think of anyone going down such a road as having made a stupid choice.

But Dylan Thomas was far from a stupid man. Stupidity is not the issue; the issue is *pain*. Go to any rehab program that has a chance of succeeding, and you will hear the same axiom: these patients are practicing a form of *self-administered anesthesia*. They have found a desperate way to make the pain stop.

As we look at the fifth house from the evolutionary perspective, we ask the critical question: *why* would someone have planets there? What is the soul's purpose in doing that? How could a soul find itself in a condition where "having a good time" might be a critical link in its evolutionary strategy?

The answer jumps out: *pleasure and joy are the antidotes to pain and suffering.* The *need for joy* implicit in any truly evolutionary perspective on the fifth house immediately points to the mysterious time before the present birth—a time in which something very painful must have happened.

This quickly brings us into karmic analysis—the territory of the lunar nodes. That is complex terrain and I will not attempt to summarize it here. As we have often mentioned, that kind of analysis plays a pivotal role in the craft of evolutionary astrology. If you are drawn to learning about it, have a look at my book *Yesterday's Sky: Astrology and Reincarnation*.

For our purposes here, it is sufficient to recognize that behind the playfulness and necessary self-indulgence of the fifth house there lies a wound in the soul.

A right response to the fifth house helps to heal that ancient hurt—while an unconscious, reflexive response to it leads to various forms of "self-administered anesthesia," some of them very dangerous.

Moving on to add Saturn to our thinking about the fifth house, we immediately collide with a very obvious dilemma: *what is this serious, hardworking planet doing in the house of fun and games?* What fun is there in resisting temptation? When did integrity and self-respect ever have much to do with having a good time?

As we will soon see, the combination of Saturn and the fifth house is not nearly as unnatural as it might seem at first.

Let me begin by aiming directly for the bull's-eye. With Saturn in the fifth house, *the great work of your life lies in learning the discipline of joy.* We might equally phrase it as the *discipline of spontaneity.* I have always enjoyed that latter phrase. It of course sounds completely contradictory. But it is not. After crippling shock, recovering spontaneity requires effort.

Pain leads to tightness. We are afraid to let go, afraid to trust. Maybe something terrible has happened. Maybe it is past, over and done, but you are still deeply shaken. A friend encourages you "to just relax." Good advice—but of course it is very difficult to follow.

With Saturn in the fifth house, that is exactly what you are up against, except on a cradle-to-grave scale. Recovering joy in being alive is your Great Work. You probably do not remember what hurt you, but your soul remembers.

What practical course might you follow to restore life to your damaged inner child?

Committing yourself to a path of *creative self-expression* is a fundamental, positive strategy here. Learning to play the piano—as distinct from learning how to "work" a piano—illustrates the point beautifully. The restoration of spontaneity and flow are the intentions.

Dance can be enormously effective here because of the way it invites the physical body to engage with this healing process.

Creative writing may be less visceral than dance or music, but it is still very helpful—no one can write very well unless he or she learns to surrender to the unconscious mind and its precious, uncontrollable visitations of energy.

AND WHAT ABOUT SEX?

Ask any honest adult to free-associate from the word "pleasure" and it is not long before sex enters the conversation. That is only natural; cutting to the chase, in many ways, the very epitome of the fifth house is *orgasm.* In orgasm, we of course experience an extreme peak of pleasure. We are also fully and totally surrendered to the present moment, fully committed to a state of unguarded, spontaneous engagement.

Nothing so captures the heart of the fifth house.

For the majority of human beings, orgasm is not so difficult to attain, one way or another. Does having Saturn in the fifth house indicate any particular difficulty there? I would not jump to that conclusion in every case—although if the karmic analysis suggested sexual damage, issues around orgasm might very well be present with this configuration.

The quality of one's sexual experience is of course inseparable from the quality of one's relationships. That would quickly lead us into broader territory than we are covering here. Suffice to say that, with Saturn in the fifth house, there is an evolutionary intention to improve one's skills at *mate selection*—that is the "love affairs" dimension of this house. Avoiding people who have a repressive effect upon our erotic impulses is critical. We are in fact very likely to meet a few of them.

Good news—that gives us a chance to break up an old karmic pattern which has only hurt us.

ICING THE CAKE

In this chapter and in the previous one, we have explored an absolutely mission-critical astrological skill: *understanding how a sign and house flavor the basic nature of a planet.* As we saw earlier in the book, the trinity of a sign, a house, and a planet forms the simplest, most elemental astrological structure that we actually find in a human mind. Lacking any one of the three, we only have an abstraction.

The word "planet" has become a bit elastic lately. Calling the Sun and the Moon planets, as astrologers always have—and including Pluto despite the predations of the International Astronomical Union, leaves us with ten of them. That at least is the system I am exploring in these four volumes.

What about Chiron—and if are using Chiron, what about the other Centaurs, such as Pholus and Nessus? What about the major asteroids? What about Eris, the size of Pluto and out beyond it in deep space?

These are real questions. I take those bodies seriously. To keep these four books down to a reasonable length—and frankly to remain solidly planted on the *terra firma* of my own professional experience with clients—I am sticking to what I view as the absolute essentials. At this point in time, that means ten "planets."

Master those ten planets, learn to contextualize them in these triads, learn to listen to their dialogue with each other, and you have made a giant step toward astrological competence.

PART THREE

VENUS, MERCURY, AND SATURN THROUGH THE TWELVE SIGNS AND HOUSES

No astrological triad breathes anything like human air on its own. A person might have a peaceful Venus in Taurus and the fourth house—and nine planets spread between Aries and Scorpio.

That peace-seeking Venus will operate in the context of a larger agenda of ferocity and honesty—and will look very differently from Venus in Taurus in a more mellow chart.

In the pages that follow, I provide a few suggestions for the interpretation of our three Earth planets in the context of the twelve signs and the twelve houses. Please take this information as a starting point for a more integrative and holistic analysis.

That is how you make the magic happen.

9

VENUS IN THE TWELVE SIGNS

VENUS IN ARIES

Underlying Intimate Agenda: I resolve to overcome any fears that stand between me and genuine intimacy. I will be direct; I will ask for what I want. When I see something limiting going on between myself and another person, I will bring it up. I will tell the truth; I expect the same. I offer my loyalty; and, again, I expect the same.

Essential Qualities in a Natural Partner: The courage to be authentic. Honesty. Directness. Fierce loyalty. Passion in the context of fidelity.

Strategy: When I am feeling an unmet need or discomfort in a relationship, I express it quickly and cleanly. I do not let bad feelings fester. I do not insist that all my needs be met —but I do insist on the right to express them clearly and to have them taken seriously.

Tools: A passionate nature, inclined to forging ahead in intimacy, taking the risks inherent in keeping love active and alive in the present tense. An ability to be clear.

Returning to Equilibrium: Above all, I benefit from the company of friends and partners as we have just described them. Vigorous exercise. Letting off steam. Dance. Passionate music played loudly. Blowing out the cobwebs. Adventures.

Dealing With The Shadow: I am aware that I might over-dramatize a point of contention. I will not let self-righteous anger limit my ability to see the other person's point of view. I cultivate forgiveness. I let the past be the past. I do not hold a grudge or seek revenge.

VENUS IN TAURUS

Underlying Intimate Agenda: In thinking about dear friends or partners, I keep my eye on the real prize for me: serenity of spirit. I want to feel genuine ease and comfort in my relationships. I am not afraid of working on a relationship, but I never want to force anything to work. I prize naturalness; I trust my instincts. I am looking for someone who helps me feel saner and more peaceful rather than crazier.

Essential Qualities in a Natural Partner: Groundedness. Reasonableness. One who prizes peace, and takes no perverse joy in intimate drama. One who "smells right." The kind of person cats, dogs, and horses seem to like.

Strategy: I make a great effort to sort out the deep passion of a true soul-bond from the hormone-addled, histrionic psychodramas which masquerade as "purple passion." I look for someone whom I simply like, with whom I can be quiet, with whom I sleep easily.

Tools: My body is a powerful sensing instrument when it comes to finding natural partners. I always consult my "inner animal" before I commit to trusting someone. My mind can fool me, but my body never will.

Returning to Equilibrium: Above all, I benefit from the company of friends and partners as we have just described them. Silence is precious. Time spent in the natural world. Yoga. Massage. Hugs. Cuddles. The quiet company of animals with whom I feel a soul-bond.

Dealing With The Shadow: I accept that intimacy sometimes involves hard work. I recognize that my own dark side will certainly be revealed to my partners. I resolve that I will learn to see it clearly too, and to take responsibility for it. I avoid taking anyone for granted. I avoid deadening intimate ruts.

VENUS IN GEMINI

Underlying Intimate Agenda: Excellent communication is critical to my experience of intimacy. The clear translation of soul-states into vocabulary and syntax is always challenging; I resolve to master that skill, both in terms of my own self-expression and in terms of my ability to listen deeply to another person without being blinded by my own preconceptions. I do not do well when I am bored; I resolve to do my part to keep all my relationships interesting, growing, and changing.

Essential Qualities in a Natural Partner: Open-mindedness. Curiosity. An eagerness for new experiences and for opportunities to learn. Listening skills. Articulateness—or at least willing verbal self-expression. A natural predilection for conversation. A willingness to discuss anything.

Strategy: I commit to two resolutions: to listen to any partner carefully and to respond clearly and forthrightly from my own heart. I do my part in keeping a relationship interesting: I suggest travel, I read books and talk about what I have learned, I dynamite deadening intimate routines for the sheer joy of seeing something different. I ask questions.

Tools: I like to talk and I like to listen, at least in intimate situations with people I love. I am naturally interested in many things. I am genuinely curious about the perspectives of others, especially those with whom I am sharing my life.

Returning to Equilibrium: Above all, I benefit from the company of friends and partners as we have just described them. Exposure to anything new, fresh, and enlivening. Quiet time with a book or an interesting program in any medium of communication. Sensory exposure to beauty.

Dealing With The Shadow: there are many interesting and attractive people in the world, but once I am committed to a particular relationship, I am careful not to be distracted by other people. I will use language as a way of building bridges to people about whom I care; I will zealously monitor myself regarding my tendency to hide my heart behind words and elaborate rationalizations.

VENUS IN CANCER

Underlying Intimate Agenda: The formation of strong, long-lasting, committed bonds with other human beings. Stability and longevity in relationship are not the only point—the deeper point is the creation of an intimate environment in which the most vulnerable parts of my being feel safe enough to be revealed. At the heart level, I am seeking home and a feeling of family in some sense of the word.

Essential Qualities in a Natural Partner: A willingness to be radically committed to me. Faithfulness, reliability, and loyalty. One who is not unduly afraid of a powerful word such as "forever." An urge to nurture—whether that nurturing is of children, pets, a garden, or the relationship itself.

Strategy: I must maintain a creative tension between, on one hand, my natural caution about getting hurt and, on the other hand, volunteering to take the risk of opening my heart. I will not be so cautious as to be unreachable.

Tools: A deep and fundamental capacity to love another human being in a spirit of familial devotion and lifelong commitment. A nearly infinite ability simply to care for another person. A natural internal marriage of sexuality with emotions of simple affection.

Returning to Equilibrium: Above all, I benefit from the company of friends and partners as we have just described them. Quiet time at home. Familiar routines: a cup of tea in a comfortable chair that has taken the shape of my own body. Time in bed, even if I am not sleepy. A distinct reduction in the level of external stimuli.

Dealing With The Shadow: I resolve to be aware of my potential for excessive caution and self protection. I will not hide my true feelings or needs behind the "parental" mask of caregiving.

VENUS IN LEO

Underlying Intimate Agenda: I resolve to not settle for anything less in my intimate life than the feeling of being cherished by someone whom I myself treasure. No one has to be perfect. The agenda here is to be perfectly loving—to celebrate each other, stand up for each other, and to consistently prioritize the relationship over other concerns.

Essential Qualities in a Natural Partner: Expressiveness. An affectionate, demonstrative nature. Supportiveness. The ability to say I love you. Attentiveness and a natural fluency in offering compliments. Self-respect—and respect for me—as demonstrated by a willingness to look and behave his or her best.

Strategy: First and foremost, I resolve never to settle for a partner whom I do not genuinely cherish. I would rather be alone than to abase myself that way. Once having found such a person, I actively commit to an active, lifelong path dedicated to preserving and nurturing the romance of our bond.

Tools: I have a certain flair for style and colorful self-expression. An ability to say what I feel in an impactful way, so it is heard deeply. A degree of healthy pride, self-respect, and dignity—all of which support me in not settling for too little in any of my relationships.

Returning to Equilibrium: Above all, I benefit from the company of friends and partners as we have just described them. My creative outlets soothe me; I cultivate some form of artistic or aesthetic self-expression. I know that it helps me feel good inwardly to look my best outwardly; when I am upset, I groom myself. I dress attractively. Perhaps I shop. Perhaps a try on a new look.

Dealing With The Shadow: I remind myself that no one's life need to revolve around mine. In a healthy relationship, we are like a double star orbiting a common center of gravity which we have created together. I express my own needs forthrightly—but I also make space to hear the needs and celebrate the victories of my friends and my partners.

VENUS IN VIRGO

Underlying Intimate Agenda: I resolve never to accept a relationship with anyone who is irresponsible or unreliable. Grown-ups only need apply. Groundedness, maturity, and reasonableness are critical ingredients if I am going to trust another person. We accept imperfections in each other and in the relationship, but at the same time, we resolve endlessly to chip away at them, making things better over time.

Essential Qualities in a Natural Partner: A hard working, responsible willingness to behave in an adult fashion. Competence. One "who has a life" in terms of having found meaningful work and responsibilities. An ability to communicate; an astute awareness of human flaws, along with a commitment to self-improvement—and enough of a sense of humor about the whole thing to survive the intensity of the process.

Strategy: I resolve to be cautious in offering my heart to anyone. My aims here are discrimination and discernment; I do not condemn anyone because he or she fails to meet my needs or standards. At the same time, I am resolved never to enter into a relationship which, deep down inside, I know in advance could never satisfy me.

Tools: I have an analytic mind, even in affairs of the heart. When emotions are involved, people often do not think clearly. I am not immune to falling into that trap—but I am more skilled at avoiding it than are most people. Once committed, I am capable of working on myself and working on the relationship, fashioning it into something which we both treasure.

Returning to Equilibrium: Above all, I benefit from the company of friends and partners as we have just described them. Work and routine have soothing effects upon me. So does the practice of any craft, from astrology to bead work. It calms me to do things with my hands. Pleasurable concentration distracts me from worry and relieves tension.

Dealing With The Shadow: I resolve to cultivate an expansive, forgiving view of human nature, my own or that of my friends or partners. I will not nitpick. Even in love, I will recognize the eternal truth that "perfect" is the enemy of "good enough." I will recognize moments when a relaxed acceptance of flawed reality is the highest course.

VENUS IN LIBRA

Underlying Intimate Agenda: To aim for a "perfect relationship" might seem like a quixotic goal, but that is truly the intimate agenda here. To bring this idea down to earth, I recognize that my agenda lies in committing to a process of development, rather than looking for a bond that works automatically, without effort, right from the beginning. Here are the qualities I seek: deep, three-dimensional *attention* to each other. Fairness in all things. The cultivation of grace and serenity. And a lifelong romantic appreciation of each other.

Essential Qualities in a Natural Partner: A civilized quality of grace and courtesy, even elegance. Politeness and evidence of respect for me, even if we are angry. A willingness to take in my point of view even if he or she sees things differently. Aesthetic sensitivities. An instinct for fairness.

Strategy: Cultivating the ability to see other people as they are—which is to say, an appreciation of the fact that they are different from me. A spirit of mutual inquiry. Genuine listening. Peacekeeping skills—but in which such skills are never employed to avoid necessary, difficult negotiations.

Tools: I was born with an affable quality of natural charm; an ability to get along with other people, to build bridges even across wide chasms of human difference. An instinct for understanding another person's point of view. A knack for diplomacy—how to express potentially difficult things in ways that diffuse a situation rather than escalating it.

Returning to Equilibrium: Above all, I benefit from the company of friends and partners as we have just described them. Immersion of my senses in beauty, whether it is the beauty of nature or the beauty created by human artistry. Civilized pleasures. Experiences of elegance, grace, and quality.

Dealing With The Shadow: I resolve never to employ my diplomatic skills in order to paper over hurt or genuine intimate challenges. I put truth on the table first, and only then do I deploy my capacity for respectful negotiation.

VENUS IN SCORPIO

Underlying Intimate Agenda: A radical commitment to honesty. And an equally radical commitment to living truthfully, forgivingly, and humbly with both my own Shadow and the Shadow of my partner. A relationship between the wholenesses of two psyches—including the unconscious minds—rather than simply between two conscious, "virtuous" personalities.

Truth above all.

Essential Qualities in a Natural Partner: Psychological savvy, even if the person is not formally educated in that way. A desire to pursue the truth. A commitment never to punish me for pointing out the truth as I see it, no matter how uncomfortable that might be. A willingness to look me directly in the eye.

Strategy: The cultivation of a level of trust sufficient to support true emotional nakedness. The cultivation of the habit of honesty and the establishment of a pattern of mutual acceptance, no matter what. Permission to think anything, with the only restrictions being those placed on behavior itself.

Tools: I have a great innate intensity of being. A capacity to deal acceptingly with emotionally challenging material. A willingness to break the mental taboos imposed by society. An unashamed sense of the power of sexuality to maintain, and even to restore, a sense of bondedness between two human beings.

Returning to Equilibrium: Above all, I benefit from the company of friends and partners as we have just described them. Serious talks with dear friends about charged subjects, such as mortality, aging, and disease. Realness. The antithesis of cocktail party chatter. Humor—often of the "gallows" fashion—plays a pivotal role in the restoration of my serenity.

Dealing With The Shadow: I resolve to learn to recognize the moment when intense emotion or need begins to distort my ability to think clearly. Similarly, I cultivate sensitivity to the signs that someone I love has reached that same point of distortion. I recognize the power of the Shadow, and respect it. Sometimes I need to step back and de-escalate a situation. I learn to let things go. I learn the fine arts of patience and timing when it comes to deep psychological work.

VENUS IN SAGITTARIUS

Underlying Intimate Agenda: The integration of that infamous polarity: love and freedom. I resolve to learn how to love voluntarily, free of the deadening hand of any oppressive sense of duty. Simultaneously, I celebrate the freedom and autonomy of those whom I love. Together, we create more of a sense of the possibility of adventure in our lives than we could ever create alone.

Essential Qualities in a Natural Partner: Independence; a high degree of self-sufficiency. A taste for the open road. A philosophical, principled nature. A powerful motivation to learn and to grow. A willingness to let me be who I am.

Strategy: Experience leads to wisdom in terms of mate selection; I am not afraid to explore intimacy and to learn from diverse experiences there. Before I grant myself love, I must grant myself freedom. I might have to "kiss a few frogs" in order to find my prince or my princess. I keep it honest, keep it loving, and then I let no one shame me for any of it.

Tools: I have a curious, resilient, energetic heart. An ability to build bridges across cultural or social divides. An emotional resilience; the ability to recover rapidly from heartbreak. Faith in life, even when individuals may have failed me.

Returning to Equilibrium: Above all, I benefit from the company of friends and partners as we have just described them. Seeing new places refreshes me. I heed the call of the open road or the far horizon. Uplifting aesthetic experiences—glorious natural scenes, heroic or anthemic music, ambitious films—all of them help me to restore and uplift my soul after some shock.

Dealing With The Shadow: I resolve to actually *find* what I am seeking; I will not hide from the real world of maturity behind the veil of an endless tragic-romantic search for someone who does not exist. I will not take cheap refuge in my incredible capacity for rationalization and explaining myself.

VENUS IN CAPRICORN

Underlying Intimate Agenda: In relationship, my aim is nothing less than a masterpiece and I know that masterpieces take time. I want to create a bond with another human being of which I am truly proud. I seek the ancient vow of a lifelong commitment—a commitment not simply to passing of years together, but rather to the kind of love that might arise between two true elders in the real world, regardless of our actual ages.

Essential Qualities in a Natural Partner: A willingness to make and keep promises. A capacity for seriousness when seriousness is appropriate. One whose already-existing history suggests that he or she places a great value upon integrity. Character is high on such a person's list of attractive qualities, never eclipsed by more transitory charms.

Strategy: Commitment over the long term is fundamental here. But such commitment is not entered spontaneously or frivolously; we earn each other's faith through a gradual, patient process. I am capable of commitment, but I do not offer it lightly.

Tools: An elevated capacity for self-discipline, maturity, and delayed gratification. I, more than most people can actually keep the intimate promises that I make. In times of difficulty, I keep my eye on the prize, which is weathering the storm, and learning from it. That which does not destroy us only makes us stronger.

Returning to Equilibrium: Above all, I benefit from the company of friends and partners as we have just described them. Paradoxically, relaxation comes most easily to me when I am engaged in some focused effort. Ambitious projects are good for me. I might work as hard at my hobbies as other people work at their jobs. I do not let anyone criticize me for that—I know that it is a reliable method for restoring my serenity of spirit after some trying or stressful experience.

Dealing With The Shadow: I resolve always to remember to be tender with myself. That resolution takes several forms. One is that I commit to expressing my needs. I am not ashamed to ask a friend or partner for help, support, or a hug. Love is a joy, not a task. I resolve to remember that—and if love does in fact become a task, I give myself gentle permission to reconsider my promises.

VENUS IN AQUARIUS

Underlying Intimate Agenda: I resolve that all of my intimate choices will be made in a spirit of self-awareness, self-possession, and on a completely voluntary basis. I will not be told what to do, intimately or sexually, by anyone. I am the ultimate authority in my own intimate life. Every community and every ethnic group always has a pre-written script for love, friendship, and sexuality; I reject the script. My choices are my own.

Essential Qualities in a Natural Partner: An unquestioning respect for my own freedom and individuality. An independence of nature, and a corresponding appreciation of my own independence. One who questions authority. A true, one-of-a-kind individual. One who is following his or her own path through life. One who loves me more than he or she needs me.

Strategy: First and foremost, I commit to sorting out my own needs and my own identity before I confuse my own path by trying to accommodate it to someone else's path. In every culture, there is a rule book of customs and assumptions about human intimacy. I toss it out; I am writing my own rule book. Nothing is required of me in any relationship I choose to be part of except honesty.

Tools: I was born with a capacity to think outside the framework of the conventionalities other people typically accept without thinking. I am tolerant of human diversity; I do not need my friends or partners to think the same way I do, or to agree with me about everything. Live and let live—that ideal comes quite naturally to me. I can respond creatively and originally to any intimate dilemma.

Returning to Equilibrium: Above all, I benefit from the company of friends and partners as we have just described them. I am friendly, but often when I am upset, the best way I can regain my serenity of spirit is just to be left alone for a while, not needing to explain myself to anyone. In terms of the arts, my tastes might seem weird to some people—but exposure to art helps me find my balance again. What works for me works for me and I do not need to explain it.

Dealing With The Shadow: I resolve, when someone has earned my trust, that I will struggle sincerely to open my vulnerable heart to that person. I will not hide behind distance, "weirdness," or detachment; I resolve to let myself be truly touched.

VENUS IN PISCES

Underlying Intimate Agenda: I resolve that I will settle for nothing less in this lifetime than relationships that have a genuinely, consciously spiritual basis. This does not mean that we must share a religion or even a philosophy; it means that we can sit together in silent communion. It means that sometimes words are not necessary to bridge the space between us. It means that we can gaze unguardedly and openly into each other's eyes.

Essential Qualities in a Natural Partner: I know that anyone who lacks an active, conscious spiritual life will only fill my heart with loneliness in the long run. The reason is simple: such a person, who may have many virtues, simply cannot grasp a very large part of what I am. My natural partner is, in some sense, a mystic. Under that banner, I include visionaries, creative people, and people of imagination. They may not be churchy, but there is strong evidence in their lives and speech of their communion with something vaster than themselves.

Strategy: I know that the quality and happiness of my intimate life is directly linked to the depth of my own personal spiritual practice. The deeper I go, the deeper my relationships are likely to be—and the deeper are the people whom I attract into my life. As I think about the pressing importance of my spiritual practice, it is helpful to recognize that art and creativity can be quite central to it.

Tools: A capacity for decoupling my consciousness from my personality arises naturally in me. Love helps me with that; so does losing myself in aesthetic rapture—listening to music, gazing at beautiful scenes, and so on. I sense that there is a wider world deep down in my psyche—and that the more I embrace it through those methods, the more my Venus will magnetize the right people into my life.

Returning to Equilibrium: Above all, I benefit from the company of friends and partners as we have just described them. I need a certain amount of time, hopefully each day, to simply sit in silence and release the day's entanglements. Listening to music, gazing at flowers or beautiful paintings, making sure that I don't miss the sunset or the moonrise—all of these experiences of aesthetic trends help to restore my lost tranquility.

Dealing With The Shadow: I resolve not to become a ghost in my own relationships. There are some things I do not need to accept in another person. I need to be clear about those boundaries—and to leave any relationship that is not serving my higher spiritual purposes. I affirm that I have the right to do exactly that. I reject the drunken torpor and toxic stability of bad love.

10

MERCURY IN THE TWELVE SIGNS

MERCURY IN ARIES

Cognitive Rocket Fuel: To stay mentally engaged and alive, I must expose my intelligence to edgy, fresh, groundbreaking information. I celebrate debate and disagreement, so long as people are still listening to each other and responding cogently. Ideas grow stronger and perceptions clearer when they are met with challenges.

Learning Strategy: I seek conversations with people who offer constructive argument and who are not afraid of my passions or my opinions. I avoid those who require me to "walk on eggshells" around them, and require me not to upset them or ever challenge their assumptions. When it comes to ideas, "blow it up and start all over again" often works fine for me.

Natural Style of Communication: Listening and speaking is most effective and comfortable for me when everyone, myself included, can just speak their minds in straightforward, spontaneous, direct fashion. "Just say it!" Just give me honesty and the truth as you see it, and we will take it from there. Sometimes I float a point just to see if it stands up or collapses. I don't necessarily even agree with myself sometimes. When I like people, I often tease them.

My Best Teachers: Those who can most effectively help me learn what I need to learn in this life are not afraid to confront my defenses and opinions directly. They do not hide behind diplomacy. They are not afraid of me, nor do they need to be. When my skull is thick, they know how to penetrate it.

Perceptual Bias: Because of my tendency to focus on the creative tensions generated by opposing ideas, I can see conflict where none is necessary or present. Thinking that "I am only having a conversation," I can miss the fact that I am actually triggering fear or defensiveness in another person without my knowing or intending it. My intensity can sometimes eclipse what I am actually trying to get across.

Defensive Strategy: When I am reflexively shutting myself down to a necessary but threatening perception, I can argue like a crooked attorney. I can win arguments even when I am wrong—and when deep down inside, I even know that myself. I can win arguments by exhausting the listener to the point that he or she simply gives up—then I can take that surrender as agreement. Using this defensive method, I am capable of learning nothing at all.

MERCURY IN TAURUS

Cognitive Rocket Fuel: To stay mentally engaged and alive, I must expose my intelligence to the natural world—and to "natural" people. Tying myself in intellectual knots gets me nowhere. There are complex truths and there are simple truths; for me, it is often the simple ones that get me to the heart of what I need to understand. Silence is my greatest teacher.

Learning Strategy: I seek the simple essence of things. I trust my instincts and my first impressions. I cultivate calm and quiet within my own mind by seeking the same things in my outward experiences. It is in that tranquil condition that I see things most clearly. Understanding requires patience and direct engagement. I find the words later.

Natural Style of Communication: Listening and speaking is most effective and comfortable for me when conversations happen patiently, with the heart of the matter stated clearly, punctuated with reflective silences. Interruption rarely adds to mutual comprehension; I appreciate it when people let me finish a sentence or a paragraph, then let me do the same for them. The best conversations are the ones in which it is safe to take a breath without fear of the other person launching in a different direction.

Best Teachers: Those who can most effectively help me learn what I need to learn in this life are earthy and grounded, full of "chicken soup" wisdom and practical understanding. They use language effectively, even beautifully—but underlying what they say is their appreciation of the fact that words and reality are not the same thing. They convey a lot with their silences.

Perceptual Bias: Because of my tendency to focus on the "grounded" and "the tried and true," I might miss the possibility of radical innovation. The unexpected can sneak up on me—or bypass my attention completely. I can resist change and fight new ideas, even if they could potentially be of benefit to me.

Defensive Strategy: When I am reflexively shutting down to a necessary but threatening perception, I can be stubborn. I can refuse to think outside the box or to question my own assumptions. I can withdraw into silence. I can say, "I don't want to talk about it" and withdraw from meaningful engagement.

MERCURY IN GEMINI

Cognitive Rocket Fuel: To stay mentally engaged and alive, I must expose my intelligence to an endless diet of wonder and amazement. Boredom is anathema to me. I trust my curiosity—and I try to keep it hungry, not by starving it, but by cultivating its bottomless appetite. Fresh wording of old truths can trigger breakthroughs for me.

Learning Strategy: I constantly seek new ideas and fresh perceptions. I read. I listen. I commit to lifelong learning. I question my own beliefs and assumptions, always entertaining perspectives which challenge them. My mantra is, whatever I see, the truth is more than that.

Natural Style of Communication: Listening and speaking is most effective and comfortable for me when two people in conversation can ramble and free-associate, and thus share a mutual process of discovery. I learn almost nothing from communication that happens without joy and spontaneity. I delight in opportunities to say, "I didn't know that I knew that . . ."

My Best Teachers: Those who can most effectively help me learn what I need to learn in this life are articulate. They beguile me with their eloquence as well as by piquing my curiosity with fresh ideas or at least new ways of phrasing older ones. They celebrate language. Typically, they speak rapidly. Underlying their most effective lessons is one foundational concept: *"There might be an entirely different way of looking at this . . ."*

Perceptual Bias: Because of my tendency to focus on words and ideas, I might miss cautionary messages arising in my own physical body—having "a bad feeling in my bones" about a person or suggestion, for example. Thinking and talking are only one way of engaging with reality; I must be careful not to ignore instinct, intuition, or the voice of angels whispering in my ear.

Defensive Strategy: When I am reflexively shutting down to a necessary but threatening perception, I can hide behind a wall of words. I can chatter, and thus prevent another person from speaking or from getting through to me. Even when no one is around, I can endlessly loop a false or limited version of reality in my head until I have totally convinced myself of its truth, even if it is a lie.

MERCURY IN CANCER

Cognitive Rocket Fuel: To stay mentally engaged and alive, I must expose my intelligence to the reality of human needs and human woundedness—both my own and that of other people. I am learning to look at the world through the eyes of the Great Mother, which is to say, with compassion and forgiveness. I see the frightened child in everyone. I think psychologically.

Learning Strategy: I seek insight into the way people are motivated by their often-unconscious emotional needs or by the "wounded child" within them. I look beneath the surface of human behavior in a spirit of gentleness and humility. In the face of the universal, unspoken realities of the human condition, I seek opportunities to be of genuine comfort to other people, knowing that the ones who need it the most are often the ones who deny it.

Natural Style of Communication: Listening and speaking is most effective and comfortable for me when people are gentle and patient with each other, when they take time to genuinely listen and to speak softly from their hearts in a spirit of trust. Psychological language comes naturally to me, as we speak unguardedly of our needs and fears.

My Best Teachers: Those who can most effectively help me learn what I need to learn in this life are people who have made progress healing from their own wounds. My best teachers are kind, gentle, and patient with me. They support me and have an uncanny sense of when I need to be pushed and when I need to go at my own pace. They feel like family to me.

Perceptual Bias: Because of my tendency to focus on what other people need, I can find myself coddling them, perhaps to a point where I become insensitive to two important realities: their innate resiliency and my own needs.

Defensive Strategy: When I am reflexively shutting down to a necessary but threatening perception, I can hide inside my shell indefinitely. It is as if I have closed my eyes tightly and put my fingers in my ears. I can also trick people into turning their scrutiny away from my own wounds or needs by my focusing helpfully on theirs. In doing this, I may look like a saint, but the reality is that I have isolated my own heart.

MERCURY IN LEO

Cognitive Rocket Fuel: To stay mentally engaged and alive, I must expose my intelligence to the risk of self-expression. I must be vulnerable. I must put my thoughts and ideas out on the stage of the world—hoping for applause, but taking the chance of criticism and rejection. Performance and creativity, in some sense, trigger my rapid evolution.

Learning Strategy: I seek avenues in which I can manifest my imagination and my ideas. I open my mouth and speak; I step out on the stage, perhaps appearing to be fearless, even if I am inwardly quaking. I find my audience and I face it in a spirit of vulnerability and sincerity, whether it is one other person or a crowd. I learn by doing.

Natural Style of Communication: Listening and speaking is most effective and comfortable for me when both people are given a lot of space and support to shine. They take turns being on stage. If I need three or four paragraphs to make a point, I appreciate someone listening attentively until I am finished. I am then happy to do the same for other people, and to enjoy their time in the spotlight. Making room for some style, some sense of "theater," enlivens and supports my unselfconscious spontaneity. I appreciate speaking with anyone who really takes joy in language itself.

My Best Teachers: Those who can most effectively help me learn what I need to learn in this life are masters of stagecraft—even if the stage is a quiet conversation between two people in a café. They know how to reach the heart; they do not hide in some dry intellectual ivory tower. Their personalities themselves are half of the message they bring.

Perceptual Bias: Because of my tendency to focus on presentation and style, I can undervalue the ideas offered by mild or introverted people. I can also be beguiled or even deceived by polished surfaces behind which there is little substantial content. I can become so enamored of my own viewpoint that I blind myself to the useful perspectives of people who disagree with me.

Defensive Strategy: When I am reflexively shutting down to a necessary but threatening perception, I can defend myself behind a brick wall of stubborn opinion. I can override and interrupt another person, perhaps without even knowing that I am doing it. I may even win arguments that it would benefit me enormously to lose.

MERCURY IN VIRGO

Cognitive Rocket Fuel: To stay mentally engaged and alive, I must expose my intelligence to methodology, technique, and craft. I must roll up my sleeves and actually learn how to do things, and to do them in a spirit of pursuing excellence. I seek to approach perfection in my work and in the execution of my responsibilities. I open like a flower in the presence of worthy teachers—masters of whatever field I am seeking to learn.

Learning Strategy: I seek teachers who embody the excellence and skill to which I aspire. I apprentice myself to them in a spirit of gratitude and humility. I burn the midnight oil; I study in a spirit of self-discipline and focused attention. I am not afraid to "read the manual," whatever form it might take.

Natural Style of Communication: Listening and speaking is most effective and comfortable for me when the presentation of ideas is orderly, logical, and detailed. I appreciate competence in anyone offering me information; I also appreciate anyone sufficiently interested in what I am saying to listen in detail. Grounded, rational criticism, coming and going, is a valued treasure in any conversation which I am likely to remember positively.

My Best Teachers: Those who can most effectively help me learn what I need to learn in this life are masters in their fields. The bottom line is that they actually "deliver" in the areas in which they claim competence. My best teachers have had teachers themselves; from time to time, they mention them respectfully and warmly.

Perceptual Bias: Because of my tendency to focus on details, I can lose perspective on the big picture. I can waste time perfecting something that will later be eliminated, rejected, or edited. My critical faculty can blind me to the reality that something, although flawed, is in fact already good enough. I can create in my mind a state of constant worry and doubt, never relaxing enough to accept things the way they actually are.

Defensive Strategy: When I am reflexively shutting down to a necessary but threatening perception, I can nitpick over trivial details and minor quibbles, rejecting a larger perspective that would in fact be useful to me. When self-doubt is making me afraid to go forward, I can defend myself against acknowledging that fact by taking refuge in endless preparation.

MERCURY IN LIBRA

Cognitive Rocket Fuel: To stay mentally engaged and alive, I must expose my intelligence to questions involving a complex balancing act: the tension between valid opposites. I revel in paradox—that humans need both love and freedom, for example. My growth is accelerated as I learn to listen to people who see things differently than I do. Nothing expands my cognitive bandwidth faster than exposure to beauty: poetics, the arts, music, and the beauty of nature itself.

Learning Strategy: I seek aesthetic experience; I immerse my senses in it regularly. I look for people who hold "the other half of the truth"—and recognize that I may have mistaken my own half-truth for the whole thing. Whenever I have a strong opinion, I discipline myself to consider the opposite perspective. I am relentlessly suspicious of any kind of fanaticism.

Natural Style of Communication: Listening and speaking is most effective and comfortable for me when people are sincerely respectful, even courteous, regarding their differences. I appreciate interpersonal grace and I attempt to practice it in all of my communications. I expect the same. Truly listening is a basic courtesy.

My Best Teachers: Those who can most effectively help me learn what I need to learn in this life radiate openness and respect towards me, even when they are offering me corrective suggestions. They are graceful people who present themselves well in terms of their behavior and their appearance. They can always see the opposite point of view. They are blessed with the ability to get along with a very wide spectrum of human types.

Perceptual Bias: Because of my tendency to focus on the creation of harmony and agreement, I can unconsciously find myself avoiding necessary—and potentially creative—conflict. My diplomacy can get in the way of the expression of necessary truths. I can feel I have stated them clearly, but the other person might have no idea of what I intended to convey.

Defensive Strategy: When I am reflexively shutting down to a necessary but threatening perception, I can be very slippery. I can dance away from a discussion, skillfully and smoothly changing the subject in such a way that the person holding the mirror before me has no idea until later about the stunt I just pulled. Maybe I use flattery; maybe I employed the bait of a fascinating diversion; maybe I simply "appeared" to agree. In any case, I can always turn attention away from myself and aim it back at the other person.

MERCURY IN SCORPIO

Cognitive Rocket Fuel: To stay mentally engaged and alive, I must expose my intelligence to the digestion of the raw and difficult truths of life. I think about realities that other people are often afraid to consider. I am exploring beyond the boundaries of customary social taboos, wrestling with subjects that are too emotionally charged for the majority of the human race to face.

Learning Strategy: I seek to unravel my own rationalizations and mechanisms of defense, both the ones I learned as a child and the ones which arise in me as an individual. I am resolved to "think anything," no matter how edgy or extreme the thought might be. From a moral perspective, I edit my behavior, but I never edit my own mind. I cannot imagine any kind of accurate thinking separate from psychoanalytical self-investigation.

Natural Style of Communication: Listening and speaking is most effective and comfortable for me when politeness and conventional customs do not inhibit the direct expression of each person's thoughts and feelings. I appreciate intensity; I am not unduly frightened by it. I am far from humorless—but my sense of humor might be a bit dark for some individuals. I am a good person to talk to when people are faced with difficult situations, but when I am faced with cocktail party chit chat, I need to monitor and restrain my own tendency towards honesty or I will just make trouble from myself and everyone else.

My Best Teachers: Those who can most effectively help me learn what I need to learn in this life look me directly in the eye and speak from their hearts, even when their hearts have a message which I am not eager to hear. They are psychologically-savvy people; many of them have a serious respect for life's darkness, having faced it directly themselves. Their words sink into my soul like a stone. I feel their truth viscerally.

Perceptual Bias: Because of my tendency to focus on charged and taboo psychological material, I may miss the lighter, happier perspectives which contribute so strongly to our ability to continue living in this crazy world. Following my own intellectual instincts, I can get deeper at a pace which is faster than I can handle, and thus sink myself into a brooding, isolated state.

Defensive Strategy: When I am reflexively shutting down to a necessary but threatening perception—which does not happen very often—I can wound people who are only trying to help me. I know where to stick the psychological dagger in anyone's psyche.

MERCURY IN SAGITTARIUS

Cognitive Rocket Fuel: To stay mentally engaged and alive, I must expose my intelligence to influences and perspectives which lie beyond my familiar horizons. In whatever level of society I was born, there are certain assumptions and behaviors which are held as obvious and right; I must break free of them. I am on an intellectual quest which will carry me into a wider world, one beyond the boundaries of the culture of my birth. The holy grail I seek is a sense of the meaning of life. It is out there in the world, waiting for me to find it.

Learning Strategy: I seek everything that is foreign or alien, everything that challenges my assumptions. I embrace the possibility of travel and encounters with people from different societies or ethnicities. I revel in education, whether it is formal or simply experiential. I try to figure out the mysterious underlying laws by which the universe operates, and arrange my moral compass in harmony with them. I seek to align my behavior with cosmic principles.

Natural Style of Communication: Listening and speaking is most effective and comfortable for me when people are obviously engaged in a passionate way with what they are saying. I do not want to listen to people who are bored with their own lectures, nor would I willingly subject anyone else to listening to me were I myself in that pitiful condition. I like speaking about principles and the underlying patterns of life; I am a "big picture" person and I am happiest in conversation with similar people, even if their version of the big picture is different from my own.

My Best Teachers: Those who can most effectively help me learn what I need to learn in this life often come from a different culture or at least a different walk of life than me. They are philosophical people, but they are not sitting alone in some tower, afraid of life. They have lived their passions and learned from their own mistakes. They have a sense of humor about themselves, but they keep their eye on the true prize, which is how to live a life that is ultimately meaningful.

Perceptual Bias: Because of my tendency to focus on the big picture, I might miss details that are important—especially details which might run counter to my own assumptions. This creates a vulnerability in me simply to jumping to conclusions. I am skillful at recognizing patterns; I can connect the dots. The danger is that I might connect two or three dots and come up with what I take for a complete cosmology.

Defensive Strategy: When I am reflexively shutting down to a necessary but threatening perception, I can rationalize any position I might take. I excel at convincing myself that I am correct, even that God is on my side. I can find a moral, even self-righteous, argument for anything I want to do, however crazy or hurtful it might be.

MERCURY IN CAPRICORN

Cognitive Rocket Fuel: To stay mentally engaged and alive, I must expose my intelligence to projects that are worthy of me and which excite my soul. I need challenges that can only be conquered with self-discipline, concentration, and persistence over time—but I have to truly want them in my heart. My mind must engage with great works—prodigious efforts of learning, and perhaps of teaching. As a metaphor, my "writing a book" serves as a fine illustration, although my great work might take many other forms.

Learning Strategy: I seek a mental mountain worth climbing. I survey my heart, asking myself where I feel like making a massive, perhaps lifelong, investment of time and energy. Only then can I commit to the process, radically and without distraction.

Natural Style of Communication: Listening and speaking is most effective and comfortable for me when people present their ideas with sequential logic and demonstrable evidence. Such communication requires patience and careful listening. I do not need to hold forth endlessly, but I do like to have the chance to complete the expression of an idea. In other words, I communicate best with people who tend not to interrupt each other. If something is worth saying, it is worth saying well and clearly.

My Best Teachers: Those who can most effectively help me learn what I need to learn in this life demonstrate their mastery concretely. Many will have already accomplished monumental works of persistence and self-discipline. Many will be elders, at least relative to me. Many fine teachers are young—but give them a few years, and they will become even better. Those are the teachers I seek.

Perceptual Bias: Because of my tendency to focus my total attention upon the project at hand, it is as if I am wearing blinders. I can miss important, unexpected, even disruptive, information emerging from the left or the right. I can also discipline myself to the point of exhaustion, allowing errors and inefficiencies to creep into my work.

Defensive Strategy: When I am reflexively shutting down to a necessary but threatening perception, I can be rigid, inappropriately authoritative, and judging. I can make the other person wrong. I can fool myself by taking refuge in impatience and a hurried resentment of "the distraction."

MERCURY IN AQUARIUS

Cognitive Rocket Fuel: To stay mentally engaged and alive, I must expose my intelligence to ideas and perceptions of a radical or at least unconventional nature. I am stimulated by thinking outside the box. Without getting an inflated head about it, I acknowledge and celebrate my own genius. My intelligence reaches orbital velocity when I recognize the blinding assumptions by which more conventional people paint themselves into corners, and I challenge them.

Learning Strategy: I seek that which has more to do with the human future then it has to do with human history. I am drawn to those who break the rules, or who at least are breaking new ground in their fields. I am willing to consider what others might view as "crazy ideas." I am wisely nervous when anyone begins a sentence with the words, "Everybody knows . . ."

Natural Style of Communication: Listening and speaking is most effective and comfortable for me when everyone is willing to float speculative ideas and to treat them with an open mind, no matter how unusual they might sound. Instinctively, I seek out people's underlying assumptions; I like to bring them out into the light and question them. Those with whom I communicate most easily enjoy this process; they are not offended or threatened by it. They grasp the fact that all human understanding is an eternal work-in-progress.

My Best Teachers: Those who can most effectively help me learn what I need to learn in this life are rebels, revolutionaries, geniuses, and troublemakers. Their favorite sound is the sound of rules breaking. They have probably been in trouble with figures of authority in whatever field of thought they are pursuing.

Perceptual Bias: Because of my tendency to focus on questioning and doubting, I am at risk of undervaluing the gifts our ancestors have provided for us. That which is new is not always better; in overthrowing the past, we may throw the baby out with the bath water. I am in danger of re-inventing the wheel, perhaps in hexagonal form.

Defensive Strategy: When I am reflexively shutting down to a necessary but threatening perception, I can detach emotionally and simply play an intellectual or verbal chess game. I can take on a superior, know-it-all posture. Regardless of my age, I can defend myself against wisdom by acting like a teenager with a bad attitude.

MERCURY IN PISCES

Cognitive Rocket Fuel: To stay mentally engaged and alive, I must expose my intelligence to non-ordinary perceptual states. Staring into space, waiting for the light bulb to light over my head leads me to many an insight I might not otherwise reach. I seek to enter into cognitive rapport with that which has been variously called the soul, God, or the unconscious mind. I am cultivating intuition, even the development of my psychic faculties. Trance states—of which meditation is perhaps the most obvious illustration—are powerful triggers for my evolution.

Learning Strategy: I seek direct experience of the larger framework of consciousness. I aim to empty my mind in order that something transcendent might enter it. I immerse myself appreciatively in the instructions kindly left for us by spiritual and visionary masters who have gone before us. Among them, there are some who speak to my heart. I trust my intuition to discern who is who. I celebrate my creative imagination.

Natural Style of Communication: Listening and speaking is most effective and comfortable for me when images, metaphors, and intuitive expressions are plentiful and welcome. Rigid, focused mental discipline only stifles me; I lose my spontaneity and my capacity for receiving inspiration. The poem is often wiser than the poet.

My Best Teachers: Those who can most effectively help me learn what I need to learn in this life are people of genuine spiritual accomplishment. They are not pretentious about it; generally, they are humble—thus demonstrating the actual reality of not being so identified with their egos. Not all of them can easily be packaged in "religious" terms—many are creative people: artists, musicians, storytellers.

Perceptual Bias: Because of my tendency to focus on receiving messages from my deeper self, I can lose my grip on this three-dimensional human reality. In extreme form, that could make me look crazy. In less dramatic fashion, that loss of groundedness in the common version of reality would simply make it hard for other people to follow what I was saying. The overlay of the psychic realms upon the world of conventional human perception can create a perceptual bias which has the effect of isolating me from other people.

Defensive Strategy: When I am reflexively shutting down to a necessary but threatening perception, I can "abuse transcendence." By that, I mean hiding from human feelings and the gritty work of personal growth by taking refuge in false or premature forgiveness, metaphysical interpretations, or "rising above" everything—just spacing out, in other words.

11

SATURN IN THE TWELVE SIGNS

SATURN IN ARIES

The Worthy Work: I resolve that reflected in the mirror of my outward biographical life, I will eventually see a concrete manifestation of my own courage. I accept that the pioneering evolutionary work I am here on earth to accomplish will attract resistance and challenges, perhaps even enemies. I will not let any of that stop me. I ride out and meet them, undaunted. I am becoming a true spiritual warrior, brave, steadfast, and committed.

Effective Strategy: In relentlessly disciplined fashion, I establish in myself the habit of never, ever giving up. Still, I recognize that in order to win the war, one must strategically accept that some battles must be lost. I compete fairly and I maintain my integrity, but I constantly keep my eye on the prize, while unashamedly valuing honest victory.

Unbreakable Moral Commitment: In this one way above all others, I will never fail myself: fear will never make any of my final decisions.

Natural Resources: In support of my Great Work, I came into this world with tenacity, doggedness, as well as a strong sense of timing. I can think strategically. I can pull victory out of the jaws of defeat. I have a sense of the heroic potential of the human spirit. I will live up to it.

The Blockage: I humbly acknowledge and resolve to get past my blockage in the area of the distortions of awareness and perspective that arise from my passions—anger, resentment, fear, and desire. I will not let them rule my life.

The Shape of the Shadow: Were I to betray my path, I recognize that my life would be fraught with an underlying sense of failure. Bitterness and an unfocused attitude of resentment and acrimony would leave scars on my soul.

SATURN IN TAURUS

The Worthy Work: I resolve that reflected in the mirror of the physical world, I will eventually see a concrete manifestation of my own commitment to building a solid foundation for peace in my own life. My aim, above all, is to provide myself with an effective basis for serenity of spirit—a safe harbor amid the chaos of human existence, a situation in which I can attune myself to the things that are truly important in life, free from petty distractions and temptations.

Effective Strategy: In relentlessly disciplined fashion, I establish in myself the habit of prioritizing my peace of mind above everything else. To that end, I will create physical and financial security for myself—but I will keep perspective, realizing that maintaining stable, loving human connections are part of my strategy too, as is taking care of my health and my soul. I cultivate a closeness to nature, knowing that it stabilizes me.

Unbreakable Moral Commitment: In this one way above all others, I will never fail myself: I resolve to discern sources of chaos and tension from afar and to avoid them, no matter how clever and tempting their disguise.

Natural Resources: In support of my Great Work, I came into this world with common sense and reason. I have an appreciation for simplicity. I can see through pretenses. I can recognize a scoundrel. I am not easily distracted. I can tolerate silence.

The Blockage: I humbly acknowledge and resolve to get past my blockage in the area of being flexible—that means an acceptance of the fact that life involves endless change. I can adjust; I can let go of people and situations which have outlived their usefulness.

The Shape of the Shadow: Were I to betray my path, I recognize that my life would reflect a stodgy, fear-driven commitment to what amounts to endless boredom. While I need material stability in order to fulfill my evolutionary work, I recognize that I can give too much power to money and security.

SATURN IN GEMINI

The Worthy Work: I resolve that reflected in the mirror of my outward biographical life, I will eventually see a concrete manifestation of my own true voice. I will find it and I will reveal it. I will be *heard* in this lifetime. My ideas will be taken seriously. I recognize that in order to attain that goal I must create a voice that is worthy of being heard.

Effective Strategy: In relentlessly disciplined fashion, I establish in myself the habit of endlessly educating myself deeply in anything that attracts my interest. I ask the hard questions and I embrace the complex answers which follow. I will speak up whenever an opportunity to be heard presents itself. I will improve my diction, delivery, and vocabulary. I will become a master of concentration. I will learn to speak with a voice of authority.

Unbreakable Moral Commitment: In this one way above all others, I will never fail myself: when I have something worth saying, no person and no circumstance will ever silence me through intimidation.

Natural Resources: In support of my Great Work, I came into this world with a serious mind capable of sustained, monumental feats of self-education and verbal self-expression.

The Blockage: I humbly acknowledge and resolve to get past my blockage in the area of having full confidence in my own voice.

The Shape of the Shadow: Were I to betray my path, I recognize that my life would reflect a sad pattern of having allowed myself to be chronically distracted from my own true goals. I would recognize that I had thereby silenced myself, and that what I came into this world to say had been left unsaid.

SATURN IN CANCER

The Worthy Work: I resolve that reflected in the mirror of my outward biographical life, I will eventually see a concrete manifestation of my commitment to living a life of kindness. I will become a shining example of that quality to my community. I will know in my heart that I have touched the lives of other people in a healing way. I will also have established a "family" in some sense of the word—a family of which I am proud and one which cherishes and appreciates me.

Effective Strategy: In relentlessly disciplined fashion, I establish in myself the habit of paying attention to my own needs. I will be kind to myself, oriented to healing myself. I understand that this self-care is the necessary foundation for my ability to effectively care for anyone else.

Unbreakable Moral Commitment: In this one way above all others, I will never fail myself: I will find the elusive balance point between caring for myself and caring for other people. Neither one will ever eclipse the other.

Natural Resources: In support of my Great Work, I came into this world with a practical sense of how the wounds of the soul reveal themselves behaviorally and how they might be healed. I am wise and patient in the face of these slow processes. I have a gift when it comes to guiding others in the process of their own self-healing.

The Blockage: I humbly acknowledge and resolve to get past my blockage in the area of trusting the fact that life does not want to hurt me. I appreciate feeling safe, but I will not allow that need to stand between me and honest, two-way street communion with the people with whom I am sharing my life.

The Shape of the Shadow: Were I to betray my path, I recognize that my life would reflect an obsessive and excessive level of self-protection. I would be lonely, even if I were surrounded by people who depended upon me. That loneliness would arise because no one had ever been allowed to see my soul.

SATURN IN LEO

The Worthy Work: I resolve that reflected in the mirror of my outward biographical life, I will eventually see a concrete manifestation of my own genuine, authentic, and original creativity. I will leave in the hands of the world some evidence of my inner life: what I valued, what I held sacred, what I found beautiful. I resolve to be brave enough to stand naked and vulnerable, with my soul exposed to other human beings.

Effective Strategy: In relentlessly disciplined fashion, I establish in myself the habit of developing my self-expressive skills. I will find a concrete outlet—perhaps an art form—for the contents of my psyche, and I will polish it until it provides a transparent window between my soul and the community around me.

Unbreakable Moral Commitment: In this one way above all others, I will never fail myself: I will leave something of myself in the hands of the world. I will gift the world with a treasure that was forged in the cauldron of my experiences.

Natural Resources: In support of my Great Work, I came into this world with the seed of a genuine self-expressive talent. As I identify it and nourish it over time, the seed blossoms.

The Blockage: I humbly acknowledge and resolve to get past my blockage in the area of performance, "stage-fright," and emotionally risky self-revelation. I must face the perils of stepping out on the stage of life.

The Shape of the Shadow: Were I to betray my path, I recognize that my life would reflect the feeling of being a flower that never opened. I would suffer from a sense of having held back something that I was supposed to give—something which other people actually needed.

SATURN IN VIRGO

The Worthy Work: I resolve that reflected in the mirror of my outward biographical life, I will eventually see a concrete manifestation of my own practical ability to make a real difference in the lives of other people. I will become truly "good at something." I will be seen as a valued master of a craft which is of genuine service to my community. I will have done work that I know truly mattered.

Effective Strategy: In relentlessly disciplined fashion, I establish in myself the habits of focus, purposefulness, and hard work. I commit to endless improvement, both in myself and in my craft. I accept that this commitment implies a constant diet of constructive self-criticism. Each day, I will become a little bit better at what I do. I will seek the presence and support of masters who have gone before me; I will learn from them in a spirit of humility.

Unbreakable Moral Commitment: In this one way above all others, I will never fail myself: I will always, without fail, strive to do my best work. Nothing less will ever be acceptable to me.

Natural Resources: In support of my Great Work, I came into this world with a capacity for concentration, an appetite for sustained effort, and a humble ability to assess myself honestly. Through sheer relentlessness, I can come out ahead of people who may have been born with more natural skill than I have.

The Blockage: I humbly acknowledge and resolve to get past my blockage in the area of self-confidence. I can cripple myself with self-criticism, perhaps slipping into a pattern of defending myself against success through the device of endless preparation. Self-doubt can leave me in a limbo of scut-work.

The Shape of the Shadow: Were I to betray my path, I recognize that my life would reflect a kind of volunteered slavery. I could exhaust myself "putting things in alphabetical order" for people I deemed (incorrectly) to be superior to myself. I could descend into a lather of fuss and worry.

SATURN IN LIBRA

The Worthy Work: I resolve that reflected in the mirror of my outward biographical life, I will eventually see the concrete flowering of three visions: my own aesthetics and taste, something approaching an ideal human partnership, and a style of life characterized by grace, taste, and serenity.

Effective Strategy: In relentlessly disciplined fashion, I establish in myself the habit of seeking balance in all things. I follow the middle path. I resolve to accept that paradox is fundamental to life, and I will not be troubled by a need to "take sides." In the words of the Navajo elders, I resolve to "walk in beauty." I seek friends and partners who don't make me crazy—mature people, capable of commitment and of reason.

Unbreakable Moral Commitment: In this one way above all others, I will never fail myself: I will live in the presence of paradox, knowing that every story has two sides. I will never fall into the illusions created by dogmatism or extremism in any form.

Natural Resources: In support of my Great Work, I came into this world with a strong sense of balance and fairness. I have an ability to endlessly deepen my appreciation of beauty. I naturally tolerate human differences. All of these qualities are supportive of my real goal: the development of inner peace.

The Blockage: I humbly acknowledge and resolve to get past my blockage in the area of facing conflict squarely and honestly. When intimacy is challenging that way, I will not take refuge in hiding my feelings. I will not let secret solitude lurk behind an appearance of acquiescence.

The Shape of the Shadow: Were I to betray my path, I recognize that my life would reflect the triumph of formality and diplomacy over genuine soul-transparency. I would simply be lonely.

SATURN IN SCORPIO

The Worthy Work: I resolve that reflected in the mirror of my outward biographical life, I will eventually see the concrete results of my own commitment to hard inner psychological and spiritual growth. I pursue truth, fearlessly. Specifically, I will be recognized—at least by some people—as a wise elder to whom they can turn confidently when nothing less than the truth will serve their evolutionary purposes.

Effective Strategy: In relentlessly disciplined fashion, I establish in myself the habit of squarely facing every emotional glitch in my life, no matter how threatening it might feel. Patiently, I sort through my emotions and my experiences, seeking what lies hidden behind them. I seek the counsel of a few other brave souls with similar dispositions, and cherish them.

Unbreakable Moral Commitment: In this one way above all others, I will never fail myself: I will never, ever, take refuge in comforting lies. Denial, rationalization, and defensiveness are anathema to me. I resolve to do my best always to recognize them in myself as quickly as possible and to dispel them.

Natural Resources: In support of my Great Work, I came into this world with an innate instinct for psychological work. I can hold steady in the face of strong emotions and situations which other people might find to be overwhelming. I can face anything and still have strength left for those who need me.

The Blockage: I humbly acknowledge and resolve to get past my blockage in the area of simply lightening up. Life is serious—but it is funny too. I will not forget to laugh and thus to maintain a degree of humorous perspective on my own psychological intensity.

The Shape of the Shadow: Were I to betray my path, I recognize that my life would reflect an exaggeratedly gloomy and suspicious view of human existence. I would become isolated, dark, and withdrawn, unable to tap into the deep well of energy that comes from shared human playfulness.

SATURN IN SAGITTARIUS

The Worthy Work: I resolve that reflected in the mirror of my outward biography, I will eventually see a concrete manifestation of everything in which I believe. I will align my life with my understanding of the meaning of life. I will, in other words, walk my talk. Fundamental to my "talk" is the idea that life must be embraced and lived as a spiritual adventure. I will always put morals and principles ahead of practical concerns—and one of my most fundamental principles is that no one gets out of here alive, so let's all seize the day and live each day as if it were a precious evolutionary opportunity.

Effective Strategy: In relentlessly disciplined fashion, I establish in myself the habit of stretching my horizons, both intellectually and experientially. I commit to a life of endless learning. I will travel, as opportunities present themselves. I will seek the meaning of life by pursuing teachers and teachings, and by studying philosophy and metaphysics. I will wrestle with the fundamental questions of human existence. I will not be distracted by petty concerns.

Unbreakable Moral Commitment: In this one way above all others, I will never fail myself: I will live in absolute accord with my principles no matter what material costs and practical indignities might arise as a result.

Natural Resources: In support of my Great Work, I came into this world with a firm faith in the fundamental meaningfulness of life. Come thick or thin, I trust in the potential purposefulness of all experience. I am resilient; I can bounce back from losses and hurtful episodes. I am philosophical—but I am always willing to subject my beliefs to practical tests.

The Blockage: I humbly acknowledge and resolve to get past my blockage in the area of exaggerated caution. I recognize that life, despite any fears to the contrary, can sometimes go smoothly. Murphy's Law—the idea that anything that can possibly go wrong will go wrong—is a tempting distortion of the truth of life for me. I will not succumb to it. I will not "count on luck" to bail me out—but I will also expect the occasional miracle.

The Shape of the Shadow: Were I to betray my path, I recognize that my life would reflect the reality of my fears smothering my growth and evolution. Caution could triumph over adventure. Vaguely, I would sense that there had been the potential of a vibrant life out there for me—one that I somehow missed living because I was afraid to take any risks.

SATURN IN CAPRICORN

The Worthy Work: I resolve that reflected in the mirror of my outward biographical life, I will eventually see a concrete manifestation of my own commitment to excellence, my capacity for inexorable focus and patience, and my highest ambitions. I will manifest a serious, impressive accomplishment, one that reveals something of my great soul to the world. In some area of life, I will aim for nothing less than perfection. I know I will never fully attain it, but my dignity and my self-respect will thrive on the persistent effort.

Effective Strategy: In relentlessly disciplined fashion, I establish in myself the habit of not allowing myself to be daunted by any difficulty. I keep going, no matter what. I intentionally undertake tasks that intimidate me. In pursuit of great works, I accept that imbalances and sacrifices will be required of me. I acknowledge that I am not here to live a balanced life. That is the price of excellence in any one area.

Unbreakable Moral Commitment: In this one way above all others, I will never fail myself: my higher intentions will always have dominion over my weaknesses, my appetites, and any temptations that might arise.

Natural Resources: In support of my Great Work, I came into this world with an elevated capacity for focus and for keeping my eye on the prize. Sustained determination arises naturally in me. I can keep pounding away when others have given up.

The Blockage: I humbly acknowledge and resolve to get past my blockage in the area of mindful self-monitoring. I will learn to be kinder to myself. Specifically, I resolve to be attentive to bodily signals of tiredness, discomfort, or hunger. I will listen to the non-rational parts of myself, such as instinct and intuition. I give them a voice in my decisions.

The Shape of the Shadow: Were I to betray my path, I recognize that my life would reflect a kind of wasted self-discipline. I would work hard at things that meant nothing to me. I would expend an enormous amount of energy getting to the top of the wrong mountain. I would realize that I had let other people eclipse my own soul's dream, replacing that dream with their own.

SATURN IN AQUARIUS

The Worthy Work: I resolve that reflected in the mirror of my outward biographical life, I will eventually see a concrete manifestation of my own genius—which is to say that I would create something that revealed my unique understanding of life, my unconventional purpose in the world, and the values which animate it. I will put my genius into my life, becoming the practical architect of my liberation from the tyranny of the normal. I will create something that has never before been seen by anyone.

Effective Strategy: In relentlessly disciplined fashion, I establish in myself the habit of always questioning authority. I will never believe anything simply because I have been told that it was true; instead, I commit to discerning people's underlying assumptions and to testing them against the backdrop of more creative, iconoclastic possibilities. I resolve to build a practical foundation which allows me to live life with more freedom and fewer conventional strictures.

Unbreakable Moral Commitment: In this one way above all others, I will never fail myself: I will never allow my behavior to be shaped by the need for anyone else's approval.

Natural Resources: In support of my Great Work, I came into this world with a willingness to ask questions. I was born with at least one strand of "genius" DNA—which is to say, an instinctive rebellion against reflexively believing what "everybody knows." I can quietly and practically build a workable escape hatch from the oppressions of conventionality.

The Blockage: I humbly acknowledge and resolve to get past my tendency to isolate myself emotionally. I do not give up on entertaining the possibility that I *can* be understood, even loved and appreciated, by at least a few people. I am not afraid to feel or to connect with others.

The Shape of the Shadow: Were I to betray my path, I recognize that my life would reflect a kind of chilly emotional dissociation, as if I had given up on tenderness. I will not allow my objectivity and independence from the crowd to degenerate into simple coldness.

SATURN IN PISCES

The Worthy Work: I resolve that reflected in the mirror of my outward biographical life, I will eventually see concrete manifestations of my own commitment to real spiritual and psychic progress. I will achieve verifiable results in those areas of development. For that reason, many of my most fundamental successes in this lifetime will be invisible to the world at large; my greatest work is inner work. The treasures I create in this lifetime will remain with me for eternity.

Effective Strategy: In relentlessly disciplined fashion, I establish in myself the habit of regularity in meditation and spiritual self-care, along with a commitment to acts of kindness, humility, and charity in the world. Using these ancient methods, each day I chip away at ego-clinging and delusion.

Unbreakable Moral Commitment: In this one way above all others, I will never fail myself: I will always remember that this life is a short dream from which I will soon awaken.

Natural Resources: In support of my Great Work, I came into this world with a precious seed in my consciousness: the capacity eventually to become a *spiritual elder* in my community. I have an instinct for spiritual practice; I hold it precious; I will explore it. I will fulfill my full evolutionary potential in this lifetime.

The Blockage: I humbly acknowledge and resolve to get past my blockage in the area of trusting my own psychic and intuitive impressions. I welcome them into my consciousness and I am willing to act on them. I will not lose heart even though I have come to a steep place on the spiritual mountain.

The Shape of the Shadow: Were I to betray my path, I recognize that my life would reflect the fact that I had come adrift spiritually, having missed an opportunity to make a major step forward —all because I gave too much power to doubt, the illusions and temptations of this world, or perhaps even to simple spiritual laziness.

12

VENUS IN THE
TWELVE HOUSES

In the following thumbnail descriptions of the meaning of Venus in each of the astrological houses, I often use the term "soul-partners." Obviously enough, the words convey notions of romance, sexuality, and variations on the theme of marriage. Yes indeed—all of that is a big part of what we are talking about here, maybe even the most central part.

But let's not forget how priceless our deepest friendships can be, or the sweetness of family relationships when they travel down good roads. Those people are "soul-partners" too, and as precious in their own ways as those brave, lucky souls with whom we might share a bed.

VENUS IN THE FIRST HOUSE

For love to thrive, I must behave . . . forthrightly. I am developing the ability to be direct, assertive, and independent. I am learning that I naturally possess "half the rights" in any relationship. Love involves compromise; I know that. But it does not mean kowtowing to anyone. In intimacy, I have a right to say yes—and I have a right to say no. I accept that attending to my personal style and my physical appearance are actually spiritual issues for me. I must carefully scrutinize any unnatural exaggerations—or self-diminishments—in those areas.

Where will I meet my soul-partners? I find them when I am not actually looking for them, but instead when I am simply intent upon following my own whimsies and interests. Bold, unilateral actions of any sort on my part—especially ones consistent with the higher intentions of the astrological sign of my Venus—often lead me to unexpected, evolution-triggering human encounters.

How might I recognize them? They are people who seem to know what they are doing, going about life with the appearance of self-confidence and active, positive engagement. They have created meaningful lives for themselves, effectively defending their autonomy. Their behavior reflects a particularly vivid expression of the nature of my Venus sign.

What actions must I avoid or at least not over-do? I need to be careful of assuming too much control over another person's life, even if my motives are benign. Selfishness—real or perceived—is a danger. Learning to listen carefully, along with forging choices jointly, is more helpful than my simply grabbing the steering wheel.

VENUS IN THE SECOND HOUSE

For love to thrive, I must behave . . . with self-confidence and a sense of my own self-worth. Without descending into arrogance, I need to remind myself that people are fortunate to have me in their lives. I need to invest in my own attractiveness. A new hairdo or wardrobe? Could be —such outward advances in confidence can reflect inward ones. But I must take the word "attractiveness" more widely than that. I am developing the ability to not underestimate my value as a partner—and thus risk settling for someone who is not on my own evolutionary level.

Where will I meet my soul-partners? If I pay close attention, I will see that there is an underlying pattern here: I tend to meet people who are important to me when I am doing something that feels like a personal stretch—betting on myself, taking a chance, in other words, acting as if I truly believe in myself. Bold, even personally scary, actions of any sort on my part, especially ones consistent with the sign of my Venus, often lead to soul-triggering human encounters. In more mundane terms, there is an underscored pattern of meeting people while I am doing anything related to money—that is almost a "fortune-telling" statement, but it often works.

How might I recognize them? Quite possibly, you will meet these people when they are facing some difficulty or challenge, when their self-confidence is under pressure. Their own behavior might reflect a particularly uncertain or tentative expression of the nature of my Venus sign—or perhaps a particularly impressive or accomplished one.

What actions must I avoid or at least not over-do? Generosity is a wonderful, natural expression of affection, but I need to be wary of hiding behind it. Famously, no one can buy love—and that notion goes way beyond money. One can try to "buy love" with supportive actions, compliments, and so on. At some point, I must stand naked and let myself be loved for my soul alone—or be rejected, and thus be free to look elsewhere for the real thing.

VENUS IN THE THIRD HOUSE

For love to thrive, I must behave . . . in a verbally revealing, self-expressive way. If I don't speak up and express myself authentically from my heart, no one will know who I am. How could they? I need to trust my curiosity and follow it down any paths of interest which reveal themselves to me, especially if those particular interests involve art, aesthetics, or the exploration of intimacy. This next point might not sound very sexy, but it works: I am developing the ability to be an active, engaged partner in a process of endless learning. Ask any truly sophisticated person: can we imagine any hope for long-term passion in the absence of meaningful, engaging conversation? Communication is one of love's highest arts. I will master it.

Where will I meet my soul-partners? Concretely, I might meet them while, for example, I am attending classes or lectures. Or in a bookstore. To say it more broadly, I am more likely to encounter these people when I am pursuing mental interests that arise naturally in me. Being out there in the great schoolhouse of the world, trusting my whimsies and my curiosity to guide me—those behaviors come naturally to me. But they also have the side effect of placing me in the orbits of the people with whom I have spiritual business. Educational aspirations on my part, especially ones consistent with the sign of my Venus, often lead to life-triggering human encounters.

How might I recognize them? My natural soul-partners show every indication of simply being interested in life. They read. They learn for the sake of learning. Fresh ideas excite them. They are actively engaged with the world. When I first encounter such people, there is an excellent chance that they simply look busy. Conversation is likely to arise quickly and spontaneously between us. "We were strangers, but we just started talking . . ."

What actions must I avoid or at least not over-do? In conversation, silences allow another person space to reflect and then speak—I must never forget that. It is important that I reveal myself verbally—but it is equally important that I support the other person in a parallel process of self-revelation. I need to remember that some of the deepest forms of communication between souls do not involve words or language at all.

VENUS IN THE FOURTH HOUSE

For love to thrive, I must behave . . . in a way that reflects the kind of person I actually am, which is to say that I am deep and rather psychological by nature. I take intimacy seriously and I understand that when it is real—and real is the only way I want it—both people must take the step-by-step risk of gradually becoming more vulnerable over time. Trust takes time. For that reason, it is only right that we are patient and gentle with each other. We let things unfold at their own pace, without any unnatural rush. I am developing the ability to be a lifelong partner, not a person whose life is a series of brief, passionate encounters, punctuated with heartbreak.

Where will I meet my soul-partners? In quiet places, places where people can relax, communicate deeply, and open up their sensitivities. I might meet these people through family—or through the kinds of friends who feel like family to me. Actions involving home or land, especially ones consistent with the sign of my Venus, often lead to life-triggering human encounters. Illustration: with Venus in Sagittarius, I might meet someone while visiting my ancestral homeland. With Venus in Taurus, such encounters might occur in the countryside, on a farm, or near animals.

How might I recognize them? My soul-partners stand out as pensive, reflective people. They do not put themselves forward loudly, theatrically, or aggressively. They do not seem to be in a hurry to connect with me or anyone else. Sexually they are not in a rush. That does not mean that they seem cold or remote—only patient and perhaps a bit cautious. Their outward behavior reflects a particularly interior or psychological expression of the nature of my Venus sign—for example, if my Venus is in Gemini, these soul-friends might bond with me by talking about the books or films that had the deepest emotional impact on them.

What actions must I avoid or at least not over-do? I do need to make myself emotionally available to people. There is an uncomfortable law of the universe which I must learn to accept: *we all date a lot more people than we marry.* There is eternally a risky dance that people must do when they feel attracted to each other. It is a dance of discovery. Some have called it dating, some have called it courtship. I need to embrace those dance steps. Without putting myself out there and taking that risk, no one will even know that I am here or what treasures I have to offer.

VENUS IN THE FIFTH HOUSE

For love to thrive, I must behave . . . in revealing, colorful ways. I am not afraid to command attention or to take up some space. I act accordingly, even dress accordingly, when I feel like it—not that I "always" feel like it. (I can be quiet too.) Bottom line, I am developing the ability to be spontaneous in my self-expression, comfortable in my body, and confident of my sexuality.

Where will I meet my soul-partners? When I am pursuing my own creativity, doing whatever it takes to feed it, I am likely to meet kindred spirits. Maybe I meet them in a theater group. Perhaps I encounter them in a club where I have gone to listen to some music. Perhaps I encounter them at art galleries or theaters. Performance-oriented actions of any sort on my part, often lead to life-triggering human encounters —and my "performance" might be as simple as my boldly donning a rakish scarf or sexy jeans. The point is that all the world is a stage, and as I bravely step out on it, I meet the souls I need to meet.

How might I recognize them? That will be easy—they are not hiding. Likely when I first lay eyes on them, they themselves are "performing" somehow—holding forth colorfully, maybe telling a joke or embellishing a tale to everyone's delight. Just possibly, they would actually be on stage in some more literal way. I might even find these soul-friends a bit intimidating or over-the-top at first, but I cannot let that perception daunt me. Their behavior reflects a particularly theatrical expression of the nature of my Venus sign—if it is Scorpio, they are sexy. If it is Gemini, they are witty and good with words. Likely, they seem more extroverted at first than I later find them to be. Performers often look like extroverts, but they aren't quite the same thing.

What actions must I avoid or at least not over-do? Everyone has characteristics which are simply boring, prototypical, predictable—and about as sexy as a dishrag. Sooner or later, in every intimate relationship, those dull dimensions of our humanity must be revealed. When people discover that kind of thing about me, I need to be careful not to let that revelation make me feel insecure or unlovable. All the world might be a stage—but sometimes we all need to take off our brilliant costumes.

VENUS IN THE SIXTH HOUSE

For love to thrive, I must behave . . . in competent, skillful, grown-up ways. There is a craft to making love work. Humans have been trying to relate to each other for millennia. Over those years, our ancestors have learned a trick or two. Much of this boils down to all the familiar "chicken soup" wisdom about marriage, gender, and sexuality. I need those skills. Therefore, I benefit from paying attention to older people in my life—my "aunts and uncles," so to speak. There is much that I can learn from them, both from their wisdom and probably from their mistakes too. I am developing the ability to be humble enough to learn how to love. That process begins as I admit my befuddlement and confusion. This is how I develop the skills and the competence to make my relationships work.

Where will I meet my soul-partners? Circumstantially, I might very well make these soul connections at work or in any other situation in which I have duties and responsibilities. Another strong possibility is that I encounter these people "by chance" when I am actively seeking the guidance of mentors—teachers, role models, even spiritual masters. As I seek such teaching and guidance, I also experience life-triggering human encounters.

How might I recognize soul-partners? The radiate a grounded quality of competence. They impress me with their simple effectiveness whatever they are doing. They are humble and unpretentious, without being obsequious or self-effacing. Regardless of their age, I sense of quality of maturity in them. Their behavior reflects helpfulness, supportiveness, and skill.

What actions must I avoid or at least not over-do? While I am always eager to be helpful and supportive of anyone I love, and while that is a virtue, I must be wary of playing a tedious role of endless responsibility and self-sacrifice in my relationships. I will set myself up for being taken for granted. I need to be emotionally available, not just a practical support. Sometimes I might even need to be demanding—if I need grease, I need to be the squeaky wheel.

VENUS IN THE SEVENTH HOUSE

For love to thrive, I must behave . . . in wide-open, fully invested, undefended ways. I must take the risk of true commitment, putting all my eggs in one basket. For this step to be safe—for it not to be an act of absolute madness, in other words—I need to develop a deeply discriminating instinct for the true, three-dimensional reality of other human beings. I must learn to think like a psychologist, or like a novelist who is terrific with characters. I must withdraw my romantic projections and resolve to see the other person clearly before I commit to the perilous path of ultimate trust. I am developing the ability to find the balance between true romance and clear-eyed perception of another person's actual evolutionary condition.

Where will I meet my soul-partners? The bottom line is that these people will find me rather than the other way around. Learning *who to trust* and *how to trust* is a major piece of my evolutionary work in this lifetime; therefore, the laws of synchronicity guarantee that these encounters will happen. I will surely meet true soul partners—and I will equally surely meet people who offer a subtle education in discrimination: the wise art of thinking twice before I trust another person. I may very well meet people in both of these categories through mutual friends. In general, spontaneous actions of human outreach on my part, especially ones consistent with the sign of my Venus, often lead to life-triggering human encounters.

How might I recognize them? My natural soul-partners are people of natural grace. They may tell a dirty joke or sometimes use the famous f-word, but they are never needlessly crude. Many are artists—or at least avid enthusiasts relative to the arts. They have outstanding "people skills," knowing how to get along diplomatically, perhaps even warmly, with human beings who are different from themselves. They probably dress becomingly, knowing, for one simple example, which colors work with their eyes or the tone of their skin. Their behavior reflects their own version of a particularly charming and engaging expression of the nature of my Venus sign —if my Venus is in Cancer, they anticipate my needs in advance. If it is in Capricorn, they know when I need to be left alone.

What actions must I avoid or at least not over-do? Compromise and meeting-in-the-middle are of course absolutely critical skills in maintaining any kind of grown-up partnership. I need to be careful that I do not locate that "middle" too far in the direction of the other person. Behaviorally, I can create the appearance of getting along with people who in fact are not good for me.

VENUS IN THE EIGHTH HOUSE

For love to thrive, I must behave . . . in psychologically courageous ways. I am developing the ability to be a lot more honest—and thus a lot more truly intimate—than most people can ever imagine. Obviously, I cannot do that alone. One behavior I must master is how to assess, as quickly and as painlessly as possible, whether another person is actually brave enough and sane enough to meet me in that same place of soul nakedness. I accept that this kind of love will naturally be difficult sometimes; it is Shadow work, after all. I resolve never to allow myself to punish another person for being truthful, even if I do not like what I am hearing.

Where will I meet my soul-partners? We might first encounter each other "by chance" in circumstances of genuine drama or emotional intensity—the sorts of raw situations where people's "true colors" show: squabbles, accidents, crisis, even deaths. Even if the scene is not so dramatic, we quickly find ourselves talking deeply about something real: sexuality, aging, disease—any of life's emotionally-charged areas. I improve the odds of encountering these soul-partners whenever I willingly undertake any kind of "self-help." In other words, as I face what is blocking me from full self-actualization, I magnetize these kinds of people into my life.

How might I recognize them? There is a certain reflectiveness and intensity around these soul-partners—qualities which I might interpret as moodiness or perhaps even a tendency toward isolation. At the same time, regardless of their physical appearance, there is an ineffable quality of simple sexiness about them. Their behavior and motivations reflect a particularly psychologically-savvy expression of the nature of my Venus sign—were my Venus in Taurus, they might reveal a real psychic bond with their cat or their dog. Were it in Libra, they might have a taste for serious film.

What actions must I avoid or at least not over-do? Genuine intimacy and deep psychological conversation are inseparable concepts for me. That is fine and natural, but I must be careful not to transgress the limits of human tolerance for inner work. Sometimes I need to simply let go of an issue: forgive and forget. Sometimes I need to just give it a break for a few days.

VENUS IN THE NINTH HOUSE

For love to thrive, I must behave . . . in adventurous, expansive, open-minded ways. Life itself is a quest; I am delighted if someone volunteers to share that quest with me—but I never forget to keep perspective: for me, the point is abundant life-experience, and not just intimacy. In fact, in my mind, those two concepts cannot be separated. Zealously I strive to avoid the claustrophobia and predictability that always threatens the vitality of any long-term committed relationship. We learn together; we travel together; we grow together—or it is just not worth the trouble and the sacrifice. I am developing the ability to pack the experiences of many lifetimes into this one lifetime. Love is one of those experiences, but it is only real if it actually enhances and supports the rest of the package.

Where will I meet my soul-partners? I may meet them on the road—literally when I am traveling. They may be foreigners themselves, or at least have their origins in a different part of the country or a different walk of life. I may meet them as I pursue education. I may meet them as I chase down any fresh or novel experience—swimming with the dolphins or spelunking in some cavern full of stalactites. Wild, adventurous, independent actions of any sort on my part, especially ones consistent with the sign of my Venus, often lead to these kinds of life-triggering human encounters.

How might I recognize them? If I can get my hands on their passports, all I have to do is count the stamps. These are adventurous people; their biographies do not lie about any of that. They may or may not be educated in the formal sense, but they are motivated to learn and often surprise me with the eclectic scope of their knowledge. Here is the biggest test: all I need to do is to just inquire about their opinion of the meaning of life. To pass the test, first, they do not look at me as if that were a dumb or even a surprising question. Second, they have thought about it and they have some kind of answer ready. Third—and in many ways foremost—they are also interested in my own answer. Finally, their philosophy of life reflects a particularly robust expression of the nature of my own Venus sign —in Cancer, it's about kindness; in Scorpio, it's about facing reality.

What actions must I avoid or at least not over-do? The quest for love, in principle, is an idealistic one. Naturally, I think about what kind of partner would be perfect for me—but perfection is not something that humans ever actually find in this world. At some point, I must stop searching and I make my stand with other human beings as imperfect as myself.

VENUS IN THE TENTH HOUSE

For love to thrive, I must behave . . . in ways that might be described as ambitious or career-oriented, even if those are not big motivators for me. More accurately, those behaviors can be framed as my sense of having a mission in this world. Words such as "community" and "social responsibility" are relevant as well. There is a kind of dignity and sense of personal empowerment that comes from touching the lives of people with whom I do not have close personal relationships—and from being appreciated for it. That deepend dignity and sense of empowerment plays a critical role in my ability to find love that works, and is worthy of me. No true soul-friend will ever ask me to choose between love and my mission. Anyone who asks that question has no idea who I am.

Where will I meet my soul-partners? The answer may be as simple as my meeting them at work. Equally, we might encounter each other in some public forum—on a political campaign, as members of the Parent Teacher Organization, or protesting against fracking the local parklands. Professional or public actions of any sort on my part, especially ones consistent with the underlying values of the sign of my Venus, often lead to these life-triggering human encounters. Conversely, if I am not meaningfully engaged with my community, I am not likely to meet the people whom I need to meet.

How might I recognize them? These people are not necessarily prominent or powerful, but they are engaged in activities which have an impact upon the direction of my society—activities in which I myself have a natural interest or investment. These activities reflect a public expression of the values inherent in the nature of my Venus sign—if my Venus is in Leo, we might meet in connection with the performing arts. In Virgo, in connection with the practical mechanics of how societies run. Because of the way these shared values are put to practical work, these people automatically trigger in me a great sense of respect for them.

What actions must I avoid or at least not over-do? There is an eternal tension between, on one hand the demands of public life—one's job, one's mission—and, on the other hand, the legitimate requirements posed by intimacy and domestic life. I need both. The trick—and it will likely be a constant battle—is to make sure that the demands of the public side of my life do not suck the vitality out of my private life.

VENUS IN THE ELEVENTH HOUSE

For love to thrive, I must behave . . . in ways that prioritize reaching my own personal goals. Love is grand, but it can be a distraction; I need to constantly guard against having my own course through life derailed by partners and friends—otherwise resentments creep into my primary relationships. I am developing the ability to keep my eyes on the prize, even when someone else's needs must be factored into the calculations. All that having been said, with Venus in my eleventh house, it is helpful to remember that building a happy, long-term relationship is in fact right near the top of any wise list of my natural aims. If I forget that or undervalue it, I have lost sight of what is truly important to me in the long run. I need to find the balance between human relationship and maintaining a relationship with my own dreams and aspirations.

Where will I meet my soul-partners? I might very well meet them in the context of our shared affiliation with a group or a tribe, whether it is a formal organization or a spontaneous assemblage of friends. Such people might emerge first as a tangential member of "the crowd." Group-related actions of any sort on my part, especially ones consistent with the sign of my Venus, often lead to life-triggering human encounters. In general, Venusian goals are the ones which arise most naturally in me. That might reflect a long-term desire to develop myself artistically. Maybe I aspire to play the violin. And guess who I might find sitting next to me in the orchestra pit?

How might I recognize them? My soul-partners are not necessarily extroverted people, but they are actively engaged in activities that require some kind of group participation. Maybe, for example, they play in a band—or on a softball team. Maybe they're members of a support group for authors or poets. Our shared goals—which have nothing to do with relationship—are what bring us together. In being true to ourselves, we find each other.

What actions must I avoid or at least not over-do? When love works out in a stable, committed way, one of its joys lies in simply planning and dreaming together. There is an uplifting and liberating alchemy that arises when two people jointly conspire to create a future they are both enthusiastic about sharing. That is indeed a gift from the universe—but I must be wary of letting it take us too far away from the present moment. Too much focus on tomorrow can pull our attention away from the here and now—and that is where love makes its moment to moment stand. I must be vigilant about not letting dreams about the future blind us to the slippery, ever-changing, immediate realities generated by two souls in complicated embrace.

VENUS IN THE TWELFTH HOUSE

For love to thrive, I must behave . . . in ways that reflect my most sacred commitment to myself: that I take my own spiritual life seriously. I am a loving person—and love is indeed part of my spiritual life—but I need mindful time alone too. Creativity—and the trance states it engenders in me—may also be a pivotal piece of my inner journey; I need time and support for that part of my life as well. I am developing the ability to fulfill my own half of an ancient bargain: to be part of a truly spiritual partnership. That involves monitoring the collision of two tectonic plates: one is being true to my own separate spiritual needs, while the other is being true to the needs of my relationships. In any case, the only kind of relationships that work well for me in the long run are ones with a basis in shared spirituality.

Where will I meet my soul-partners? Wherever people gather for the sake of their souls, I am likely to meet the sorts of individuals with whom I resonate. Depending upon the specific qualities of my own nature, these places could quite possibly be literal religious institutions—meeting in a church or a temple, for example. Just as easily, I might think of a meditation group, a yoga class, or a presentation by a spiritual teacher. Voluntary actions motivated by my broad interest in the exploration of consciousness—especially ones consistent with the underlying values of the sign of my Venus—often lead to these life-triggering human encounters.

How might I recognize them? Every one of my true soul-partners has an independent, pre-existing spiritual life of his or her own. That is bedrock. Our theologies may not overlap at all, but we are capable of shared, comfortable silences with each other. Our *souls can communicate*, in other words. As we look into each other's eyes, I experience spaciousness, compassion, and a sense of undefended mutual acceptance. When I mention my spiritual perspectives or my psychic experiences, I am met with unfailing support and the kind of understanding that can only be born in parallel experiences.

What actions must I avoid or at least not over-do? What is the role of ego in human intimacy? For me, that question is the source of deep and fruitful meditation. Too much ego is obviously perilous in any loving relationship—but too little is dangerous too. And that latter pitfall is the one regarding which I must be particularly cautious. Being "agreeable," when carried to an extreme, is equivalent to being invisible. We might say the same for runaway expressions of pliability, conflict avoidance—even of forgiveness. In moderation, these qualities are love's vitamins. In excess, they become toxic conditions, conditions in which we feel like we are living with the ghost or at least someone who is not fully, humanly, present.

13

MERCURY IN THE TWELVE HOUSES

MERCURY IN THE FIRST HOUSE

What actual behaviors expose me to what I really need to learn—and thus help me to find my true voice? Making bold, independent statements, so long as I truly believe them—even statements which might appear to be selfish, presumptuous, or rebellious. Displaying receptivity to intellectual risk. Openness to challenging existing authorities or customs. Taking charge of my own thoughts. Standing up for myself verbally. Opening my mouth and seeing what comes out. Writing. Speaking on the spot in front of an audience. Being willing to lead and to teach.

What is my greatest cognitive strength? The courage and confidence simply to try things out. Innovation. A willingness to be "the first one to say it." The capacity to lead—and thus to attract the helpful energies and ideas of followers. How to learn by teaching. Improvisation; confidence that I can successfully "make it up as I go along." A good ability to express myself in writing.

How does the universe correct me? By giving me a lot of latitude to make interesting, instructive mistakes. By my tricking me into opening my mouth before my thoughts are fully baked. By making me listen to my own lectures.

How might I defend myself against growth and learning? By needing to be right all the time. By becoming too enamored of the role of leader or expert—and thus believing flattering delusions which other people hold about me. By mistaking charisma and authority in myself for actual wisdom.

MERCURY IN THE SECOND HOUSE

What actual behaviors expose me to what I really need to learn—and thus help me to find my true voice? Committing to learning things that I am afraid might be too hard for me to learn. Building a foundation of concrete skills and knowledge that lend me a real basis for self-confidence; that might mean mastering tools, techniques, and vocabularies. Proving my own intellectual legitimacy to myself, perhaps by gaining credentials or academic certification. Systematically building the skills, resources, and alliances that empower me with a genuine foundation for self-confidence—qualities which attract people who can help me because they see that I can also help them.

What is my greatest cognitive strength? The potential for dogged intellectual persistence over time. Through sheer determination, I can gain access to the full power of my intelligence. An ability to assess resource-bases, strengthening them where they need to be strengthened, and recognizing their potential weaknesses. Good financial instincts. An ability to assess where talents lie in other people.

How does the universe correct me? It spotlights errors and failures whose origin lie in my under-extending myself, or in excessive hesitation or caution. My painful therapy is to think back on my life in a spirit of analytic honesty, looking for the opportunities that I missed, but should have taken.

How might I defend myself against growth and learning? Endless preparation can be a trick I play on myself in order to avoid actually diving into a subject or an endeavor. Crippling self-doubt which leads to my "not even trying." Failure to acquire the skills and assets which are necessary for my evolutionary work.

MERCURY IN THE THIRD HOUSE

What actual behaviors expose me to what I really need to learn—and thus help me to find my true voice? Exposing myself to educational opportunities is a good start, but there is so much to learn that I need more focused guidance than that. On exactly what should I focus my learning efforts? For me, the guiding star is to trust my curiosity. I go where it leads me; it is wiser than me. As I gain experience, especially experience that surprises me and stretches my horizons, my natural voice arises. That voice is spontaneous, engaging, and clear, and it conveys to people not only information, but also childlike enthusiasm for the information.

What is my greatest cognitive strength? A willingness to be surprised. A willingness to entertain perspectives that I had never before considered, even ones regarding which I might feel resistance. A natural ability to teach. Natural ability as a story-teller; a sense of the enchantment of language. An elevated capacity to translate experience into vocabulary, syntax, and grammar. An ability to explain things clearly. Eloquence and articulation.

How does the universe correct me? By presenting me with cognitive dissonance—things that do not "make sense" because the facts and perspectives run contrary to my blinding assumptions. This cognitive dissonance might arise from books, articles, and conversations which I encounter "by chance." These unexpected synchronicities are my correcting guides, if I can let myself take in their messages.

How might I defend myself against growth and learning? By using language as a wall rather than as bridge. Simply talking too much, and never letting the other person get a word in—or simply by not listening. Rationalizing. Slippery avoidance through distraction, subject changes, or deflecting subjects through the use of my humor and wit. Giving too much power to my "inner crooked lawyer."

MERCURY IN THE FOURTH HOUSE

What actual behaviors expose me to what I really need to learn—and thus help me to find my true voice? My single most powerful evolutionary tool here lies in my powerful capacity for psychological analysis, both of myself and of others. As I fearlessly explore my own mind in a spirit of openness and curiosity, I discover what I need to know in order to empower and activate my true voice. In second place, and not very far behind, is everything I learn from being attentive to the psychodynamics of my own family, however I might define "family." I resolve to learn about its myths and assumptions—and I prepare myself to be startled by the clarity of the mirror they hold before my own existential assumptions.

What is my greatest cognitive strength? An elevated capacity to understand how the underlying emotions, wounds, and archetypes arising in everyone's unconscious minds shape their unwitting conscious personalities. This strength applies to my own self-analysis, but equally it indicates a powerful ability to understand what makes other people tick. I do not necessarily need to become a psychologist, but it is fair to say that I have the mind of a psychologist.

How does the universe correct me? By poking at me from my unconscious mind; nagging intuitions sneak up on me, giving me a bad feeling about something I may have already decided, but would be wise to reconsider. This correction, if I learn to heed it, can give me almost supernatural wisdom. I am learning to take advantage of the fact that my actual consciousness is much vaster than my normal conscious mind. Cooperation with that larger self is what best corrects me.

How might I defend myself against growth and learning? By withdrawing into my interior world, becoming so subjective that I defend myself against any objective learning or useful external guidance. I can dive so deeply into myself that I close my mind—and my ears—to all counsel. Because of my psychological sensitivity to family dynamics, I could fall into the trap of living the life that my family trained me to live—which may have very little to do with my own natural path.

MERCURY IN THE FIFTH HOUSE

What actual behaviors expose me to what I really need to learn—and thus help me to find my true voice? Above all, my path revolves around creative self-expression. Sometimes I just need to open my mouth and see what comes out. Whether or not I know it, I am energized by an audience—and if I do not know that, I can soon learn it by stepping out onto the stage. I need to speak up. I need to polish my skills of presentation. Writing is good for me; so is storytelling—even telling a joke. Unless I am willing to feel vulnerable in front of others, I will never find my true voice. That audience might be one person or it might fill a theater; it works either way.

What is my greatest cognitive strength? The ability to create vivid metaphors, images, and figures of speech—devices which not only skillfully convey information to other people, but also beguile them into listening, identifying with me, even agreeing with me. The ability to simply enjoy a conversation, and to have that joy be contagious—soon others are enjoying it too, opening up, and revealing themselves.

How does the universe correct me? By getting me to just "put it out there," right or wrong, ugly or beautiful. Perhaps I bluster or rant in ways that vividly reveal my own mistaken ideas. Perhaps people laugh at me or treat me dismissively—and in some cases, that is useful feedback. If I am deathly afraid of ever making a fool of myself, I will learn very little in this lifetime.

How might I defend myself against growth and learning? I can grandstand effectively and thus shut down other people's contrary views or opinions—views or opinions which might actually be very useful for me to hear, were I only to listen to them. I can distract myself from everything important in life via an addiction to trivial amusements. I can "sell ice to Eskimos," I can defend dumb ideas and win—but is that really winning and what is the prize?

MERCURY IN THE SIXTH HOUSE

What actual behaviors expose me to what I really need to learn—and thus help me to find my true voice? Above all, in order to find my true voice, I must sit at the feet of masters—people who have already found their own voices, and the well of wisdom underlying those voices. In this lifetime, it is fundamental to my spiritual health that I seek mentors. I recognize them by the authenticity and beguiling power of their language. More importantly, I sense that their voices are linked directly to their souls. I humbly discipline myself to absorb these teachings; I recognize that it is my destiny to carry the flame of this teaching forward into future generations. That is how I thank my mentors.

What is my greatest cognitive strength? I have an uncanny ability to absorb knowledge and wisdom directly from people who have already attained them. I have the "receptor cells" for direct transmission from those who are more evolved than myself. I can discipline myself to learn; I keep my eye on the prize: the ultimate purpose of this learning lies in serving those who will eventually receive these teachings from me. My mind is orderly; I have an elevated ability to make sense of complexity and to organize it cogently. My skills grow exponentially when faced with genuine need in another person; I can rise to the occasion, and be more helpful than I might have imagined.

How does the universe correct me? By arranging for me to be in the presence of those who are more evolved than myself. This is a powerful method, but it is tough on my poor ego. Therefore, in order to withstand these corrections, I must concentrate on loving myself. I should never judge myself—intellectually or in any other way—in comparison to my teachers; I should only judge myself by the standard of the intensity of my effort. The universe also helps me by arranging for me to be in the presence of those whose needs are pressing and genuine. My skills rise to such challenges.

How might I defend myself against growth and learning? Above all, I can stymie my evolution by failing to recognize those guides and teachers with whom life presents me. Arrogance—or thinly disguised insecurity masquerading as arrogance—can insulate me from these effective triggers for my own growth. If I slip into the grips of my own dark side, I can value being seen as an expert more than the humble process of actually becoming one.

MERCURY IN THE SEVENTH HOUSE

What actual behaviors expose me to what I really need to learn—and thus help me to find my true voice? I need to learn who to trust and how to trust. Most of what I need to learn in this life, I learn from other people. I must spontaneously express myself to them and learn to listen carefully and attentively to their responses. Those who are worthy of my trust are generally verbal people, curious about life, and eager to compare notes about it. They enjoy conversation. They are quick. They are not preoccupied with "trying to be my teachers;" the flow between us is more balanced and natural than that. But they do have a lot to teach me. One sure sign that I have actually found such people is that I will sometimes remember the exact words they said. Their words, which might've been simple at the time, somehow sunk into me like a stone. Those words will then work like the kernel of an idea around which a great body of wisdom coalesces—and out of the wisdom, my true voice arises.

What is my greatest cognitive strength? The ability to truly listen; a genuine fascination with the minds of certain people with whom I recognize a special cognitive rapport. The ability, through animated conversation, to co-create insights I could never generate alone. I have an ear for dialogue; I have an ear for language—and by that, I do not simply mean foreign languages, although I do have the ability to learn them. What I mean is the ability to really understand another person, to let their wisdom enter me, and *vice versa*.

How does the universe correct me? By sending me trusted people who hold the mirror of truth before me. They catch me in my contradictions and my rationalizations, and they typically accomplish that supportive aim in a spirit of respect, even of friendship. I am beguiled into spontaneous dialogue. As such conversations unfold, my errors are revealed—and very typically so are better answers.

How might I defend myself against growth and learning? By avoiding friendships with people who have anything important to say. By squandering my time in pointless chit chat. By using humor and wit as a way of avoiding authentic mental chemistry. By talking too much and not listening enough. By wasting my time with childish human beings.

MERCURY IN THE EIGHTH HOUSE

What actual behaviors expose me to what I really need to learn—and thus help me to find my true voice? Above all, the behavior that best triggers wisdom in me lies in my willingness to initiate difficult conversations. There are many subjects so charged with strong emotions that they are functionally taboo in human society. Illustrations of those subjects are death, sexuality, aging, and disease, although there are many others. Some are more purely personal. Synchronicity guarantees that I will be presented in this lifetime with a few people who are capable of entering into deep dialogue with me in these kinds of areas. I need to seek them out and, with their help and support, cross these lines of verbal taboo. These are my comrades on the path. One of the greatest gifts I could offer myself in this lifetime is a life-partnership with such a person—one with whom I can talk about anything, one with whom the only taboos are silence and avoidance.

What is my greatest cognitive strength? An ability to steady my mind in the face of strong emotional stimulus. I can look penetratingly at difficult subjects. With the right people, I can also discuss them in a spirit of honesty, directness, and shared mutual vulnerability. I think like a psychoanalyst—or perhaps like a police detective. I have a strong stomach for hard truths. It is difficult for anyone to lie to me; I see through them.

How does the universe correct me? When I am avoiding some unpleasant truth, many signs and omens arise, seemingly doing their best to help me face what I must face. These signs and omens often come in the form of conversations with intimate friends who say things that are meaningful to me in ways that the friends probably do not themselves understand. Just as commonly, these signs and omens might take the form of "books falling off shelves, open to the exact page I need to read." It can get spooky, in other words. It is helpful for me to recognize that, contrary to what I might've learned in high school, this is how the universe actually operates.

How might I defend myself against growth and learning? Much of my learning in this lifetime is connected with evolution that takes place specifically in my emotional body. Feelings typically arise before insights. I can avoid growth through the device of escaping these emotions by living in my head—intellectualizing, arguing, rationalizing. Just imagine someone with a brilliant PhD in psychology who is still actually as crazy as a soup sandwich: there, in a nutshell, is my Shadow.

MERCURY IN THE NINTH HOUSE

What actual behaviors expose me to what I really need to learn—and thus help me to find my true voice? Cross-cultural experience is a pivotal trigger for what I need to learn in this lifetime. Underlying that statement is the realization that I have been blinded by some of the assumptions of my own culture and upbringing. To find my true voice, I must get past that particular myopia. Going further, great minds throughout history have wrestled with life's knottiest questions. Their insights are available in books, via educational experiences, and above all in living lineages—I can, in other words, study with their students, or their students' students. If I do all that and absorb these teachings, I will find the basis for my true voice. These boundary-stretching experiences are the yeast in my bread.

What is my greatest cognitive strength? An ability to recognize patterns. An ability to connect the dots and draw generalizable conclusions. An ability to think in terms of first principles—morals, ethics, metaphysical bedrock. A mind-expanding ability to place myself in cross-cultural frameworks—there are problems a Chinese person might solve more quickly than a French person, and *vice versa*. With cross-cultural experience, I can find both of these people in my own head and make allies of them.

How does the universe correct me? By confronting me with questions that I cannot answer, at least not without questioning my own assumptions. Sometimes I "connect the dots" without realizing that there are other dots that I have ignored. Those "dots" then present themselves to me as loose ends and cognitive dissonance. As I pay attention to that errant data rather than defending my previous position, I allow myself to be corrected.

How might I defend myself against growth and learning? I can play the role of teacher in order to avoid learning; I can preach rather than humbling myself before those whose wisdom is beyond my own. I can perceive new, helpful, and necessary information as heresy against which I must defend my faith. I can place too much value on being right, to the point that I become impervious to actual evolution.

MERCURY IN THE TENTH HOUSE

What actual behaviors expose me to what I really need to learn—and thus help me to find my true voice? My highest mission in this world is to become a pipeline of information into the community—a "teacher," in some sense of the word, although that can take many different forms: novelist, journalist, media work—or simply someone whose voice is heard somehow in the community. As I step up to the plate and make sure that people *whom I do not know personally* are being impacted by my thoughts and my ideas, I gain the confidence, authority, and style that support the development of my true voice. My evolutionary trajectory begins with my being some kind of student and evolves into one in which the fruits of my own mind have nourished the minds of many other people.

What is my greatest cognitive strength? I have an almost supernatural sense of what my community needs to hear. Simultaneously I have a good instinct for how I need to phrase it in order that the message be received clearly—even if it is unexpected or unwelcome. More than most people, I understand how the world works, and how there is nothing more powerful than an idea whose time has come. I can bring such ideas before my community.

How does the universe correct me? Everything I misunderstand and misinterpret will be revealed in my public behavior. When I am wrong, I will speak up, imagining that I am right. There will be no way for me to keep my errors secret. If I persist in them, everyone will know it. The universe allows everyone a certain quotient of secrets; I am allowed fewer of them than most people.

How might I defend myself against growth and learning? I can become very skillful at a profession or some other public role that has no personal meaning for me at all. Perhaps this role garners me respect and stability, even a reputation as a great authority. This is a soul-cage in which I could be trapped, stymieing my evolution.

MERCURY IN THE ELEVENTH HOUSE

What actual behaviors expose me to what I really need to learn—and thus help me to find my true voice? First and foremost, I must devote myself *long-term* to the process of finding my voice. I realize that it is a step-by-step process, unfolding over decades—endlessly, really. I must approach the effort strategically: seeking education or experience of writing and public speaking—knowing that such skills gather momentum over time. I accept the fact that my voice will be heard most widely only in the second half of my journey. I seek association with people who are intelligent and interested in life, willing to learn and to grow in their understanding. Perhaps I meet them in classes or while attending lectures—these natural associates and allies are the kinds of people who would be drawn to such situations.

What is my greatest cognitive strength? I have a good ability to think strategically. I know how to set priorities and how to frame long-term plans for achieving them. I know which battles must be won and which ones can be sacrificed. If we define "politics" as what happens whenever more than three or four people are engaged in the same project, then I have a great strength when it comes to understanding politics. I can negotiate; I can bring people together with my words. I can speak for a group; I can also teach a group about their own internal dynamics.

How does the universe correct me? When I feel flummoxed, as if I have lost my track in life, often the problem lies in my tendency to let other people and the social obligations they create to distract me from my true priorities. In that situation, I find myself busy—and yet I am accomplishing nothing of actual importance. If I notice that uncomfortable reality and make the necessary adjustments to address the problem, the universe, via that feedback, has corrected me.

How might I defend myself against growth and learning? There was a time when everyone agreed that the earth was flat. That belief was prevalent despite great evidence to the contrary. This illustrates the deadening power of collective belief-systems and their ability to control, blind, and seduce the "herd animal" inside all of us. I can cripple my own evolutionary journey by not thinking for myself, instead succumbing to the perspective foisted upon me by the social world around me.

MERCURY IN THE TWELFTH HOUSE

What actual behaviors expose me to what I really need to learn—and thus help me to find my true voice? Above all, I benefit from deeper forms of mind-training. Some of that can be understood as meditation practice. While meditation itself helps, I also need teachers and teachings who correct and improve my understanding of the true nature of the mind. Reading metaphysics is good for me. My understanding of life, consciousness, and the universe is being elevated. There is, in other words, a significant intellectual or cognitive component to my spiritual evolution in this lifetime. Words cannot encompass these ultimate mysteries—but for me, certain words and teachings work as magical catalysts, accelerating my growth dramatically. As that process unfolds and my understanding deepens, the archetype of the spiritual teacher begins to crystallize in me. That archetype is the heart of my true voice.

What is my greatest cognitive strength? We are all acclimated to a three-dimensional "common sense" perception of the universe, but our consciousness actually exists in a far more multidimensional framework. Mystics have always said that; for the last century, the physicists have been in agreement. Intuitively, I grasp this mystery. I have an understanding of the vast psychic realms which lie beyond the narrow boundaries of what other people might call "the obvious facts." I can extend the field of my perceptions beyond the obvious framework of everyday reality.

How does the universe correct me? In the course of this lifetime, I will have many uncanny, inexplicable experiences—things that I just know without having any idea how I know them. Some of these experiences may be shocking or unpleasant, while others are simply impossible to explain. Seeing a ghost would be an example. So would dreaming of someone I haven't seen in years and then running into them the next day. So would knowing in advance about someone's death. Whenever I begin to succumb to "common sense"—which is to say the collective mis-definition of reality—I will receive perceptual corrections of this surprising and very psychic nature.

How might I defend myself against growth and learning? Ultimately the deepest mysteries of the universe can only be witnessed, never understood. When I begin to believe my own sermons, as if I had everything figured out, I become stuck in my own delusional certainties. I have the ability to do the sacred work of a spiritual teacher. I should not turn away from that responsibility toward other humans—but when I teach, I must resolve to be vigilant about those "delusional certainties." Whatever I understand, the truth is always beyond that.

14

SATURN IN THE
TWELVE HOUSES

SATURN IN THE FIRST HOUSE

The Great Work: Self-respect and dignity earned through success at difficult accomplishments—ones which I have chosen personally, freely and in soul-centered fashion. Attaining a state of self-sufficient, self-directed autonomy. This is not to be confused with lovelessness, isolation, or coldness—only with being free of any driving desperation for others' support or approval.

The Strategy For Achieving It: Single-minded, undistracted focus on the goals that are actually important to me, even if people call them selfish. Relentless effort sustained over time, sometimes without external rewards or attention. Remaining impervious to all external manipulations aimed at distracting me, however cunning and guilt-inducing they might be. Developing the ability to endure disapproval and isolation for the sake of fulfilling a task that is a worthy expression of the best I have to offer. Success is its own reward; anything more is welcome, but not necessary.

The Blockage That Must Be Faced Squarely: The personal insecurity and self-doubt that arise naturally in the face of anything difficult. The fear of loneliness, rejection, or alienation. The fear of failure.

The Price of Failure: A feeling of having "missed the boat" in my life, of being a flower that never opened. Soul-isolation—a condition which may still see me surrounded by people, but ones who have no idea of what my actual potential had been. And that is because I never gave any manifestation to the reality of my true nature; I never revealed myself to the community through my Great Work.

SATURN IN THE SECOND HOUSE

The Great Work: Metaphorically speaking, I must climb an intimidatingly tall mountain in this lifetime. Initially, that Great Work appears to be too much for me. That daunted feeling, by the way, is one of the signs by which I actually recognize my mountain. I must prove myself to myself through this concrete, visible accomplishment. The inward side of the work lies in the development of self-confidence and a sense of my own power—but I can only attain those inward victories through an impressive outward effort of sustained self-discipline aimed at completing a project that is truly worthy of me and expressive of my soul.

The Strategy For Achieving It: I start by realizing that my feelings of insecurity do not have their fundamental origin in my psychological make-up; instead, they derive directly from rational assessments of my own weak points in terms of skills, resources, and necessary alliances. Once I focus on shoring up that base of necessary supports, an increasing confidence that I can successfully "climb the mountain" arises naturally in me.

The Blockage That Must Be Faced Squarely: The deep-down fearful feeling that I simply do not "have what it takes." Unaddressed, that attitude could lead me to climb lesser peaks. By way of compensation for this sense of spiritual failure, I could take on time-serving, difficult, undertakings— but ones which serve no true spiritual purpose for me at all. I might spend my life counting beans for other people.

The Price of Failure: Getting to the top of the wrong mountain, and finding that it leaves me empty and unsatisfied. Down that path, I find myself mired in sticky duties and cascading responsibilities which leave me feeling robotic, exhausted—and probably resentful of those whom I am serving.

SATURN IN THE THIRD HOUSE

The Great Work: Bringing forth my true voice, which is the voice of the Elder or the Sage. Developing a style of self-expression that is inherently commanding and authoritative without ever sounding arrogant. Creating, over a long period of time, a body of verbal work—the product of my intellect leavened by all that I have learned in life. That work might be written; it might take the form of teaching; just as easily, it might be a set of helpful ideas and insights which are always ready to roll off my tongue skillfully and compellingly when presented with some genuine human need.

The Strategy For Achieving It: Study is critical here; I must not be afraid to "burn the midnight oil," learning what I need to learn. I must cut through mental laziness or any lack of sustained focus. The discipline of long-term concentration is pivotal to me. Through it, I can outperform people who might be more innately gifted than myself. I celebrate language; I develop my vocabulary and my ability to speak confidently and in complete paragraphs.

The Blockage That Must Be Faced Squarely: Fear and insecurity about my voice and my intelligence can silence me; I am not here on this earth to be silenced. I affirm that I have something important to say, and that I can express it seriously and authoritatively, and thus be taken seriously by others. Whenever I lose sight of those truths, it is a sign that I have succumbed to my area of blockage.

The Price of Failure: Being haunted by the repetitive experience of a feeling that "I should have said that." Knowing that in many situations I had real insights that were never shared—and not because I failed to love other people enough to care about them, but rather because I failed to honor myself and my own wisdom. In extreme form, I might die knowing that "I had a book in me" that I never wrote.

SATURN IN THE FOURTH HOUSE

The Great Work: Building roots; finding and building a true soul-home for myself in this world. That home may very well include a physical house, along with a spiritual relationship with the land on which it sits. Beyond that, certainly such a home includes "family" in some sense of the word— committed relationships with people, and perhaps with animal companions with whom I share my life. Deep inner work aimed at establishing a conscious connection with my vivid inner archetype of the Wise Elder. Eventually I resolve to fulfill the guiding role of "grandmother" or "grandfather," figuratively if not literally.

The Strategy For Achieving It: Sustaining human commitments over long periods of time; doing the necessary maintenance work that nourishes stable, long-term relationships—deep shared processes, including forgiveness and tolerance for differences, along with the work on my own psyche that underlies my own ability to love skillfully in the real world. The long, shared story with other souls. Realizing that romantic love is sweet and real, but that it is ultimately only a bridge I cross to where I will do my real evolutionary work. Building a sense of family. Putting down physical roots; commitment to a community, to a tribe, or to a physical place.

The Blockage That Must Be Faced Squarely: The most frightening words anyone can possibly utter are, "I will never leave you." I recognize that natural fear inside myself; I recognize that it is based on realistic wisdom. But I will never let that fear block me from my evolutionary path, which lies down the road of the long, shared story with a few other human beings. Even in long-term relationship, I will not hide from intimacy behind my psychological walls.

The Price of Failure: A feeling of rootlessness; a feeling that I have no true home in this world, that I have always been a displaced person—an alienated outsider. A pervasive, and rather stoic, mood of unending sadness in my life. Distance from my own heart. My silence may have been mistaken for depth, but I know in my heart that it was truly the face of my fear of being seen or deeply known.

SATURN IN THE FIFTH HOUSE

The Great Work: Giving some concrete outward manifestation to the contents of my inner world. Leaving tangible evidence of my imagination and my values in the hands of my community. My Great Work, in a nutshell, lies in cultivating and expanding my creativity. This creative process may take the form of "art" in the conventional sense of that word—but, just as easily, I might leave the fingerprints of my aspirations, tastes, and my nature upon an institution or an event. Whatever form this creative self-expression takes, I will constantly strive to polish, mature, and improve it.

The Strategy For Achieving It: I commit myself to the discipline of mastering the technical foundations underlying whatever creative field I am drawn to explore. I will learn from those who have gone before me. I respect the tradition in which I practice; I do not seek to copy anyone, but I will humble myself and discipline myself sufficiently to learn what my forebears have learned, and so build upon the solid ground they have shown me.

The Blockage That Must Be Faced Squarely: There is a wild god or goddess behind all creative inspiration. I acknowledge that I fear surrendering to such chaotic forces; I also understand that unless I do, my work will be mechanical and derivative. I resolve to learn the discipline of spontaneity. I resolve to surrender to my muse.

The Price of Failure: Were I to fail to learn how to surf these Dionysian waves of creativity, melancholia would suffuse my life. I would feel bottled up and inhibited when faced with any of life's wild joys. My soul would remain invisible; I would feel as if the best parts of myself were unknown.

SATURN IN THE SIXTH HOUSE

The Great Work: Finding meaningful responsibilities. Finding work that truly matters. I am capable of making enormous, focused effort when presented with a worthy task. I understand that in so doing I will experience exhaustion; I accept that exhaustion. I even celebrate it—but only if the work passes two tests: it expresses my soul and it makes a real difference in someone else's life. Nothing else is worth the monumental efforts of which I am capable.

The Strategy For Achieving It: I will find my true teachers, mentors, and role models no matter how difficult it is to locate them. I accept that part of my Great Work eventually lies in passing on what they have taught me—but first, I must sit at their feet and learn it directly from them. Always, I view the work itself as more important to me than any recognition or appreciation which I might achieve; I want those things too, but they are always secondary. The work comes first.

The Blockage That Must Be Faced Squarely: I am part of a lineage; that means that I am blocked from meaningful progress unless I first humbly recognize my need for the guidance of certain specific teachers. Nothing will stand between me and finding them—not my arrogance, nor any sense of unworthiness or self-doubt. I affirm that, with their triggering help, I am capable of this Great Work—and of passing on the treasure of this knowledge before I leave this world.

The Price of Failure: Slavery, in a nutshell. Some slaves have expensive automobiles and corner offices, but they are still slaves. I will not be one of them. Work exacts a blood-price from anyone's life—so much of our time and energy is absorbed that way; it is only worth that price if the work pays me a lot more than mere money. If I fail on this path, I will pour my life down the rat-hole of meaningless duty and responsibility.

SATURN IN THE SEVENTH HOUSE

The Great Work: Restoring my ability to trust other people—which in turn depends upon deepening my skill when it comes to judging character. I must learn to discern who is worthy of my trust. Having done that, I must take the risk of radical commitment to a few other human beings—ones who have made similar commitments to me. The Great Work manifests as an honorable, life-long vow, kept and cherished. Such vows are not limited to marriage; lasting friendships of great depth are part of them as well.

The Strategy For Achieving It: Learning reliably to sense a quality of trustworthiness in another person. Recognizing and fully appreciating steadiness, maturity, and reasonableness in somebody—and valuing those qualities above more transitory temptations, such as glamour or sexiness. Taking time to build genuine psychological familiarity; patience; not rushing intimacy—and learning to value people who do not rush me into it.

The Blockage That Must Be Faced Squarely: Due to unresolved abandonment or grievous bereavement in a prior lifetime, I was born with a defended heart. There is no shame in this; I came by this blockage honestly, as a result of tragedy. I resolve to heal that wound in this lifetime; I realize that I can only succeed in that process with the consistent help of someone who does not fail me or abandon me.

The Price of Failure: If I fail in this Great Work of recovering my ability to trust, two dark roads lie ahead of me. I will travel down one, or possibly both, of them. The first is a life of isolation and loneliness, as I simply defend myself against the possibility of pain by avoiding entanglements. The second lies in choosing people whom it would not be too hard to lose—those who are either unworthy of me or otherwise unreachable. They are the way I keep the stakes low; they are only symbols of my unresolved fear.

SATURN IN THE EIGHTH HOUSE

The Great Work: A focused and disciplined approach to facing certain specific and fundamental wounds in my psyche. It is not that I am more wounded than other people; it is only that I am ready now to face this deep work, while others might not be. I will in this lifetime reestablish my ability to trust existence itself, along with trusting a carefully selected group of humans who are worthy of my love and my fierce honesty.

The Strategy For Achieving It: I commit radically to that honesty. Simultaneously, I commit to what we might call "a lifetime of psychoanalysis," even if that is just a metaphor for an examined life. Perhaps I will do much of that psychoanalytic work all by myself—that is fine and natural. But I resolve in the course of this life to bare my soul to at least one other human being, with nothing hidden and nothing held back. I will choose that person with great care.

The Blockage That Must Be Faced Squarely: Due to painful prior life experiences with human sexuality, I am blocked when it comes to bonding deeply with another human being. Due to a tragic, violent, lingering, or untimely prior life experiences of death, I have fears around my physical mortality in this lifetime. I will face them honestly. (Note that this is not a "fear of death" *per se*; more accurately, it is a fear of *dying* whose origins lie in the deep memory banks of my soul.)

The Price of Failure: A morbid feeling of pessimism and foreboding; an unfocused sense that something dreadful always lies just around the corner. An inability to be wide open and vulnerable to the healing touch of human love. Loneliness. Sexuality suffused with the archetypes of tragic romance—that, or simple asexuality.

SATURN IN THE NINTH HOUSE

The Great Work: Education, in the largest sense of the word. I will exercise and expand my intelligence; I commit to achieving mastery in fields that intimidate me intellectually. I seek only truths which are supported by my own direct experience; if some belief has not worked for me personally, I put it on the back burner. I am never afraid of questions. For me, "faith" is subordinate to the realities of experience. I resolve to expand my understanding of life beyond the horizons of my own culture and training.

The Strategy For Achieving It: Institutions of higher education attract me; that might include universities—but it also applies to less formal paths, so long as they are serious: ongoing classes or training programs count as well. In other words, at least for a while, I am willing to humble myself before experts, to learn what they have to teach. I am eager to travel and to cross cultural boundaries, knowing that my own society has blinded me with its unconscious assumptions and prejudices to some things I must understand.

The Blockage That Must Be Faced Squarely: I like order, coherence, and rationality, but I must remember that the universe operates by more mysterious laws and principles. I resolve to avoid rigidity in my thinking and in my beliefs. I allow space for questions and for that which I do not yet comprehend. I am not offended by loose ends, nor by the irrational, nor by the miraculous.

The Price of Failure: Crippling conservatism in my views; a narrow mind, committed to defending its preexisting beliefs and its own identity as an expert. A lack of imagination. Bad religion. A parochial perspective, unable to escape the narrow bandwidth of "what was good enough for my grandparents."

SATURN IN THE TENTH HOUSE

The Great Work: Finding my true, meaningful mission in the community. Creating a purposeful role for myself in society, one to which I can willingly submit. In some broad sense, this mission will be filed under the archetype of the Elder or the Priest— words which I do not need to take literally since they are only references to a shepherding, guiding role—one which I aspire to be worthy of playing in my community. Through that role, I will touch the lives of people with whom I do not necessarily share personal karma.

The Strategy For Achieving It: I initially affirm that I simply *have* a mission; my sense of having "a Calling" is real and authentic. Part of my evolutionary work in this lifetime lies in turning myself into a worthy gift for my people. I accept that path; I surrender to it. Like a good priest, I recognize that my treasure is not necessarily in this world—it might not, in other words, be about money or prestige. It is the work itself that matters; I recognize that sacrifices will be demanded of me. I accept that part too.

The Blockage That Must Be Faced Squarely: The requirements of my mission daunt me; in order to succeed at it, I must develop skills that do not arise naturally in my personality. Faced with the pathway to my natural work, I am plagued by feelings of insecurity, ineptitude, and illegitimacy. Through sustained discipline, I must face those feelings down. One seductive way my blockages might manifest is by presenting me with "alternative careers"—ones which make practical sense to every part of me except to my own soul.

The Price of Failure: Playing a time-serving, ultimately boring role in the world—one in which my unthinkingly mechanical or automatic skills dominate while my soul hibernates. Looking like a success, while feeling like a failure. Illustrating the old proverb: it's lonely at the top. Actual failure, having never found my path and thus having just given up.

SATURN IN THE ELEVENTH HOUSE

The Great Work: Living a life structured in accord with the actual long-term priorities of my soul. Keeping first things first, regardless of pressures, distractions, or temptations. Setting goals, both spiritually and practically—and keeping my eye on the prize consistently over the decades of my life. A life lived intentionally, navigated by the guiding stars of my soul's inspiration. Seeking the support of a community of people who share these same guiding stars; my helping them—and in turn being helped by them. My aim is that at the end of my life, I will have accomplished something concrete and real of which I am very proud, and of which I may very well have dimly dreamed when I was young.

The Strategy For Achieving It: Even though Saturn is a rational planet, I must first suspend rationality and ask my heart one pressing question: *when I am old, what kind of life do I want to look back upon?* Once I have that answer, I must formulate a practical strategy for embodying such a life over time. I must set fierce and focused priorities—and honor them by avoiding all tempting distractions and side tracks. It is critical that I seek creative, supportive alliances with people who are traveling a similar road.

The Blockage That Must Be Faced Squarely: I acknowledge that I am hesitant about relating to groups of people. I tend to not trust them or feel comfortable in them. I need to overcome this blockage—carefully. The aim is not that I try to transform myself into some kind of extroverted party animal; rather, the aim is that I recognize that certain other people are holding cards that I need, just as I am holding cards which they themselves need. Thus, fruitful alliances can arise—but only if I am first clear about my own direction and what I want to achieve in this lifetime. That knowledge must come first; these alliances are a natural side-effect of this initial self-knowledge. If I want to play third violin, I am going to need an orchestra.

The Price of Failure: A feeling of being lost at sea, without any guiding stars. Directionlessness. A life of tactics, lacking any larger strategy. Coping and reacting rather than keeping my eyes on a defined prize. Squandering my energy with a similarly lost and directionless crowd—or simply feeling a kind of urban anonymity, *ennui*, and Kafka-esque alienation.

SATURN IN THE TWELFTH HOUSE

The Great Work: A profound commitment to a lifetime of practical spiritual progress, based upon effort, self-discipline, and, above all, *consistency* of practice. Strange as this might sound to religious people, in this lifetime I am casting off any need for faith. My "faith" is strong enough just as it is; now what benefits me are *proofs* based on my own inner experience. To find those proofs, I will cultivate direct experience of the Divine. I will undertake certain established spiritual practices in a spirit of regularity; I am not afraid of austerity and self-sacrifice. I know the prize is worth ten times the effort.

The Strategy For Achieving It: Consistency of spiritual effort is critical to my success. I will, for example, meditate not because I want to, but because it is six o'clock in the morning and that is when I have promised myself I will meditate. Fasting might be of benefit to me, as is a periodic vow of silence. My spirituality is supported by times of solitude, away from the buzz of the world. I will not lose sight of compassion for myself—but the bottom line is that I am teaching "my inner monkey" who is the boss.

The Blockage That Must Be Faced Squarely: People often use the metaphor of "climbing a mountain" for the spiritual path. If so, I must recognize that I have come to a steep stage in that ascent. For me, the next steps involve a challenging, but potentially very fruitful battle with my fears, my appetites, and my own laziness. Facing that "steepness" is hard, humbling work—but the good news is, when climbing a steep mountain, a little bit of forward progress puts a person on much higher ground.

The Price of Failure: A feeling of spiritual stagnation, as if my forward progress has been stymied, and my inner psychic experience—whatever level of it I may have attained—has become predictable and routine. At its worst, failure here can lead to a loss of active spiritual engagement—a feeling of having been "abandoned by God." Cynicism might arise in me. A dark night of the soul potentially looms—but only if I lose sight of my Great Work and the strategies I must employ consistently for attaining it.

15

ASTROLOGICAL ASPECTS
IN THE NATAL CHART

In *The Book of Fire*, we introduced the astrological aspects mostly as they related to astrology's "moving parts"—transits, progressions, and solar arcs. Once we understand them in that moving context, it is a short step to understanding them in the natal chart—and *vice versa*. Either way, it is always about two different energies trying to accomplish something that neither one could ever accomplish all by itself.

Here, in *The Book of Earth*, we are introducing aspects a little earlier in the story. At this stage, we are still thinking about the role of the Earth planets in the birthchart rather than their role in transits, progressions, or solar arcs.

You may have been born with Pluto opposite the Moon. That is a stable installation, at least for as long as you remain in your present physical body. That means that the Intelligence of the universe wants to "invite you to do some reflection"—not just for a couple of years, but rather cradle to grave. That Pluto-Moon aspect is fundamental to how you feel, think, and perceive the world. And like everything else in astrology, there are ways to get it right and ways to get it wrong. You will likely explore some of the "wrong" ways—and no shame there! We're all here to learn, and your chart shows exactly what you need to learn. Since you "need to learn it," it follows that you do not already know it—and that is your Get Out of Jail Free card when it comes to errors.

Because you are reading this book, I have reason to believe that you are living an examined life. That is enough evidence to give me confidence in saying that you will also discover some of the ways to get that Moon-Pluto aspect right as well.

The underlying point is that these natal aspects do not go away like transits and progressions do. That's what makes them different.

Still, most of what we need to say about natal aspects is pretty similar to what we have already said about the moving ones. Because of that, much of what follows in this chapter overlaps with the aspects chapters of *The Book of Fire*. As I've mentioned previously, in this four-volume Elements series, I am sometimes going to commit the Sin of Redundancy in order to avoid Sins of Omission. As I wrote earlier in the book, I am hoping that readers want all four volumes—but I am aware that some will only acquire the volume that relates to their Sun Sign. I want each book to stand alone.

If you have absorbed the previous volume, much of what follows is likely to feel familiar.

KEEPING PERSPECTIVE ON ASPECTS

Aspects bind a chart together—but they are not the only thing that does. If, for example, a person has Venus in opposition to Saturn in her natal chart, her happiness in intimacy is bound to her need for solitude—thus, we might helpfully speak with her about claiming time alone in her relationships, along with the helpful advantage of choosing partners who tend to be self-sufficient rather than "needy."

Now let's say we have a person who is a solar Taurus with Venus conjunct his Sun—but with Saturn in his seventh house. Saturn forms no aspect to his Sun-Venus alignment, *but it has to be included in any useful perspectives we might offer about his intimate style.* Any helpful reading of his chart must include a similar synthesis of his relationship needs and his need for some time to himself.

There are two principles implicit in this example:

To say it formally, everything in the birthchart is interactive with everything else, even when no aspects are involved..

To say it more simply: ultimately, you have only one head between your ears.

Aspects, in other words, are only one mechanism by which we spot the most vigorous planetary interactions in a birth chart. As astrologers, we must master aspects—but we must also never forget that there are other integrative processes at work.

ALL ASPECTS ARE ABOUT INTEGRATION

If you forget everything else and simply let that integrative principle guide your thinking, then your work with aspects will be helpful, accurate, and profound. And if you forget that all aspects—even the so-called "bad" ones—are still all about integration, you lapse into a far more limiting form of astrological work—one that is not only less sophisticated, but is also unnecessarily depressing a lot of the time.

I emphasize this principle in order to counter the ubiquitous idea that there are "good" aspects and "bad" aspects. We see this idea everywhere in the astrological literature, and it has never once helped anyone become wiser or more self accepting. That Saturn-Venus opposition we just used as an example would be considered "unfortunate" by many conventional astrologers. "Bad luck in love" would be the general formula—and fair enough: if you get involved with a clinging vine who needs constant attention and reassurance, you will surely prove the gloomiest astrologers right.

But that is bad luck that you have created for yourself. It didn't need to be that way.

Good and bad aspects are not useless concepts, but I would love to declare a ten-year moratorium on astrologers using the words. It is far more accurate—and really just as simple—to say "easy aspects" and "hard aspects."

And let's remember that "hard" equals "bad" only for lazy people. We have all done hard things that were good for us. We have all even done hard things that we enjoyed doing. Why would anyone paddle up the tributaries of the Orinoco River in the Amazon Basin? Why would anyone read the complete works of Shakespeare? Or *Ulysses*? Why would anyone bother to learn to play the mandolin?

The pivotal concept here is not some pop-psychological stricture against using "judgmental words" or "being negative." It is simply that when two planets are in aspect, the reality is always that they are trying to work together. They are trying to integrate their energies.

Your job is to figure how to help them do that.

If the planets are linked by a so-called "bad aspect," that integration is indeed more difficult. If it is an "easy" aspect, the integration is easier—but there is also a danger of laziness or a lack of pressing motivation.

Bottom line, my suggestion is that when you are confronted with any astrological aspect, that you try to organize your thinking in four steps, as follows:

* Step One: Start by contemplating the energies the planetary archetypes represent. (Examples: Saturn is *solitude* and Venus is *love*). Realize that if they are linked by any aspect at all, they are trying to cooperate—and your evolution depends upon them working together. (Think: *solitude and love are not truly opposites*; everyone knows that sometimes "absence makes the heart grow fonder.)

* Step Two: Imagine what such an integration might look like if it were successful.

* Step Three: Pay attention to what it would look like if the planetary partnership became unhealthy—that is always a possibility too. (*If I am not getting time alone in a healthy, straightforward way, I might cut myself off from you emotionally.*)

  (Notice that everything I have said so far is totally independent of exactly what aspect we are talking about—it could be a trine, a square, or a sesquiquadrate; so far, the specific nature of the aspect does not matter. Regardless of the aspect, it is all about integration, always, period.)

* Step Four: Next, for the first time, consider the nature of the aspect itself. Are we talking about friction or complimentary tensions between the two archetypes? Or are we in the realm of the easy aspects? Are we thus talking about mutual enhancement and support—and the possibility of laziness, a lack of motivation, and dark collusion? *In a nutshell, put the planetary integration first and the nature of the aspect last.*

ASPECTUAL ORBS

There is nothing rigid about the orbs of aspects—except perhaps astrologers' opinions. Some of us use tight orbs in order to strategically reduce the number of aspects in a chart and thus focus narrowly on the most pressing ones. Other astrologers use wider orbs and thus have more aspects in order to paint a more subtle portrait.

Two general principles reliably guide us as we consider how we might best relate to orbs:

* Aspects are not all equal in strength. Use wider orbs for the more energetic aspects. Here, in my experience, is the hierarchy of aspectual strength in descending order of power: conjunctions, oppositions, squares, trines, sextiles, quincunxes—followed by sesquiquadrates, quintiles, semi-sextiles and the rest of the minor series.

  (Another astrologer might list them differently, especially as we get further down the list toward the minor ones. I don't mean to sound dogmatic here; these are just my impressions.)

* The more charged the astrological planet or point, the wider the orb it casts. Almost universally, for example, astrologers use wider orbs for the Sun than they do for Saturn or Neptune. But be careful; other factors can intervene—if, for example, Capricorn is rising, then that Saturn "rules the chart." That strengthens it enormously, dictating wider orbs for any aspects it makes. But you still need to take it further: where exactly is that chart-ruling Saturn placed and how central is it? Is it conjunct the Midheaven—or hiding out in a corner somewhere?

Many factors, in other words, come together to determine the "power" of a planet, and thus we understand that any hard and fast rules about the orbs of aspects represent a dangerous over-simplification of astrological reality.

TAILORING ORBS TO FIT YOUR OWN NATURE

Your own cognitive style is a major factor here. It is wise to include some self-knowledge in your considerations about how you choose to work with aspects and their orbs. Here is what I mean by that:

* As we mentioned earlier, tighter orbs mean fewer aspects. That approach might suit you very well if your nature dictates that your thinking works best if you can go deeply into a few aspects, having narrowed your list down to include only the most pivotal ones. That "editing" is something you can accomplish by the simple device of using tighter orbs.

* On the other hand, you might be the sort of person who can happily surf over large sets of data, with your intuitive function pulling it all together. If that is who you are, then use wider orbs. You will have more aspects then, but your consciousness is wired to be able to handle that complexity.

Let us immediately blow the trumpet for both of these approaches. It is a question of style and self-knowledge, not a question of skill. It is not about intelligence, it is about the *nature* of your intelligence.

I suspect you are beginning to have a sense of why I shake my head when I read an astrological text that tells me authoritatively—and completely erroneously—that "trines should have an orb of 7° while sextiles should have an orb of 5°," and so on. Reality is simply not that rigid, and neither is your head.

Furthermore such a dogmatic approach completely ignores the critical factor of adapting aspects to your own cognitive nature.

WHOLE SIGNS VERSUS GEOMETRY

Be sensitive to "whole sign aspects," no matter what the orbs might be. Anything anywhere in Leo is going to experience some "squaring" by anything anywhere in Scorpio. The underlying sign archetypes suffuse the two planets—and thus the archetypal square makes itself felt.

That situation gets particularly curious when a planet in 29° Scorpio "trines" a planet in 1° Leo. We call that an *out of quality* aspect—that is, one that involves planets in the "wrong" signs, even though the geometrical angle is correct.

Out of quality aspects are always tricky to interpret because you have two incompatible principles interacting: the geometrical aspect and the whole sign aspect. Are they in 'easy" or "hard" relationship to each other?

My approach is to pay attention to both perspectives; each of them will make itself felt in life and in consciousness.

IS IT A QUINCUNX OR IS IT A QUINTILE?

Similar ambiguity can arise when two different aspects overlap. That happens because of orbs. However we define them, there are always fuzzy zones where one aspect blends into another one. You do not see that much if you limit your attention to the major aspects—but add the minor ones, and you will collide with some irresolvable arguments.

Illustration: we might have two planets separated by 147°. Do we call that aspect a 150° quincunx—or a 144° bi-quintile? As with the previous "squared trine" example, both interpretations can cast light on the experienced reality.

If you are starting to sense that reading aspects is a very personal thing, and really more an art than a science, you are getting the picture. We have to weigh many factors, and make a lot of judgement calls.

APPLYING VERSUS SEPARATING, WAXING VERSUS WANING

When an aspect is approaching exactitude in real time, we say that it is *applying*. When it is past its peak, but still within orbs, we say that it is *separating*. These two situations have distinctly different energetic textures. Applying aspects feel like an in-breath and separating ones an out-breath. Applying ones are more urgent, active and intense, while separating ones are more reflective, cautious, and passive.

Similar statements can be made about *waxing* aspects in contrast with *waning* ones. Geometrically, our thinking here works just like the phases of the Moon—New Moon to Full Moon is waxing, and from there on, it is waning. To determine waxing/waning status between any two planets, the general rule is to take the slower body as the anchor point—treat it like the Sun, in other words. For example, since Venus moves faster than Mars, see if Venus is waxing relative to Mars—that is, between 0° and 180° ahead of Mars in the zodiac. That would then be a waxing Venus-Mars aspect—and it has some of the same active and "forward" quality we see with applying aspects. If Venus were beyond 180° ahead of Mars in the natural order of the signs, it would then be waning aspect.

There are some important wrinkles here, and some unsettled ambivalence. Even though the Sun moves faster than all the planets from Mars on out, it works best to take it as the anchor point, no matter what. Ditto in even more extreme fashion for aspects involving the Moon.

Here we are deferring to the established astrological practice of treating "the Lights" as a special case simply because they are so intrinsically powerful.

ASPECTS IN A NUTSHELL

Each aspect has its own texture and feeling. A book could be written about them. Bil Tierney's Dynamics of Aspect Analysis is good start for deeper understanding of their individual natures. Here, for a start, are some keywords to get you going.

Aspect	Separation	Action
Conjunction	0°	Fusion; formation of one "meta-planet"
Semi-sextile	30°	Clash; annoyance. Waning: Letting go.
Semi-square	45°	Fighting for freedom; endings, awkward transitions.
Sextile	60°	Mutual excitation and stimulus
Quintile	72°	Creativity; inspiration
Square	90°	Blocking; challenge; contradiction
Trine	120°	Mutual enhancement; support
Sesquiquadrate	135°	Tension; breakthrough or breakdown; sacrifice
Bi-quintile	144°	Demands toward transcendence; "the Call"
Quincunx	150°	Adjustment; shared creativity; romance
Opposition	180°	Polarization or Complementarity

PART FOUR

SEEING POSSIBLE FUTURES

For all of us, there is a time to make a stand. There is a time to "make it real."
No matter if your astrological makeup is as Fiery as the heart of the Sun or as
Watery as the bottom of the sea, you will go through these Earth-dominated
crossroads in your life. Often they are times when 51% of you wants to turn right
and 49% of you wants to turn left—only you are afraid you might possibly have
the numbers backwards.

Navigating these forks in the road wisely, in a way that feeds your soul in
the long run, is what this book is all about.

What signals the arrival of these periods? And how can we best prepare for
them and use them intentionally and consciously?

Against the backdrop of your natal chart, there is a constant tidal flow of
moving points: transits, progressions, and solar arcs. They provide the keys to
understanding the dynamics of our journey through life, on a day-by-day, year-
by-year basis.

Sometimes these astrological triggers move into Earth signs or into the
"Earth" houses—two, six and ten. Sometimes they form aspects to Venus, Mer-
cury, or Saturn. At such times, the universe is asking us to put our cards on the
table. To make our stand in a world of hard, imperfect choices.

Meanwhile, those three Earth planets are themselves moving through your
natal chart, hitting sensitive points via their own transits, progressions, and
solar arcs.

All or any of these astrological events mark the outset of Earthy chapters in your journey. These are times when you make the concrete decisions that define the actual shape of your future. As it said on a movie poster I once saw, "What we do in life echoes in eternity."

Astrologers are still often expected to make predictions. Many still do; many are sometimes even correct. But we are not puppets dangling from planetary strings; we are human beings, endowed with magical powers of creativity, learning, aspiration, and—just possibly—wisdom. Those are powerful forces to have on your side. With them as allies, you can regularly make a monkey out of such an astrologer, especially if he or she is predicting doom and gloom for you.

In the pages that follow, we throw away the astrologers' traditional crystal ball. Instead, we use these Earthy events to predict the questions that you will face, and to suggest the answers—which is to say, the conscious choices—that lead you to the higher ground.

You have many possible futures. Astrology can describe them all, and their consequences. It can help you navigate wisely among them. It hands you the menu, in other words. What you choose to eat is up to you.

There is, however, one possibility that does not exist: that these astrological events will not impact you at all. Their energy has been created; it cannot be destroyed, only changed in form. But what actually determines the form these celestial events will take is your own choice —and your own responsibility.

In all of what follows, your ace in the hole is your own magic. You and the planets are co-creating your story. Real-life astrology happens at the interface of consciousness and the vast archetypal fields of possibility that the symbols represent.

You are as powerful as they are.

16

THE EARTH FAMILY AND ASTROLOGY'S CRYSTAL BALL

Okay, win a new Lexus on me—which will hit you harder, a transit of Mercury or a transit of Saturn?

Despite its "no-brainer" appearance, this is actually a trick question. The right answer, at least on an hour by hour basis, is that their powers are approximately equal.

Our reflex—which is of course to point to Saturn—is sound enough in practical terms. Everyone with any astrological experience knows that a Saturn transit is much more likely to alter your direction in life than is a Mercury transit. But here's the deeper point: during that transit of Mercury, your cell phone is ringing and your email inbox is as busy as Gemini on steroids. Friends run into you on the street and talk your ear off. One article surfs off into the next one on the Internet. Somehow, a sudden fascination with aardvarks led you to the history of avocados, and three hours have gone by.

Then, after three or four days, it is all over. Mercury has moved on.

Meanwhile, that Saturn transit is just getting started. It has months left to go—plenty of time to develop *depth and complexity of meaning*.

Time is what makes the difference. That is why, in practical terms, a Saturn transit is a more significant event than a Mercury transit. *It all boils down to how long your consciousness is exposed to the energy.* But we should never lose sight of the fact that while Mercury is passing through a sensitive zone, its impact on your life is every bit as palpable as Saturn's.

One line from our introduction to Part Four really says it all: *real-life astrology happens at the interface of consciousness and the vast archetypal fields of possibility that the symbols represent.* At our human end of the pipeline, it is all about consciousness.

And consciousness is swimming in the river of time.

Maybe once you had a romantic fling with someone. Even though you were ships in the night, the memory is sweet, even tender, and the soul-encounter was intense. It all happened many years ago. It's not forgotten—but months, even years go by when you don't even think of the memories.

On the other hand, perhaps you were partners with someone for a decade or two—married, or something similar. Perhaps you parted many years ago. As we all know, that is a whole different psychological reality. That long relationship shaped you in ways you are probably still figuring out.

Think about the difference: minute by minute, the experience of the fling was almost certainly far more intense than any random sample of minutes from the long partnership.

And yet which sinks more deeply into your bones, a fling or a marriage?

Comparing the impacts of these two human bonds takes us straight to the heart of the matter. *The underlying insights they generate in us about the relationship of consciousness to time underlie the practical application of all predictive theory in astrology.*

At a practical level, everything boils down to this: all the planets, nodes, and angles move through your chart at varying speeds. And in predictive astrology, slowness equals power and impact. Speed, in contrast, equates with transitoriness.

Planets in slow motion establish the grand thematic scheme of a life, while the fast-moving ones operate as triggers, precipitating these themes as specific events.

SOME QUICK DEFINITIONS

There are many different techniques for moving planets and points against the backdrop of the natal chart. In this chapter, my aim is to explore them in broad terms, focusing on the astronomy behind them. It is through the astronomy—their actual observed motions through the sky—that we gain our mission-critical insights into their speed.

In my own practice, I use three of these techniques: *transits, progressions, and solar arcs*. Most readers probably already know the definitions, but I want to make sure that anyone who is new to astrology is up to speed. So here are a few brief words of methodological explanation.

Transits are the actual motions of planets in the sky. If, for example, Venus is currently in Pisces by transit, that is true for everyone. Transits, in other words, are external factors. They are like the weather. Everyone shares them. We just respond to them differently—just like some people find a gray day gloomy, while others may find it poignant and romantic.

Where does Pisces fall in your chart? Do you have any planets in Pisces? The transit of Venus through Pisces is like the radio signal, while your own natal chart is the radio receiver. Are you tuned to the Pisces station? If so, that transit is more likely to have some personal meaning for you.

Progressions work more like an internal biological clock. They are unique to you; while your Mercury is progressing through Virgo, my Mercury might be progressing through Aries.

The theory behind progressions sounds strange—even suspect—but it works reliably: *days are set symbolically equal to years.* If you want to know the positions of your progressed planets on your fortieth birthday, you find out where those planets were in the sky literally forty days after your birth. *Voilà:* those are your progressed planetary positions.

Admittedly, that seems crazy. But the proof is in the pudding: you can count on progressions working as well as you can count on transits, which is to say, very reliably. We are taking the two most fundamental Earth-rhythms—the daily rotational cycle of Earth on its axis and the yearly cycle of Earth's revolution around the Sun—and drawing an equal sign between them. Progressions are a bit like saying, "In human years, our dog Fido is one hundred and two." A symbolic analogy is set up between a human life cycle and the canine one.

Why do progressions work? In all honesty, I have no idea. But I do suspect that progressions sound dubious to me for exactly the same reason that I probably seem as mad as a hatter to the angels.

Another way to say it is that once the notion that the Earth was not flat seemed like lunacy—but science marched on. Well, human science has some more marching ahead of it—we are, in other words, in thinking about progressions talking about one of those actual laws of the universe that we did not hear one word about in high school.

Let's move on to solar arcs.

Solar arcs are really a subset of progressions. We note the distance in degrees that the Sun has progressed by the methods we have just described. Then we add exactly that same "arc" to the rest of the planets, equally. All solar arcs—planets, nodes, the Ascendant, the Midheaven, plus several thousand named asteroids if you really want to drive yourself crazy—move at *exactly the same speed* by this technique.

With small variations, the Sun progresses approximately 1° for every year of your life, so when you turn thirty, it has moved about 30° ahead of where was when you were born. To calculate your solar arcs on your thirtieth birthday, we would then add that same 30° to your Moon, your Mercury, your Ascendant, and all the rest.

(One quick technical note: Earth's orbit around the Sun is elliptical. The effect is that we are moving more slowly during the northern hemisphere summer and more quickly six months later. *So if you were born with the Sun in Capricorn, your solar arcs move slightly faster than someone born with the Sun in Cancer.* The idea that Solar arcs move 1° per year is only a useful approximation. Yours will vary slightly. The average annual motion of the progressed Sun is 59'08".)

Since solar arcs are slaved to the Sun, they reflect the Sun's nature—which is to say they tend, like the Sun, to be more *biographical* and *outward* in their manifestations. Meanwhile, progressions are often more sensitive to evolutions occurring beyond the boundaries of the human ego and the conscious, rational mind. Most of us have had the mysterious experience of waking up one morning and suddenly everything looks very different to us, even though we cannot put our finger on exactly why. Somehow our attitude has shifted. Progressions are more likely to mirror those kinds of deep psychic events. They are not, in other words, quite as linked to the reasoning parts of our minds.

At the same time, let's give your poor ego a break. You need it and it needs you, and solar arcs are its astrological reflecting pool.

THE RHYTHMS OF THE HEAVENS

Throughout the rest of the book, we will fathom all three of these developmental techniques as they relate to the Earth Family. Exploring the grounding, crystallizing, and maturing effects of the transits, progressions, and solar arcs of Venus, Mercury, and Saturn is a big part of it. You will find all of that in the subsequent chapters.

In the rest of this chapter, our focus is more astronomical than astrological. Cycles have rhythms; and before we can do any affective interpretations, we need to get with the Earth beat.

Remember our comparison of the transit of Mercury to a transit of Saturn at the beginning of this chapter? As we saw then, the speed of such events plays a critical role in determining how seriously to take such a configuration interpretively. The core principle is that slower events have time to develop depth and complexity of meaning as they interact with your consciousness over months or years instead of hours or days. That insight about planetary speed leads to bedrock predictive theory: by progression and solar arc, planets move slowly, so these rhythms are all close to the fundamental heartbeat of life.

It is folly to ignore progressions or solar arcs.

With transits, it is more complicated since some of them—Saturn, for example—move slowly enough to sink deeply into us. Others, such as Mercury, will press our buzzer for a few days, then move on, completely forgotten. At the extremes, the Moon transits through all twelve signs in a little less than a month, while languorous Pluto takes two hundred forty eight years to do the same thing.

VENUS AND MERCURY LIVE DOWNTOWN

In the words of the immortal electric guitarist, Jimi Hendrix, Earth is "the third stone from the Sun." It may be a simple poetic statement about our home-world's point of view on the rest of the solar system—but its practical astrological effects are dramatic.

Think of an archery target with its familiar concentric rings. Since the Sun lies at the center of the solar system, let's call it the bull's eye. Since Mercury and Venus orbit closer to the Sun than does the Earth, it is as if they are placed on the first and second rings of the target. Meanwhile, we earthlings are standing out on the third ring—while all the Martians occupy the fourth one, and so on out to the edge of deep space.

Want a peek at Mercury or Venus? Because their orbits circle inside of ours, to look in their general direction is to look, more or less, in the direction of the Sun.

They "live downtown," so to speak.

Just like the rest of the planets, Mercury and Venus frequently form conjunctions with our central star—but unlike the rest of the planets, these conjunctions come in two flavors: *inferior* conjunctions and *superior* conjunctions. Here is what those terms mean: an inferior conjunction occurs when Mercury or Venus lie directly between us and the Sun. A superior conjunction, on the other hand, occurs when they are as far away from us as they can possibly be—on the other side of the Sun, in other words. Either way, they are lined up. As you might imagine, these two kinds of conjunctions are rather different beasts.

No planets other than Mercury and Venus, can possibly form inferior conjunctions with the Sun. For the rest of them, their orbits lie far out in space and the only way they can line up with the Sun is by being directly opposite us, on the other side of the solar system, on the other side of the Sun.

Another practical effect of all of the "downtown" status of Mercury and Venus is that, from our point of view, they can never lie *very far* from the Sun. Again, they are downtown— if we want to see them, that is where we have to look.

* The maximum *elongation* of Mercury from the Sun is 27°—that is as far as it can ever be from the Sun in any astrological chart.
* For Venus, the figure is 47°.
* The only *major* aspect that either of them can ever form with the Sun is the conjunction.

Unless you are working in synastry, and thus entering the fascinating and sometimes surreal "virtual-reality" of the composite chart, you will never in your astrological career have to give a second thought to the meaning of a Venus-Sun square or a Sun-Mercury opposition. They simply do not exist in nature. The geometry of the solar system forbids them.

SPEED

With planets, speed is everything. We have already explored that principle. And Mercury and Venus—at least by transit—are speed demons. They do not have much time to develop the "depth and complexity of meaning" that is characteristic of slower astrological events. For that reason, neither one of them steps full force into the status of true theme-builders until we see them operating by progression or by solar arc.

The solar arcs of Mercury and Venus unfold at the standard pace of about one degree each year. Their progressions, however, are much more complex. As we saw earlier, the actual positions of the planets thirty days after you were born are their progressed positions on your thirtieth birthday. How far have Mercury and Venus moved in the first month of your infancy?

That, as we will soon discover, is a rather slippery question.

Since Mercury and Venus are slaved to the Sun, their *average* daily motion is exactly the same as that of the Sun—59'08", or very slightly less than one degree.

Now, before anybody sends me an email about how his or her Venus is faster than that or slower than that, let me explain myself. What I just wrote is actually accurate, but it is also wildly misleading. The critical word there was "average." The *actual* daily motions of Mercury and Venus vary enormously. They slow down, even stop—or *make a station,* to use the technical term—as they prepare to turn retrograde. And they do the same thing again when they turn direct. Near stations, they are very slow. At stations, they are stopped. Midway between these "stations," they attain impressive speeds.

Their daily motions are, in other words, all over the map. You really need to look at it case-by-case.

Here is an analogy: in the year 2011, the average age of all the humans on the planet was a little bit under thirty-two years. Now, does that fact give you any insight into my age—or into yours? And can you think of a single practical use for that information, even though it is true?

"Average" is a word that can get us into worlds of trouble.

Cutting to the chase, Mercury's maximum daily motion is 1°40', while that of Venus is 1°22'. That is as fast as they can ever go. Their speeds range downward from there— all the way to zero if they happen to be making a station.

Those are daily figures. They refer to *transiting* Mercury and Venus, in other words. For progressions, those same numbers refer to their *yearly* motions. If you happened to be born near a Venus station, the planet might only progress five or six degrees in the first twenty years of your life. If you were born during a faster part of its cycle, Venus might make it through an entire sign in that same length of time.

Venus is retrograde for about forty days out of its 584-day cycle—that is the length of time between successive inferior conjunctions. So, by progression, once Venus turns retrograde, it will stay that way for about forty *years*. This, by the way, is very likely the source of many Biblical references, such as the children of Israel wandering in the wilderness for forty years before entering the Promised Land, or Jesus fasting in the wilderness for forty days—not to mention Noah experiencing some monumentally sour weather for "forty days and forty nights."

That is a big subject, but not one for this book. Bottom line, there is a lot more astrology in the Bible than meets the eye.

By the way, that long Venus cycle has some rather amazing features. After five inferior conjunctions, the planet has traced out a nearly perfect five-pointed star—a *pentangle*. It takes almost exactly eight years to do that by transit, and this is a powerful and relatively underutilized Venus cycle.

I am going to save that subject for *The Book of Air*—we will naturally be taking another look at Venus there due to its rulership of Libra. In that volume, we will also explore the personal meaning of having progressed Venus retrograde during any portion of your life.

In the sky, Mercury is retrograde for an average of about three weeks. Thus, by progression, it remains retrograde for a bit over two decades—a fascinating period of life that we will explore in chapter nineteen. Right now, we are still only getting grounded in the basic rhythms of these Earth-planets. An exploration of their human meaning lies ahead.

In summary, we have learned that, by transit, Mercury and Venus move too quickly to be of very deep evolutionary consequence. In that fashion, they only operate as event-triggers for more important, slower moving, factors. It is only by progression and by solar arc that these two "downtown" planets really begin to shine.

For now, we have one more Earth planet to consider. That is Saturn— and as we will soon see, it is an entirely different creature than Mercury or Venus.

SATURN IN MOTION

The further a planet lies from the Sun, the more slowly it moves forward in its orbit— that, plus its actual trek around the circuit is a lot longer too. The effect is that outer planets take a whole lot longer to move through the twelves signs than do the inner ones. We shift from the realm of months to the realm of decades.

Saturn's distance from the Sun ranges between eight and ten times further out into space than Earth. The result is that Saturn is a slow boat, taking just a little under three decades to make it around the Sun a single time. The precise figure is 29.457 years. That works out to an average daily motion of 2'01"—only about 1/30 of a degree.

Hopefully, you jumped a little bit when you read the term *average* daily motion. As we learned with Mercury and Venus, that figure can be quite misleading. And indeed, in common with the rest of the planets, Saturn slows down, makes a station, and slowly takes off in the opposite direction.

If Saturn takes almost thirty years to transit around the Zodiac, how long would it take to do the same thing by progression? For practical purposes, you can put that one on the back burner. The answer is just under 11,000 years.

As I write these words, I am about seventy years old. Saturn turned retrograde about three weeks before I was born. In all the time I have been alive, Saturn has progressed only about five degrees. For me to experience progressed Saturn coming to a station and turning direct, I would have to live to approximately the age of 115.

Think I will make it? Me neither.

Bottom line, by progression Saturn simply doesn't do very much. Even when it does form an aspect, the event unfolds so slowly that any awareness we might have of it is quite abstract.

I recommend ignoring the progressions of Saturn—and for similar reasons, I would also ignore the progressions of Jupiter, Uranus, Neptune, and Pluto. There is more than enough in astrology that can be relied upon to hit you like the proverbial ton of bricks; given a couple of hours in the counseling room, no practical astrologer has the slightest need to go scraping up subtleties of which humans can be only barely aware.

Never fear: that leaves two faces of Saturn that are capable of changing the direction of your life—Saturn's transits and Saturn's solar arcs.

By transit, as we have seen, Saturn takes about twenty-nine years to get through the twelve signs, and averages approximately 2' of motion per day. That languorous motion gives it plenty of time to develop depth and complexity of meaning. We will detail all of that in psychological and evolutionary terms in subsequent chapters.

Watching Saturn night after night against the starry background, we would see it lose speed, stop in its tracks, then loop backwards in retrograde motion for a while before turning around and advancing again. Just like the rest of the planets, it takes two steps forward, then one step back, then two more steps forward, eternally.

In approximate terms, Saturn generally remains in direct motion for about eight months, followed by four or five months of retrograde motion. The exact figures vary somewhat because of the elliptical qualities of its orbit.

Natally, that means about one out of every three people is born with Saturn retrograde—and of course that means that by transit, Saturn is retrograde about one third of the time.

For our practical purposes, we need to be mindful of Saturn's stations. At these times, its energies are particularly focused and intense. Transiting Saturn making a station conjunct your natal Sun is going to hit you a lot harder than Saturn moving pedal-to-the-metal through the same aspect.

Many an astrologer, seeing either version of that Saturn-Sun conjunction coming up, would likely terrorize you. No need to fear it. That event, in common with all other astrological events, has a higher purpose. It represents an *evolutionary necessity* in the unfolding journey of your soul.

If you get it right—and emphatically you can do that—it can be sweet, if a little tiring, while you are passing through it and precious as you look back upon it.

How can you get it right? Just turn to chapters twenty-one and twenty-two, where all the secrets are revealed.

17

CELESTIAL NAVIGATION I: VENUS TIMES, TAURUS TIMES

No matter how you are wired astrologically, sooner or later Venus is going to step into the spotlight—that, or something in your chart is going to enter Taurus. These are very different events, but they do share common ground. In both cases, it is time to take a deep breath, to quiet yourself enough that you can hear the whispers of your heart, and to trust your deepest animal instincts.

In this chapter, we aim for a global understanding of these two initial kinds of Earth family events, whether they are happening by transit, by progression, or by solar arc.

In the next chapter, we continue our exploration of Venusian or Taurean times, planet by planet, in cookbook fashion.

Let's start with the mysteries of Venus.

STAY MINDFUL OF THE FULL VENUSIAN SPECTRUM

Venus is not just about love and love is not just about romance and sexuality. In working effectively with this planet, we need to remember that its foundations lie even deeper in the psyche than our bonding instincts.

Still, a million years of evolution has hardwired us humans to cling to each other—sometimes sweetly and other times like crazy people. It is difficult for us to look beyond love when Venus rears its beguiling head.

When I am preparing to record astrological readings for clients who live far away, I always invite them to fill me in on any questions or concerns they might currently have. Almost invariably, people ask about their relationships—or their lack of relationships. This is of course completely understandable and appropriate. Our sense of well-being is permanently hooked to our love-lives. I am like that; you are probably like that too. So much of the human journey really boils down to the dance we do with people we love, or are trying to love.

This is definitely Venus territory. We will soon attempt to fathom it. The trouble is, issues around love are so emotionally pressing that they can eclipse other dimensions of Venus. And as we will soon see, some of those other dimensions are not only hugely significant—but they must also be gotten right if our intimate lives are going to rest on a solid foundation.

VENUS AND STRESS REDUCTION

Life is stressful and stress kills. There's a train wreck for you.

Self-help gurus living in ivory towers counsel us to avoid people and situations that spike our blood pressure. Good luck with that one. It is impossible to live in a human body in the human world without a significant amount of headbanging.

Even worse, the effects of all that stress are cumulative; they build up inside us, damaging our entire body-mind-spirit ecology. If we do not find some kind of safety valve, eventually our hearts explode—sometimes literally.

Everything that happens in your chart represents an evolutionary necessity. You *need* your transits, progressions, and solar arcs to happen, even if it does not feel that way. When Venus comes along, necessity *numero uno* is to monitor your stress levels as mindfully as you can. Necessity *numero dos* is to actually do something about them. Ultimately everything depends upon those two steps—even, as we will soon see, your love life.

The quintessential Venusian act is simply to take a deep breath and let it out. If you do that right now as you are reading these words, you will experience something very much like a mini-Venus transit, especially on that out-breath. You can feel your body relaxing; you can probably feel your mind relaxing too.

Friends supporting each other in times of stress often say, "Remember to breathe." And it is excellent advice.

Speaking of breathing has perhaps already triggered thoughts of *meditation* in you. "Follow the breath" is of course a familiar spiritual instruction, and well it should be. In a Venusian time, meditation practice can be a powerful support in reducing your stress levels.

Meditation, however, comes in a variety of flavors, and some of them can be unsettling. I am thinking of shamanic practices, vision quests in the wilderness, or some of the fiercer insight-oriented techniques such as *vipassana*. These techniques, however effective they are as spiritual practices, can run counter to what you actually need during a Venusian time. What you need then, above all, is simply a dose of *serenity*. If meditation leaves you feeling peaceful during a Venusian or Taurean time, it is serving your soul very well.

If it makes the hair on the back of your neck stand up, save that spiritual practice for a Plutonian period in your life.

Always, before you think of relationships, remember the heart of the matter: when Venus steps into the spotlight, your most pressing evolutionary necessity is stress reduction.

The wisest move you can make is to prioritize peace.

VENUSIAN TRANSITS, PROGRESSIONS, SOLAR ARCS

A Venus transit, as we saw in the previous chapter, is a brief event. It is probably not going to change your life in any significant way—it just doesn't stick around long enough to accomplish that. In common with the rest of the inner planet transits, such a Venus transit functions primarily as a trigger in the context of larger developmental themes.

Illustration: you might, for example, be experiencing transiting Uranian earthquakes—major moves, relationship changes, and so on. Those existential temblors may be necessary, but they are also very likely to be pegging your stress meter in its red zone.

In the midst of that Uranian year, along comes a brief Venus transit. It only lasts for a few days—but in those few days, the immutable laws of synchronicity assure us that an opportunity to reduce stress will arise. Your job is to recognize it and seize it. A friend offers you a quiet weekend at the beach. Your favorite songwriter comes to town. Your partner offers to rub your feet.

By progression and solar arc, Venus is slow enough to emerge in its full archetypal glory. We will then see the entire spectrum of Venusian possibilities emerging. We will detail all of that in the next few pages, but underlying it all is that core principle: whether we know it or not, Venus times are always about the familiar quest for psychic and existential equilibrium.

Astrologers generally do not associate Venus with crisis, and yet the word has some hidden relevance here. Again, we invoke the notion of the basic Venusian evolutionary necessity: *calming down*. You may not be "in crisis" in any obvious sense of the word, but the hidden crisis is that you are actually at risk of becoming estranged from your own soul. Your heart is trying desperately to get your attention. It is wise to make time to hear it.

The irony is that, while you might not be in an obvious crisis, you could be setting yourself up for a crisis down the road. Your ego might be making choices that your soul would never make—and which you will need to undo somehow as the pages of the calendar turn.

How can you avoid falling into that snare? Take a breath. Go for a walk. Quiet your mind. Get off the treadmill. Feel rather than think. Ask your body for its opinion.

French war hero and later president, Charles de Gaulle, lost a valued member of his cabinet to death— a man who was viewed as "indispensable." Queried about how he could possibly go forward without this man's able assistance, de Gaulle had an utterly Scorpionic response: "The graveyards of the world are full of indispensable men."

In a Venus time or a Taurus time, just go "be dead somewhere" for a little while. The world will muddle through somehow without your assistance.

IMMERSING YOUR SENSES IN BEAUTY

You are walking south on a city street in late afternoon. You make a right turn, so now you are heading west—directly into the face of a glorious, once-in-a-blue-moon, psychedelic sunset. The sheer beauty of it stops you in your tracks. Your eyes widen.

And you sigh.

The ballerina leaps to the center of the stage; she pirouettes; she looks otherworldly, as if she were made of vapor. You have rarely seen anything so lovely. Your eyes widen; you settle into your seat.

Again, you sigh.

Physiologically, what is a sigh? It is a release of tension. And that, as we have seen, is exactly the evolutionary purpose of a Venusian period. When our senses perceive anything harmonious, we embrace the object. We internalize its harmony; it thus turns into inner harmony. We sigh; in other words, we release tension in order to get into synch with the desirable perception.

The beauty of nature and the beauty that humans create—during a Venus time, immersing our senses in either one of them is an effective remedy for accumulated stress. And because of synchronicity, such opportunities are very likely to abound. The universe is trying its best to take care of us. Go out and hear some music. Buy a piece of art. Sit in a garden. Vacation in some knockout beautiful place.

You can further supercharge these Venusian stress-reducing techniques by *actively pursuing your own creativity*. Dust off that old guitar. Pluck one string—and listen until you can't hear it anymore. Write poetry. Arrange flowers. Cook a fancy meal. Take a painting class.

You will find peace in the beauty that you create.

HOW'S ABOUT A HUG?

A few pages back I wrote, "Venus is not just about love and love is not just about romance and sexuality." So far, we have been trying to keep our spectrum of inquiry broad by focusing on Venus in two of its archetypal manifestations: the goddess of *peace* and the goddess of the *arts*.

With the word "hug," we begin to edge into that classic Venusian territory: human intimacy. We meet Venus as the goddess of *love*.

Friends hug. Family members hug. Lovers hug. We hug our pets. Lately we even hug relative strangers.

The meaning of that primal human gesture varies from relationship to relationship, but it pretty much always feels good. A hug lowers our blood pressure, it comforts us in grief or defeat, and it dots the "i" in our happiness. When it comes to stress reduction, a hug is one of the sovereign human remedies—and that is the link in the chain that ties everything we have explored so far to where we are going . . .

YOU ARE GOING TO MEET SOMEONE . . .

As we contemplate our spiritual and psychological journeys, is there any category of experience more fundamental to us than the dance we do with our loved ones? For most of us, love—for better or for worse—defines the chapters of our lives.

And with astrology being the mirror of the soul, it follows that the timing and the meaning of our intimate encounters is unerringly reflected in our charts.

In all my years of astrological practice, I have never seen a significant relationship start unless it was heralded by transits, progressions, or solar arcs. That is a principal which seems never to fail. Someone might "meet a soul mate" on Thursday and be broken up by Sunday afternoon—that probably has more to do with hormones, need, and opportunity than with any major astrological activity.

But every now and then the Real Deal comes along. The outset of that new relationship marks the first sentence in one of the major chapters in the book of your life.

No surprise: the astrological events behind those kinds of developments often involve Venus, either by progression or arc, or via some stimulus of its natal placement.

The words "meeting someone" of course immediately invoke images of romance—and romance is indeed part of the picture we are painting here. But let's also remember to honor other sorts of significant relationships. The angels are paying close attention on the day you meet someone who will become your dearest friend. How could it be otherwise? Ditto for the day you meet a significant creative partner, or someone with whom you might build a business. Carl Jung, for one example, met Sigmund Freud on February 27, 1907—exactly one week after his progressed Moon made a conjunction with his natal Venus.

In working skillfully with this planet, it is imperative that we do not allow our compelling fascination with sexuality to blind us to the priceless treasure of other forms of intimacy. We all know how precious our friends are to us. Haven't they fed our souls? Aren't we different because of them?

Wouldn't our lives be diminished without them? Friendships hit all the Venusian evolutionary bases, in other words.

Bottom line: always keep one eye on friendship when you are looking at any imminent progressions or solar arcs of the planet Venus. Otherwise you might miss something important.

Be careful not to fall into the trap of "predicting romance" for a client, who later comes back complaining that she hasn't even "had a date"—all the while you both ignore the fact that she's a lyricist who just found a compatible composer. They're now writing songs together, and doors are opening for both of them that neither one of them could ever have opened on her own.

Underlying that little anecdote, is another basic point: *fundamental to the evolutionary reality of a Venusian time is that in order for us to go forward, we need some help.* We are learning about trust and interdependency, and no one can do that work alone. There is no harm in giving yourself a hug, but it is markedly more satisfying if you have a helping hand.

Furthermore, because of the ever-reliable principle of synchronicity, we can count on such help actually being available. The only question is, do we recognize it? Are we humble enough to ask for it? And always remember that the help might not come packaged as a romance. Sigmund Freud's spiritual impact on the youthful Carl Jung was life-changing. Even though they eventually parted on unpleasant terms, Jung could not have formulated his understanding of the human psyche without Freud. Jung "couldn't have done it without him."

And, to my knowledge, they never slept together.

CUTTING TO THE CHASE

We may love our friends—that's what we have just been celebrating—but most of us would crawl over forty miles of broken glass to be with our beloved. The love between life-partners is a different beast than friendship. Calling that *coupling* kind of relationship "sexual" intimacy is of course accurate, but the term sounds a little bit too biological for me. Sexual intercourse is naturally part of such a relationship, but only a pornographer would ignore the other 99% of the recipe.

Being called a "friend" usually feels good—but there is one circumstance in which the word feels like a kick in the belly. That is when our lover suggests that perhaps we should "just be friends."

In that context, everyone understands that "friend" indicates a serious demotion.

Do the math: *subtract "friend" from "lover" and the remaining quotient is the particular Venusian mystery we are trying to fathom here.* Very little in life is more compelling.

So far in this chapter, my strategy has been to avoid writing very much about sexual love. That was because I know that once we fall into its gravitational field, other subjects quickly fade into the background.

Now that we are standing on a broad enough theoretical foundation, let's jump into that wild, ancient ocean—a place in our lives where our mammal-brains and our immortal souls are trying to hammer out a deal that works for both of them: sexual love.

UH OH . . .

"You're going to meet someone"—I say those words to a young person, and I am typically met with a look of joy and hope.

I say exactly the same words to someone who is forty-five years old, and I might hear, *"uh oh . . ."*

Not to be cynical here, but how often in your life has "meeting someone" led ultimately to happiness? By the time we are in life's long middle, we have all had our hearts broken. Sexual love is dangerous. People sometimes commit suicide or homicide over it—or, in order to steer clear of those grisly temptations, they spend thousands of dollars on psychotherapy.

In the jungles of sexual love, there are predators. The walking-wounded abound, looking for love—and fearing it too. Sex and love are famously easy to confuse. Two good people fall in love—and six months later, after investing their hearts in the relationship, they realize that it is just not going to work. With every heartbreak, trusting becomes a little bit more difficult.

Working with the planet Venus is not for the faint-hearted.

Still, when true love flowers, there is no greater treasure available to anyone on this earth. The comfort of a soul-companion on the journey— ask a lonely or ill-married rich person how the value of such a bond compares to the value of money. Life is sweeter when it is shared. Memories held by two people put more smiles on faces than memories that no one else recalls or cares about. These are ancient human truths.

With Venus, the stakes are very high. That's why you can walk into any bookstore and find a shelf twenty feet long full of self-help books about relationships. All of us—with very few exceptions—are highly motivated to get Venus right.

But how?

In the first few pages of this chapter, we recognized that when Venus comes along, we must remember to breathe. We must cultivate serenity. Such a progression or solar arc indicates that the level of buzz in our heads has reached dangerous proportions. Specifically, we are at risk of no longer being able to hear the soft, wise voice of our own souls.

And it is the voice of the soul which we must hear clearly and without distortion if we are going to make healthy intimate choices.

This is the critical connection. This insight is an essential link in our chain. This is where all the various threads in our understanding of Venus come together in a single tapestry. *It is only in the silence of the soul that we can recognize our natural partner.* It is only there that we can sort through the biological noise of our sexuality, the madness of our childhoods, and the erotic toxins of our culture.

Love is exciting. We need to be careful of that. When love looms, close your eyes. Take a breath. Take a moment to love yourself. When you are as still as a lake at dawn, ask your heart: *are my path and this person's path one and the same?*

WHEN THE BULL BELLOWS: TAURUS

The sign Taurus and the planet Venus are not interchangeable, but they are connected. They share a lot of common ground. They have an affinity for each other. As we translate astrological symbolism into English, we naturally find ourselves using many of the same words to describe both of them. Here, in *The Book of Earth*, I have emphasized the Taurean side of the Venusian equation—hence the focus on calm, the wisdom of the body, and staying grounded.

In *The Book of Air*, we will explore the Libran face of Venus. That will give us a different perspective on the planet—one that is complementary rather than contradictory, but which will take us down some fresh roads.

Even if you were born with nothing in Taurus, the sign impacts your natal chart. Taurus is probably on the cusp of a house. If not, then it is certainly intercepted—that is, swallowed up—by a house. In either case, its energy and motivational agenda are relevant to that part of your life. Taurus may not be a central theme from the evolutionary perspective, but the Taurean stamp is always there in everyone's chart. We are all built from the same twelve signs; it is only the roles, ratios, and mixture of them that make us different from each other.

Taurus might only play a bit part in the drama of your life—but even if that is true in general, there will be times when that bit player takes center stage. That happens when, by transit, progression, or solar arc, a planet is passing through that territory.

By transit, if I currently have a planet in Taurus, so do you. Transits are universal. As I write these words in 2019, the planet Uranus is passing through Taurus. It is affecting everyone; it is shaping history. But what does that mean for you personally? We answer that question by considering which of your astrological houses Uranus is currently occupying, along with what particular aspects it is forming to your natal chart.

Here is a quick personal example: Uranus is currently in my sixth house. That suggests the need for changes in my daily routines and my patterns of responsibility. If I heed my own heart, those changes would reflect my placing more value on serenity.

Sure enough, this year I have cut out quite a lot of my teaching-related travel in order to make time to write this series of Elements books. In the grounding spirit of Taurus, that decision has been a stress-reducing move for me. I love being home in the beautiful Anza-Borrego desert with my partner Michelle, and I love writing. I also mightily relish spending less time in TSA queues at various airports—and having less exposure to the tender mercies of the airline industry is an added stress-reduction boon.

We will take a long, deep look at the planet Uranus in *The Book of Air*. In a word, you cannot simultaneously be true to the Uranian impulses and win every popularity contest. Not everyone has been happy about my teaching less—I myself have not been entirely happy about it. But it was the right thing to do: in a nutshell, it was time for a *revolution* (Uranus) in my *routines* (sixth house) that edged me toward the possibility of greater *serenity* (Taurus)— with the mysterious underlying promise that, in that serenity, I would better hear the voice of my soul as it aimed me in some new, unimagined directions.

TAURUS COMES AFTER ARIES

That simple statement about the natural order of the Zodiacal signs provides a key that unlocks a big part of our understanding of a planet passing through Taurus. Back in *The Book of Fire*, we explored Aries deeply. In those pages, we conjured up an image—not of a testosterone-addled Viking warrior—but rather of a feisty, newly-hatched robin. Against all the odds, that little bird is fighting to survive. That's Aries—it is about *claiming a right to exist.* It is about *assertiveness.* It is about *courage*—and the challenging experiences which might teach us about courage.

Aries territory: *every organism has a right to defend itself.*

More Aries territory: if we love, there is also an implicit contract of *mutual defense*—only the lowest kind of traitor would run from a friend in need.

No matter how peaceful our instincts might be, sooner or later something comes along that wants to eat our lunch. If we don't fight, we will surely starve. That is Aries too.

After any such episode, you would naturally welcome a little peace and quiet.

There's Taurus.

Famously, to win a war is difficult—but winning the peace is even more difficult. After great effort comes the need for rest. After stress comes healing and renewal. After noise, we appreciate silence. If you have had an awful, exhausting, combative day, maybe you've been dreaming of finally being able to get into bed, to relax and sleep. But come bed time, your nervous system is so buzzed that you cannot fall asleep.

It takes conscious effort to release Aries and enter Taurus. There is an art to it.

When planets are passing through Aries, the lessons the soul is trying to learn are fiery ones. Inevitably, they create stress. It cannot be avoided. No matter if we succeed or fail—in either case the aftermath leaves us over-stimulated and shaky.

Taurus is the remedy. *Taurus, in other words, can be understood as a reaction against the excesses or extremes of Aries.*

That is actually a principal which can be followed productively around the entire circle of the twelve signs—Gemini can cure the excesses or extremes of Taurus, for example. Cancer cures Gemini, Leo cures Cancer, Virgo cures Leo . . . and so on around the circle.

As a planet crosses into Taurus, we echo the point that we underscored about Venus at the outset of this chapter: the bottom line is *stress reduction*. Coming as it does on the heels of Aries, we recognize that the evolutionary purpose of Taurus revolves around *healing, recovery, and restoration*. Many of the positive strategies we explored in connection with Venus are operative here in Taurus as well: it is time to take a deep breath and let it out slowly. We benefit from exposure to art. We are calmed by meaningful touch and the presence of people whom we love.

To that Venusian list, we would add some additional—and particularly Taurean—strategies. Any of them can help you. Try them all, and you will be breathing easily again before you know it.

* *The healing power of silence* is fundamental to our understanding of the psychic mysteries of this sign.
* Paradoxically, *music*—even though it is obviously not silent—has the effect of silencing us inwardly, and that inner silence is really the point. Time spent listening to music is a potent Taurean remedy.
* Hours or days spent in *nature* are precious and effective in such times.
* *Working with our hands*, especially with *natural materials*, soothes the Taurean soul: thus, for example, weaving, making pottery, woodworking, and gardening all come to mind.
* *Yoga, tai chi*, and *dance* are all indicated.
* Contact with our *four-footed, winged, and finny friends* is enormously comforting and helpful as well.

And you really, really need a hug.

The last couple of lines are intended as a set of specific behavioral suggestions that can effectively assist us during times of Taurean stimulation. I am much happier, by the way, presenting astrological counsel that way—as suggestions—rather than dictating a set of predictions.

Still, because of synchronicity, we can with some confidence foresee that opportunities for the kinds of healing experiences I have just cataloged are likely to present themselves. As ever, the universe—as it emerges in the practice of astrology—is an incubator of consciousness. It is, in other words, always trying to help us. That help works best if we are willing to help ourselves.

We can confidently predict the emergence of these kind of supportive opportunities. What we cannot predict—but perhaps we can actively support—is whether the horse will drink from the water to which it has been so kindly led.

Going further, periods of Taurean stimulus reflect an evolutionary intention to ground ourselves in our instinctual natures. We need to hear that proverbial *still, small voice within*—that unique and trans-rational set of inner promptings that can potentially guide us unerringly through life's various mazes and conundrums: whom should we love and trust, in what should we believe, where should we live, and so on.

To attain that level of quiet inner attunement, we must dump some of our load of stress. There is too much noise in your head. Over-thinking is tying you in knots. And the whole mess is propelled by that underlying stress.

The ultimate aim is always the same: to tune in to that quiet place of simple knowing that exists in every human heart. Such a Taurean time plants an inner, transrational, instinctual sense in hearts—a psychic compass needle that eventually points to the Capricorn mountains we need to climb and the Virgoan teachers, mentors, and methods that will help us scale the peak.

We vex ourselves with foolish ambitions, frivolous desires, and the internalized craziness of our societies and our families. After a while, the madness metastasizes into a lifestyle. We may sense that we are entangled in situations that seem to be beyond our control. How did I get here? Whose life is this anyway? And how do I escape from this bizarre estrangement from my true self?

All of the right answers begin with Taurean silence.

18

TAURUS TIMES, VENUS TIMES: THE BUILDING BLOCKS

The moving Venus can step onto center stage in your life by transit, by progression, or by solar arc. Each one of those techniques plucks a different string on your psychic harp.

The transits of Venus, as we have just seen, are brief. They may be intense while they are happening, but they soon pass. Think of a romantic film that puts tears in your eyes for two hours. Then compare it to an affair that puts tears in your eyes, perhaps in a different way, for two years. Both are impactful—but which one are you going to recall in a past-life regression five hundred years from now? That's one way to compare the transits of Venus with its solar arcs and progressions. The latter two hang around a lot longer. They get into your bones. They change you in fundamental ways.

Venus changing house or changing sign by either of these slower methods is a real game-changer. Back in chapters nine and twelve, we looked at Venus in the twelve signs and houses in the context of the natal chart. With a little imagination, you can reframe all that material in terms of progressions and solar arcs. Read such changes as the emergence of a new developmental stage in your life—one with a new set of alliances, new fascinations, new underlying evolutionary aims, and new methods of rest and recovery.

Maybe you can skillfully see such a change as natural evolution. For example, imagine years of Venus progressing through hot, passionate Aries. Might you get to a point in your life when you could use a little peace, stability, and normalcy in your relationships? Easily, huh? That's Venus exiting Aries and entering Taurus.

In milder, more transitory ways, we can apply similar thinking to the transits of Venus into new signs or houses.

As Venus travels around the chart, it also interacts with your natal planets via aspects. That will be our particular focus in much of this chapter. Long ago, astrologers realized that when a planet crosses a position that was previously held by another planet on the day you were born, things got busy in your life—and that what happened seemed to reflect a blend of the natal planet and the moving one. Thus was born the doctrine of astrological aspects.

As our understanding deepened, our astrological grandparents also figured out that a planet moving opposite the position another one occupied at birth worked pretty well too—thus the *opposition* aspect entered collective awareness. And the system proliferated from there. As we saw in our chapter about aspects, there are now a large number of these triggering geometrical angles in our arsenal of astrological theory, each with its own texture and significance.

You do not want to read an encyclopedia and I don't want to write one. And that is what it would take to describe all of the possibilities. In chapter fifteen, we described eleven aspects, with five of them viewed as "major." All but the conjunction and the opposition have waxing and waning forms, making a total of twenty distinct aspects all together—and that's limiting ourselves to the eleven I described. There are others as well—*deciles, quindeciles, noviles, bi-noviles* . . .

There are ten things we currently call planets, plus the lunar nodes, plus the four Angles. Each one of them can form most of those twenty aspects with any one of the others, as well as with their own natal positions.

I don't want to do the arithmetic, let alone write it all out. You probably don't want to read about the arithmetic either.

Even that long list would be incomplete: Venus squaring a Libran Sun presents a very different prospect than Venus squaring a Sagittarian one.

The brain quickly boggles. Even publishing a short paragraph about each one of these possibilities would lead to serious deforestation somewhere.

Faced with such complexity, our only hope is to learn how to *think astrologically*. Otherwise the sheer number of possible astrological combinations overwhelms the mind.

Fear not; we do have an ace in the hole. Never forget our North Star when it comes to aspects: *every one of them, regardless of its nature, is ultimately about integration*. Keep that one principle foremost in your mind and the whole situation becomes a lot less daunting. Regardless of the specifics, two archetypal fields are trying to find a way to cooperate in your head. Understand those two symbols—and the shape of their possible dance—and you are off to a solid start.

Maybe transiting Saturn (*your need for solitude*) is interacting aspectually with your natal Venus—*you love your partner, but you need a little space*.

Maybe solar arc Venus is making an aspect with Mars, the "war god." Can you learn the art of *constructive conflict*? Can you do your part in injecting a little *more passion* into the intimate mix?

These are big subjects, but those few words really demonstrate how you actually put the pieces together. That is how we "think astrologically." It is not that difficult; it is not like you have to learn the secret handshake or some magical password. You have actually been thinking this way all your life—all we are really doing is taking plain-English words such as "love" and "solitude," looking at them through the X-ray machine of astrology—and with its help, becoming about ten times smarter than any of us would otherwise be.

In the "cookbook" pages that follow, we offer some hints, key words, and general guidelines about how the moving Venus might best integrate—via any aspect—with each one of the other planets. Later on in the chapter, we take a look at the impact of each planet as it moves through Taurus.

True astrological mastery arises only when we can skillfully hear all the grace notes and subtleties. My hope is that these simple formulas help you make a good start in that direction.

VENUS CONTACTING THE SUN

How Best to Reduce Your Stress Load: Stand up for yourself. Ask for what you want. Insist on having your critical needs met. Look your best. Dress as if you are proud of yourself—it affects how people see you. Hold your head high. Expect to be taken seriously—and to be liked. Do something creative—and make sure that at least a few people know about it. Reach out to someone; make yourself available and obvious.

Most Beneficial Aesthetic Input: Anything big and bright. Spectacles; heroism; drama. Anything noble, reflecting high aspirations and the basis for human dignity. Anything that dramatizes someone prevailing against the odds, injustice, or resistance.

What You Need To Learn About Love and Trust: That you are still worthy of love even when you are up front about your needs. Ditto, when you are clear about what is not acceptable to you. That you must put yourself forward if there is to be any chance of your being seen and appreciated. That it is not fair of you to expect that others will understand your needs via some supernatural power of perception. Speak up and be straightforward.

How to Identify Your Soul-Helpers: They are colorful and direct. You know exactly where you stand with them. They can "perform," even when you are the only one in the audience—and they clap generously for your performances too. They are spontaneous; they seem to move comfortably and without self-consciousness through the social world. They have a certain animal magnetism, *gravitas,* or charisma.

What Happens If You Squander the Opportunity: A tense feeling arises, as if you needed some release that never came. Insecurity triggers outward displays which others read as vanity. You feel caught in "playing a part," perhaps representing a character whom you do not like very much.

VENUS CONTACTING THE MOON

How Best To Reduce Your Stress Load: Spend time at home, if your home is peaceful—and if it's not peaceful, move if you can! Be self-indulgent. Be kind to yourself. Listen to your body. Sleep a lot—dreams are restorative, and sleep is how to have them. Eat well. Go see your soul-family, even if they live far away.

Most Beneficial Aesthetic Input: Soft light: candlelight, firelight, literal moonlight. Silence. Trancing out to beautiful music. Being near bodies of water. Spending time outside at night. Fine fabrics; quilts; comforters. Romantic films and literature, especially familiar ones.

What You Need To Learn About Love and Trust: That real trust comes slowly and is earned over time. That there is no one as precious as an old friend, tried and true. That you need family—and that the meaning of the word "family" might be different for you from what is written in the dictionary. That the ultimate expression of love and trust is shared vulnerability in a spirit of long-term commitment.

How to Identify Your Soul-Helpers: They are comfortable expressing emotions of tenderness and vulnerability. They are comfortable when you do the same thing; they make that kind of sharing easy for you. They have a personal history of long-term relationships. There is a good chance that they love their families and are involved with them in ongoing ways. They are not afraid of commitment.

What Happens If You Squander the Opportunity: A spirit of lassitude arises—not quite depression—rather something more like just not caring very much. Temptations become harder to resist; it is as if your defenses against your own runaway appetites has collapsed. You make self-destructive intimate choices as laziness and emotionality eclipse your ability to make sober assessments of reality.

VENUS CONTACTING MERCURY

How Best To Reduce Your Stress Load: Deep, open-ended conversation with someone you love and whose company you enjoy. Arrange a situation in which you are confident that you are truly being heard by someone who cares about you. You need to engage your mind and your senses with a fresh face of the world. Get out and do things that expose you to new ideas and new experiences, especially ones with significant aesthetic dimensions.

Most Beneficial Aesthetic Input: Read poetry. Read literary novels. Watch films made for grown-ups. Travel to beautiful places. Pick up the house, make it pretty. Go to museums. Visit a planetarium. Look through a telescope at the heavens. Gaze at anything beautiful.

What You Need To Learn About Love and Trust: That love and trust thrive on a diet of patient, respectful communication conducted in a spirit of genuine mutual interest and inquiry. That being heard—and your words being remembered—builds a bond of trust between people. That feeling ignored, dismissed, taken for granted—or simply not heard at all—erode the bridge of affection.

How to Identify Your Soul-Helpers: Words come easily to them; they can express themselves fluently and clearly. They display a vibration of mental quickness. They listen well too. They are probably witty; they make you laugh—and to think in new ways.

What Happens If You Squander the Opportunity: Your words begin to feel scripted and phony, as if you are simply saying your lines in a play of manners. Talk, talk, talk—and it is all forgotten by the next day. The triumph of propriety over honesty; the triumph of diplomatic stability over genuine process. Polite words building a wall between souls.

VENUS CONTACTING VENUS

How Best To Reduce Your Stress Load: Say "I love you" to someone who deserves to hear it. Hear the same words yourself—and believe them. Take the risk of making genuine heart-contact with someone whom you hold in affection; blow out the walls of deadening habit; freshen your love. Meet new people, but only if they really interest you. Trust any instinctual feelings of fondness that arise in you toward anyone. Pretty yourself up and look approvingly at yourself in the mirror.

Most Beneficial Aesthetic Input: Anything that makes you sigh when you hear it, see it, feel it, or smell it. Shared aesthetic experiences are more effective than solo ones—attend a concert with a friend whose company gives you pleasure, for example. Go to art galleries. Enjoy something expensive; share it, if possible.

What You Need To Learn About Love and Trust: That courtship, displays of respect, and simple courtesy nurture love and trust. That when people love each other they savor their hours together; they are patient; they take time with each other. In the kind of sexuality that is meaningful and lasting, the eyes are more important than the genitals.

How to Identify Your Soul-Helpers: They are naturally courteous and comfortable to be around—polite without being formal or stiff about it. They move fluidly through varying social landscapes; they seem to know how to get along with different kinds of people. They present themselves well and gracefully; their grooming and clothing reflect mindfulness and taste without pretense.

What Happens If You Squander the Opportunity: Your life devolves into something resembling a boring cocktail party, full of empty chit-chat and obligatory social interactions. Your appetites loom pressingly in exaggerated fashion, promising relief, as a kind of low-level social anxiety takes its subliminal toll on you.

VENUS CONTACTING MARS

How Best To Reduce Your Stress Load: Get all sweaty. Exercise. Dance. Enthusiastic, uninhibited sexual expression works magic. Walk on the wild side. Have an adventure. Break up your intimate routines; do something different—or, if you are doing something familiar, do it in a different place.. Above all, if an issue has been festering in any of your primary relationships, now is the time to put it on the table and deal with it.

Most Beneficial Aesthetic Input: Passionate, loud music—whether it is Beethoven, hip hop, or rock 'n roll, *turn it up* and move your body to it. Anger crystallized in art; bright colors, bold contrasts. Novels and films portraying courage, heroic scenes, and grand adventures. Tales of conflict, especially ones where the good guys win in the end.

What You Need To Learn About Love and Trust: That love and anger are not opposites, but rather a complementary pair. Without the healthy expression of anger and resentment, love and trust are diminished. If you are in a sexual partnership, you are invited to participate in an ancient mystery: that humans can literally *make* love—that is, enhance and deepen their sense of connection—in sexual union.

How to Identify Your Soul-Helpers: They are direct and honest with you. They have presence and intensity. Often, no matter their physical appearance, they possess an ineffable quality of sexiness. You know where you stand with them. They are fiercely loyal—but if you do something which displeases them, you will quickly hear about it.

What Happens If You Squander the Opportunity: Pointless conflicts arise. People blow off steam—which is to say, squabbles arise which have little to do with any of the actual issues underlying the tensions: arguments about money that are sublimated arguments about sex or family dynamics. Alternatively, necessary negotiations are entirely avoided, leading to a mood of frustration and unspoken resentment.

VENUS CONTACTING JUPITER

How Best To Reduce Your Stress Load: Be your own Santa Claus. Give yourself a gift; spend some money on yourself; blow off responsibilities and have some fun. Dress in bright colors. Take center stage, at least in front of your friends—tell a joke. Tell a mostly-true story about yourself, one that puts you in a good light, and do not be afraid to embellish it a bit for effect.

Most Beneficial Aesthetic Input: Something "above your pay grade" in any category: buy a beautiful painting, upgrade your sound system, go shopping and purchase something personal of impressive quality that you can barely afford. Buy yourself expensive tickets to a performance that attracts you. Dress up when you attend it. Do everything you can to like what you see when you look in the mirror.

What You Need To Learn About Love and Trust: That generosity of spirit is precious and essential to the maintenance of an attitude of love and trust. By generosity of spirit, we mean a supportive attitude, a spirit of forgiveness and radical acceptance, and the expression of sincere joy at the other person's victories. You must both offer and receive this kind of affirmation. Now is the time to assure that it is flowing. Shared laughter builds love and trust; make time for some giggles.

How to Identify Your Soul-Helpers: They are big-hearted, generous spirits. They laugh easily. Look carefully and you will also detect a hint of *star quality* in them, as if in a parallel universe, they could be in the film industry. They *believe in you*, perhaps even more than you believe in yourself. Their presence lifts your spirits; when they walk into the room, your reflex is to smile.

What Happens If You Squander the Opportunity: You overreach in a relationship, making unconsciously-selfish assumptions about another person's generosity—or level of duty—toward you. You lord it over someone, creating a reaction of resentment in them. Without realizing it, you make yourself look silly, "entitled," or foolish.

VENUS CONTACTING SATURN

How Best To Reduce Your Stress Load: Even if you are in a happy, satisfying relationships, you might simply need some time to yourself. Do not let a misguided sense of duty or responsibility prevent you from asking for it. Laughter and fun feed the life-force—but so does seriousness. You need some of that seriousness with your partner or your friends right now. What is the *next developmental stage* in these intimacies? It is time to take those steps together. That may not be easy—but the thus-far unmet need to take those steps is the source of the underlying tension that you are feeling.

Most Beneficial Aesthetic Input: Some artists in every discipline have functioned almost like a priesthood, mediating between human beings and the enormity of life's real issues: love's difficulties, the reality of loss and defeat, mortality. Exposure to such serious art is helpful to you now; mere entertainment will seem hopelessly trivial. Listening carefully and deeply to a symphony utilizes a different part of your consciousness than does tapping your feet to a pop song; that "symphonic" place is the part of your consciousness which needs to be fed at this juncture of your life.

What You Need To Learn About Love and Trust: That loyalty, reliability, and commitment are essential to the maintenance of love and trust. That people need to keep their word. That vows and promises kept and honored are the life-blood of any lasting human bond in the adult world. That relationships, just like people, need to grow up—and that the process never ends. What worked just fine in a high school fling no longer works in our forties or our fifties.

How to Identify Your Soul-Helpers: They radiate competence. You can trust them—not only to have good intentions, but also to execute those intentions effectively. They are good at what they do. They show up on time. They can laugh—but they can also be serious. They do not hide from life behind humor. They will never make a joke out of your attempts to be serious.

What Happens If You Squander the Opportunity: Loneliness arises. That word might have its usual, straightforward meaning: you might find yourself isolated or alone. What you are not recognizing, if that is the case, is the evolutionary necessity of some solitude now. Try to appreciate it. Alternatively, loneliness can arise within a relationship or a crowd. That happens when we are still interacting with people whom we have outgrown, or when we have failed to do the hard work of actually growing the relationship.

VENUS CONTACTING URANUS

How Best To Reduce Your Stress Load: Break out of the tyranny of your own routines and habits. You are at risk of becoming a victim of your own predictability. Deep down, you are sick and tired of it. Trust those feelings. You need change in terms of your circumstances, your memorized daily patterns, and above all, your attitude. You need more of a sense of freedom in your life, and you need to be its author or it will not happen. This edgy feeling is most pressing in your primary relationships. Astrologers often use these aspects to predict breakups; here, we are turning it around, talking about how to *avoid* breakups.

Most Beneficial Aesthetic Input: Your tastes are at risk of becoming jaded. It is time to stretch your aesthetic horizons. You need fresh input—something that perks up your ears or your eyes, something new. If you like pop music, try listening to an opera. If you like modern abstract painting, make a study of Rembrandt, Velasquez or Delacroix.

What You Need To Learn About Love and Trust: Nothing sustains a relationship more effectively than blessing our partners' natural right to follow their evolutionary threads wherever they lead. As the U2 song says, "We are one, but we are not the same." Love and trust should enhance our freedom rather than diminishing it. Change is equivalent to being fully alive; partners celebrate that aliveness in each other: they support each others' changes.

How to Identify Your Soul-Helpers: They hear a different drummer and dance to a different tune than most people. From the conventional point of view, they are probably at least a little bit strange. They regale you with unexpected perspectives and unusual understandings. They may seem "not to be your type," although the opposite is the actual truth.

What Happens If You Squander the Opportunity: Your relationships move in the direction of becoming stale and predictable. Perhaps consciously, perhaps subliminally, you begin to lose interest in each other. People do drift apart, and sometimes that is what this aspect indicates. But it can also be something darker: a failure to do the work of keeping up with each other's changes. Then a love that does not need to die, dies.

VENUS CONTACTING NEPTUNE

How Best To Reduce Your Stress Load: Meditation—especially meditation upon serenity—is the sovereign remedy. Similarly effective is sitting quietly in a garden or watching as a beautiful sunset slowly unfolds. Those are "meditations" too, just not so formal. The aim is to empty your mind. A Buddhist metaphor comes to mind: let a glass full of turbid water sit for an hour. Watch it become clear as gravity settles the suspended particles of dirt to the bottom. The same thing will happen to your mind if you sit for an hour. Try gazing at a flower or a beautiful stone—that will make the sustained focus easier to maintain..

Most Beneficial Aesthetic Input: Romantic, idealistic art that uplifts your spirits. Art that elevates your consciousness. There are worlds beyond this physical one; visionary artists since the beginning of time have attempted to represent those worlds in imagery, poetic language, and sound. Turn your attention now to those artists. You are ready to understand and appreciate them—and to be helped toward serenity by them.

What You Need To Learn About Love and Trust: That love, for you, must have a spiritual basis—that is to say, two spirits must experience a sense of psychic connection. This does not imply mental telepathy or shared religion; those things are neither here nor there. It does imply easy shared silence. It implies an underlying sense of resonance and empathy linking the two partners, one that does not require discussion or physical contact.

How to Identify Your Soul-Helpers: They are sensitive souls, perhaps a bit otherworldly at times. They respond knowingly and avidly if you bring up metaphysical topics: psychic phenomena, life after death, seeing ghosts. They have vivid dreams and vivid imaginations. They often have a faraway look in their eyes; they often seem to return from "elsewhere" when you call their names.

What Happens If You Squander the Opportunity: You might find yourself falling in love with an illusion—that is to say, a person whom you are misreading or one who is not what he or she seems to be. You might "hang on the cross" of loneliness feeling sorry for yourself, all the while not making any practical attempt to reach out and connect with anyone. You might experience an exaggeration of any of your innate tendencies towards escapism.

VENUS CONTACTING PLUTO

How Best To Reduce Your Stress Load: There is a paradox here: in order to reduce the level of stress you are carrying, you will probably first have to increase it. Psychological realizations—some of them difficult—are pressing at you from the unconscious. They are most likely uncomfortable insights into issues underlying your primary relationships. Some of these insights are about you; some are about people whom you love. You ultimately reduce your stress load through the often-stressful process of facing these emerging truths squarely.

Most Beneficial Aesthetic Input: Everything you are facing has been faced by other people before you. Some of them have been successful, some have failed. And some have turned their experiences into art: serious books and films, for example. You benefit from exposure to those art-forms; you may even create some yourself now. Humor plays a very helpful role here as well. At first, that sounds like a very different notion, but actually, humor is one of the most effective art forms humans have ever created for dealing with subjects which make them nervous or uncomfortable. You may find humor very helpful at this point in your journey.

What You Need To Learn About Love and Trust: That without honesty, there is no such thing as trust. Love may exist without it, but only in the form of kindness. Right now, you need the whole package: love—but also enough honesty that you can trust what you are hearing. This is a two-way street: you must speak the truth that is actually in your heart, but you must also strive to become the kind of person who can hear truth without punishing the person who is telling it.

How to Identify Your Soul-Helpers: They look you directly in the eye. They are not trying to win a staring contest with you, but they are trying to make sure that you are linked by an authentic soul-to-soul connection. They tell you things you might not want to hear. They can keep your secrets; they offer you some secrets of their own. Whether or not they are formally educated, they have a natural ability to speak in psychological terms.

What Happens If You Squander the Opportunity: Relationships rot because of festering issues left unaddressed. Suspicions grow; people begin to generate "psychiatric" interpretations of each other, generally characterized by a sense of hopelessness or resignation about the other person ever improving. We fail to look at ourselves; we imagine the issue to have its sole origin in the other person's intransigence.

ENTERING TAURUS

When planets enter Taurus, whether by transit, progression or by solar arc, there is a distinctly Venusian vibration to the period—but this time with some added Taurean fingerprints. It is, in other words, similar to what we have been looking at so far in this chapter—but a little different too. In any case, we are again faced with the need to integrate two archetypes: the specific nature of the moving planet and the Earthy, grounding, calming motivational agenda of the sign of the Bull.

Jupiter, for example, might have been in Aries by solar arc for the past thirty years. During that time, a woman's ambition to *do something big* with her life—such a grand desire is pure Jupiter—has been on fire with Arian competitive drive. Very likely, that combination of energies has produced impressive results.

But the poor thing has probably gotten pretty tired too . . .

As Jupiter arcs into Taurus, it is still of course Jupiter—still a planet that thinks big. But now the structure of its motivations becomes different—calmer, more Taurean. At an inner level, the woman's evolutionary logic has now gone through a significant change of direction. Taurus seeks peace.

So what happens?

Perhaps she takes some of the money she has earned and buys a second home—a place in the country where it is easier for her to relax. Maybe she makes friends with the local birds and squirrels. She works fewer hours; she passes lucrative contracts on to younger, hungrier colleagues. Her more competitive, ambition-driven period—which is now behind her—has in fact been her authentic spiritual path. While there, she has developed a healthy kind of pride and confidence in herself, based on her very real accomplishments. She has probably also had to wrestle with some of the shadow dimensions that arise when anyone "dances with the archetype of the Warrior Queen."

But as Jupiter passes into Taurus, all of that changes. Suddenly the soul's lessons in *ambition*—Jupiter territory—become significantly less heated. It is time for her to learn how to care for herself, how to listen to the messages of her body, how to prioritize a simple sense of well-being.

She has made some money.

Now she might very well need to learn how to spend it.

Earlier in this chapter we explored Venus interacting by aspect with the rest of the planets. Now let us investigate what it means for any planet to enter Taurus.

As per our earlier lamentations, this "cookbook" format precludes the inclusion of the full spectrum of astrological details that flesh these structures out and make them human. When a planet enters Taurus, which house in your chart is it impacting? What aspects will it make while it passes through that sign?

Always remember to take those variations into account as you apply the following guidelines.

A Reminder: Transits of the Sun, Moon, Mercury, Venus, and Mars are fast-moving astrological triggers. They do not have time to develop the depth and complexity of meaning that are characteristic of progressions and solar arcs. That deeper complexity is also characteristic of the transits of Jupiter, Saturn, Uranus, Neptune, and Pluto.

In the material that follows, we are mostly focusing on the deeper theme-building kinds of events. At the end of each section about the five fast-moving "trigger-planets," you will find a few lines about their effects under the heading "by transit."

THE SUN ENTERING TAURUS

Your New School: Recovering simplicity. Prioritizing serenity. Paying attention to your body and trusting your animal instincts. Letting silence speak to you. Calming down. Immersive experiences in Mother Nature. Music as a spiritual path. Animals as teachers; four-footed friends. Not sweating the small stuff. Focusing on the true essentials.

Don't Hold Onto . . . old grudges. Competitiveness. An endless, unreasoning sense of urgency about everything. Anger and resentment. Drama. The need to be number one.

What To Expect: Opportunities to withdraw from intense situations. A chance to relax, perhaps in nature. Doors opening for the active pursuit of peace. Body work. Less drama and stress. Exposure to art; exposure to animals. Greater financial stability and predictability.

The Shape of Failure: Becoming so driven by an obsession with an unreachable level of material security and stability that you are afflicted by chronic anxiety. Achieving such a degree of stability in your life that it stifles your soul. Boring yourself to death.

By Transit: Much here depends upon what house of your chart is contacted by the Sun and what aspects form and separate. As you answer those questions, recognize that opportunities are arising for you to make a positive, active stand in defending yourself against undue stress in those particular areas.

THE MOON ENTERING TAURUS

Your New School: Finding safe harbors in your heart. Finding pockets of peace hidden in daily life. The secret of Enlightenment: eating when you are hungry; sleeping when you are tired. Prioritizing your soul-family. Making your home more comfortable—and making time to enjoy it. Actually tasting your food. Inviting your physical body to speak to you.

Don't Hold Onto . . . a rushed attitude of endless, anxious crisis. Competitiveness. Resentments. Judgements. Realize that a certain battle is as over as it is ever going to be. You can therefore safely drop some of what was once necessary vigilance.

What To Expect: Opportunities for rest, restoration, and peace—and "expecting" them is actually a form of effective mindfulness which will help you recognize them. Sometimes these opportunities are obvious; other times, you must actively try to recognize them and seize them.

Encounters with soul-friends arise, and can calm your jagged nerves. Opportunities to "walk in beauty."

The Shape of Failure: Getting stuck in the momentum of a stressed-out mood that you already could have released. Stubbornly defending an attitude that is not doing you any good at all. Staying mad.

By Transit: Much here depends upon what house of your chart is contacted by the Moon and what aspects form and separate—in any case, it will all happen quickly since the Moon only takes a couple of days to pass through Taurus or any other sign. As you answer those astrological questions, recognize and honor your heart's call to relax and take care of yourself in those particular areas, even if it means postponing responsibilities or tiring tasks.

MERCURY ENTERING TAURUS

Your New School: Grounding your thinking in two fresh ways: one is simply to come to practical, real-world decisions. The other is to make sure that your gut instincts had a voice in those decisions. To some degree, logic and reason must guide you now—and that is because you are emerging from a time in which Arian emotions have distorted your perceptions. Anger, fear, passion, and angst are rarely clear-eyed counselors. Take a breath before you make a decision—then make the decision.

Don't Hold Onto . . . those fiery Arian emotions we just listed. They had a purpose, but they have served it. A time has come for making your best deal with reality as it is—and letting go of any mental dramas that are now only serving to drain your brain and dissipate your vitality in bursts of pointless nervous energy.

What To Expect: A chance to sit quietly, perhaps in nature, certainly in silence. This respite, if you seize it, provides an opportunity to reflect on a longer, more forgiving view of things, and to regain some lost perspective.

The Shape of Failure: Endless, repetitive fugues of memorized inner dialog looping ceaselessly in your head. Stubborn, defensive adherence to ideas and speeches which, if you listen to your heart, you no longer actually fully believe.

By Transit: Much here depends upon what house of your chart is contacted by Mercury and what aspects form and separate. As you answer those questions, recognize opportunities to speak up and to claim your right to reject certain stressful situations. If you listen to your heart, you can follow your own instincts in those particular areas.

VENUS ENTERING TAURUS

Your New School: The serene rapture we can experience as we surrender to the sheer beauty of nature. Precious moments of transcendent peace that arise as we are uplifted by art. Loving your physical body; being kind to it. Gentleness; kindness; the healing, soothing mysteries of physical touch.

Don't Hold Onto . . . anything ugly, whether it is an emotional state or a physical object. Maybe now, for example, is when you recognize the unpleasant feelings you get when you consider your worn-out living room sofa. Softening the textures of your immediate domestic world is now a path of mindful kindness toward yourself.

What To Expect: Opportunities arise to pass time peacefully with some dear, familiar souls—people whose simple presence soothes you even if you are just "talking about the weather." In those relationships, more healing is conveyed to you via touch, gesture, and silence than can ever be conveyed by words. Opportunities to immerse your senses in beauty present themselves—surrender gratefully to them.

The Shape of Failure: Rigid adherence to fixed patterns of behavior—even ones based upon your actual responsibilities—can block you from claiming these necessary islands of serenity. Give yourself a break; the world will not end if you take time to show yourself a little kindness.

By Transit: Much here depends upon what house of your chart is contacted by Venus and what aspects form and separate. As you answer those questions, recognize opportunities to reach out and ask for help and support in those areas. That assistance is very likely available—and a helping hand will cut the stress-load in half.

MARS ENTERING TAURUS

Your New School: Fighting for peace—that's a dangerous phrase, but it makes the point. It is time for you to take steps to defend your serenity of spirit against anything that might erode it with petty annoyances. Only you can calm yourself down; only you can create a situation conducive to that needed serenity. Prioritize achieving mellowness; focus more on what you need, and less on what you want. Faced with what you cannot control, try just letting it be.

Don't Hold Onto . . . the momentum of old battles, efforts, and conflicts that can actually be dropped now. Declare victory and go home. In *karate*, the famous first move is simply to walk away. Be mindful of how you are holding onto unnecessary levels of stress in your body. Relax your neck and shoulders.

What To Expect: Signals of accumulated stress arising in your physical body—again, be particularly mindful of your neck and shoulders. Appreciate these signals too—they are not a "bad report card." They are just reminders that your evolutionary focus is shifting from one chapter to another. Expect chances to exercise, especially in nature or with animal-friends.

The Shape of Failure: Stubborn attachment to old angers and resentments, not registering that they are only running on momentum. Holding onto "high school" grudges. Burn out. Surrendering to destructive behaviors, giving them semi-permanent status in your head.

By Transit: Much here depends upon what house of your chart is contacted by Mars and what aspects form and separate. As you answer those questions, recognize opportunities to make a clear and forceful stand regarding limits and boundaries, especially in areas of your life that are sources of ongoing stress.

JUPITER ENTERING TAURUS

Your New School: What is simply being comfortable worth to you? What price to pay for soothing your soul and your body? You need to pamper yourself now, to recover and recoup your energies. Some luxury helps; so does *quality* in anything you acquire. Keep one eye on simplicity and immediacy though—a $10,000 easy chair might feel great, but in balance, you might have created more stress than you dissipated.

Don't Hold Onto . . . austerity in any area of your life. Let go of making a virtue out of "doing without." It is time to cash in some of your chips—make a dream or two come true. Use effective physical methods for releasing the tension you carry in your muscles. Try a bubble bath, for example—and don't listen to that tough, steely-eyed part of yourself that can "survive" without a bubble bath. Of course you can "survive" without one—but why? Laugh at that part of yourself, draw the bath, and you will feel better.

What To Expect: A chance to indulge yourself. A chance to relax. Material gifts, some coming from the universe and some coming directly from you to yourself. Contact with luxury. Opportunities to enhance your health, both physical and mental.

The Shape of Failure: Mere materialism. Conspicuous consumption. Mistaking sources of pleasure for sources of actual happiness. Blustering. Forgetting that happiness is an inward condition of consciousness, and instead imagining that it lies in material objects; pursuing those objects endlessly. "You can never get enough of what you don't really need."

SATURN ENTERING TAURUS

Your New School: A steady, relentless slog to the mountaintop. Taking aim at actually manifesting your best work and not stopping until you have accomplished it. Earning the soul-comfort of having achieved excellence in some visible way. Getting to a place where you can look back and genuinely feel that you did well. Making changes in relation to your physical body that enhance your long-term well-being.

Don't Hold Onto . . . dreams that cannot come true. Face reality—then negotiate hard, make your best deal, and be content with it. Release futility; withdraw from Quixotic battles; accept loss if that is relevant, and move on. Look to tomorrow, not to yesterday. Release dreams and behaviors which no longer suit you, given the fact of your maturation. Realize that hanging onto anger is just a way of punishing yourself for someone else's sins.

What To Expect: Practical life-enhancing paths of genuine maturational development open before you. To travel them, you must be open both to compromise and to hard work. The person you have actually become can recognize these pathways, while the outworn, memorized, habitual version of yourself is blind to them.

The Shape of Failure: Stubborn adherence to the past. Beating dead horses, hoping that they will rise up and whinny. Caution verging into fear, crippling your ability to improvise creatively in the face of emerging circumstances. Stability is your right to be just as stuck a year from now as you are today.

URANUS ENTERING TAURUS

Your New School: Asking your body what your next move in life should be—and trusting its message, even if it seems a little strange. Maybe, for example, moving to a new place sounds logically like a good idea—but whenever you visualize being there, a subtle hint of a headache makes itself felt at the base of your skull. Wisdom and guidance are rising up from your instinctual side. Remember that your inner animal is smarter than you are.

Don't Hold Onto . . . an exaggeratedly rebellious or pugnacious attitude. Do not think of forgiveness simply as a spiritual virtue—instead, think of it as a form of self-liberation. You may have been conscripted into someone else's war. It is time to go AWOL. Peace is of more spiritual value to you now than victory.

What To Expect: Opportunities, many of them arising suddenly and unexpectedly, to escape constraints generated by other people's expectations of you. Take advantage of these "exit ramps," and you will breathe a sigh of relief. It is time to lay those burdens down. A chance to return to nature, perhaps literally, and certainly in the sense of returning to your true essence.

The Shape of Failure: Stubborn persistence in lost causes and failed battles. "Getting on with the past." Immature behavior manifesting as symbolic rebellions—while the genuinely necessary rebellions go unaddressed. Defense of your quirks, as if they were important. Mistaking your quirks or your rebellions for individuality.

NEPTUNE ENTERING TAURUS

Your New School: Nature mysticism; communing with earth spirits and local deities. Pilgrimage to magical locations. The body as a portal to higher states: thus, yoga, *tai chi*, ecstatic dance, shamanic drumming. The convergence of spirit and flesh. Sexual magic. Animal messengers. Tree-hugging—literally.

Don't Hold Onto . . . limiting models of "rational" thought. Escape the tyranny of common sense. Don't hold onto a subliminal mood of hurried emergency—you need to slow down. Calm is a perceptual portal that reveals truths otherwise invisible.

What To Expect: A chance to breathe in and breathe out—and never underestimate its magical powers. Opportunities to practice yoga, dance, etc. Mysterious encounters with animals. Contact with 'earth wisdom" traditions—for example, Native American practices, Taoism, divining rods, crystals. A sweat lodge. A drumming circle.

The Shape of Failure: Dissociation from the physical realm; dissociation from the body. Unreleased, chronic tension. Ignoring obvious omens meant to guide you. Lassitude; laziness. Strange physical symptoms whose diagnoses are elusive.

PLUTO ENTERING TAURUS

Your New School: Body work, in the broadest sense. Signs arise in your physical body that indicate the presence of unconscious or semi-conscious psychic wounds; deep truths, some of them uncomfortable, are emerging—and your flesh recognizes them before your mind does. Ultimately, this work is about healing your soul—but the process might start with a headache or a stiff neck. Follow them down, down, down.

Don't Hold Onto . . . denial and rationalization. Your need to be "right;" your need to be pitied; your need to be seen as wise. Don't live in your head. Don't be afraid of strong emotions. Don't escape into abstraction or a metaphysical fairyland. Stand naked and humble before the mirror of truth.

What To Expect: Omens and synchronicities involving natural phenomena—rays of sunshine, gusts of wind, or dark clouds "answering your thoughts," commenting moment-by-moment on their truth or their falsehood. Getting "a feeling in your bones" about a choice or an insight. Physical symptoms—not necessarily dire!—that can lead to psychic revelations. Example: a stiff neck? Look for a "pain in the neck" in your life—and act to remove it.

The Shape of Failure: Messages from the physical body getting louder and perhaps more dangerous if you continue to ignore them. Stubborn patterns of denial, compartmentalization, or rationalization calcifying into stable structures of blindness or limitation. Making a dead religion out of your personal complexes. An unconscious resolution never to evolve or change.

19

CELESTIAL NAVIGATION II: MERCURY TIMES, VIRGO TIMES

Transiting Mercury speeds around your chart, returning to its starting point after about one year. Unlike the Sun's stately annual passage through the twelve signs, Mercury's path is frenetic. It slows down, stops, turns around and goes forward again—in retrograde motion, back to direct motion—looping along that way three or even four times each calendar year.

By progression and solar arc, its motion is naturally much more majestic—once again, it is moving slowly enough to have real impact upon your experience.

In any of its three moving forms, Mercury always signals the same advice: *keep your eyes open, look closely at what lies before you, observe it objectively and without prejudice, and you will surely learn something that you need to learn.*

Mercury represents, above all, that elemental jet fuel for the evolution of consciousness: *fresh data.* In Mercury times, turn your attention outward. It is time to forget the usual bias, common among people who view themselves as being on the spiritual path, toward inner life. The action is out there in the world.

During these Mercury times, the universe interrupts your normal programming for an important message . . .

A HAPPY FANTASY

A professional astrophysicist falls in love. One day, his new partner mentions a run of minor hard luck: her refrigerator and the transmission in her automobile both failed in the same month. She casually blames her misfortune on a current Saturn transit she is experiencing.

Her astrophysicist boyfriend responds according to his socialization—he points out that since Saturn is actually about a billion miles away, it probably does not have much bearing on her refrigerator or her car.

He respects his new sweetheart, but he is a bit incredulous that a smart cookie such as herself could believe in something as dumb as astrology.

(Meanwhile, unbeknownst to our astrophysicist, his progressed Mercury is entering his ninth house, while forming a square to his natal Saturn in the twelfth house. And because of the advent of the new partner in his life, there is probably something of a Venusian nature going on too—see the previous chapters for those details.)

Already in this story, we see the basic structure of Mercury's archetypal field: our protagonist is facing *cognitive dissonance*. That is to say, he is facing tension and contradiction in his perceptions—he believes his girlfriend to be highly intelligent; but simultaneously, he believes that only stupid people believe in astrology.

Something has to give. There is only one conceivable way that his mind can accommodate both of these perceptions: it must expand.

Welcome to a progressed Mercury event.

Will his mind expand? Will he open his thinking to the possibility that astrology actually works? There is no way to answer that question astrologically. All we know is that, through synchronicity, this opportunity is presenting itself.

The astrophysicist challenges his girlfriend about her belief that Saturn is to blame for her current pattern of difficulty. She in turn challenges him to see for himself—she offers to gift him with a session with her astrologer.

At first, he wonders out loud why he should waste his time that way. She presses him, inviting him to challenge his own assumptions—and asking him if he actually, truly, *knows anything* about a subject regarding which he has so many preconceived opinions.

To his credit, the astrophysicist accepts the challenge. He is doubtful, but with the rudiments of an open mind, he sits down with her astrologer—who of course shocks and disarms him with the accuracy and relevance of his chart interpretation. *Put that in your pipe and smoke it,* says the universe. And, to his credit, he does.

How can he reconcile the apparent efficacy of astrology with his education? As he thinks about it, he realizes that quite possibly the only reason that astronomy and astrology appear to be antagonistic to each other is a social one. He knows that planets obviously affect us—otherwise, we couldn't even *see* them. Who has a right to say *ex cathedra* that they cannot affect us in ways other than visually? That closed-minded attitude is only a collective agreement; there is no true opposition between astrology and astronomy. It is only a belief system in which the astrophysicist was trained, nothing more.

But if astrology is real, then . . . *I have some thinking to do.*

In that moment, our astrophysicist has accepted Mercury's most precious gift: *surprise..* The planet has entered his ninth house: *new data* (Mercury) is stretching and informing *his understanding of life* (the ninth house). Meanwhile, Mercury is also squaring his natal Saturn, challenging his need to *control the universe* by being right about everything all the time.

Two nights later, the astrophysicist and his sweetheart find themselves gazing at the starry sky. He has seen it before. He can describe the nuclear fusion blazing in Rigel, Sirius, and Aldebaran; he can speak eruditely about the physics of collapsing clouds of hydrogen and dust in the Magellanic clouds.

But now he looks up at the sky as if he had never seen it before.

He is beginning to realize what astrologers have believed since the beginning of human time: that sky and mind are like two mirrors facing each other, locked in an active resonance. .

And what does our astrophysicist have to say about that? His thoughts begin with the holiest words in Mercury's sacred liturgy:

"Wow, I never thought of that before . . ."

REALITY AS A COGNITIVE STRUCTURE

Whether you are a British art historian or a Swahili shaman, if you stub your toe on a rock, the experience is the same: it hurts. We cannot dismiss reality simply as an attitude or a belief; there is *something* out there—even Buddhists squeal, despite some of their views on the emptiness of all phenomena, when they stub their toes.

Still, an awful lot of what we think of as reality is composed more of interpretation, bias, interests, misunderstandings, wishes, misinterpretations, and fears than it is of atoms and molecules.

Ask a physicist: an atom is composed almost entirely of empty space. There is actually very little "there" out there—but that brings us straight back to stubbing our toes. The illusion of the solidity of the rock is extremely convincing. It goes back and forth—Niels Bohr, one of the founders of quantum mechanics once said, "Everything we call real is made of things that cannot be regarded as real."

But tell that to your throbbing toe.

The bottom line, is that we all live in two worlds: the world out there, whatever its ultimate nature might be. And, on the other hand, the "theory of everything" that we create in our minds.

"The ultimate nature of reality" is a daunting subject. To bring our Mercury theory down to earth, try this more mundane expression of exactly the same notion: *compare your own story of what it was like growing up in your family to the stories told by your brothers or your sisters—or your parents,* for that matter. Everyone will tell the tale with his or her own spin; that is only natural—and yet let me warn you: if you actually try this experiment with a sibling or a parent, you might soon have a fight on your hands. People cling passionately to their version of things, however illusory that version might be—in fact, the more illusory it is, typically the more passionately they cling to it.

That human tendency to cling to illusions is the problem addressed—we hope—by the transits, progressions, and solar arcs of Mercury. During such times, the world presents us with new data—data custom-designed to *shatter our faith in the errors of perception* which currently blind us to what we must now understand if we are going to go forward in our journeys.

It is as if we are being offered corrective lenses, hearing aids, and an education all at once.

SIGN AND OMENS

Many of us are familiar with the so-called Viking runes. At one level, they were simply the Norse alphabet. At another level, they functioned as a method of divination, much like Tarot cards. The Norse god, Odin, hung from the world tree, *Yggdrasil*, for nine days and nights in order to obtain them—such was his "passion for literature."

Perhaps you detect a Mercury connection?

These same "gods" arise in almost every culture. Once we get past their specific names and folklore, we realize that each one of them represents some fundamental part of the human mind. For that reason, they are generally quite obviously astrological, once you scratch the surface. It does not take long, for example, to realize that Odin and Mercury are equivalent.

Still, much has been forgotten. The very Romanized Mercury which we modern astrologers have inherited is a rather academic fellow. Those more scholarly parts of Mercury are all true and essential to our understanding—but Odin reminds us, with his passion for the runes, that there is another dimension to this archetype: *divination* and the *reading of signs and omens*.

Any astrologer will tell you that Mercury is about communication. Trouble is, when we hear that word, we tend to think of people talking. That is definitely part of what Mercury represents—but what we must remember here is that the *universe itself is constantly talking to us*. It is not just about human chattering.

Illustration: in the same week, three different friends independently suggest that you need to read the same book. Even we modern people, with no war-paint on our faces or shamanic drums beating, would react the same way. We understand that the universe has given us a sign. After the third time, we probably say, "I guess I need to read that book."

Even though few people say it out loud, at some level, we all take the existence—and purpose—of these synchronistic patterns for granted.

Illustration: you are discussing next year's vacation with your partner. You are torn between a trip to Mexico and a trip to Hawaii. You tentatively decide on Hawaii—and right in that instant, the sky suddenly grows dark, there is a flash of lightning, and two seconds later an ominous growl of thunder.

Perhaps we should go to Mexico after all . . .

The point of these anecdotes is that, even though reading signs and omens sounds like some exotic anthropological practice, we all still are pretty good at it. Such divination may not be an official part of our culture at this point, but it is hardwired into human nature.

During Mercury times, reading such omens and taking them seriously can save you quite a lot of trouble. The gods are trying to help you.

Perhaps Mercury is entering your seventh house. You eat at a new Italian restaurant and freshen your appreciation for that yummy Mediterranean cuisine. A week later, you see an Italian film and really enjoy it. Then, at a party, you are introduced to a stranger whom you like right away. His last name is Marinucci—his ancestors were Italian.

Do you ever see him again? We all meet a lot of people at parties . . .

If you have heeded Mercury's omens, you follow up with lunch with *signore* Marinucci—and you have made an important friend who will open doors for you and probably trigger helpful, unexpected insights in your consciousness.

SPEAKING AND LISTENING

Ask any astrologer: Mercury is about *speech.* I have intentionally avoided that fundamental truth for these last few pages. I did not want to get bogged down in it right away. While Mercury is indeed about communication, the points I have made so far are much closer to the evolutionary heart of the matter.

Bottom line, Mercury is about *learning what we do not already know.* There are many ways to do that; listening is certainly one of them—and of course, we famously learn a lot more with our mouths closed than with our mouths open.

We put the act of listening—especially listening with an open mind—first, before talking. Speaking can be part of the Mercury process, provided we do not let it get in the way. In terms of active speech, Mercury's most powerful tool lies in asking *questions*—sincere questions, questions to which we genuinely do not have a prefabricated answer.

Again, everything boils down to getting our own opinions and interpretations out of the way, allowing our minds to be fed by the unexpected, the unanticipated, and the miraculous.

A FRIEND WITH A BROKEN HEART

A dear soul-friend of yours has been unexpectedly abandoned by her partner. She feels that her life has fallen apart; her heart is broken. We have all been there. You know that she will survive, but you want to be there for her and support her.

One evening you are sitting with her, listening, just letting her vent. She has created an elaborate—and rather psychiatric—interpretation of her partner's behavior. You know her partner; you actually do not really think he is quite that crazy. You love your friend, but you also know her quirks and have some understanding of the difficulties her partner must have faced in intimacy with her.

But you do not say any of that. You are being a good friend. You know that your job is mostly to listen and to agree. At this point in her grieving process, she needs your support a lot more than she needs any confrontive insights.

Three days later, she phones you at 10:20 in the evening. She apologizes for the late hour, but she really needs to talk. She says that she has come to significant new insights which she wants to run past you. You love her, so you listen. Her "new insights" tonight turn out to be pretty much the same as her previous insights three nights back.

Perhaps over the next couple of weeks you hear her make exactly the same speech three or four more times. You have the impression that she keeps repeating it in hopes that she will actually come to believe it herself. You also understand that her description of her ex's "psychiatric issues" is a strategic oversimplification. She probably does not even understand why she is doing it—but you do. Since the actual nature of her reality is too painful for her to endure, she is attempting to create an alternative reality in her mind, one in which losing "that crazy, worthless, defensive person" is not quite so painful.

We all do this sometimes. This "talking defense" is fundamental to the dark side of Mercury. In the long run, defending ourselves against the truth is obviously not helpful—illusions may comfort us for a while, but in the end, they are always costly. Still, a little compassion is not remiss here. Could anyone survive without the occasional rationalization, compartmentalization, or comforting delusion? *Mercury can talk itself out of seeing what lies directly before its eyes.*

The "tell" when someone is traveling down that all-too-human road is that they invariably need to enlist others in their delusory beliefs and understandings.

That's why your friend called you at 10:20 that night. She was giving herself a message, not you.

A point we have been making so far is that, during Mercury times, we are always offered a chance to learn something beyond what we already know. Sometimes that new knowledge is simply interesting, even fascinating. Our curiosity is nourished. Other times, what we need to learn is cognitively dissonant—that is to say, it clashes with our preexistent views and opinions.

In extreme cases, Mercury's message might be profoundly threatening to the ego. This is often the case when Mercury is involved with the natal Pluto, the sign Scorpio, or the eighth house. In a milder way, it is more characteristic of Mercury's hard aspects than of the soft ones.

At all such times, we are desperate—or at least highly motivated—to avoid the new data. So we simply deny it. We rationalize and compartmentalize. We argue. We also typically try to rally others to the flag of our self-preserving version of things—again, that is exactly what your friend is doing in the foregoing story. By endlessly repeating her argument to you, she hopes to enlist your support. At the most fundamental level, she is of course also trying to convince herself of this less ego-threatening mental model of the circumstances, as if through mere repetition she could magically turn a lie into a truth.

As always, there is no spiritual medicine equal to mindful self-awareness. If, during a Mercury time, you find yourself nervous and talking too much, it is helpful to read the "omen" of that symptom for what it actually is—it is the effort of your mind to prevent your soul from learning something it really needs to learn.

DISTRACTION: THE BAD NEWS

In this moment, I am Mister Mercury: I am engaged in writing. Words are trying to form themselves into sentences, paragraphs, and chapters in my head. The process is not at all threatening to my ego—I am not living the kind of story we were just telling. I actually like to write, but that does not make it easy. The lazy part of my mind can think of many things it would rather be doing. Earlier in this volume, we saw how Mr. Yeats put it when faced with the similar dilemma of writing poetry, "All things can tempt me from this craft of verse."

As I write these words, I am sitting right here at my computer. Temptations abound. What could be easier than to check my email or to have a quick look at Facebook? What about the news? What harm could come from a quick peek at the headlines? I have also been thinking about how, living out here in the desert, we could really use a Jeep. Maybe I should Google around a bit and see if I can learn anything interesting about Jeeps . . .

You can easily see where succumbing to those temptations would lead me. If I had fallen for those distractions, you would not be reading these words. I never would have finished writing this book.

These reflections upon distraction actually lead us into some exceedingly complex territory. Distraction has a positive side as well, but we will get to that in a moment.

If you started this book on page one, all that I just wrote probably rings a familiar bell. I used very similar language in talking about natal Mercury many chapters ago. That should be no surprise. This issue of potential distraction is a "permanent installation" where your natal Mercury lies, and a temporary one when Mercury is just passing through town.

The obvious exhortation here would be that, in either case, we need to stay focused. And indeed, if we truly want to learn anything during a Mercury time, some degree of *sustained mental discipline* is helpful. If we allow ourselves to be distracted by every whimsy, we doom ourselves to perpetual superficiality—which is a classic Mercury trap.

To that caution, we can add a deeper one. If the universe is leading you toward data that might be threatening to the ego—remember your broken-hearted friend—then this kind of distraction takes on a more diabolical tone: as we get near a truly deep insight, we might suddenly be consumed with a fascination about The History of Pizza Pie in North America. Let's just Google pizza pie and see where it leads . . . which is likely to be right down a rabbit hole.

Changing the subject, in other words, is a Mercurial way of keeping the ego's illusions safe.

DISTRACTION: THE GOOD NEWS

Still, even acknowledging those two cautions, there is another side to this "distractible" dimension of Mercury. *Just as too little mental discipline can be a terrible enemy here, so can too much of it.*

Keeping militantly "on the subject" may be a tyrannical way of avoiding other, less pleasant subjects. One can fall into that snare with no one else anywhere around—but it works like a charm with other people too. Keep talking, keep hammering away at the same themes, maybe add some wit and a few red herrings . . . soon enough, everyone is too exhausted to ask you any hard questions.

The larger point is that free-association is sometimes a legitimate and effective Mercury tool. Often relaxing control and allowing the mind to drift on its own mysterious currents leads us to understandings we might not otherwise encounter.

Sorting all this out can be tricky. There is no rigid formula for getting it right. But here is a rule of thumb: when, during a Mercury time, you are dealing with emotionally-charged psychological questions, such free association is not likely to produce much genuine insight. The problem is that the unconscious mind underlies and shapes that "free" association in ways that likely serve its darker, repressive purposes. Something inside of you is doing its level best to *keep* the material unconscious. Guaranteed, if you let your mind drift naturally, it will "drift" away from exactly what you need to know.

On the other hand, when you are faced with creative, scientific, professional, or practical existential questions, such free association during a Mercury time can be highly productive. More disciplined thought often goes down tired, established pathways; in a Mercury time, you are always looking for serendipity. The unknown, the unimagined, and the unexpected are what feed you.

Free association, unencumbered by any snakes in your head, can be a terrific tool at such a time. Insight comes wrapped in surprise.

A FEW MERCURY LINES AND PROVERBS

* *Whatever you see, it is more than that.*
* *We learn more with our mouths closed than with our mouths open.*
* *Expect to be amazed.*
* *Zen mind, beginner's mind.*
* *Consistency is your right to be just as stupid next year as you were last year.*
* *Better to learn something new than to be seen as right.*
* *Academics behave that way because the stakes are so low.*
* *Words are only a finger pointing at the Moon.*
* *What a fool believe, he sees.*
* *Sailors: Here lies the body of Michael O'Day. He died maintaining the right of way.*
* *Aviators: Minds are like parachutes; they only work when they are open*
* *Southern: she could talk the legs off a table*
* *Irish: He is a terrible man for knowing everything.*
* *India: When the pickpocket meets a saint, he sees pockets.*

MERCURY RETROGRADE

By transit, Mercury's retrograde periods have entered the popular mind as a time of high jinx. And indeed, there is a noticeable tendency for anything of a Mercury nature to go awry during such times. As I write these words, for example, Microsoft just compelled me to update my Windows 10 laptop computer during a Mercury retrograde time. I was nervous, but the new regime gives us no choice in the matter. My fears were confirmed: when the computer rebooted, the software on which I depend for recording astrological readings had crashed and I could not recover it. The machine is now with a technician. All I can say is that I am hopeful that it will make a full recovery.

Beyond terrorizing laptop computers, one general astrological counsel is to "avoid signing anything important" while Mercury is retrograde;

similarly it is not the best time to buy a new computer, communications equipment—or really anything electronic.

Positively, these same Mercury retrograde periods are viewed as splendid opportunities for *review* and *reflection.*

On November 11, 2006, the New York *Times* published an unusually open-minded piece about Mercury retrograde periods. As you will see, it provides us with a little bit of perspective—Mercury retrograde is a caution, not a death sentence.

According to figures from the federal Bureau of Transportation Statistics, the percentage of late flights into and out of La Guardia Airport in New York City during the past three summers rose to 24.6 during retrograde periods from 22.8 during non-retrograde periods. What's more, during the past three years, claims of mishandled domestic baggage rose to 5.44 per 1,000 passengers during months when Mercury spent more than half the time in retrograde from 5.38 per 1,000 in months when the planet was not in retrograde. That works out to one extra lost bag per 15,000 passengers.

I suspect this news story is substantially accurate—but for the sake of keeping perspective, please note that flying during a Mercury retrograde period does not exactly spell "kiss your luggage goodbye." The effect is real, but modest—one extra lost bag per every 15,000 passengers.

You'll probably be OK, in other words.

Personally, I respect these times, but I do not cringe before them. If I have the option of delay, I take advantage of it. If that option is not practical or possible, I am willing to take my chances with Mercury retrograde. I have some bruises to prove it—but things have also often worked out just fine.

Here in America, in the presidential election in the year 2000, Mercury was retrograde. What followed was a result so tangled that it required the United States Supreme Court to eventually award victory to George W. Bush over his opponent Al Gore. As I write these words, special counsel Robert Mueller has just released his long-awaited report on the Donald Trump campaign's alleged obstruction of justice and collusion with Russia—and Mercury is currently retrograde. The House voted unanimously that the report should be released, but Atty. Gen. William Barr is sitting on it. At this point, no one knows its actual contents; no one knows if we ever will.

I have no idea how all that will play out—but I do know that right now, Mercury retrograde has once again left its fingerprints on history.

Here's another example: on March 10, 2019, an Ethiopain Airlines Boeing 737 MAX crashed, killing 157 people. Mercury had turned retrograde just a few days earlier. This was the second lethal crash of this kind of jet in five month, and triggered a world-wide grounding of the aircraft. (Mercury was not retrograde at the time of the first crash.) Upon investigation, it emerged that a faulty sensor (*Mercury*) had fed bad data (*retrograde*) to an onboard computer (*Mercury again*), throwing the plane into an uncontrollable nosedive. The subsequent tangle of denials and rationalizations by the Boeing company further illustrates the garbled communications that are so characteristic of this astrological phenomenon.

PROGRESSED MERCURY RETROGRADE

So far, in speaking of Mercury retrograde periods, we have been operating in the category of transits—here today, gone tomorrow, in other words. Ultimately, there is a triviality to almost anything that is so transitory.

Where this Mercury phenomenon emerges as a serious player in the realm of evolutionary astrology is by progression.

In the actual sky—again, by transit, in other words—Mercury is retrograde for three weeks or so, perhaps a day or two longer. With progressions, those days turn into years. Once progressed Mercury gets going "in the wrong direction," it will typically stay that way for something between twenty-one and twenty-five years: a long time, in other words.

The majority of us will experience such a period at some point in our lives. And don't worry, such a situation does not portend two decades of failed computers and lost luggage.

Naturally, some people are born *during* Mercury retrograde periods. Depending on exactly when they were born during that retrograde cycle, the planet will remain in that reversed condition throughout some portion of their youth, then turn around and begin advancing. For other people, Mercury might turn retrograde only in their old age. Then perhaps they do not live long enough to see it go direct again.

So what does it mean? To answer that question, we need to marry two points:

* The fundamental quality of a planet in retrograde motion lies in the most obvious fact about it—that it is returning to degrees of the Zodiac through which it has already passed. It is, in other words, heading back toward bygone times. For any planet in retrograde motion, there is therefore an element of "review" about the process.
* Mercury specifically represents our cognitive functions, memory included. It is about the ideas and concepts that populate our intelligence and our imagination about ourselves. Thus, when Mercury is retrograde, it is about *remembering the past*. It is a trip down memory lane.

This Mercurial process of recollection, however, is more active than passive. One way to say it is that we are invited during that entire Mercury retrograde period to *rewrite our personal history*. On the face of it, that sounds terrible—as if we were going to try to erase all our most embarrassing or shameful moments and replace them with heroics that never actually happened. No worry; the Mercury retrograde process of "rewriting our histories" is not about whitewashing or distorting anything; in fact, as we will soon see, its purpose is precisely opposite that.

A MERCURY RETROGRADE PARABLE

A man who was abused physically by his father when he was a child is currently in psychotherapy. As a kid, our protagonist was three feet tall, weighed forty pounds—and was *brutalized by a giant upon whom he was dependent for food and shelter.*

That was his reality; that was how it actually was and that is how he remembers it. That is how he laid down the memories.

In therapy, this man realizes that his father was simply a bully. Studying old family photographs, he comes to understand that the man was physically short—and a fine example of so-called "short man syndrome." He had a chip on his shoulder, in other words; he was driven to compensate for his "lack of stature" in the world—and of course, that reaction was purely psychological, and had almost nothing to do with his physical height. On reflection, our subject realizes that his father did not have much going for him professionally or socially. He was treated dismissively by the world and ignored by other men—*and the pitiful wimp took out his frustrations on his little boy.*

The real truth is that the "giant monster" in our subject's memory was actually psychopathological weakling. *But that was not how he looked when the initial memories were being laid down;* that is just how he really was.

* In psychotherapy, our protagonist *rewrites his personal history.*
* He alters his memories of his father *in the direction of more truth, not less.*
* He inserts a viewpoint into his memories that did not exist at the time the memories were laid down.

This present-tense viewpoint is wiser and more accurate by far than the original one.

Here is a little trick I use with my clients in order to get this idea across quickly. I ask them to imagine a *feminist perspective on Shakespearean England.* Given the patriarchal, male-dominated structure of that long-gone world—Queen Elizabeth herself excepted, of course—such a perspective would be highly productive.

Then I point out a problem: there actually *were no feminists in Shakespearean England;* that helpful, productive perspective simply did not exist in those days.

(This is probably a slight over-simplification, but it makes the point.)

In thinking this way, *we are inserting a viewpoint into history which did not exist when those history books were written.* As a result, we are seeing the history much more clearly than did the Elizabethans themselves.

It is famously wise to think before we speak. That is a fine principle to remember as we live our lives moment to moment—and it is even more profoundly relevant to Mercury's retrograde progressions. This period of "thinking" may strain your patience somewhat—*with Mercury retrograde, the universe invites you to reflect and hold your tongue for two decades.*

Patience!

Real insights are baking in you. People will appreciate them less if you serve them half-baked.

A PERSONAL TALE

In my own life, progressed Mercury made a station and began its long retrograde cycle in the summer right after I graduated from high school. Just a few months earlier, at age seventeen, I had a tonsillectomy—an interesting Mercurial synchronicity: I literally could not talk for a couple of weeks.

While I was lying in bed recovering, my mother offered to buy me something to read. I asked for an astrology book. She got me a couple of them; one of them, Joseph P. Goodavage's *Write Your Own Horoscope*, marked my entry into the field. With progressed Mercury making a station, I lost my tonsils, but I gained astrology.

There is more to this story, but let us stop and reflect for a moment.

First, whenever a planet makes a station, its energies are markedly focused and intensified. Any Mercury station, no matter whether it is turning retrograde or direct, represents a time when critical new information is presenting itself. Waves of new data are crashing against your preconceived belief systems—*it is Mercury City*, in other words. Stations are like that.

As a kid, I was kind of an egghead, tending toward a science track. I was an amateur astronomer—not an astrologer at all.

But when Mercury stationed, astrology shocked its way into my head. The universe "interrupted my normal programming . . ."

There is another practical point I would like to make about Mercury's stations: contrary to the date that you see on your computer screen, *they actually last a long time.* By progression, Mercury slows down very slowly, comes very gradually to a halt, and begins very slowly to accelerate in the other direction.

The computer gives you a specific date and minute for a Mercury station; don't take it seriously. Mathematically, it is accurate, but the reality is that Mercury is effectively stationary—and thus greatly intensified—for a period of several years. *During that entire time it might not move much more than one degree.*

Back to my story. With Mercury progressed to a station and about to turn retrograde, I began reading astrology obsessively. When I got to college, there were no astrology classes offered, so I did the next best thing: I quickly switched my major from economics to religion.

Even though I had swallowed the astrology hook, I felt that there was something systematically wrong with all the books I was reading. I also had a strange *woo-woo* feeling that I was *remembering* astrology rather than learning it freshly—as if I had learned in a past life..

The universe gave me a couple of decades to think about all that.

Two decades later, as progressed Mercury was turning direct, I published my first astrology book. Having reflected on what was right and what was wrong with astrology during the entire time that Mercury was retrograde, it was now time for me to speak. Here are the first lines of the first chapter of my first book, *The Inner Sky*: *"People change. Yet one assumption runs like a virus through most astrological writing: people do not change."*

To this day, I cannot think of a way to improve upon those words. At the deepest level, they explain why I call myself an "evolutionary" astrologer. It is not only about reincarnation—even more so, it is about the fact we are all evolving year to year, even minute to minute.

I am also grateful that the universe did not allow me to publish anything until I had all that figured out. That was a gift progressed Mercury retrograde gave to me.

Remember that Mercury's progressed stations are best understood as *periods of a few years* rather than as the specific dates on which they nominally occur. While reading my first astrology book coincided closely with progressed Mercury's station—within six or seven months—*The Inner Sky* was actually published about four years *before* my progressed Mercury actually stationed and turned direct.

That sounds like a long time—but the reality is that when the book came out, the planet was only 1° from its turning point: very close, in other words. That illustrates why it is so helpful to view these stationary periods as "chapters" of life, rather than as "dates."

Without getting too windy about it, let me say that for me personally, progressed Mercury turning direct actually referred more broadly to my active emergence as an astrological writer and teacher. It coincided with the publication of my entire "Sky" trilogy and all that the appearance of those three books and their attendant hubbub implied for my life.

Bottom line: when progressed Mercury is retrograde, it is a time to think, reflect, and correct our understanding. We are "inserting a point of view into our thoughts and memories" that was not there at the time they were first laid down. Once we have succeeded in that corrective process, and when Mercury goes direct, we have something fresh to say—and it is usually something which other people will find worth hearing.

ENTERING VIRGO

Even though Mercury remains Mercury no matter where it is in your chart, when it enters a new sign its underlying motivational agenda changes. In Sagittarius, for example, the natural curiosity of the planet is aimed at wondering what might lie over the next horizon. When it crosses into Capricorn, it becomes curious about how we might become more productive or efficient. That is still a form of curiosity, but of a very different nature. That is how signs leave their fingerprints on planets.

So what happens when a planet enters Virgo by transit, progression, or solar arc? No matter what planet we are talking about, its behavior—at least its potential for healthy, evolutionary behavior—becomes temporarily suffused with Virgo's motivational agenda. As ever, we need to remember that Virgo has a dark side as well as a bright one. If the planet entering Virgo does not head for the higher ground, then it will surely become entangled in less healthy possibilities.

What does Virgo want? For one thing, it loves making lists. So let's make one. Here are the energies, motivations, and values by which the better side of Virgo navigates.

* A hunger for precision and clarity.
* A compelling drive to improve.
* Eagerness to learn.
* Self-discipline and hard work.
* A respect for competence and skill.
* A distaste for abstraction; a preferred focus on practical applications.
* Honest self-assessment.
* Attraction to highly accomplished mentors.
* Eagerness to be of practical use to others.

As we learned earlier, each sign is a reaction against the potential excesses or errors of the previous sign. Leo comes before Virgo, and its shadow dimension lies in the direction of self-centeredness, self-aggran-dizement, and the unhealthy face of pride. Each item on our list of Virgo's motivations is a natural remedy for those kinds of potential Leo problems. Inevitably however, these remedies bring their own dangers and possible excesses. As a planet enters Virgo, it might become crippled with doubts and insecurities. Perfection is always an unreachable standard; a planet en-tering Virgo might become painfully exacting, demanding too much of itself—then beat itself up as a "failure." It is a short step from there to becoming similarly exacting relative to other people.

Say a planet enters Virgo in your chart. Imagine you find yourself slipping into some of those shadow traps. What is the cure?

The answers are simple and ancient: *loving yourself.* Forgiving yourself. Accepting yourself. Judging yourself only by the standard of your level of sincere effort rather than by the impossible standard of perfection. Getting over yourself by means of the ancient device of being of meaningful service to someone else.

In the next several pages, we look at each of the planets, one by one, as they cross the Virgo frontier.

20

VIRGO TIMES, MERCURY TIMES: THE BUILDING BLOCKS

As Mercury whiplashes around your chart by transit or waltzes in more stately fashion by solar arc or progression, it forms a predictable series of aspects with the planets and sensitive points in your natal chart. Here is a way to frame any such an event in your mind: each one of those planets and points, at the deepest level, represents a lofty evolutionary intention. And each one of them can benefit enormously from a visit by "the messenger of the gods."

Each one of them, in other words, needs a dose of fresh, accurate information.

People joke about "God appearing in a flash of light," offering some liberating insight or advice. That is essentially what Mercury does—but only if we are willing to listen. What stops us? Ignorance can get in the way, that's true—but Mercury is a skillful teacher, adept at dispelling ignorance.

More often, what blocks us is simply our own ego. We all love to be "right." We are all attached to a carefully constructed narrative about who we are and how we came to this point in our lives—a narrative that is inevitably fraught with distortions, rationalizations, lies we have been told, blame, misperceptions, accusations, judgements, and so on.

We all carry a *description of reality* in our heads—and often mistake it for the actual nature of reality, even when actual reality stares us in the face.

Mercury is typically one of the less popular lecture topics at astrology conferences. That has always baffled me. *Aligning mind and truth:* can there ultimately be anything more exciting than that?

In the pages that follow, we consider the effects of Mercury as it moves through any kind of aspect to any of the rest of the natal planets. That's a complex undertaking since there are a vast number of possible combinations. For example, solar arc Mercury in Gemini and the 4th house might form a quincunx aspect to your Jupiter-Neptune conjunction in Scorpio and the 9th house. *Switch any single one of those variables and you are in a very different astrological situation.* There would be no way to cover each of them individually without writing the fattest book in the history of human literature.

We have to approach the subject more systematically, looking at the core principles that unlock the individual configurations.

Here's a good start on that strategic simplification: as with Venus in the previous chapter, let's reiterate that all aspects are about integration, no matter whether they are soft ones or hard ones. So, as a starting point, we can forget about the distinctions between a quincunx and a quintile, and focus instead upon the *core integration* any such aspect represents. Always, for the sake of our psychological and spiritual well-being, the moving planet and the natal planet simply need to find a way to cooperate. Each aspect, at the highest level of evolutionary intention, suggests *a specific method for that cooperation.* Any aspect can work; any of them can also get us into trouble if we don't engage them with proper effort and skillful methods. Despite what you might read or hear, there are no inherently "bad" aspects—or "good" ones.

If you are fuzzy about any of that, you might review chapter fifteen, where we look at aspects in a deeper way. Here, we focus on the essential elements of the various integrative processes as Mercury dances with the Sun, the Moon, and the rest of them. The basic synthesis is always present regardless of the technical aspect. That technical aspect only serves to describe the *nature of the negotiations* that can lead to the helpful, if temporary, merger of the two planets.

Once we are done with Mercury's aspects to the other planets, we will look in similar cookbook fashion at what to expect when any of them enter the sign Virgo.

MERCURY CONTACTING THE SUN

What I Need to Learn: How to speak up and let people know who I am. How to step up to the plate verbally. How to express my values and opinions clearly and forthrightly. How to command attention without being seen as strident or pushy. How to think critically. How to defend a point. In doing all of this, I must pay attention to my impact on other people—I have something new to learn about how they are reading me.

Potential Blindspot: Mistaking my opinions for reality. Mistaking subjectivity for objectivity. Not realizing that I have said too much or spoken too long. My mouth might be revealing my ego.

Omens and Synchronicities: The world is my mirror now; I see myself reflected in it. It is time to look for feedback about how I appear to other people. Surprises, signs, and omens arise—I notice them, and I interpret them as clues to something I need to learn.

How to Recognize Your Teachers: They express themselves with natural authority. People want to listen to them. They can use themselves as examples without seeming egocentric. Their own story is a teaching device. They are notably articulate.

Squandered: Compulsive nervous chatter. Distraction standing in the way of actual accomplishment. Mental fugues in my head; rationalization. "Convincing others" as a way of trying to convince myself.

MERCURY CONTACTING THE MOON

What I Need to Learn: How to speak straight from my heart. How to accurately articulate the precise nature of my needs so others can grasp them clearly. How to effectively translate my feelings into words. How to verbally express tenderness and vulnerability. How to think about what I feel before I blurt out statements that only create confusion and misunderstanding.

Potential Blindspot: Emotions clouding reason. Strong feelings distorting my sense of reality. Mood and attitude poisoning communication.

My own needs blinding me to the legitimate needs and perspectives of other people.

Omens and Synchronicities: Heart to heart conversations leading to revelations and fresh understanding. Emotional outbursts in myself or other people which offer clues as to the nature of energies moving in either of our unconscious minds. Messages from family. Insights which arise in candlelight, moonlight, or twilight.

How to Recognize Your Teachers: They are emotionally present. They express themselves fluently with immediacy and vulnerability. Even upon my first meeting them, they feel familiar—as if they were already family. Literal family members may have much to teach me now.

Squandered: Talk can build bridges between two hearts, but it can also build walls. If there is something that I am afraid to feel now, nervousness arises in me and I release it in compulsive chatter. I am being more defensive than I realize.

MERCURY CONTACTING MERCURY

What I Need to Learn: I am ready to take a great leap forward in terms of my skill and confidence as a speaker, a teacher, or a writer. I resolve to say exactly what I mean, taking as much time as I need to express myself clearly. I enunciate my words; I am articulate. I speak in complete sentences; I am interesting. I am always willing to learn something new. I am not afraid to use my full vocabulary.

Potential Blindspot: Compulsively describing reality does not change reality at all. I resolve to be wary of my own defense mechanisms as they reveal themselves in a need to argue or to convince other people of my version of things. I take note of my present tendency to be distracted; I use it as a clue to help me understand what I am avoiding knowing.

Omens and Synchronicities: Signs and synchronicities are abundant now. I resolve to be alert to the messages inherent in patterns of "coincidence." I note carefully the correlation between thoughts arising in my mind and external changes in the light, the wind, and the flights of birds. I realize and appreciate that I am being actively guided now. I am grateful for these signs and I acknowledge their Source.

How to Recognize Your Teachers: They trigger fresh thoughts and fresh understandings in you. They may say things that you already know—but they say them in such an unexpected way that you hear them as if it were the first time. They are masters of language—articulate, engaging, and fascinating. They themselves are curious, always willing to learn. They may, for example, display genuine interest and excitement about something that you can teach them.

Squandered: Talk that has nothing to do with communication. Empty conversation with no one really listening. Distraction; running around in circles. The heart eclipsed by the mind; the heart drowning in a sea of meaningless words.

MERCURY CONTACTING VENUS

What I Need to Learn: How to use language to build genuine bridges to other people—and that is at least as much about listening and responding as it is about talking. How to say I love you. How to listen well and help others feel that I have actually heard them and understood them. How to be more eloquent and graceful in my speech. How to express myself without profanity, if that is what I choose. How to pay constant attention to my listeners, monitoring their level of engagement with what I am saying.

Potential Blindspot: Talking "at" others rather than "speaking with" them. Becoming narcissistically enamored of my own eloquence. Concentrating so much on reaching the other person and eliciting his or her agreement that I have lost my moorings in my own feelings about reality. Diplomacy eclipsing truth.

Omens and Synchronicities: I resolve to pay close attention to messages coming to me from people whom I love. I will not let my familiarity with them blind me to the fact that they have something new and important to say to me. Messages come to me woven into art—films, novels, music—which I "happen" to encounter now.

How to Recognize Your Teachers: They immediately elicit strong feelings of affection and affinity in me towards them. They may be artists. They are "beautiful" in some sense of that very multidimensional word. They are easy with other people, getting along with them even if they are very different. Love is more important to them than insight.

Squandered: Papering over genuine differences with empty, agreeable words. Wasting time with forgettable chit-chat. "Preaching to the choir"—

that is, endlessly reiterating that which is already obvious to everyone. Telling people what they want to hear rather than what actually feels true.

MERCURY CONTACTING MARS

What I Need to Learn: How to express opinions which I hold passionately in an engaging, effective way—that is to say, in a way that intrigues and convinces other people rather than triggering their defensive reflexes. How to argue effectively. How to express anger without seeming strident, out of control, or merely silly.

Potential Blindspot: Not seeing how my edgy style of verbal delivery can create resistance in other people to hearing what I am actually saying. My own passion can create a blockage to mutual understanding and the effective resolution of conflict.

Omens and Synchronicities: Annoying circumstances arise which potentially trigger shoot-from-the-hip reactions in myself or in other people. Stressful messages appear unexpectedly. Trivial conflicts burst on the scene; by not reacting reflexively in anger to them I can follow them down to the roots of the real issue.

How to Recognize Your Teachers: They may make you angry. They may appear as rivals or competitors, even as enemies. In argument or disagreement, they are your worthy opponents, compelling you to clarify your own thoughts and to express your views effectively.

Squandered: Fights, disagreements, or tiffs whose apparent content is actually unrelated to the true, underlying issues. Displacement; misdirection. Example: arguing about politics because you are angry about sex. Blowing off steam. Saying things we later wish that we could unsay.

MERCURY CONTACTING JUPITER

What I Need to Learn: That I have something significant to say. That I have underestimated my persuasiveness and my natural authority. That without seeming arrogant, I can speak with the voice of a king or a queen. That an attitude of generosity and positiveness towards other people can open their minds to me. That humor often builds bridges of heart-to-heart communication. That I am worthy of further education.

Potential Blindspot: Blustering. Taking up more than my fair share of people's time or attention. Flogging a point that has already been expressed and understood. Overestimating my knowledge, authority, or entertainment value.

Omens and Synchronicities: Messages arrive opening doors for me. These messages might be obvious, such as a phone call offering me a better job. They might be more subtle, such as reading an article about an emerging technology—and suddenly realizing that it is the missing ingredient in a creative idea I have been entertaining. The message could take the form of a hopeful, open glance from someone in whom I am interested. Always, the key to success here lies in acting boldly and audaciously upon the opportunity of the moment.

How to Recognize Your Teachers: They display a certain "star quality" without seeming arrogant about it. Their natures are generous and expansive. They radiate contagious optimism and faith in future possibilities—and probably faith in me as well. They tell better jokes than I do.

Squandered: Talking an idea to death. Alienating potential support through an appearance of arrogance or self-importance. Reaching for that which is truly impossible or unreachable. Jumping to conclusions, then using those shaky conclusions as the foundation of strategy.

MERCURY CONTACTING SATURN

What I Need to Learn: That this is a time in my life when the only true way forward lies in a sustained, disciplined effort to master new information and new skills. Education opens doors for me now. Knowledge—especially knowledge not easily won—is power. In terms of my speech, I need to move forward to my next natural stage of verbal maturation. At some level, my style of self-expression must become more "adult"—that is to say, more authoritative, clear, and confident. It is time for my intelligence to manifest some kind of Great Work.

Potential Blindspot: Any hesitation I might feel in regard to monumental intellectual effort can cripple me now. Insecurity and fear can distort my sense of the nature of the road ahead. Laziness—especially mental laziness—is catastrophic at this point. I might not see that the perceived immaturity of my voice is having a negative impact upon people's perceptions of me.

Omens and Synchronicities: Situations arise indicating that my own ignorance or lack of necessary skill is blocking my evolution. The purpose of these signals is not to discourage me; it is to steel my resolve to dispel the ignorance and to develop the skills I need. Opportunities to do exactly that materialize before me. Attention turns to me; chances to speak up with greater quiet authority than ever before arise.

How to Recognize Your Teachers: They are serious people, probably enough older than me that I notice the age difference. They may be true elders. They may have a "wizardly" quality. They may or may not be "intellectuals" in the academic sense, but they radiate high intelligence.

Squandered: Missing a real chance to arm myself with missing knowledge or valuable education. Indulging in mental laziness. Believing that what worked for me last year will work for me next year. Failure to speak up. Masking intellectual insecurity behind silence. The single most fatal line at such a time is, "I don't want to talk about it."

MERCURY CONTACTING URANUS

What I Need to Learn: That my truth is my truth even if others disagree with me. I appreciate their support, but I do not need it. I have a natural right to my own understanding of things, and I have a right to express it— even if it does not elicit applause. I am currently experiencing a genuine "genius" stage in my development, which means that some very original and unprecedented insights are arising in me. I may not be right about everything, but I need to trust these insights and follow them to the natural conclusions.

Potential Blindspot: Am I mistaking mere contrariness for genuine intellectual independence? I might come across to other people now as simply cranky, stubborn, and opinionated, thereby creating an emotional reaction in them of negativity towards me—a reaction which might eclipse the potential of their actual agreeing with me, or learning anything from me.

Omens and Synchronicities: Patterns of weird coincidence arise now, conveying important messages and guidance to me. For example, in the same week three different people happen to mention Papua, New Guinea. That means that maybe it is time for me to go there. During this time, the universe labels all of its pivotal communications with me in the same way:

they all have the fingerprints of the weird, the unlikely, and the improbable on them.

How to Recognize Your Teachers: They dance to the beat of a different drummer. It is not that they do not care about other people; it is only that they will not modify their behavior or their understanding of life in order to win the approval of others. They think outside the box. Some might call them weird or peculiar.

Squandered: Reflexive contrariness. Wasting time trying to garner the approval and support of other people. Equally, wasting time by trying to trigger a reaction of shock or judgment in others. Either way, I have enslaved myself to other people's reactions to me. I have turned my back on true freedom.

MERCURY CONTACTING NEPTUNE

What I Need to Learn: That reality is far more complex than common sense would indicate. That psychic phenomena are real. That there are other dimensions folded into the three dimensions that we can see; that those dimensions contain unimaginable energies, wellsprings of information—and even inhabitants with whom I can interact. I am presently receiving an accelerated spiritual or metaphysical education. It may come to me through books or teachers; it will certainly come to me now via direct, mysterious, inexplicable experience.

Potential Blindspot: Not trusting the reality of my own senses or my own actual experience; instead, pasting consensual reality over them, fearing that the place where my own soul is trying to lead me is madness rather than a higher state of evolution. Alternatively, escaping reality through fanciful, ungrounded "spiritual" ideas—taking a "flight into light," in which comforting delusions prevent me from facing reality head on.

Omens and Synchronicities: Look for "impossible" experiences. Knowing a twelve will come up on the dice just before I toss them. Knowing who is on the phone just before I answer it. Seeing light around the head of a lecturer. "Thinking" I saw something moving in the corner of my eye. Try trusting these perceptions; they are now leading you deeper into the mystery. Teachers and teachings appear abundantly.

How to Recognize Your Teachers: They are classic mystics—sensitive people, with a dreamlike quality about them. They may be psychic; they are certainly compassionate. They are warm when they meet me, but they seem to need a lot of time alone as well. I feel protective towards them, even though they actually seem to be doing fine without my help.

Squandered: Getting lost in an endless, ever-expanding labyrinth of delusion and misperception. Substituting comfortable fantasy for genuine spiritual experience and authentic learning. Becoming hypnotized by mere ideas; confusing thinking with actual meditation.

MERCURY CONTACTING PLUTO

What I Need to Learn: How to speak difficult truths in ways that can actually be heard and received. That my understanding of my own life has been flawed and incomplete; that I am now ready to see myself and my personal history more deeply and more honestly than ever before. That sometimes "the truth will set you free, but first it will make you miserable." That I do not need to be afraid of reality as it actually is; that I am now strong enough to deal with it.

Potential Blindspot: As this psycho-spiritual development begins to unfold, there is something fundamental which I am not allowing myself to see. That is my blindspot, and it is always present at the outset of such events for everyone. There is no shame in that—but it would indeed be a shame if I were still maintaining that same blindness by the end of this contact.

Omens and Synchronicities: Hidden or buried truths emerge; lies and rationalizations are revealed in their true natures. Pivotal conversations occur. Pieces of the puzzle come together. Old letters, emails, photographs, and fragments of memory are shared, triggering revelation.

How to Recognize Your Teachers: I feel that I can say anything to them and that, so long as I am honest, I will not be judged. They are not so much "good" as they are "real." They look me directly in the eye. There is a certain intensity around them; they are too much for some people. They have made some instructive mistakes in their lives—and learned from them. They have not been afraid of their own passions.

Squandered: Enormous creative energy can be wasted now in maintaining lies and creating new ones. "Pride"—which is really only enslavement to the need for other people's approval—attempts to sustain a false narrative of my life. It may succeed; then my ego survives behind a lonely wall of disinformation and delusion. In an effort to defend myself, my words and my insights can become offensive weapons, doing hurtful damage to the souls of anyone who gets near enough to me to begin to get the scent of my buried truths.

ENTERING VIRGO

Planets are like people; each one has its own personality. And just like people, those planetary personalities are not fixed and immutable. Like you, they respond to circumstances. You are probably not quite the same person in conversation with your grandmother as you are in conversation with your friends. Colleagues at work understand you differently than does your mate or partner. When the policeman stops you for speeding, you might display a different attitude towards figures of civic authority than you might while sitting in a bar with your pals.

It is not a question of hypocrisy; we are not faking anything. We are simply adapting our personalities to different social environments. These adjustments are so natural that we barely registered making them.

For planets, the equivalents to the social environments are the signs, houses, and aspects. Each one modifies the planet's expression. A planet passing through the sign Leo responds to the values, potential misfirings, and underlying evolutionary agenda of that sign. It has come to a point in its unfolding journey in which it needs to express itself more fluidly, to celebrate itself, to attract to itself the life giving energy of other people's attention. We covered all that deeply back in *The Book of Fire*.

After Leo comes Virgo, and that is very much like leaving the bar with your friends and going directly to tea with your grandmother—that analogy is imperfect, but it does convey the shock of reorientation required of the planet.

When a planet enters Virgo *by transit*, it is happening for everybody at the same time. With the slow-moving transits—Jupiter, Saturn, and on out to Pluto—the new energy makes itself felt in the collective spirit of the times. We see its fingerprints in the headlines, in fashion, and in popular culture.

The same is true in a milder way with the quick transits; they just do not have enough time to develop into major social forces.

At the personal level, much of the meaning of a planet *transiting* through Virgo derives from its impact upon the particular house through which it is passing, along with the aspects it forms to any of your natal planets.

The point is to remember that the nature of that transiting planet is not going to be quite the same in Virgo as it was in Leo.

The impact of planets entering Virgo by *progression* or by *solar arc* is much more individual and personal. Unless you and I were born on the same day and year, my progressions and solar arcs are different from yours. While such a moving planet in my chart might be entering Virgo, that same planet in your chart might be in the middle of Sagittarius.

Bottom line: the material we are about to cover works with transits as well as with the other two methods, but in practice, you will probably find it more personally useful with the arcs and the progressions.

FROM LEO TO VIRGO

Sometimes a planet enters Virgo through the back door—that is to say, it retrogrades back into Virgo from Libra. That can happen by transit or by progression, but never by solar arc (solar arcs are never retrograde.) Most of the time, however, we are looking at the natural, archetypal flow of Leo energy turning into Virgo energy. The exact meaning of that transformation varies from planet to planet, but there are certain core principles which pervade all of the possibilities. Let's lay the foundation for the cookbook section which follows by understanding them.

"Pride goes before a fall" is a familiar old proverb. Its tone is too narrowly negative to embrace all of the Leo-to-Virgo evolutions, but it does definitely capture one of the darker ones. The Sun rules Leo and astrologically the Sun represents ego. We have to be careful here: ego is not always a bad word—but we all recognize its dark side. When ego gets inflated or overextended, it usually winds up getting taken down a peg or two. We think we are the best—then we meet someone even better. We are the toast of the town—then we are yesterday's news. We say, "Mirror, mirror, on the wall, who's the fairest of them all?"– and along comes Snow White.

These Leo-to-Virgo "corrections" reflect fundamental laws of the universe. Excesses of pride or arrogance are what attracts them, and they hurt. But not every planet succumbs to these kinds of ego-mistakes while passing through Leo. *The point is, getting Leo right sets us up for an easier passage through Virgo.*

The young guitarist practices hard and becomes a small town musical hero.

He enjoys performing and plays confidently. His heroes are the masters whose recordings he cherishes. When his Moon is progressing through Leo, he gets his first standing ovation. It's at a church talent show, with an audience packed with friends and family: not exactly a tough crowd. When his Moon hits Virgo, he has an opportunity to hear one of those masters perform—and he is humbled, but also inspired in a practical way. He has always played music by ear; now he learns to read score. He is self-taught. Now he seeks a teacher. He can impress anyone while playing in the key of E. Now he learns to play in E-flat—and if you play a stringed instrument, just think for ten seconds about what it takes to rise to that challenge and you will soon understand the meaning of Virgo.

Just as Leo has a higher purpose and dark side, it is the same with Virgo. In the dark version of our guitarist's Moon progressing into Virgo, he gives up music. He feels that he could never play like his heroes, so why bother?

Instead he focuses on criticizing other players.

THE SUN ENTERING VIRGO

I accept the reality that . . . I am imperfect, but that with right effort and skillful means, I am capable of effective step-by-step improvement. I am a work in progress. There is no magic bullet which would allow me to bypass the need for disciplined hard work on myself. I resolve to see myself and my karmic predicament clearly and honestly.

Where My Skills Must Improve: To have the strength to sustain this evolutionary effort, I must above all practice self-love. I judge myself only by the standard of my effort, never against the impossible standard of perfection. I recognize that a bulwark of my self-respect lies in my being of skillful, competent service to others. I resolve to improve those skills.

Identifying My Teachers and Mentors: I recognize these precious helpers who appear now in my life by the way they combine trenchant observations about where I need to improve with an absolute faith in my ability to improve. Typically, they are people whose lives have been dominated and defined by a particular set of remarkable skills with which they were born.

My Path of Self-Sabotage: Falling into a crippling pattern of hesitation, self-doubt, and self-criticism. Failing to love myself. Endless preparation operating as a way of avoiding actually getting started on anything real.

THE MOON ENTERING VIRGO

I accept the reality that . . . I am ill at ease with myself now, and that the time has come for me to bite the bullet and make some changes in my attitude toward myself and toward my possibilities in life. There are actually concrete reasons for my discomfort and feeling of insecurity. The good news is that I can do something about them. Once I part the distorting veil of my uncomfortable mood, those reasons can be effectively addressed. I do that by acquiring new skills of emotional self-expression— skills which allow me to better understand my own changing needs and to ensure that those needs are met.

Where My Skills Must Improve: I must deepen my ability to be kind to myself and to care for myself wisely and skillfully. The wisdom that animates that kindness lies in the realization that I am capable of becoming a better person, better able to make a meaningful difference in the lives of other people as well as in my own life. Claiming that spiritual victory requires effort on my part. That effort is the precise nature of my wise kindness toward myself.

Identifying My Teachers and Mentors: I recognize these precious helpers who appear now in my life by the way they make it relatively easy for me to talk about how I really feel in fresh ways. They listen well. They offer grounded, psychologically meaningful, advice and guidance. They do not judge me, but I have the feeling that they see me very clearly.

My Path of Self-Sabotage: Succumbing to a defeated mood of resignation, and confusing it with factual external reality. Giving up on myself. Endless fugues of worry. Dwelling on past errors, shortcomings, and failures instead of setting the attitudinal stage now for tomorrow to be a better day.

MERCURY ENTERING VIRGO

I accept the reality that . . . in order to go forward meaningfully in my life, I have reached a point where I need more education, at least in some sense of the word. This may not mean "school," but it does imply that without further knowledge, information, and the mastering of some new skill-sets, I will simply become mechanical and bored with myself.

Where My Skills Must Improve: Sustained, disciplined mental focus is the heart of the matter. I will not allow tedium, distraction, or mental fatigue to break my concentration. I will not be intimidated by complexity or by details. I will keep my eye on the prize, no matter how much coffee it takes.

Identifying My Teachers and Mentors: I recognize these precious helpers who appear now in my life by the fact that they are simply very good at what they do. These are skillful people. The community recognizes and celebrates them for the benefits they bring to everyone around them.

My Path of Self-Sabotage: If I fail to further nourish my innate talents with education at this point, an element of merely "going through the motions" creeps into my work and my responsibilities. It would be as if I were ready for college, but instead started over again as a freshman in high school.

VENUS ENTERING VIRGO

I accept the reality that . . . loving is not only an emotional state; it is also a skill I can develop and deepen over time. "Love," by the way, does not refer narrowly here to romance—it is about my friendships as well. The time is come for me to move my intimate partnerships to the next level. I take active responsibility for initiating that process. If these relationships are not growing, they are dying. Even though I cannot do that work alone, I resolve to do my part to help them thrive, understanding and accepting the hard reality of the alternative path. And if any friends or partners will not do their share of the work, I resolve to see that reality clearly and to make a fiercely rational response to the situation.

Where My Skills Must Improve: I humbly recognize the parts of myself that are difficult for anyone to love. I make an honest inventory of them. I will not beat myself up over any of it, but during this period, I resolve to activate more of my better self and to offer those improvements as a gift to anyone who loves me.

Identifying My Teachers and Mentors: I recognize these precious helpers who appear now in my life in two ways. Some of them, without knowing it, are models for the very skills I am actively attempting to develop. They show me the way forward, and for that I am grateful. Others hold the mirror of truth before me by acting out, often almost in cartoon fashion, the very traits I am trying to shed in myself. Even if they are annoying, I am grateful for them as well— they reveal to me what I must get past in myself.

My Path of Self-Sabotage: Entering into relationships with people who are unworthy of me. Displacing these helpful energies of self-correction into a cascade of corrections aimed at other people. Niggling criticism of my partners or my friends, reflecting my own discontent with myself.

MARS ENTERING VIRGO

I accept the reality that . . . mere emotional courage *without a mature set of supporting skills* is only dangerous bravado, and very likely to hurt me and people about whom I care. Assertiveness without the warrior-resources to back it up only leads to humiliation and defeat. I have come to a point in my journey where my "inner warrior" needs some practical, logistical support. I accept the reality that my next step is more wise than bold—I will prepare myself for victory with a set of skills, alliances, and resources rather than going off "half-cocked."

Where My Skills Must Improve: While they remain safely locked in the realm of my imagination, I let my passionate desires speak privately to my mind. What is it that I really want? Once I am clear about those intentions and aspirations, I take a hard look at reality, along with a brutally practical inventory of my existing resources. What must I develop *first* if I am going to have a real shot at making those dreams come true? What tools, skills, and alliances must be created as the initial practical step?

Identifying My Teachers and Mentors: I recognize these precious helpers who appear now in my life by the way they have kept their eyes on the prize over the years. These are people who knew what they wanted and went after it relentlessly. They have functioned with integrity and dignity—no scoundrels need apply—but their single-mindedness has blossomed into impressive accomplishment. They show me the way.

My Path of Self-Sabotage: Slipping into a mental pattern of endlessly recycling petty resentments. Blowing off steam in criticism of others— then wasting time dealing with their reactions. Allowing tensions to accumulate in my body to the point that they damage me psychologically or physically.

JUPITER ENTERING VIRGO

I accept the reality that . . . I really need a victory of some sort now and that I am going to have to work hard to achieve it. Compared to my actual capabilities, I am underachieving; I know that— no denial, no rationalization, no pinning my failures on other people. What stands between me and the breakthrough I need is partly just having enough confidence in myself to make my move. At a practical level, there are initially also some skills I need to develop, perhaps through training or some form of education. I believe in myself enough to go out and get them.

Where My Skills Must Improve: Pride is a word that sometimes has a negative connotation; for me, at this point, it is a completely positive word: it means owning a deepening sense of my own unrealized potentials, along with faith that I can fulfill them. I dare to dream of what I might become if I opened fully to my calling in life. Once I have let my imagination soar that way, I roll up my sleeves and begin to think of the logistics and tactics that will get me there.

Identifying My Teachers and Mentors: I recognize these precious helpers who appear now in my life by the way they have brought their own dreams into manifestation. At one level, they are people with impressive skills. They have earned their victories. They deserve them. But they have something more, some kind of magic: their faith in themselves—and their unspoken faith that the universe favors them and supports their success— is a quality that I am currently cultivating in myself.

My Path of Self-Sabotage: A person might set out to be the first human being to swim solo across the Pacific Ocean. Very likely, he or she will drown long before Hawaii. Lofty, inspiring goals are good for me now— but setting impossible ones, ones that are so lofty that I cannot realistically ever reach them, is a form of self-sabotage. I must be wary of it. It is a way of setting myself up for failure—and thus whitewashing the underlying karma with which I am dealing now: the fear of making practical success a reality in my life.

SATURN ENTERING VIRGO

I accept the reality that . . . it is time for me to take a big step forward in terms of maturation. That does not mean that I am currently behaving childishly— only that I am ready to move onward to the next stage of my journey. This process entails a major redefinition of my responsibilities, along with the realization that I am now capable of carrying more weight—but that the right weight for me to carry involves defining a fresh task, one that is worthy of what I have become. As I take on this major effort, it feeds back into my consciousness new maturity and increased self-respect. The effort is the outward yoga; the inward fruits grow in that soil.

Where My Skills Must Improve: A fine rule of thumb now is that you must do the most difficult thing, within reason, that you can imagine. The skills necessary for you to go forward in a meaningful way are not easily acquired. They require sustained concentration, commitment over time, and the use of the farthest frontiers of your intelligence. You are capable of more than you think.

Identifying My Teachers and Mentors: I recognize these precious helpers who appear now in my life by the way they carry themselves with quiet authority. Their heads are held high; they move with dignity and self-possession, without a hint of arrogance. They do not need to prove anything to anyone; their competence and their absolute integrity simply radiates from them.

My Path of Self-Sabotage: Losing heart as I stand poised at the base of the mountain I know I should climb. Turning to lesser tasks—ones that are simply not worthy of me. Making myself smaller. Turning my back on my highest potentials.

URANUS ENTERING VIRGO

I accept the reality that . . . sometimes you have to fight to be free. I am sick and tired of the endless slog through my ever-metastasizing daily responsibilities. I am not lazy, but I need more liberty and more latitude for improvisation and independence in my life. I accept the fact that turning this desire from a pointless, futile longing for things to be different into practical reality will require some difficult concrete measures, some risks, and considerable courage. I may have to blow up some bridges behind me.

Where My Skills Must Improve: I must devise survival methods that support a more independent style of life. Very possibly, self-employment of some sort looms on my horizon. Downsizing and simplifying my circumstances can liberate me from the grind—or at least reduce its hold on my existence. I need to become better at saying no to people who have come to depend upon me, perhaps to a point that is harmful to both of us.

Identifying My Teachers and Mentors: I recognize these precious helpers who appear now in my life by the way they seem to have escaped some of the tarted-up slavery that plagues much of the rat race of modern life. They are not simply "free spirits." They are in fact responsible, productive human beings making a contribution to their communities—but doing it in their own independent, individualized way.

My Path of Self-Sabotage: Symbolic rebellions that actually change nothing at all. For example, showing up late to work, wearing inappropriate clothing, radiating "attitude." These kinds of behaviors have virtually no impact on the reality of my life except to make me look silly. They only blow off steam—steam that might be better employed in plotting a more effective revolution.

NEPTUNE ENTERING VIRGO

I accept the reality that . . . there are many human beings on the earth who are far more advanced than me spiritually. I immerse myself in gratitude that many of these lofty souls are compassionate enough to help me. In this spirit of grateful humility, I seek these teachers and their teachings. If I am very fortunate, I might actually meet them. Failing that, I devote myself to reading their words or perhaps learning directly from those who have learned from them. I am open to the notion that some of them might not have physical bodies at this point, but that they can still help me.

Where My Skills Must Improve: Accurate, humble self-assessment is critical here. I must walk a tightrope between spiritual ego-inflation on one hand, and on the other hand, settling for teachers and methods insufficiently advanced to actually help me. Regularity, repetition, and self-discipline are the keys to successful transformative inner practice now.

Identifying My Teachers and Mentors: I recognize these precious helpers who appear now in my life by the way their eyes seem to go back forever when I look into them, even in photographs. I recognize them by their vibration of all-embracing, non-resistant openness. I understand that many of my most impactful teachers may not be labeled as "certified spiritual giants" by the community. It is those eyes and that open vibration by which I recognize them, not by some "funny hat" issued to them by a religious organization or by popular vote in the marketplace.

My Path of Self-Sabotage: Imagining myself to be more spiritually self-sufficient then I actually am. Failure to recognize the proffered hand of those more advanced than me. Not asking for help. Not sufficiently valuing the treasure of generations of practical spiritual teaching. Practicing methods more suitable to souls less advanced than myself on the journey.

PLUTO ENTERING VIRGO

I accept the reality that . . . no psychological problem in the history of the world has ever been solved until a person was brave enough to recognize its existence. I have come to a point in my journey where I need to see myself clearly, free of denial, compartmentalization, and suppression. Simultaneously, I must be free of the distortions generated by shame, childhood wounds, and any humiliations I may have suffered. I seek a middle path of truth, and truth alone. Clarity and honesty reign—and I accept the reality that in order to achieve them I may very well need to seek the support and insight of someone wiser than myself.

Where My Skills Must Improve: Being brave, open, and steady in the face of threatening psychological stimuli—the kinds of stimuli that might otherwise trigger a defensive reaction in me. I must hear things that I do not want to hear, feel things I do not want to feel—and keep an even keel in the face of some very strong emotions. Faith can sustain me, even in a dark time—and, as they say, "it is always darkest before the dawn."

Identifying My Teachers and Mentors: I recognize these precious helpers who appear now in my life by the way they cut to the heart of any matter presented to them. They value kindness, but not as much as they value the zealous pursuit of truth. There is a quality of penetrating intensity about them.

My Path of Self-Sabotage: To punish myself rather than healing myself. Failing to recognize that behind almost every negative behavior in myself or anyone else there lies a wound. That is true of almost everyone who has ever hurt me, just as it is true of me. If I misunderstand that point, healing energy turns into punitive energy, and even more damage is added to the pile. If I am unduly afraid of powerful emotions, I will find ways to escape from them and thus short-circuit the entire process.

21

CELESTIAL NAVIGATION III: SATURN TIMES, CAPRICORN TIMES

Beautiful, ringed Saturn—a planet almost universally acclaimed as the loveliest object in the solar system—could easily sue Earth's astrologers for slander and defamation. For years, poor Saturn was vilified as the Greater Malefic: the purveyor of everything from bankruptcy to loneliness to the common cold. Astrologers often still fill their clients with fear when Saturn steps into the spotlight. Heavy times ahead is the typical prognosis.

But Saturn is actually quite light. In fact, it is physically the least dense planet in the solar system. (Earth, by the way, is the densest of them all—a source of much obvious humor among the angels, I suspect.) While Saturn outweighs the Earth by almost a hundred times, it is also much larger—put a coin next to a soccer ball and you get a sense of the comparison. The effect is that Saturn's mass is spread out quite thinly through all of that puffy hugeness.

Saturn is, in fact, so light that it would float on water. No other planet can make that claim.

As we have seen, Mars is red like blood, like the color of passion. Venus is beautiful. The Moon goes through moods and changes. The solar system—or rather the great Intelligence behind it—was not trying to make astrology difficult. The hints it offers are often very broad. Beautiful

Saturn, so light that it could float . . . did the Intelligence behind the universe make a metaphorical mistake there?

Or is it perhaps the astrologers themselves who have gotten Saturn wrong?

I am betting on the latter interpretation. I hope I began to convince you of a more benign understanding of Saturn back in chapter five. I intend to make the case even more strongly in the next three chapters.

We do not need to fear this planet—nor any other planet.

CLUES IN SATURN'S ORBIT

Every 10,759 days, Saturn completes another long slog around the Sun. That works out to slightly less than twenty-nine and a half years. That's a long time—especially knowing that Saturn is moving forward in its orbit at a brisk 22,000 mph. That velocity would definitely get you a speeding ticket here on earth, but in space, such a speed is not so impressive. Our own planet, for example, is actually moving about three times faster than that.

Johannes Kepler figured all of this out about four hundred years ago: one of his most critical insights is that the further a planet lies from the Sun, the more slowly it is actually moving forward in its orbit. Saturn is about nine and a half times further from the Sun than we are. That makes it the slowest of the planets about which our ancestors knew—Uranus, Neptune, and Pluto of course move even more slowly, but they were only discovered much later.

Not only is Saturn's physical velocity much less than that of our own planet, it also has a lot further to travel. Being that much further from the Sun, the circuit of its orbit is far longer—would you rather walk around a race track or around Australia? With the diameter of its orbit nine or ten times wider than Earth's, to get back to where it started Saturn needs to travel about five and a half billion miles.

Even at 22,000 mph, Saturn must be really glad not to have kids in the back seat.

So, for all practical astronomical purposes, Saturn is the slow boat of the solar system—or so thought our astrological ancestors, whose knowledge of the solar system ended there. With the discovery of the planet Uranus in 1781, everything was shaken up. There are many fascinating mysteries around the discovery of that first "new" planet. We will explore them in the next volume of this series, *The Book of Air*. For now, our focus remains on Saturn.

And to our ancestors, with no telescopes and only their eyes, the sky, and their hearts to go on, *Saturn's slowness compared to the other planets was the biggest hint about its nature that the night sky gave them.*

GRANDPA SATURN

Used to be, if I dropped a quarter, I would just bend down and pick it up. Nowadays, at age seventy, I ask myself if it's really worth the trip. A quarter isn't worth what it was when I was a kid, but of course that is beside the point. The real issue is that I am stiffer and slower. With the exception of a few nonagenarian yogis balancing upside-down on one hand, these complaints about ageing are pretty universal.

No wonder our ancestors made the connection between Saturn's slowness and the physical realities of getting older.

Before my mom passed away at the age of almost ninety-six, grocery shopping with her was a real exercise in patience. She bravely insisted on shopping, but her forward speed was about a tenth of a mile-per-hour. God bless her, she knew she was in a use-it-or-lose-it situation. Walking was difficult for her, but she knew that if she stopped trying, she might never walk at all again. I respected her pluck, her self-discipline, and her determination—and those are Saturn qualities too.

As the body ages, we all need more of exactly those same qualities, or we pay the ultimate price for our laziness. That last comment has Saturn's signature on it as well: as we saw earlier in this book, astrologer Grant Lewi pointed out a few generations ago that Saturn's transits deliver "the cosmic paycheck." What he meant was that, with Saturn, *you get what you have earned.*

My mom was mobile until very nearly the end of her life—but only because she had made that Saturnian effort. She earned her mobility with hard work, patience, and determination. She also "kept all her marbles," as she put it, by never leaving the house until she had first completed a crossword puzzle. The unused mind goes the way of the unused body, and often goes there even faster.

MATURATION

Saturn, in common with the rest of the planets, represents a vast archetypal field of possibility. Old age is only one of its dimensions. Synchronistically, regardless of our age, by transit or by solar arc Saturn times may very well see us *interacting with older people*. But that is only a footnote in the story; the real issue is considerably more universal in its application. Old age is really just a clue here.

An eleven-year-old child goes through a Saturn transit. Perhaps the planet is conjuncting her Sun—and maybe grandma comes for an extended visit that summer. That contact with the geriatric world is part of the Saturn experience for the little girl. But here is the real heart of the matter: not interaction with grandma, but rather t*he daunting realization in the child's mind that she is soon going to have to transform herself into one of those goddesses of urbanity and sophistication: a teenager.*

And she has no idea of how to do that.

Most of us do not think of teenagers in those "urbane" and "sophisticated" terms. But the point is that such a view is completely legitimate on the part of our eleven-year-old. For that child, becoming a teenager is *her next developmental stage*. And that is exactly what a Saturn transit demands of us all: however old or young we may be, it is time to take that next step forward in life's chronological cycle.

Saturn is not narrowly about old age; it is simply about *whatever is the next step for us.*

I had a female client who was a real party animal. She often made brave speeches about how marriage was an outdated medieval custom, sexist to boot, and definitely not her style. Then Saturn crossed her Ascendant and she fell truly in love for the first time.

While it would not be fair to say that married people as a group are more mature than single people, for her in particular, marriage represented her next developmental stage. It was a struggle for her too. After all those years as an enthusiastically single person, she had many old habits to break.

She rose to the challenge and she and her husband lived "deeply" ever after.

Here is the same story, only backwards: during Saturn times, I have often seen relationships come to an end. Breaking up is hard to do, especially if we have shared life with another person in a multidimensional, adult way, getting enmeshed in all of the usual practical entanglements as well as the emotional ones.

And yet sometimes, in order to move ahead authentically in our lives, we may need to recognize that we have *outgrown a relationship*. Welcome to Saturn, beckoning us to take that next step in our maturational journey.

* With Saturn in the spotlight, I sat with a young waitress who was a client, supporting her scary realization that she needed to go to law school.
* I spoke with a popular musician who realized that in order to move forward authentically in his life, he needed classical music training.
* More times than I can count, sitting with clients in Saturn times, I have seen them recognize that it was time to commit to in-depth psychotherapy.
* Or to move across the country.
* Not long ago, I sat with a woman who realized that she needed literally to climb a mountain—Denali in Alaska, in her case.

In every one of these instances, we see the same pattern: *through undertaking a great work, a person moves forward to the next maturational stage*. During Saturn transits and solar arcs, that fundamental idea—that inward self- transformation can be triggered by a monumental outward effort—is the core symbolic DNA of the event. The details are as varied as human beings, but that maturational transformation is always the heart of the matter—at least when a person gets it right.

DO YOU WANT TO BE EXHAUSTED OR DO YOU WANT TO BE DEPRESSED?

Sitting with people facing such a Saturn time, I often tell them that they face *a choice between exhaustion or depression*. That may not be the cheeriest comment they have ever heard—but they all quickly come to the same conclusion: while exhaustion never sounds very appealing, it always beats depression.

Then we open the gift box.

Exhaustion arises when we have given everything we've got. For that reason, no one ever achieves excellence without exhausting themselves—at least not excellence in their own eyes. We may fool the world, but we cannot fool ourselves.

And that is a major point with Saturn: *giving everything you are capable of giving.* Literally doing your best.

Going further, Saturn is the planet that looks you right in the eye and says, "I know you want it—*but how badly do you want it?*" Its energy is hungry—and, famously, hunger is the best sauce.

We are talking about serious motivation.

Another way to express it is to use a line we first saw in thinking about natal Saturn. It works just fine with transits and solar arcs too—*Saturn gives us the power to do what we do not feel like doing.* That giant step that takes us to the next maturational stage never comes easily—but its benefits in the long run make it a bargain. The joys of Saturn are not exactly paroxysms of ecstacy, but they are still profound: the satisfaction of self-respect, feelings of real accomplishment, of promises kept and meaningful victories achieved.

Those are truths that stand on their own two feet, but Saturn's prizes are vividly underscored when we contemplate the alternative: *depression.* How do you feel when you are ostensibly on a diet—but you couldn't resist that bowl of ice cream? Or you quit smoking ten days ago—and you just bummed a cigarette? Or your zipper was down when it really should have been up?

We can talk about guilt, shame, and a sense of failure. But it all boils down to simply feeling bad and somehow defeated. Depressed, in other words.

My young waitress contemplating law school was around twenty-five. I asked her how she felt about being a waitress. She said it was OK. Then I asked how she might feel about becoming a *thirty*-five year old waitress.

The blood drained from her face.

There is no shame in being a wait person, but she was in the midst of a Saturn transit. It was time for her to move on in life. Next stop: law school. Three or four years later, she passed the bar. There were many material improvements in her life as a result, but the heart of the matter was that she had climbed the right mountain, and she knew it.

Imagine being hurled back via some evil magic to the eighth grade. You retain your present consciousness, but your circumstances are that of a schoolkid. The good news is that you have that limber, youthful body again. All the rest of the news is bad: you are still under the tyrannical thumb of your parents' rule, your friends are dolts who want to talk about television shows, and you are trapped in the opportunity-space of a fourteen-year-old child.

Whatever your present age, that teenage opportunity-space represents awfully thin soup. You would quickly realize what a long prison sentence childhood is, and how narrow a world it represents, at least from an adult perspective. Such a fantasy sojourn back into your youth would be interesting for maybe three days—but if you were truly trapped there, it would not be very long before you were thinking of jumping off a bridge.

In that little anecdote, we see the outlines of Saturn's formula for depression. When it steps into the spotlight by transit or solar arc, deep down inside, you are ready to move to the next developmental stage. To do that will take a lot of effort. The idea of law school really frightened my client. Ditto for the party-animal contemplating marriage. Or the woman envisioning herself on top of Denali. But the alternative is horrendous: *it means being caught in what we used to be.* To be caught in the past. To have somehow missed the bus. To continue to go through the motions of a stage of life that has outlived its purposefulness.

There is our depressed thirty-five year old waitress.

Here is a Rogues Gallery of failed responses to Saturn's transits or solar arcs:
* A dead-end conversation in a marriage that should have ended ten years ago.
* A bitter, disengaged college professor who should have retired many years back. She is going through the motions of teaching, all the while boring, shaming, and otherwise ignoring her students.
* A tired fifty-year-old musical star performing his thirty-year-old hit song for the ten thousandth time.
* The old guy with a comb-over flirting with the young receptionist, with no idea how ridiculous he looks to her.
* People trying and failing via surgery, cosmetics, clothing, and slang to look twenty-five years younger than they actually are.

I promised depression, right? We recognize all of these sad types. They are straight out of central casting. Every one of them came to a cross-roads in life at which, if they had been willing to climb the mountain that lay before them, they could have avoided this spiritual miasma.

Saturn is not bad—but it is quite fair to say that it is hard. And only for very lazy people is there an equal sign between those two words.

Just to end this section on a positive note, here is an Angels Gallery illustrating successful responses to Saturn's transits and solar arcs:

* A kid from a ghetto who just got an acceptance letter from Harvard.
* A married man or woman who just walked away, zippers still up, from a guaranteed-not- to-get-caught sexual opportunity.
* A novelist putting the final period on a 700-page manuscript.
* A magnificent old man with a beard hiking down the mountain trail shortly after dawn.
* An old woman dancing alone with the sea-wind, a faraway look in her eyes.

SOLITUDE

Here are two words that are often confused: *solitude* and *loneliness*. During Saturn times, we often find ourselves alone, left to our own devices, and solely responsible for whether we sink or swim. That is an objective existential reality, easily verified by astrological observation. How we *experience* that reality subjectively says quite a lot about who we are.

In simple terms, introverts typically enjoy this Saturnian alone-time more than extroverts.

But for all of us during such periods, the path to the higher ground requires that we "turn lead into gold in the alchemical cauldrons of our hearts." Specifically, we must *transmute loneliness into the precious evolutionary elixir of solitude.* If we then drink deeply of it, the vision for the exact nature of our next developmental stage appears before us. Our hearts reveal to us the nature of the right mountain—the one which is actually ours to climb.

Just to get grounded here, let me offer a commonplace example. Earlier I mentioned that divorce and breakups are not unusual features of Saturn periods. Perhaps two people have simply outgrown each other and they are both now ready to move down different pathways. Still, even if such a parting is right and necessary, it is almost always a hard time, fraught with emotional and psychological challenges.

Imagine two people who have been together for ten or twenty years. They come to such an ending—*and just two weeks later, one of them announces an engagement to someone he or she just met.*

Judging others is not our business—but how do you feel about that precipitous development? What is your instinctive reaction? Doesn't that new relationship seem a little fast—perhaps dangerously fast? Don't we naturally assume that when a serious, long-term partnership collapses, *that a period of solitude might be beneficial?* Individual exceptions abound—but the part of you that understands what I am saying here is called Saturn. *Periods of mindful, solitary reflection at any of life's crossroads are classic signature of a high, conscious response to Saturn's transits and solar arcs.*

And these periods are not always about the endings of long relationships. As easily, they can represent periods of intentional renewal within established relationships. Ultimately, They can be about any kind of "graduation" from any serious, extended chapter of life: a new career direction, a first pregnancy. Those are new beginnings, obviously—but we are also looking at a "graduation" from the old career or from a long period of not being a parent.

Often, during such Saturn times, these seasons of solitude seem to arise "by chance." We do not have to look for them, in other words. They find us. That is often simply how life works under such symbolic stimulus. Under Saturn's rays, a person might take her next big career step—which, incidentally, entails moving to a distant city. Ostensibly, that step is a professional one, but of course she has no friends yet in that new city.

Even though the universe often supplies such solitude "free of charge" during Saturn times, I think it is helpful for us to *consciously embrace solitude*—to actively choose it—whenever Saturn rings our doorbell. Such solitude is often the incubator of the kind of wisdom that moves us along maturation's road. A little time alone can work wonders in terms of insight and updated self-knowledge.

One quick bow in the direction of the dark side: how often in human history has a desperate *fear of being alone* ever lead anyone in a healthy direction? Love and friendship are precious, and a life lived without them would be an empty one. But Saturn weaves its own threads into the tapestry too. There is an ancient symbiosis between love and solitude. To love well, we need time alone. And when mere loneliness grabs the steering wheel, it almost always drives us into the arms of someone who is not good for us.

THE SATURN CYCLE

All through human history, anyone approaching his or her thirtieth birthday is guaranteed to be experiencing transiting Saturn conjunct natal Saturn. It is just like watching the minute hand go around the clock—after sixty seconds, you know exactly where it is going to be: back home again. The same is true with Saturn: after twenty-nine and a half years, it arrives back to where it started. Let the minute hand run another "sixty seconds," and Saturn again returns to its starting point. That second Saturn return happens when are about fifty-nine years old.

Eat your organic veggies, and you just might hit a third Saturn return when you are eighty-eight.

These are eternal, universal, inescapable human realities, with no exceptions. Even among those who have never heard of astrology, while they do not use the term "Saturn return," they still understand the reality behind it. Everyone knows that turning thirty, turning sixty, and turning ninety are major milestones in life. And everyone who is twenty-nine and who didn't badly flunk high school math can see their thirtieth birthday looming on the horizon. They interpret the feelings they are experiencing as "dealing with turning thirty." By the thirtieth birthday—or the sixtieth—the show is over. That's why those birthdays actually often feel a bit anticlimactic. The real truth is that the whole psychological process is keyed to Saturn's orbit, which actually takes slightly less than three decades. By the time we hit those "milestone" birthdays, we have already been through the initiation.

These Saturn returns are of such monumental significance that they merit a separate chapter. We will explore them in depth in chapter twenty-three.

CAPRICORN TIMES

Sooner or later, all the planets pass through Capricorn by transit, progression, or solar arc. In a few cases, we may not live long enough to experience such an event personally. For example, as I write these words, all the newborn children have Uranus in Taurus. For them to experience its *solar arc* into Capricorn, they will have to live a couple more centuries—and for their Uranus to *progress* into Capricorn, their wait will be closer to 90,000 years.

We can be more optimistic about most of them experiencing a transit of Uranus through Capricorn. That event begins in 2072, when they are in their fifties.

In the next chapter, we will catalog all the possibilities one by one. Here, in these next few pages, let's reflect on such Capricorn ingresses at the level of theory and principle. As ever, this is the most productive way to think astrologically. My hope is that the thumbnail sketches of each event that you will find in the next chapter can interact with some deeper understanding we generate over the next several paragraphs.

As always, the core principle remains the same: *as a planet enters a new sign, it takes on the values and motivations that are characteristic of that sign.* Mars is always Mars and Pluto is always Pluto—but put them in the sign Cancer and their innate fierceness is directed toward protective and nurturing behaviors. Put them in Leo and their underlying values and intentions shift: they will not be content until they "rule the world," or at least some part of it.

Back in chapter five, we got to know Capricorn. It is "fascinated with what is difficult;" it is disciplined and focused. Above all, to remain healthy, Capricorn must remember to consult its heart before it chooses the mountain it will climb. When a planet enters Capricorn, it is hungry to make its mark—hungry to get its teeth into something, to manifest excellence, and to move concretely forward in terms of maturation, empowerment, and recognition.

We can understand all of this more vividly if we recall that the planet entering Capricorn is most likely simultaneously emerging from the sign Sagittarius. That is always true with solar arcs. With progressions and transits, it is always possible that a planet enters Capricorn "backwards," via retrograde motion, from the sign Aquarius. Here, we focus on the more common situation: leaving Sagittarius and crossing into Capricorn.

EXITING SAGITTARIUS; ENTERING CAPRICORN

Back in *The Book of Fire*, we got to know Sagittarius. If I had to summarize the evolutionary purpose of that sign in two words, I would choose *gathering experience*. We all come to places in the journey where we simply need to live, to enrich our lives with stimulating variety—to "educate" ourselves in the broadest possible sense of that word. That is Sagittarius the Archer. I always think simply of an arrow flying through the air, going fast—but not exactly knowing where it is going. That sounds like I am teasing the Sagittarians, but that's not my intention: no one ever really learns anything new if they are sure that they already know what they are setting out to learn. Sagittarius is about *discovery*, with all of its risks and uncertainties.

As ever, adjacent signs tend to clash, just like two adjacent keys on a piano. We saw this principle earlier in the book: each sign can be understood as a reaction against the excesses or darker dimensions of the previous one.

Sagittarius can be flighty and irresponsible; that is obviously not its higher purpose, only the shadow it casts. Capricorn reacts against that Sagittarian shadow, focusing on integrity, maturity, and responsibility.

In aspiring to those virtues, Capricorn can become stodgy and predictable—which is why God created the next sign, Aquarius.

The circle goes around and around, eternally.

After an education, we expect a person to get a job. That is one of those simple "everyone knows that" kinds of statements—and it elegantly telegraphs the nature of the Sagittarius-Capricorn cusp. That cusp is hardwired into human consciousness, even if someone knows nothing about astrology.

Here is another illustration of the same principle: youth is truly misspent if it is not at least slightly wild and experiential; that is how we grow up; that is one way that we find ourselves. (Those words are purely Sagittarian.) At some point, we need to cross the line into life's long middle. We do not need to become boring, but we do need to make a stand somehow. (There's the voice of Capricorn.)

Think of a young woman of twenty who has, shall we say, "entertained three gentlemen" during the past year. Do we judge her? Probably only if we "misspent our own youth," as I described it a few lines ago—by failing to entertain a few ladies and gentlemen of our own.

Now let us cross a dangerous, and very Capricornian line: *how do we feel about a person of forty-five who is living the same way?*

Obviously there are many nuances in life and hopefully none of us want to rush to judgment—but for most of us, promiscuous behavior is more suspect in midlife than it was in youth.

That is another illustration of the organic reality of the Sagittarius-Capricorn cusp.

When a planet enters Capricorn, it needs to take what it has learned while it was in Sagittarius and make it real somehow. All that experience must figure out a way to become *useful*. It needs to get serious. It needs to focus on the attainment of a *worthy goal*. It is time to *make a stand*.

The young woman in our previous example might have Venus progressing through Sagittarius. A hunger for the kind of wisdom that comes only from life-experience is motivating her sexuality. We all famously have to "kiss a lot of frogs" in order to find our prince or our princess. Her condition, in other words, is honorable and she deserves our respect.

When her Venus progresses into Capricorn, it is time for her to take what she has learned and, once again, make a stand in the world. Fundamentally, this transition represents a shift in values and attitude. It would not be unusual, however, for this progression to coincide with her embarking upon the great Venusian work of a committed, long-term partnership.

We can view all of this as "the good news." *In this evolutionary story line, we see a healthy response to Venus in Sagittarius metamorphosing naturally into a healthy response to Venus in Capricorn.*

But what about the bad news? How might these evolutionary opportunities be squandered, their point missed?

A dark response to Venus in Sagittarius can simply be promiscuity in the trashy sense of the word. That kind of exploitive behavior leads eventually to burn-out, not to mention a tell-tale trail of other people's blood behind you. If your life depended on the answer, how would you rate the general long-term marital success of porn stars? It is not difficult to surmise that, as Venus progressed into Capricorn, such pointless experience would devolve into loneliness and isolation—darker Capricornian possibilities.

Here is another possible weak response to Venus in Sagittarius: we become so demandingly idealistic in the pursuit of "perfect love" that we never find it. We become that familiar Venusian archetype: the *tragic romantic*. How many heartbreaks can we survive before we lose our ability to have the faith that fuels love in the real world? Once again, when Venus progresses into Capricorn, we might see such burnout leading directly to loneliness and isolation.

In thinking soberly about the lower ground, let's not lose sight of the higher ground: Sagittarian experience leading to Capricornian accomplishment.

In these simple illustrations, we can glimpse the dance of the underlying archetypal transitions as Capricorn succeeds Sagittarius, for good or for ill.

In the next chapter, we contemplate each of the planets as it crosses this sign frontier. We will also consider, similar in cookbook fashion, the meaning of Saturn as it moves through aspects to the rest of the birthchart.

22

SATURN TIMES, CAPRICORN TIMES: THE BUILDING BLOCKS

Old-fashioned astrologers tend to become obsessed with prediction. They want to look into the crystal ball and tell you in advance what is going to happen. To my knowledge, the fact that they are quite often dead wrong has not slowed them down even once in the past two or three millennia. I suspect that the underlying, unconscious motivation is nothing less than a need to have some comforting, if delusional, *sense of control over the future*—as if mere prediction could ever actually offer that kind of control.

One crowning irony, as these astrologers surrender human freedom to the whimsies of the planets, is that we all actually *do* have some capacity to control the future—or at least to influence it in significant ways. As I wrote many years ago in my second book, *The Changing Sky,* our job is "not to predict the future, but to create it."

We perform that miracle by working on ourselves, by committing to the process of gradually becoming less crazy—and therefore less likely to make decisions which lead us to painful places. As we consciously and intentionally change our beliefs and attitudes, our sense of the very nature of reality changes. We navigate differently, more wisely. The result is a better future than the one we would have landed in had we been lazier.

Underlying that very real spiritual progress, there is another level of mystery: as we intentionally change our energies, we begin to magnetize different kinds of experiences into our lives. Faith in ourselves, for example, leads to open doors in our lives. You can call that phenomenon New Age thinking if you want; Carl Jung called it *synchronicity*; our ancestors had a simpler term: *magic*.

If someone said that *The Book of Earth* was all about how to make predictions, I would frown censoriously and say that we can predict the nature and the timing of the *questions* that life will ask, but we can never predict the answers that people will give.

If, on the other hand, someone suggested that *The Book of Earth* was a handbook of practical magic, I would smile and say, "you know me very well."

Of all the planets, Saturn is the one with the greatest affinity for *manifestation* in the material world. It is also "the cosmic paycheck," as we saw earlier. Often it is present when the inevitable results of previous actions come home to roost.

I believe everything I just wrote about the power and dignity of human freedom—but if someone jumped off a bridge a half a second ago, those lectures about freedom are a little late. Once wheels are turning, sometimes it is difficult to stop them. And Saturn does often trigger the *manifestation of the results of actions we have already undertaken*—hence, the "cosmic paycheck" metaphor. All this does give Saturn an enhanced affinity with material prediction.

There's more.

Outward events happen during Neptune transits, for example—but the real action with Neptune often occurs invisibly, deep in the mystical caverns of consciousness, in dream-time, in meditation, in the arising of inexplicable insights and understandings.

Not so with Saturn—this planet, above all others, is concerned with *making it real*. It loves to rearrange the atoms and the molecules of the physical world right before your eyes, often in ways that take the form of obstacles—mountains you need to climb, challenges you need to face. If a problem arises, Saturn wants to know *what you are going to do about it*, not how you feel about it. If you are disciplined and determined, Saturn rewards you with wisdom, empowerment, and deeper maturity. If you are lazy, Saturn has no mercy at all. It is never cruel; it simply lets the eternal law of consequences take its toll.

Here is what all of this boils down to:

I would not use Saturn to "make predictions" in the old sense of that term, not any more than I would use any of the other planets for that shaky purpose.

But if for some dark reason I had to hazard a material prediction, Saturn is the demigod to whom I would turn.

SATURN TRANSITS

By transit, Saturn spends an average of about two and a half years in a sign. It advances for approximately eight months, makes a station, then turns retrograde. The retrograde motion lasts about four months. Then it turns around again and advances for another eight months—so, *two steps forward, and one step back.*

Right there in the sky, we see Saturn's emotional fingerprint.

In common with the rest of the planets, when Saturn is *stationary*, its impact is focused and exaggerated. In working with Saturn's transits, we must always be mindful of these stations. They are powerful. Saturn making a station conjunct your Sun or your Moon is an entirely different beast than Saturn passing through those aspects, full speed ahead, on its way to a station many degrees away from that sensitive point.

SATURN BY SOLAR ARC

By solar arc, Saturn of course advances at the standard speed of all such astrological events: about 1° per year. It would be foolish to ignore the solar arcs of Saturn. They are as impactful as its transits.

Just to flesh all this out, here is another personal example: the year that solar arc Saturn made an opposition to my Aries Moon was a critical one for me. Right on schedule, just as the aspect was exact, I found myself in "Saturn city." I was deep in my twenties, working a profoundly mind-numbing clerical job at a university. But I had a good Aries Moon reason for my volunteered slavery: I was working that job in order to make enough money to buy my getaway vehicle: a sailboat.

After a while, I had earned the money, quit the job, and bought *Puffin*, a 22' sloop. I then spent a summer with my girlfriend sailing slowly from New York Harbor down to the Virginia line in Chesapeake Bay.

In the course of that voyage, I came to three Saturnian realizations:

* The first was that I was not Jimmy Buffett and that I was not going to sail my life away.
* The second one was that there was no way I was going to "have a job" ever again in my life—I could not stand it.
* The third realization was that I was going to take a crack at starting a full-time astrological practice.

You can feel all of Saturn's fingerprints in this story. I had to "climb a mountain"—working that deadening job, earning the money to buy the boat. The universe was asking me, "how badly do you want it?"

The voyage itself was an adventure, and often arduous —there is the synthesized signature of my Aries Moon, along with the Saturn.

All that is a fine example, by the way, of how aspects operate integratively: for me, Saturn's *hard work* triggered and supported an Arian *adventure*. Neither planet alone can account for what actually happened. Saturn would have kept the job, while my Aries Moon would have jumped in precipitously and probably tried to *swim* to Virginia.

Here's the heart of the matter, and the real point of this story: in the end, I emerged from being a minor clerk working in a university, and instead came out as a professional astrologer—and in that, I would say that I made a major Saturn-step forward in my maturation as an individual.

SATURN BY PROGRESSION

In practical terms, Saturn's progressions move so slowly that I would be suspicious of anyone claiming to feel them or experience them in any substantial way. It would be as if someone were to say that he could "feel the Sun slowly orbiting around the black hole at the center of our galaxy."

Give us a break, in other words.

Sigmund Freud was born with Saturn near the end of Gemini. He lived to be eighty-two; during all those years his Saturn only progressed about ten degrees. It crossed into Cancer. It squared Jupiter and it squared Mars. We can draw some correlations—in 1877, when his Saturn entered

Cancer, for example, he was looking for male reproductive organs in eels. That is Saturn work, for sure—and Cancer does relate to reproduction.

But in practical terms, we must reckon with his Saturn taking a little more than eight years to move through a single degree. The symbolism is there, but, given any kind of reasonable orbs, it is hard to focus it on the calendar.

Astrology is rich and complicated enough without our needing to deal with such subtleties. I recommend ignoring Saturn's progressions. Its transits and solar arcs will keep you busy enough.

What follows is a quick aspect-by-aspect look at what happens when Saturn triggers each one of the planets. All of this applies equally to its transits and to solar arcs.

Remember: what we are looking at are the basic *underlying integrations* as Saturn and another planet try to figure out a way to work together cooperatively.

* If it is a hard aspect, they will have to do some serious negotiating.
* If it is an easy one, they will need to keep a cautious eye on temptingly lazy solutions, dodges, and cheap avoidance.

Each aspect represents a distinct sort of conversation between planets, each with its purpose and its pitfalls. Chapter fifteen details all of that if you need a quick review.

SATURN CONTACTING THE SUN

*Growing Pains . . . a*re striking my entire self-image. I am not who I once was. The endless internal process of maturation is bringing both pressure and a lot of real developmental opportunity to bear upon the core values that underlie all of my existing choices in life. Every structure I have created questioned—work, relationships, residence, everything. I am feeling heavy for a good reason: I am caught in old habits and patterns that no longer serve me. I have outgrown my old self. I am ready for whatever is next in my life and I am willing to make a monumental effort to achieve it.

The Task: I must honestly acknowledge that underlying my feelings of simple tiredness is something deeper and darker: I feel burdened because I have grown bored with myself. Instead of wallowing in self-pity or dead-end thinking, I resolve to do something about it. I acknowledge that I am caught in the past. I am ready to remodel my life, recreating it at a more mature and self-actualized level. I want this badly enough to pay any price for it. Nothing will distract me from this effort. I am quietly—and effectively—fighting for my life.

The Fruits of Right Effort: If I get this right, my outward circumstances will become re-engaged with my soul in a fresh way. My biographical life will catch up with the reality of my inner evolutionary state—it will, in other words, become a life worthy of who I have really already become inside of myself. I will align my place in the world with the emerging accomplishments of my soul and my evolving nature.

The Price of Laziness: If I turn away from the mountain I must climb, I will begin to feel like a machine—or a zombie. I will become enmeshed in the endless repetition of past patterns that I have now outgrown. I will spend my life "going through the motions." With my soul not truly embodied in the realities of my life, no one will see who I really am. Because of that, I will feel lonely. Resignation and a black mood of emptiness will arise and be difficult to dispel.

SATURN CONTACTING THE MOON

Growing Pains . . . are striking me via my mood and my attitude. The endless internal process of maturation is putting tremendous evolutionary pressure on my heart. A "memorized" mood needs to be challenged; those habits are no longer serving me, if it ever was. I feel weighed down and burdened. I need not to wallow, but rather to get on with my life. The path forward lies in defining as precisely as possible what I am feeling that I now need, and then creating a rational strategy for positive change. Emotional energy is strong in me at this crossroads, and my relationship with it is complicated: on one hand, my heart holds an intuitive sense of what I need to become, while on the other hand, my reasoning function needs to actually execute the plan. I may have outgrown my physical home; there may need to be some role-changes in relation to my family.

The Task: I must honestly acknowledge that there are no magic bullets for me now. Only hard work and sustained effort will free me from these feelings of entrapment and resignation. In order to dispel this feeling of being lonely or misunderstood, I need to find new language to express what is in my heart—and discipline myself to speak up about my needs or my feelings with dignity and self-possession. I need to keep my eye on the prize—but what exactly is the prize? Here is how I can answer that critical question: I visualize an older, wiser version of myself— say, me ten years down the road. I ask him or her what my next move should be *right now* if I want to successfully arrive there a decade from now. I will know that I can trust the answer I receive by this sign: *I had hoped to hear something easier.*

The Fruits of Right Effort: If I get this right, I can find a basis for happiness, engagement, and meaning in a new stage of my life. I will have taken a major step forward in the endless process of growing up. I can identify what actually makes me happy today, as opposed to reciting old "position papers" about needs and desires that I have actually outgrown.

The Price of Laziness: If I turn away from the mountain I must climb, a sodden mood of quiet, resigned self-pity arises in me. I lose my spark. A feeling of tiredness dominates my mood—but it is a kind of tiredness that sleep does not cure. Part of my soul surrenders—unnecessarily—to endless feelings of loneliness and isolation. I feel chronically misunderstood—and that is because I did not make the effort to understand myself.

SATURN CONTACTING MERCURY

Growing Pains . . . are striking my intellect and the voice I use to express it. My understanding has gotten ahead of my vocabulary, while a hunger for deeper understanding—a hunger for education, in some broad sense of the word—threatens to widen the gap even further unless I make the effort to satisfy it. Through synchronicity, a chance now looms for me to learn something that will be a great support to my evolution and my maturational process. I recognize that there is always an element of "theater" inherent in speech; I am ready to outgrow the now-immature role in which I am habitually cast.

The Task: I must commit to two great efforts: one is to simply get my teeth into some serious intellectual commitment. I must exercise my mind. I must learn something that is worthy of the far limits of my intelligence. Deep down inside, I recognize that I actually want to do that now. I am hungry for that struggle. My second great effort lies in updating my verbal style. I am ready to speak with more confidence, precision, and quiet authority.

The Fruits of Right Effort: If I get this right, when I speak, people will listen to me appreciatively and take my words seriously, even if they disagree with them. I will actually know what I am talking about. I will strip my speaking style of muttering, of any slang that puts a date on me, and all unnecessary apologies. I will finish my sentences. I will know how to speak in paragraphs.

The Price of Laziness: If I turn away from the mountain I must climb, I will feel as if I have been silenced. I will blame other people for not listening and taking me seriously, while denying my own responsibility for creating the negative situation. A frustrated sense of not being heard will degenerate into resignation, resentment and silence.

SATURN CONTACTING VENUS

Growing Pains . . . are striking both my existing relationships and my larger attitude towards intimacy and friendship in general. The love between teenagers and the love between two octogenarians are different beasts. Wherever I find myself on that spectrum of evolution, the time is come for me to take the next step. This relates strongly to my own beliefs, assumptions, and attitudes about sex and intimacy. But it also relates to my existing relationships, both in terms of sexuality and of friendship—both of those must now grow, or they will begin to die.

The Task: I must honestly acknowledge that I am the source of half the difficulty facing me in any relationship. In taking responsibility for what I bring to the table, I recognize that I am ready to release some old habits and to take some steps in the general direction of wisdom and greater maturity. I also recognize that it takes two to tango—if a partner refuses to acknowledge the need for evolutionary work, I need to consider coldly the possibility that we have outgrown each other.

The Fruits of Right Effort: If I get this right, my healthy intimacies are updated and enlivened, while relationships that are no longer serving me loosen their hold on my life. In the updated version, we will have grown together and rediscovered each other at a new level of maturity. Whether or not we go through any kind of formal ritual observance, our vows are renewed. Sometimes the fruit is more bitter than sweet: as we have seen, these aspects can also bring partings. Such events can be heartbreaking at the time—but keep perspective: the alternative is living a relationship that died long ago, but never had sense enough to fall over. That takes more of a bite out of your soul than temporary heartbreak.

The Price of Laziness: If I turn away from the mountain I must climb, self-inflicted loneliness arises. Perhaps a relationship that could have been saved through evolutionary work and growth failed to take those steps. That is a quiet tragedy. Perhaps a relationship that needed to go through a conscious ending, either ends in an ugly, unresolved way—or, even worse, endlessly repeats the same failed script.

SATURN CONTACTING MARS

Growing Pains . . . are striking at the seat of all my passions. That list obviously includes my sexual energy, but also my capacity for enthusiasm in general, along with my angers and resentments. In every case, it is time to re-think them and see them in a new light. I have matured. It is helpful to notice how the tone, texture and motivation of all of these passions is trying to evolve to its next developmental stage. Habitual activities that used to fill me with enthusiasm might pall now. That does not mean that I should kiss the fire in my belly goodbye—it just means that somewhere in my life a new source of that kind of stimulation is arising. I need to look for it. Ditto for my sexual energies—they change with time too. What about anger? With mindfulness, I will realize that some of my old anger-scripts have simply run out of gas. I let them go; those energies were never my friends anyway.

The Task: Regardless of my age, I must honestly acknowledge that the passing years are having an impact upon my energy. Unless I am of advanced age, this is probably not simply about physical energy fading—it is more about changes in its source than it is about reductions or diminishment. Here is the question that reveals my new path of fire: *what challenges me to marry my sense of adventure with my sense of dogged determination?* What next step in my life would require both of those qualities in me? What new mountain should I now climb, in other words? *Hint: it frightens me. Hint: I want to do it anyway.*

The Fruits of Right Effort: If I get this right, I have taken a critical step toward eventually becoming one of those fiery elders who inspire us all—even if I am young. I have found a way to be full of life, even when life changes. I have updated my passions.

The Price of Laziness: If I turn away from the mountain I must climb, I turn away from something even bigger: my passion for life. Something inside of me gives up, surrenders in shame and resignation. Anger and resentment are bottled up, triggering a mood of ill-defined stress and tension. Sex goes flat.

SATURN CONTACTING JUPITER

Growing Pains . . . are striking my dreams and my ambitions. At one level, it is time to actually do something about them—to make them real, which might involve some deal-making and also some compromise. At another level, I need to review them critically, with one fundamental question in mind: are these dreams and ambitions worthy of the person I have now become? Do they still really move me—or is that just a speech I have memorized and repeated for so long that I actually think that I still believe it? I am ready for a truly monumental effort now—I just need to make sure that it is the right effort.

The Task: I must honestly acknowledge that I need a victory in my life now, and that it will not come easily. I make three resolutions: one, I resolve to make whatever sacrifices are required to achieve that victory. Two, I resolve to stay focused and to keep myself free from tempting distractions. And, three, I will make this an inner victory as much as it is an outer one— I am feeding my soul here, not just my ego. Wherever I am in the cycle of life, I cast a very "adult" eye on the dreams of my "youth," questioning them—and updating them where necessary. I will not "turn eighty, still hoping to the Queen of the Prom."

The Fruits of Right Effort: If I get this process right, I gain a rational, compelling basis for deepening levels of personal dignity. In principle, everyone deserves respect—but there is a special satisfaction available to those who have actually earned that respect by doing something extraordinary and impressive. It is time for me to join that elite tribe.

The Price of Laziness: If I turn away from the mountain I must climb, I become like the famous fox who decided that those hard-to-reach grapes "were sour anyway." The sound that dreams make when they die is nearly silent; in other words, failure here might not look like much, unless we view it through the teary eyes of the angels.

SATURN CONTACTING SATURN

The conjunctions are of such profound importance that they warrant an entire chapter of their own. It appears right after this one.

Growing Pains . . . are striking you in the most pure and direct way possible. You are ready to move forward to a fundamentally new developmental stage in your life. You are therefore currently trapped by the momentum of the past, caught up in "what you used to be." It hurts—and the only path open to you is straight up. You will be exhausted—or you will be depressed. Go for exhausted.

The Task: I must honestly acknowledge that dullness and predictability are nipping at my heels. No one can save me from this soul-cage except for myself. I resolve to extricate myself from the past that I have created— and to create a future that mirrors what I have already begun to become internally.

The Fruits of Right Effort: If I get this right, I am comfortable with my life, my body, and the natural behaviors of a person of my age. I move gracefully into my next decade of life, anticipating the future in a spirit of happiness and engagement.

The Price of Laziness: If I turn away from the mountain I must climb, I will feel as if I have lost the thread of my spiritual path; I will feel silly, awkward, and self-conscious; I will seem like a depleted version of what I was five or ten years ago.

SATURN CONTACTING URANUS

Growing Pains . . . are striking the heart of my right to be an individual. Perspective: even children "feel as if they know who they are." I am realizing how much of an illusion that certainty is. Lately, I am discovering so much that is new and unexpected about myself—and realizing how much I have unintentionally compromised myself because of other people's expectations over the years. I take responsibility for that, blaming no one, not even myself. But I resolve, now that I know more about who I truly am, to be true to myself whatever the cost. Were I to do otherwise, what was previously honest error would quickly metamorphose into hypocrisy.

The Task: I must honestly acknowledge that I feel trapped in a sticky net composed of other people's plans, needs, and expectations. As I claim my freedom, I must walk a tightrope. On one hand, I recognize that I must re-frame my life so that it accords with what I now actually know of myself and of the true purpose of my earthly journey. On the other hand, I must find a way to maintain my integrity regarding some promises and commitments that I have made, even though I perhaps should not have made them in the first place.

The Fruits of Right Effort: If I get this right, I gain an exhilarating sense of freedom, honesty, and authenticity in my life. I move forward, not only in maturity, but also in terms of my outward life's attunement to my inner guidance, not to mention what I might call my "genius."

The Price of Laziness: If I turn away from the mountain I must climb, I will know that I have volunteered for slavery. Something in me will be broken. I may not have actually "missed my last chance," but I may begin to play that game in my head as an unconscious way of never trying again.

SATURN CONTACTING NEPTUNE

Growing Pains . . . are striking my spirituality. What is the nature of my *next effective step* on that sacred journey? All we know for sure is that it will be a challenging one, requiring significant effort and serious self-discipline. A three-day fast or a solitary vision quest in the wilderness are useful illustrations, even though my own path may be very different. I know that the spiritual experiences of young people tend toward extremities, while the spiritual experiences of older people tend to be more quiet and more easily integrated with everyday life. Wherever I am on that evolutionary spectrum, it is time to take the next maturational step, moving myself in that more "integrative" direction.

The Task: I must honestly acknowledge that through repetition and familiarity, I have lost some of the freshness of my inner life. I am fully capable of correcting the situation, and the time has come for me to do that. How? I need to push the edges of my consciousness a little harder. If the Mysteries could talk, they would now be asking me how badly I wanted to take that next step. I resolve to answer, "Very badly . . ."

The Fruits of Right Effort: If I get this right, I will have earned what is truly the ultimate grand prize: a genuine step forward in the depth of my spiritual life. Maturity, wisdom, and stability come to pervade my awareness of the deep luminosity that is my true nature. Not that it has anything to do with ego or pride, but a quality of *spiritual authority* makes itself felt in my character, visible to anyone who is sensitive to such realities.

The Price of Laziness: If I turn away from the mountain I must climb, a kind of soul-numbness sets in. It is not simply that I failed to take a step forward; it is worse than that. Something in me gives up and surrenders to this three-dimensional world, as if it were the entirety of reality. I become bored by my own spirituality, deadened by its predictability. Without this step forward, I lose heart for my path.

SATURN CONTACTING PLUTO

Growing Pains . . . are striking upwards from my unconscious mind. Difficult, truthful realizations are creating cracks in my resistance, my denial, and my capacity for rationalization. Genuine *repressions* (where charged material is actually held outside my conscious mind without my knowledge) are metamorphosing into more active *suppressions*, where insights are nipping at me even though I am fighting with them. That is good news, at least in the long run: these suppressions can then potentially be resolved into liberating understanding about my actual story. I am now sufficiently mature to handle these insights. I am ready to face the truth of my life.

The Task: I must honestly and humbly acknowledge that part of me simply does not want to do this work. Part of my own mind has become antagonistic to my evolutionary intentions. The unconscious mind does not willingly give up its contents; my hope lies in relentless effort, disciplined self-inquiry, and looking into the mirror of my own history with a clear, cold eye. I may enlist the support of a wise and experienced counselor at this time.

The Fruits of Right Effort: If I get this process right, having dealt with my own woundedness, I make a giant step in the direction of becoming a wise man or a wise woman. The archetypes of the Shaman and the Elder marry in the alchemical cauldron of my consciousness, turning me into someone who will be held precious wherever I go.

The Price of Laziness: If I turn away from the mountain I must climb, I stay exactly as crazy as I was a year or two ago, only a bit more tired. There is no insult implicit in those words; only a lamentation about a missed chance. Furthermore, in wasting this energy, I will have bolstered my defenses against the very insights that were trying to break through to me.

The next time such an opportunity looms, the challenge will be that much greater, simply because those walls have grown thicker and taller.

ENTERING CAPRICORN

Sooner or later each one of the planets will enter Capricorn by transit, by progression, or by solar arc. As they do, their natures change subtly, touched by the energy of the new sign. Mars remains Mars, for example—but suddenly it is Mars with a Capricorn agenda instead of a Sagittarian one.

We explored this transition from Sagittarius to Capricorn in some detail in the previous chapter. No need to repeat all that here. Instead, let's begin to consider each individual planet, case-by-case, as it clicks the Zodiacal dial in this new way.

SUN ENTERING CAPRICORN

By transit, this is an annual event. Its personal meaning for you actually depends mostly upon which house of your birth chart is getting hit, along with whatever natal planets the Sun will contact by aspect during that month. Most of what you are about to read here applies more directly to the progression (or equivalent solar arc) of the Sun into this new sign.

My New North Star: Accomplishments worthy of my actual capabilities and truly reflecting my values. Putting what I have learned in my life to some practical use. Making my stand. Leaving my mark upon the world—or my community. Building something that lasts. Crystallizations of my self-discipline, my vision, and my integrity. Whatever my age, stepping into the role of elder, caring for others, guiding them if they request it.

Claiming My Necessary Tools: Focus. The ability to resist distraction and other temptations. Self-sufficiency; being a self-starter; initiative. A taste for great works. A fascination with what is difficult. Conscience and moral values. Valuing integrity highly in myself and in others. Taking the long view. Patience; determination; strategic self-sacrifice.

Missing The Point; Misusing The Energy: Instead of controlling myself, attempting to control everyone else. Pointless, timeserving slavery. Whining self-pity—all the while resisting offers of help. Self-righteousness; judging others; a crippling fear of the uncontrollable future.

MOON ENTERING CAPRICORN

The transits of the Moon are very brief. You can definitely feel them! But they do not have time enough to become deep events. Below, we are mostly concerned with the progressed Moon, which takes about two and a half years to get through Capricorn, along with the solar arc Moon, which requires about thirty years.

My New North Star: Listening carefully to my heart, asking for guidance about the best next steps for me to take in my life. Once I have that information, focusing practically and relentlessly upon achieving the goal that my heart has declared. The paradox here is that in order to accomplish all that, I need to keep my emotions in check, not allowing moods, fears, or temptations to grab the steering wheel. The heart declares the course, then sheer, focused determination takes over.

Claiming My Necessary Tools: Attunement to the trans-rational messages of my heart and my soul: that must be the first step; without it, I am an unguided missile. Once I have allowed my heart to determine my priorities, then a capacity for absolute single-mindedness must take over. That requires emotional self-discipline and some capacity to put my feelings aside and focus on the task at hand.

Missing The Point; Misusing The Energy: A melancholic mood pervades the psyche; unspoken self-pity arises. Feelings of frustration arise, while feelings of somehow having been checkmated by life blind me to the reality of paths forward which are actually open to me.

MERCURY ENTERING CAPRICORN

Transiting Mercury is quick. It rarely indicates major evolutionary steps. Instead it supports those steps with fresh information and significant conversations. The deeper material here is more associated with Mercury's progressions and solar arcs.

My New North Star: Orderly, sustained mental discipline. Through sheer determination, pressing my intelligence to operate at the extreme limits of its potential. Speaking my mind clearly and with authority.

Claiming My Necessary Tools: A willingness to burn the midnight oil—to study, to memorize, and to think critically. I humbly appreciate those who have gone before me down the road that I am following; I am willing to learn from them. I am grateful to stand on their shoulders; I honor them with my effort and determination to emulate them. Then I take it further.

Missing the Point; Misusing The Energy: Learning things that I do not need to learn, things that do not serve my higher purpose even though it might require much (wasted) effort to absorb them. Playing video games when I should be learning to fly an actual airplane—or learning to do astrology at a professional level.

VENUS ENTERING CAPRICORN

Transiting Venus, like Mercury, is quick. It rarely indicates major evolutionary steps, instead supporting those steps with fresh input from other people, along with opportunities to take a breath and catch up with yourself. The deeper material here is more associated with progressions and solar arcs.

My New North Star: An appreciation of the unique opportunities for self-knowledge posed by lasting relationships—ones characterized by mutual commitment and a long, shared story. These need not be romantic connections; precious friendships count too. I recognize that such bonds sometimes require effort and maintenance, and that they thrive on promises kept. Over time, people can help each other mature, rising together in awareness and wisdom, holding the mirror of truth before each other.

Claiming My Necessary Tools: A mature sense of accepting the reality of human limitations, both in myself and in the people whom I love. Everyone, myself included, has foibles. I forgive them and I accept them. A deepened sense of gratitude towards people who have loved me through thick and thin, despite everything. A sober perspective on the sorts of romantic delusions that can be created in the "magic of the moment" between strangers. I will sing a few hearty choruses of *Auld Lang Syne* and let the beautiful old words sink directly into my heart.

Missing the Point; Misusing The Energy: Becoming too demanding of my loved ones, and using their "failures" as an excuse for avoiding looking at my own fear of intimate vulnerability. Not recognizing the healing impact upon any relationship of unstructured time and simple fun. Confusing taking responsibility with the expression of love.

MARS ENTERING CAPRICORN

Transiting Mars does not move as fast as the previous bodies, but it too rarely indicates truly major evolutionary steps, although it can precipitate dramatic events. Instead, transiting Mars supports those deeper steps with acts of courage and self-assertion which move situations forward—or dramatic events that break up logjams or reveal underlying issues. Still, the deeper material we explore here is more associated with progressions and solar arcs.

My New North Star: Calculated boldness and audacity; a willingness to assert my values and to take a clear stand in their defense. I resolve to consider my natural rights judiciously, without inflation—and then to claim them; I resolve to ensure that my legitimate needs are well met. I can wield the Elder's sword to defend that which is worth defending in my life.

Claiming My Necessary Tools: Anyone can get angry and yell. That is not my goal here; my goal is to win. I accept that in order to win, I need strategy, sobriety, and the right weapons. I am patient; I choose the time to act rather than reacting impulsively. I read Sun Tzu's *The Art of War* cover to cover. I apply its principles coldly, but always within the framework of my beliefs, values, and the maintenance of my sense of integrity.

Missing the Point; Misusing The Energy: Anger bottled up to the point that when it explodes, the results are spectacular, but ineffective. Colluding co-dependently and in a state of self-delusion with war-makers by "exercising patience" and "trying to maintain the peace" in a way that only worsens the inevitable confrontation.

JUPITER ENTERING CAPRICORN

With Jupiter, we enter the realm of true theme-building transits. What you read below definitely applies to Jupiter's transits, along with its solar arcs. Meanwhile, its progressions have slowed to the point they are effectively imperceptible.

My New North Star: The happy and familiar combo-platter of hard work and success. Success sometimes comes without hard work, and sadly hard work sometimes leads a person nowhere—but that is not the energy of Jupiter in Capricorn. Here, if I am willing to make great efforts, the universe rewards me. Is there a catch? I must make sure that it is my heart rather than either my ego or someone else's dreams that have chosen the mountain that I am now intending to climb.

Claiming My Necessary Tools: A robust confidence in my ability to do extraordinary things. Belief in myself. I am willing to contribute the famous *99% perspiration*—but I am guided and encouraged by a full commitment to faith in my *1% of inspiration*.

Missing the Point; Misusing The Energy: Going for mere glitter; striving too hard to win the approval of others through accomplishments that have no other personal meaning for myself at all. Haughtiness; the abrogation of authorities that are not truly mine. Telling other people what to do.

SATURN ENTERING CAPRICORN

With Saturn, we are interested in transits and solar arcs. The progressions only amount to a few degrees in a lifetime—too slow to notice.

My New North Star: I resolve to show the universe what I am made of. It is time for my masterwork to take concrete form. That is true in whatever category of excellence I choose to make my stand—it could be my work, but just as easily it could be my family, my inner life, or some form of art. I accept as reality the sense that I am being called to a mission. I do not recognize failure as an option. Whatever my age, I am willing to play the role of Elder, offering wise and balanced guidance to anyone who requests it.

Claiming My Necessary Tools: A willingness to give everything that I have in order to reach this "pearl of great price." Success here is more important to me than any of my personal needs; I accept that the great work is simply bigger than I am. I surrender to that reality. I will pay any price without hesitation.

Missing the Point; Misusing The Energy: Devoting this monumental outpouring of energy and self-discipline to an unworthy goal. Such a goal does not necessarily have to be immoral or unethical; all that is required for it to be unworthy is that it did not arise naturally in my heart, but instead reflects the public values that animate consensual reality—everybody else's definition of "my" success.

URANUS ENTERING CAPRICORN

Transits and solar arcs are our focus here. Once again, the progressions are too slow to be of practical use.

My New North Star: Building practical structures and supports for my eventual escape from the tyranny of normalcy. I will not waste my time being a "rebel without a clue." As I move in the direction of creating a life that more freely reflects my true individuality, I understand the need for a rational, long-term strategy. I resolve to get my escape plans right—and to enjoy my dessert later.

Claiming My Necessary Tools: First and foremost, I need to listen to my soul—and my soul alone—about the kind of life that I actually want to live. Only with that deeply-seated, independent vision firmly in mind will I be able to muster the kind of long-term focus that I now need. I need to want it that badly. After that, I resolve to embrace the practical realities of actually getting there and making it happen: earning seed money, hammering nails, whatever it takes.

Missing the Point; Misusing The Energy: Symbolic attacks on normalcy or conventionality, attacks which say almost nothing about who I am except that I am frustrated and angry. Suppressing my sense of entrapment to the point that I become dissociated, simply going through the motions of a life which holds little true interest for me.

NEPTUNE ENTERING CAPRICORN

Transits and solar arcs are our focus here. Once again, the progressions are too slow to be of any real use.

My New North Star: A single-minded commitment to my own spiritual evolution. All other needs, drives, and considerations are now secondary to that goal. I recognize that the term "spiritual evolution" embraces many disciplines beyond obvious references to prayer and meditation; it also includes acts of charity, kindness, and compassion aimed at the support of others. I will not fall into the false "spiritual" illusion of turning my back on the needs of this world, coldly separating myself from the realities of other people's needs.

Claiming My Necessary Tools: Structuring my daily life in such a way that it includes sufficient time for inner work: meditation, prayer, yoga, chanting, perhaps religious ritual. Figuring out some concrete way to channel my compassion into the effective alleviation of pain and hurt in the world. I meditate upon the archetype of the spiritual elder; whatever my present age, and I embrace it as my own destiny.

Missing the Point; Misusing The Energy: Bossing other people around spiritually; "correcting" their beliefs and their practices. Arrogating a kind of theological authority to myself which I have not yet actually earned. Mistaking mere memorization for wisdom. Mistaking mere austerity for spiritual progress.

PLUTO ENTERING CAPRICORN

As with Uranus and Neptune, transits and solar arcs are our focus here. Once again, the progressions of Pluto are too slow to be of any practical use.

My New North Star: A sober understanding of the exact nature of my karmic predicament; I adjust myself to the idea that it may have taken thousands of years for me to become as crazy as I presently am—and that if I work hard on myself, I might get beyond that craziness in a few hundred more years. (The numbers may be totally wrong here; what is not wrong is the idea of seeing my issues and my delusions clearly, and of resolving to do whatever it takes, for however long it takes, to face them down.) I celebrate my evolutionary *relentlessness.*

Claiming My Necessary Tools: The great twentieth-century masterpiece of modern, non-pharmaceutical psychology and psychotherapy can be a huge help to me now. There are things I need to feel and to talk through. Having a person of wisdom on the other side of the conversation can help me cut through the fog of my own defenses. Beyond psychology, the tools of past life regression, psychic readings, and evolutionary astrology can help me get to the substratum of wounds that I am seeking to heal. I recognize that some of them predate my childhood in this present body.

Missing the Point; Misusing The Energy: Disciplining myself to not feel. Holding back necessary tears. Toughing out negative emotional states rather than following them down into the secret chambers of my heart. Attacking others for having the same wounds that I do, all the while having no idea that I am looking into a perfect mirror of my own condition.

SATURN THROUGH THE HOUSES

By transit, Saturn spends an average of two and a half years in each house of your chart. Houses of course vary rather extremely in width, especially for people born at high latitudes, so those numbers vary widely too.

Bottom line, your own Saturn's passage through each house may be as short as a year or as long as five or six years. In all cases, however, Saturn's transit through a house lasts long enough to be a real turning point in your life. Such transits also move fast enough that as we look back, they usually form up rather neatly and naturally into convenient "life chapters."

With Saturn's three decade orbit, on average we all get about three passes of Saturn through each one of the houses—each passage hitting us at a very different stage of life, and so having a rather different meaning each time.

Meanwhile, by solar arc, Saturn moves at the usual 1° annual pace. Depending on the geometry of your birth chart and your longevity, by solar arc Saturn typically touches only three or four houses. Its entry into a new house is then a rather epochal development. It is as if you have entered a new school with new rules and new lessons.

Let us look briefly at each of these passages.

SATURN ENTERING THE FIRST HOUSE

In the first house we see the results of the interaction of two active factors: our self-image and the choices we make as a result of it. Who we think we are, rightly or wrongly, determines what we do. Those are obviously very broad categories, but the deeper point is that they are also subject to evolutionary change. That is what is happening for you now. You are changing in Saturn direction, and to get it right, all of the Saturn basics take on emphasized relevance: solitude, realism, self-discipline. For you, everything ultimately centers now on the process of maturation. There is a need to take on some kind of great work in order to accomplish that big step forward in life. A good rule of thumb here is that you need to do the most difficult thing that lies before you. That is very probably "your mountain"—and you would not want to find yourself on top of a shorter, easier mountain that was not actually yours. During these times, people start new careers, move, have babies, get married, get single—life's most obvious milestones abound now.

SATURN ENTERING THE SECOND HOUSE

Despite conventional astrological wisdom, money is not always the central issue in the second house, although it often does play a role in the emerging situation. The real issue is that whatever effort you initiated with Saturn in the first house was probably a sound enough idea—but it now needs a little bit more than faith to make it happen at the practical level. Here is the key question before you: *what new resources must you acquire in order to support your intentions—and simultaneously to banish this pesky underlying feeling of insecurity?* At such a time, it might feel as if you have made a big mistake somewhere along the line. Don't worry; that is probably not actually true—but those fearful, insecure feelings have a practical basis in fact. The key is that all of these issues are *addressable* in practical ways. None are truly fatal. Reorganizing our finances can easily play a role here—money is of course a fundamental resource. But so are mutually helpful alliances, new tools along with the skills to use them, and appropriate training. All these things build a *practical foundation for self-confidence* as you go forward—and the lack of them does exactly the opposite.

SATURN ENTERING THE THIRD HOUSE

"Not all those who wander are lost," as the famous wizard said. If you have done well with the previous two houses, your new vision is established. You have forward momentum. The question becomes, *what possibilities are there that you have not seen yet?* That applies both to dangers and to opportunities. This developmental stage calls for a time of disciplined learning and serious investigation—but learning what exactly? That is where our line about "wandering" comes into play. Despite any anxious instincts, resist the temptation to be totally practical now; *resist the illusion of thinking you already know what you need to know.* Your learning must now be studious and focused—but do not ignore the voice of your intuition in terms of deciding precisely what it is that you need to learn. Your best instincts are now disguised cleverly as whimsical curiosity. At a purely practical level, there is a great need at this point to improve your vocabulary and your skills regarding verbal or written presentation. Your voice needs to catch up with your mind. Some "wandering" can work miracles there.

SATURN ENTERING THE FOURTH HOUSE

Time to turn your attention inward, both toward your own soul and toward your human roots—your home, your family, your people. They all need your attention now. While you were preoccupied elsewhere, all three have gone through some changes. Even your soul is not what it was the last time you checked. That was not a mistake on your part—Saturn's passage through the last three houses has kept you busy with the material world. But that is not the only world there is. You now need some quiet, reflective time. Meanwhile, people you love—your family, in any sense of that word—have been changing too. It is a perfect time to sit around the fire with them, to hear their stories, to soak up their changes, to pay them some attention. Meanwhile, take a look at your physical home. Does it suit what you have become? Homes sometimes need to grow up too. Is it time for a move? A remodel? New furniture? A kitten? A baby?

SATURN ENTERING THE FIFTH HOUSE

See if you can wrap your head around this paradoxical idea: the *discipline of spontaneity*. That strange phrase encapsulates the ambiguous nature of this house passage. Saturn has a serious tone, while the fifth house is playful and fun. The key here is to realize that simple playfulness serves a serious developmental purpose. Of course, if we get too serious about play, it does not work very well! There are two interlocking points to understand. The first one is straightforward: if you keep on working at the same pace, this tiredness you are feeling is going to seep into your soul and dye it gray. You really need some relaxation. Go on vacation, buy yourself some toys, enjoy a bubble bath. The second, deeper, point is that your inner child has a better sense than you do of the major developmental stages that lie ahead for you. Trust that inner child of yours and encourage him or her to play. Illustration: perhaps you find yourself "wasting time" watching movies about adventures in outer space. *And perhaps those fantasies lay the foundation for a big idea that has not yet actually dawned on you: that just a little bit down the road, you are going to get your pilots license.* Without saving the galaxy piloting that X-Wing Flyer, there will be no Cessna 150 in your future . . .

SATURN ENTERING THE SIXTH HOUSE

Hard work is definitely part of the picture here. The sixth house and Saturn share an affinity for responsibilities—dangerously, even ones they do not actually need to take on. In other words, use a little discrimination before you sign up for any new commitments now. Are they really the best use of your energy, especially in the light of—and here is the big Saturn piece—your recent pulse of maturation? When you were fourteen, maybe you made some money mowing lawns. That was a legitimate responsibility and it was probably good for you. Nowadays, there is surely a better use of your time. Be mindful; there must be maturation on your part now in terms of how you *define* your appropriate commitments—and how you set smart limits by using that magic word, "No." There is always lots of genuine satisfaction in a job well done; if you are not honestly feeling that satisfaction, the job you did was probably not yours to do. Older mentors may appear in your life now, people who have been down the road you are now facing. Pay attention to them; they have a lot to teach you. Do that, and you might not have to pay the same price that they paid.

SATURN ENTERING THE SEVENTH HOUSE

This astrological event has led many an astrologer to blunder into frightening people about the imminent ending of important partnerships: "you will get a divorce." Be careful not to make that same mistake. In actual fact, assuming that a relationship is reasonably intact and healthy in the first place, this transit or solar arc is only a call to a new level of intimacy, commitment—and very probably happiness. The only hitch is that for this more encouraging prediction to come true, the bond between the two people needs to mature. The perspective is that stable relationships tend to be conservative; patterns established early tend to persist: using baby names for each other is good example. After a while, those habits can begin to blind one person to what the other one has become. Familiarity can be numbing, in other words. This is the wall that must be torn down. The fundamental question is, *if we met for the first time today, would there be energy between us?* If we are busy staring at a brick wall of preconceived notions about each other, we cannot know the answer. Our only hope is to tear down the wall—and that mindful destruction is an excellent definition of Saturn's work as it passes through this house. Some couples enter into counseling; others simply go on a long vacation, thus breaking up the patterns of their daily routines, liberating their spontaneity with each other. Some re-discover the underlying spark that brought them together in the first place. Others discover that, with the wall down, they do not actually have much to say to each other anymore. That is sad, but it often spells a clean, resolved ending rather than a messy, unresolved one.

SATURN ENTERING THE EIGHTH HOUSE

There is a strange interplay of opposites here: the eighth house is the most intimate of the houses, while Saturn is the most solitary of the planets. Deep mating bonds are very much in the eighth house domain—but if we begin there, we will only hit a brick wall in our thinking. The eighth house is one of the gateways that connects the conscious mind to the unsettling realm of the unconscious. Our point is that there are times in life—Saturn times—when we need to go down into that dark realm all by ourselves, with no one to hold our hands. Here is the key that holds everything together, both the solitary inner work and sexual bonding: *the issues, demons and complexes that we face in that inward process are exactly the ones that tend to rise up later on to scuttle the ship of love: jealousy, insecurity, anger*. Sometimes a solitary journey into the land of our own shadow can serve a preemptive purpose—in other words, that which we have healed in advance, before we dare to love, will not rise up later to suck the life out of a marriage or a partnership. I am visualizing a self-aware man or a woman with Saturn entering the eighth house; he or she is courageously entering into something like psychotherapy, all alone. I am visualizing them a little bit further down the road, living deeply and happily with another human being, having defused the potential bomb in advance.

SATURN ENTERING THE NINTH HOUSE

Imagine being in a prison cell, gazing longingly out through a window at the wider world. Dial that image back a little bit; it is too extreme—but as Saturn enters your ninth house, look for that same kind of entrapped feeling arising in your own heart. You will find it—and the time has come to do something about it. You need to widen your horizons. It is a fine time for a jailbreak. Some of that run for freedom might involve travel and cross-cultural experience; some of it may very well be educational. In both cases, breaking free requires an enormous commitment of energy on your part. Duties and responsibilities may be holding you back from the adventures that you need. This is a philosophical house—so here is some philosophy for you to put in your pipe and smoke: *what about honoring your duties and responsibilities to your own soul for a change?* Life is just too short for you to risk not spreading your wings—however costly that might be—at this critical crossroads.

SATURN ENTERING THE TENTH HOUSE

Houses always interlock; they flow developmentally from one to the next. In the previous paragraph, discussing Saturn in the ninth house, we cautioned you about the folly of not spreading your wings at "this critical crossroads." With Saturn now entering the tenth house, we can understand how much rests upon getting the ninth house right. In conventional astrology, the tenth house is related to career. Fair enough, but I prefer to use the word *mission*—your "cosmic job description," so to speak. Here is the point: *before we get a job, we typically need an education.* And an education, once deeply internalized, usually triggers in a person an urge to be useful somehow to the community. It is time now for the role you have been playing for the past few years in the world to mature; you may very well be ready to take the next concrete step forward in your career—or more broadly, your next step in terms of the hat you are wearing in the world. In any case, you have simply outgrown your accustomed role. Those shoes have grown too tight for you. The mind-stretching work that you did with Saturn in the ninth house is the foundation upon which you are standing today—assuming that your jailbreak was successful. If not, then you have some catch-up ahead of you.

SATURN ENTERING THE ELEVENTH HOUSE

At one level, the eleventh house refers to our "tribal identity"—the groups of people who recognize us as peers, and *vice versa.* These tribes can take any social form, from a corporation to a *Sangha* to an orchestra to a base-ball team. *Here is the question you are facing: is that tribe still serving your highest spiritual purpose or is it holding you back?* Have you outgrown your socially-defined and universally-expected role in that tribal context? It may be time to move on. There is a second level to the eleventh house—one that casts a telling light on its social dimensions. This is the house that refers to your *direction in life*—your goals and aspirations. In a world full of hard choices, the eleventh house clarifies the nature of your most natural and appropriate *priorities*. With Saturn passing through this territory, begin your inquiry with a long-range question: *where do you want to be in your life in ten years time?* As you ask the question, make sure that you are centered, mindful, and very "present-tense" as you listen to your heart. If you succeed there, you will realize that your priorities have shifted since the last time you set them. *Now go back and review your relationship with your tribe in the light of these emerging, more mature, goals. Are these people helping you or hindering you?*

SATURN ENTERING THE TWELFTH HOUSE

The preacher in the pulpit intones, *O death, where is thy sting?* And the congregation responds predictably, in happy, prerecorded accord. Not to make fun of churches—but how will any one of those congregants react on Monday morning when a doctor looks them straight in the eye and announces some really bad medical news? Faith is a funny thing. Without it, life would be almost unbearable—but people often hide from the truth behind their faith, taking refuge in collective agreements about things they have not actually directly experienced. Truth often then creeps up on them in shocking fashion. Saturn is, above all, profoundly realistic. It wants you to be prepared for anything and everything. As it enters your twelfth house, your faith will be cast into the alchemical cauldron of life's fiercest truths. All that will stand its ground in the face of that onslaught of pressing life-and-death questions is that which you have truly seen, felt, and experienced in your own soul. Your faith may well be stripped down to its very bones—but every single one of those bones is absolutely honest. You can count on them forever. If you surf the wave of this onslaught, you will find yourself inspired toward systematic, disciplined and absolutely authentic spiritual investigations. Your aim here has nothing to do with mastering fancy metaphysical chatter; it is 100% about the truth—and nothing but the truth—of your own mind and your own soul.

23

SATURN RETURNS

Nearly everybody—even people who do not believe in astrology—knows his or her Sun sign. Avoiding that knowledge is nearly impossible nowadays. As astrology has increasingly entered the mainstream over the past few decades, I've been entertained to see how a few more technical pieces of the astrological puzzle have also caught the public's imagination. People everywhere, for one example, seem to live in abject dread of Mercury retrograde. Anything goes wrong and you instantly hear, "Is Mercury retrograde?"

. . . even if it isn't.

Ditto for "Oh no, the Moon must be Void . . . "

In a similar way, "Saturn returns" have entered popular parlance. Everyone seems to have at least heard about them. In a lot of ways, this is much less surprising than what's happened with Mercury retrograde or the Moon being Void of Course. That is because everyone seems to understand intuitively that turning thirty years old is a very big deal. We can say the same for turning sixty.

Those big birthdays align fairly closely with the Saturn cycle, and so the simple convergence of "a-birthday-with-a-zero-in-it" and a deep astrological rhythm have created a natural and obvious association between the two.

When I was a kid back in the wild and woolly 1960s, we had a saying: *Never Trust Anyone Over Thirty*. It was, of course, a monumentally stupid thing to say, but it did have a certain resonance with the times. After a decade or so, I began to hear a tongue-in-cheek variant: Never Trust Anyone *Under* Thirty. That was dumb too—but *why thirty?* Why not twenty-five or some other round number? Even then, at some intuitive level, we realized that when a person turned thirty, he or she had crossed some kind of line.

No profession yet? No committed relationship? In your twenties, most people will cut you some slack. Turn thirty, and they start worrying about you—or just writing you off.

There are deep waters here. We will fathom them soon.

Some of you readers have experienced your second Saturn return; many of you have not. It takes six decades to get there. That is another line to cross. At that time, our faithful friends will gather around to help us celebrate. They will merrily present us with rubber pants, dead flowers, and a fake Viagra prescription. They will call us grandma or grandpa, while regaling us with exaggerated grotesqueries of *r-e-s-p-e-c-t.*

Beneath their playful teasing, there is a ritual recognition of the fact that, here at age sixty, we are experiencing another serious passage: *we are entering life's third cycle.* It is different than the first Saturn return, but there is a similar *right of passage* sense to it. As with the idea of never trusting anyone under or over thirty, the social recognition of the second Saturn return is typically presented as a joke—but behind the joke there is something deeper happening. In a way, your tribe is putting you through a ritual initiation.

MAIDEN, MOTHER, AND CRONE

In the archetypal feminist psychoanalysis, it is often stated that there are three stages in a woman's life: *maiden, mother, and crone.* I would not want to handle the public relations account on the word "crone" nowadays. It is a hard sell, even though it is a word with an honorable history. Getting a bit ahead of myself here, I prefer the term "elder" in reference to the third Saturn cycle since it is both respectful and gender neutral.

Many of you have been *maidens*—courted, desired, sexualized. Then perhaps you become a *mother*—and suddenly the social interpretation of your identity was significantly altered. You felt it and so did everyone else. Finally, there is a standard joke—or complaint—among women as they get older and start moving into the third Saturn cycle: that they become *invis-*

ible. No one notices a "crone." Famously, there is no better disguise if you want to be a shoplifter than to be a "respectable" woman in her sixties. You can walk out of that store wearing three watches and a diamond necklace dangling a price tag, and all you will hear is a vague, "thank you . . ."

Again, in these simple, human observations, we sense some of the deeper, darker waters of the Saturn cycle, although nothing I have written so far brings us close to the heart of the matter. All we have demonstrated so far is how universal this astrological experience actually is.

Unlike most transits, progressions, and solar arcs, to know if someone is experiencing a Saturn return, all we need to know is how old that person is. Everyone hits these passages at exactly the same age. Transiting Saturn square natal Venus? That can happen at any time. But Saturn returns: always, like clockwork, they happen every twenty-nine and a half years.

This universality of experience has hammered these returns deeply into the collective consciousness. At the level of folklore and custom, everyone knows about them, even people who do not consciously relate them to astrology. We don't need astrology to know about them, in other words. Our ancestors have passed on their understanding—and their misunderstanding—of the ageing process since the beginning of human time.

YOUTH, MID-LIFE, AND THE CYCLE OF THE ELDER

Taking the Saturn cycles beyond the context of feminine psychology, we can offer more universal labels for these three organic and distinct periods of human life. Let's drop maiden, mother, and crone, replacing them with *youth, mid-life, and the cycle of the elder.*

Each one, as we will see, has its own logic, nature, and developmental purpose. The Saturn returns themselves are the *punctuation marks* in the long, archetypal process of human maturation. They mark the *boundaries* between these longer stages.

Another way to say it is that the first Saturn return is the initiation into life's *long middle*, while the second Saturn return is the initiation into *elderhood.*

Some of us will experience a third Saturn return as we near the age of ninety. Let us call that one an initiation into the Great Mystery since everyone knows that by then death is not far away.

When I use the word "initiation" here, I am thinking like an anthropologist studying indigenous people. In such cultures, an initiation often has elements of an ordeal or a test. The boy or girl experiencing puberty, for example, might be expected to fast alone in the wilderness for three days and three nights. That is not easy; it is possible to fail. Similarly, Saturn returns are serious initiations. They place the evolving psyche under considerable stress; they too can fail—or succeed, and move us forward gracefully and meaningfully in life. In order to succeed, it is helpful to have the map that astrology provides.

Jokes about never trusting anyone under thirty and fake Viagra prescriptions can only take us so far.

LEARNING CHINESE

Usually when I travel in a foreign country, I make some effort to learn how to say please and thank you in the local language. Generally, I pick up a few more phrases fairly easily. In China, I have found that process to be far more difficult than usual. The basic sounds of that language are strange to my ears; a change of pitch changes the meaning of a word. It is a difficult tongue to master for anyone raised on European languages.

And yet, I marvel: currently there are literally millions of people learning to speak perfect, unaccented Chinese. I am humbled by their linguistic brilliance.

I would only add that most of them are three years old and Chinese.

In practice, we know that little kids are likely to do dumb things—cross the street without looking, put their finger in an electric socket. As adults, we have to take care of them or we know that they will hurt themselves. No one says it out loud, but basically we treat children as if they didn't have brains in their heads. And yet in some specific ways—learning to speak Chinese, for example—little kids are absolutely brilliant, and much smarter than we adults. *When it comes to learning language, the brain is optimized for the process before we are seven years old.* Blessed are those who are exposed to a second language when they are young. They will speak it like a native for the rest of their lives.

The broad point here is that at different stages of the life cycle, human intelligence experiences the rising of certain necessary skill-sets. For a while, we are particularly good at something, exactly when we *need* to be good at it. We must seize that opportunity right then and there. It will not last; with time those skills will fade—and be replaced by the rising of another set of skills, ones that are appropriate to the next developmental stage of life.

I could study Chinese every day for the next ten years. Eventually I could probably learn to understand it and to express myself—but no one would ever mistake me for a native.

"Learning Chinese" is simply a metaphor here. We will discover that there are far wider-ranging qualities of intelligence that arise powerfully in youth, then fade away at the first Saturn return. Never again in our lives will we match them. We need to use those skills while we are young—or we will be in trouble in mid-life. Then we would be in the same boat as someone who had never heard human language until he was thirty years old. It would, in other words, be too late for mastery. The first Saturn return marks the rapid fading of certain youthful skills—and the arising of fresh ones, appropriate to success in our middle years. Something very similar happens at the second Saturn return as well—the skills of life's middle years begin to fade, while something fresh and precious begins to arise in their place: let's call it "the wisdom of the elder."

Structurally, it is helpful to think of the Saturn cycle as *three long, thematically coherent periods punctuated by two brief, intense periods of transition.*
  * Youth, mid-life, and elderhood are the long, coherent periods.
  * The first and second Saturn returns are the periods of transition

We could add the third Saturn return as an initiation into a final, more extended phase of life—although our prospects for it being a long one are less certain.

Diving into an analysis of the Saturn cycle, we will look at youth, mid-life, and the cycle of the elder in terms of their global evolutionary purposes. We will catalog the skills that arise naturally—and which must be exploited while they are available—in order for us to continue developing our potential as human beings throughout the life-cycle.

Once those broad "chronic" patterns are understood, we penetrate the more "tactical" Saturn returns themselves, seeing them as specific initiations or punctuation marks separating these broad epochs of life.

THE PURPOSE AND UNIQUE SKILLS OF YOUTH

Little Johnny is wearing a cape and a mask. If you call him Johnny, he will sternly correct you: "I am not Johnny. I am *Batman*." And by ancient unfailing instinct, you apologize: "Excuse me, Batman. For a minute there, you looked a lot like my nephew Johnny."

How many times has such a scene been replayed in human history? At some hardwired level of our psyches, we recognize that children must play or they will not grow up right. Instinctively, we pitch in and help them.

Johnny will be a man someday. As such, we hope he can make a stand in this world, defending the principles he holds sacred and competently protecting those whom he loves—just like Batman . . . more or less.

Pretending to be Batman can be understood as a kind of *neurological rehearsal for* what Johnny will eventually become. He gets into the role-playing adamantly, but there's another layer to it: *as fervently as the young lad engages in the fantasy of being a superhero, somehow we have faith that he is not going to try jumping off a roof.*

He still has one eye on reality, while the other one is *dreaming his future.*

If Johnny turns sixteen and he still wearing his cape and mask, we begin to have some serious concerns about his mental state. Hopefully, by then his dream- track and his reality-track are beginning to converge. But if we ask him at age sixteen what he wants to be when he grows up, it would not surprise us to hear him express something grandly ambitious: he wants to be a movie star or an environmental crusader who changes the world—or, more likely, both. Those may be unlikely developments, but, unlike Johnny actually becoming Batman, they are within the realm of possibility. His dream-track and his reality-track are converging.

So far, so good.

Parents who are terrific with very young children often blow it badly with their teenagers. So long as Johnny is a little kid pretending to be Batman, everything is copacetic. But if, in pursuit of his dream of becoming a movie star, he announces that he wants to major in theater when he attends university, he may very well be discouraged by his parents, while being pressured to choose something "more practical."

Let us hope he defies his parents and sticks with his dream. *Because the whole purpose of youth—and its most unique special skill—lies in dreaming.* That is our critical idea here.

    * *During the first Saturn cycle, our intelligence is optimized for listening to the voice of our soul as it guides us toward an understanding of our natural path through life.*

Johnny will never become Batman—but he just might possibly become a movie star. More likely, "movie star" is simply a metaphor his soul is using to guide him, just as Batman was a metaphor for the eventual empowerments of adulthood. Even if Johnny never makes it to Hollywood, that dream is as precious to him as the North Star is to the sailor lost somewhere out on the dark ocean. His parents do him a terrible disservice by not taking his dream seriously. It is only natural at Johnny's present developmental stage—now, starting college, about mid-way through his first Saturn cycle—that his dream-track and his reality-track have not yet fully converged.

    In youth, the gap between reality and dreams is precious; it is where the soul makes its voice heard. That simple idea is one of the most precious and fundamental insights astrology can offer into the purpose—and special skill-set—of life's first three decades.

Maybe in college, Johnny's language changes. He no longer speaks of wanting to be a movie star; instead, he describes himself as an actor. It's essentially the same idea—but his perspective is updated, along with his advancing maturation. He enjoys acting; he has discovered that he has some talent there. Becoming "rich and famous" like a movie star still appeals to him—but he also recognizes that it might not happen. He is accepting of that. He has begun to find a path through life that might feed his soul a diet richer than mere money and glamour.

    * Note the way the dream-track and the reality-track are approaching each other. Note also the way the dream-track is *actively informing* the nature of the reality-track: right there, we see the core logic of the first Saturn cycle. From birth to age twenty-nine, it is the dream that guides the evolving psyche.

As the first Saturn return approaches, the strictures reality imposes upon the dreams get tighter and tighter. Perhaps after college, Johnny finds himself making a living as a waiter in Los Angeles. Perhaps he has had a few crowd-scene parts in movies. Maybe he has a lead in a play in some *boho* converted warehouse downtown. There is no money in it, but that doesn't matter much to him: he is acting, and that is what counts.

Perhaps eventually Johnny lands a role in a deodorant commercial— and it pays him thirty thousand dollars.

Ask any aspiring actor waiting on tables: that is a happy day.

I am thinking of all of those three-year-olds in China learning to speak perfect Chinese. Similarly, in life's first Saturn cycle, *our minds are optimized for something like a long vision quest.* For that process to succeed, the capacity to dream must be cut loose from the fetters of practical reality. It must enjoy some "youthful unrealism." It must be free to soar—and to explore wild possibilities. No matter if we are unrealistic or impractical. No matter if our dreams are too grand. The aim is simply to let the soul speak in its own natural language—the language it learned in its luminous, multidimensional home beyond the veils of this world.

There is a special circle in hell for older people who try to clip the wings of their children's dreams. Their intentions might be good, but the damage that they can potentially do to the life of another human being is incalculable.

This is the fabled *idealism of youth.* It is not only natural and psychologically inevitable; it is also a critical vitamin in the development of a healthy adult psyche.

Pity the young ones who never dreamed. They are the ones who never knew themselves.

THE FIRST SATURN RETURN

When transiting Saturn first conjuncts its natal position, the dream-track and the reality-track collide—sometimes with a loud bang. It can be a very difficult time. That difficulty is predictable, of course—as we have seen, the first Saturn return is a major spiritual initiation. The stakes are very high. Failure is possible, as is success. This is a station on the way to someone eventually attaining elderhood, with all of its powers and responsibilities.

The angels don't want any wimps getting through that door.

Maybe Johnny realizes that his part in that deodorant commercial marked the height of his fame as an actor. Reality is notoriously hard on dreams, especially the idealistic dreams of younger people. But let's say that while waiting around for yet another bit part in a crowd scene on a movie set, Johnny picked up some knowledge of lighting. Maybe he made a friend of an older man who happened to be the head lighting technician. Maybe Johnny helped out a bit. Maybe after the filming was done, he and that lighting technician stayed in touch. Maybe they drank a beer together from time to time.

Let's go further down Johnny's road by a leap and a bound. Maybe, when we tune into his life around his fortieth birthday, he has become *a lighting technician in the film industry.*

He loves his work. He does not hate Mondays.

Johnny's childhood dream guided him straight to the Saturn return initiation, and out the other end of it—which is true adulthood, or mid-life. There, at the first Saturn return, his dream collided with reality. In common with all the dreams of youth for everyone everywhere, this collision battered the dream. *But enough of Johnny's dream survived to give him a meaningful experience of mid-life.* He has come through his initiation with flying colors. He made a deal with reality; that is as good as it ever gets—and that is good enough.

If twelve-year-old Johnny—our aspiring young movie star—could look into a crystal ball and see where he would be at age forty, it would have broken his heart. That is the crowning irony of this whole Saturn initiation. *Johnny the lighting technician is happy man.* His dream has guided him to where he needs to be in life.

ENTER SYNCHRONICITY

There is more to this story —in Johnny's thirties, he is doing the lighting for a television commercial. While working on that set, he meets a boom operator with whom he spends the rest of his life. Those two souls were "destined" to meet—but people sometimes fall short of their destinies. People get lost in life, wind up being in the wrong place—and the most reliable trigger for that disaster is not following their dreams. If Johnny had not dared to trust his youthful inspiration, to major in theater, and then to head for Hollywood, he would not have been doing the lighting for that commercial.

He would not have been there to meet his true love.

THE PURPOSE AND UNIQUE SKILLS OF MID-LIFE

If the purpose of youth is dreaming, then the purpose of life's long middle lies in *making the dream come true*. This second Saturn cycle is the domain of the Earth Element, pure and simple. The whole cyclical system with Saturn can, in fact, be neatly summarized in a single sentence: *first we dream it, then we make it real, then we let it go.*

That is life in a nutshell.

There is an art to getting each one of these phases right. The dreams of youth must be bold; if they are also a bit ungrounded, no problem: the first Saturn return offers us an opportunity to fix that ungroundedness. In making our dream come true, we have to wheel and deal. Reality drives a hard bargain, always claiming its eternal *mordida*: compromise.

There is a hidden treasure in all of this: while compromise is often anathema to the young, it sits more comfortably with us after the first Saturn return. In fact, it no longer really feels very much like compromise at all. That adjustment to reality—that radical acceptance of its true, flawed nature—is one of the special Earth sign skills of mid-life.

Remember: *Johnny the lighting technician does not hate Mondays.*

We get older, moving past the first Saturn return into life's second cycle, and the room does not have to be painted red or orange anymore. Pastels work just fine. The music does not have to be so loud. Our true love does not have to be quite so perfect. As we come to accept life's imperfections, we are simultaneously becoming more comfortable with our own flaws—and with the imperfections of those whom we love.

That's another mid-life superpower.

At the first Saturn return, it is time to make our imperfect stand in this imperfect world. We are transitioning into mid-life. To call the first Saturn return a "crisis" over-dramatizes it, but it definitely gets your attention. Events that define that next three decades of life often happen right now. Bridges are burned behind us. At this passage, people often find themselves committing deeply to a relationship or to a career path. It is common to be having children, with all that they imply in terms of commitments.

Other people begin to see us differently too. At your first Saturn return, your boss, let's call her Ms. Deborah Garcia, one day spontaneously announces, "Call me Debbie." She's never offered that invitation before; the energy is changing between you. She senses it. You are becoming more equal.

Maybe your parents ask *you* for advice for the first time.

And, again for the first time, *an attractive stranger several years your junior calls you sir or ma'am.* That classic Saturn return event can be kind of a shock—but basically it is more welcome than not. In common with our general theory of Saturn, we are now *psychologically ready* to move onward to our next maturational stage.

Such comfortable acceptance of a new, more mature role is always true during any kind of Saturn time as we have seen in the previous two chapters—at least if we are making a conscious, mindful response to the transit or solar arc. Invariably, such Saturn events signal that it is time to move on in life. That "moving on" can take many forms.

With the first Saturn return specifically, the only difference is that the next stage is clearly defined: it is *mid-life.*

BEFORE AND AFTER THE FIRST SATURN RETURN

A young woman of twenty-five breaks up with her boyfriend. She says that she loves him, but her reason for leaving the relationship is that she does not feel ready yet to make a commitment as serious as marriage. The boyfriend has expressed a desire for a family; the young woman has not yet decided if motherhood is for her or not.

Unless you happen to be the boyfriend, you probably have no problem accepting this young woman's choice. She is still fairly young, still in her first Saturn cycle; much of life lies ahead of her, unformed and unimagined. Let her live for a while; let her *dream* for a while; that is how she will find out who she is. Saturn has still not conjuncted itself; she still needs space to imagine her future.

Before she can live it, there is no choice but to dream it. That is the way it is and the way it needs to be, before the first Saturn return.

What about *after* the first Saturn return? Passing this astrological marker changes everything. Here is an example. A woman of forty-five leaves her husband of six years. Her reason is exactly the same as the younger woman's: she does not feel ready to make a commitment as serious as marriage. This is the second time she has "learned" this lesson; she married fifteen years ago and had a baby. The baby now lives with dad.

Not to get up on a high horse and start judging people, but I think it is fair to say that we would form a less charitable interpretation of the second woman than we did of the first one.

What is the difference?

In literal terms, it is only mathematical: twenty years.

But in the juxtaposition of these two images, we trigger our intuitive understanding of how the pan-human logic of the first Saturn cycle contrasts with the pan-human logic of the second Saturn cycle. The first Saturn return itself is what divides them. It is the border, and once we cross it, the only way to go back involves reincarnation. Everything changes. *What is the natural freedom to dream in the first cycle emerges as irresponsibility and immaturity in the second cycle.* What looks like courage in youth often looks like cowardice in mid-life.

Without changing a syllable, youth's wisdom can turn to folly after the first Saturn return.

In a word, as Saturn returns to its natal place, we begin to realize that *this is really it*—this is my real life. We may still use the phrase "when I grow up"—but when we use it now, we are smiling.

It is time to make your best deal, time to make your stand.

If you have dreamed boldly for the first three decades of your life, those dreams will have guided you well—probably better than you realize. Live with your "best deal" for a while and you will come to appreciate that it is an unexpected treasure.

A SUBURBAN BARBECUE

It is a summer Saturday night in the suburbs. A group of people are chattering around the barbecue pit, cocktails in their hands. Their ages range from thirty to fifty; they are normal, middle-class types, pretty much straight out of any shopping mall. As we tune in, they are reminiscing about their college days. If we listen carefully, we might note a characteristic mix of nostalgia and bitterness.

One of them says, "When I was a sophomore, my roommates and I would pool our fortunes and by the biggest bottle of cheap wine we could find. Then we would sit around talking about how blockheaded everyone in authority was, and how obvious all the solutions to the world's problems were."

Everyone is smiling and nodding their heads; they all remember those days very well themselves.

Then the speaker comes to his punchline: *"I was nineteen years old and I was going to save the world. Now I am forty, and I pray to God that I can save my ass."*

They all laugh; they all feel grown-up—wise and sophisticated regarding the realities of life.

Underlying the speaker's punchline is another declaration, this one left unspoken because it is so painful: *"I used to dream, but now I only cope."*

And underlying that unspoken line is another one: *I failed my first Saturn return.* I let reality win. I didn't even put up a fight. I either had no dream at all—or I abandoned the one that I had.

One thing about life in the modern, industrialized world: if you have no dream and nothing to inspire you, if you are willing to become a drone, to live a life that has no meaning to you at all, *someone will pay you a reasonably comfortable salary to do it.* That is how all those people wound up around that suburban barbecue pit.

I am aware that what I just wrote is an oversimplification; there are social inequities about which we do need to be mindful. But fundamentally, if we are not bothered and burdened by a dream, we do tend to be very employable.

PHYSICAL AGEING

Get a group of people together in their late teens or twenties. Guess their ages, one at a time. I bet that you will do quite well. I doubt that you would often be wrong by more than a couple of years.

Try the same thing with a group of people ranging in age from thirty-five to sixty. Guaranteed, your guesses will include some big mistakes.

As we move on in life, attitude and energy begin to interact powerfully with the aging process. People who are chronically bored or always sad tend to look older than people who are enthusiastically engaged with daily existence. I cannot help but think of the proverb, "*When you are old, you will have the face you deserve.*" Call it cruel, but remember—Saturn is about the law of consequences. It is not a *mean* planet, it simply gives us *exactly what we have earned*: Grant Lewi's "cosmic paycheck.."

Justice, rather than mercy, is Saturn's *forte*.

In youth, we are all offered a bountiful gift: it is the power to discern a future path through life that will continue to give us a compelling reason to get out of bed in the morning, even when we are in our forties or fifties and beyond. The gift might come to us wrapped in unrealistic youthful fantasies. It might initially even suggest to us that we will grow up and become Batman or at least a movie star.

If we take it literally, we eventually crash headlong into the brick wall of reality.

But if we live with that dream, following its "slender threads," letting it whisper in our ears whenever we come to forks in the road during the first thirty years of life, *that dream works like a lighthouse on a stormy night.* Following its beam until we come to our first Saturn return, the ship of our days arrives at the safe harbor of a meaningful path through life's long middle.

That is a treasure that the human soul takes almost thirty years to construct. *That guiding dream is the great masterpiece of youth.* Remember those three-year-olds in China learning to speak perfect Chinese—in both cases, *no one over thirty has any idea any longer how to work this miracle.*

Do you remember how you learned to speak English? Do you remember how you learned to walk?

For a while, the human mind is optimized for this particular great work. The saddest thing in the world is for someone to squander this chance.

And the second-saddest thing in this world is for someone who has dreamed such a dream to abandon it at the crossroads of the first Saturn return. In true Saturn fashion—true Earth Family fashion—that is the moment when the dream must make its stand. This is how we enter mid-life with some sense of inspiration and higher purpose intact. This is how we make a meaningful stand in the world.

We all understand intuitively how powerfully the experiences of infancy impact the adult personality. If we are held and loved and cherished in the first year of life, we are off on a good foot for the rest of the journey. The first Saturn return parallels infancy in many ways, except that it marks the *infancy of mid-life*. During that year or so, you set the tone for everything that follows.

If mid-life is the movie, the first Saturn return is the trailer. All the seeds of what lies ahead germinate then. We begin to live out the dream we have dreamed in our youth— or at least enough of it that we don't hate Mondays.

Before we know it, thirty years have gone by, and we are facing . . .

THE SECOND SATURN RETURN

As the second Saturn return looms, we see our sixtieth birthday on the horizon. Since we weren't born yesterday, we know that our friends are stockpiling those rubber pants, dead flowers, and fake Viagra prescriptions. We are getting braced emotionally for all of that buffoonery, but we already sense that the wind in our sails is shifting direction.

Right now, we are just fifty-nine—no big deal, unless we are trying to blow out that many candles on our birthday cake. Fifty-nine is one of those birthdays that can slip by without much fanfare. Nobody even notices it unless other people feel the need to make a fuss. By then, you have had a lot of birthdays.

Actually, however, we are at that very moment in the midst of an extraordinary psychic transformation—and by the time we are opening those gag gifts, it will be all over. Strange to say, but psychically we all "turn sixty" when we are fifty-nine. The math sounds funny, but that is the way it works. For obvious round-number reasons, the epochal psychic process of transformation represented by the second Saturn return is encoded in our culture as "turning sixty."

When I sit with the client in her second Saturn return, I often glance at the exact date of the first contact between transiting Saturn and natal Saturn, then I announce that on that date there will be one brief nanosecond of time in which she will be *the world's youngest old lady*.

The line always gets a laugh—and the laugh serves a helpful purpose. Obviously, "entering the cycle of the elder" is not something that happens in any meaningful way on a single day. The process is far more multidimensional and complicated than that. The second Saturn return is merely a marker, telling us that we have crossed an important line in life—and that from now on, rules that used to work for us are not going to work so well any longer.

The mind itself is becoming something radically different from what it has been for the past three decades. All the old bets are off. Fresh "unique skills" are arising; the mind is now optimized for different processes—ones that people in mid-life might not readily be able to imagine.

MY PASSION FOR MADNESS

I have been a professional astrologer for my entire adult life. When I was younger, that often entailed working with clients older than myself. In other words, I had spent many years counseling people about "turning sixty" long before I had any direct personal experience of it. As my own turn approached, I found myself hoping that what I had been telling everybody actually had some truth in it. When I got into my own second Saturn return, I was relieved to realize that the counsel I had been offering others actually worked pretty well for me too.

But of course I also learned something new—something I had not fully understood until I went through this second Saturn return *initiation into elderhood* on my own. The new understanding came to me in the form of a phrase that kept repeating of its own accord in my mind: *my passion for madness is diminishing.* Now, a few years down the line, I realize that this simple sentence takes us to the heart of the matter with the second Saturn return—and, just as with the first Saturn return, the event itself only lasts for a year or so, but it sets the tone for the three decades that follow. It too is the trailer for the movie.

So what makes us feel crazy?

Everyone has his or her own list, but here is a pretty good guess about three items that are almost guaranteed to make your Top Ten: *sex, money, and power.*

Let's take them one at a time in the light of the second Saturn return, starting with sex.

Scene #1: You are in your twenties and you fall in love. Your expectations of your beloved and the magic that he or she will bring into your life are probably so high that they almost constitute cruelty. Who could ever live up to those romantic expectations?

Scene #2: You are single in your sixties, tempered by life experience. Again, you fall in love. If I say that "your expectations are now lower," a younger person might entirely miss the point of those words. She or he might imagine that your heart had been so battered over the years that you were afraid to get your hopes up again. But that is the polar opposite of the truth: *in your sixties, you no longer expect that other person to automatically give meaning to your life.* You are simply happy to have the creature comforts and the companionship—the solace of a good friend, warts and all. *As you have learned to forgive yourself for your own faults, you are much more forgiving towards your new partner.* That is why "your expectations are lower." *Translation*: your expectations are more realistic, more forgiving, and ultimately more compassionate.

Your passion for what made you crazy forty years earlier is much diminished. Sex—in the broad, human sense of that word—is still compelling for you. But it will not knock you off your even keel the way it did when you were younger.

Everything is clearer now. You are less crazy than you were.

What about *money?* That stuff makes people crazy too.

Imagine that a lazy, but profoundly heterosexual bartender with a penchant for cocaine wins $138 million in a lottery when he is twenty-seven years old. How would that giant influx of cash interact with his insecurities and his appetites? Can you confidently guarantee that the money would make him happier?

How could there possibly be a problem?

I doubt that anyone with enough brains to be reading this book would hesitate for one moment in answering that question.

Now let's imagine a man in his middle sixties. He has done well with his first two Saturn cycles; he has created a life that is meaningful to him. Let's say he has a stable relationship, maybe some grown kids launched on their own lives. He wins that $138 million. What happens? *He buys a few toys and a few experiences for himself and his partner. His favorite charities benefit; he helps out his children.*

The point is that, unlike our young bartender, all that money cannot knock him off the solid foundation of the life he has built. Perhaps not that much actually changes. Maybe the money does actually enhance his happiness.

When we enter the third Saturn cycle, money is probably still a pivotal force in our lives; that does not necessarily change. But the *power of money to make us crazy* is much diminished.

There we again see our key principle: our passion for madness has less hold on our lives.

What about *power*? (Or we could say "reputation" or "what other people think of us.") It is all really the same thing.)

Your face appears on the cover of a national magazine when you are in your twenties. Everyone is really impressed with you. That is a lot of ego-adrenaline. If the same thing happens when you are older, that dose of fame probably feels more like it is about your work, not about you yourself. You are happy—but you are far less likely to let that magazine cover go to your head.

You are bumped up to First Class on an airline flight. You find yourself sitting next to a popular film star, whom you recognize immediately. It's a long flight; the two of you get to talking. The relationship feels natural; you like each other. You stay in touch. Pretty soon, you are "close personal friends with—(*fill in the blank*.). Some of his or her *star-status* rubs off on you. Maybe *paparazzi* photograph you together and the picture gets in that national magazine.

How might that big boost in your worldly "coolness factor" go to your head when you were twenty-five? And what would it mean when you were seventy?

Feel the difference?

Again, that increase in power, status, or coolness simply *does not have the power to beguile you* that it had when you were younger. That kind of "shine" has lost some of its hold on you; your passion for that ancient madness has now diminished.

You are beginning to pack your bags for another world; the tempting power of the treasures of this world are rapidly diminishing.

WISDOM AND OBSCURATIONS

In Buddhism, there is a mysterious paradox. On one hand, we are told that the Buddha-nature is simply intrinsic to consciousness. Everyone has it, even ants and monkeys have it. Relax. You do not need to develop it; you were born with it.

On the other hand, we are told that a human birth is a precious opportunity, not to be wasted. We are exhorted to make serious spiritual effort at all times, not to squander a minute.

So which one is true—that we are *already there* or that we need to *struggle to get there?*

The Dharma teaching is that, even though we are truly already there, that *obscurations* prevent us from knowing it. In other words, there is "dirty Vaseline" on the window pane between your conscious mind and your deepest nature.

And what is the nature of those obscurations?

Well, here are three of them that are almost certain to make your Top Ten: sex, money, and power.

Sound familiar?

This is why, as our passion for madness diminishes at the second Saturn return, we see the rising of the fabled *wisdom of old age.* That is one of the "superpowers" that arise in life's third cycle, and really only then. This is why we always like our wizards to be old. Like the Buddha nature, this wisdom was there inside you all along, but it was having a hard time shining through the seductive, life-sucking, madness-inducing power of your attachments—your fears, your insecurities, your angers, and your desires. With the second Saturn return, their hold on you loosens. You calm down. You don't sweat the small stuff so much anymore. You worry less. The mosquito-buzz of your ego fades.

The cobra of your own craziness loses some of its ability to hypnotize you.

A REMEDY FOR THE FEAR OF AGEING

The world teaches us to fear ageing, and there is no way to separate an awareness of ageing from the second Saturn return nor the cycle that follows. You turn sixty, and somebody welcomes you to your "golden years"— and as soon as you hear a loaded phrase like that one, you immediately smell a con artist trying to sell you snake-oil. Instantly you are convinced that he is trying to foist something unto you that you really do not want.

Entering the cycle of the elder? Let's cut to the chase and call it what it is: *getting old.*

What can you expect? What does this next chapter of your life promise?

Ask almost anyone on the streets of this world: *infirmities, weakness, and wrinkles. Different pairs of glasses for every situation. Hearing aids—assuming you still want to hear anything, that is. Needing to pee all the time. Kiss trying to look sexy goodbye or you will look like a joke. Welcome to the world of the clueless. Welcome to a world of machines you do not understand. Welcome to blank looks when you mention song lyrics or any of the pop-stars of your youth. Welcome to being tragically unhip, presumably useless—and definitely abysmally boring to anyone under fifty.*

Hey, what's not to like?

All that is the conventional, consensual picture of aging. It is totally fear-based. Clearly, if that is what they are selling, none of us are buying. The only pro-ageing argument that seems to hold any water at all is that tired old chestnut: *if you do not like aging, just consider the alternative.*

OK, so death would be worse. Probably.

Earlier, we promised a remedy for the fear of ageing. Here it comes.

Remember that diminished passion for everything that made you crazy? That leads us directly to a second question: *has being crazy ever made you happier*—I mean, in the long run?

And once you have answered that question, we start to get the picture:

* *If the things that have made you unhappy in the past now have less hold over you, it seems that the third Saturn cycle promises the potential of being the happiest time in your life.*

I know that sounds strangely counterintuitive, but there is considerable logic in it. I actually do not think it is so much counter to intuition as it is counter to cultural expectations.

As we contemplate life's third Saturn cycle, half the work lies in clearing our path of all the social detritus that blinds us to the truths of the human heart.

I remember a night in my twenties, the result of which was that I could not drink tequila again for about five years. It was fun, and I don't really regret the memory—but it was not the sanest evening of my life. In speaking of increased happiness in connection with Saturn's third cycle, I am not talking about our capacity for wild flights of ecstasy. I suspect our ability to ride those particular Dionysian waves reaches a kind of crescendo sometime late in Saturn's first cycle—in our late twenties, in other words.

Here, with the third Saturn cycle, I am talking about happiness in its purest form: *a peaceful feeling of fulfillment, ease, and contentment.* Those "obscurations" really make it a lot harder to get there—but after the second Saturn return, many of those self-imposed blockages to well-being simply go poof. We don't fall for their tricks quite so easily.

And so, here it is once again: reason and self-observation dictate that the third Saturn cycle promises the potential of being the happiest time in your life.

Someone might counter this line of reasoning by referring to *health challenges* that almost inevitably arise at some point in the ageing process.

Fair enough; illness can definitely suck the joy out of existence.

Without becoming too doctrinaire or simple-minded about any of this, I think it is worth saying that if we have taken care of our souls through the two previous Saturn cycles, that the resultant health of the soul has a supportive influence upon the health of the body. Simply said, *a meaningful life gives you a reason to live, and that is good for your health.*

I want to be careful here though—shaming anyone for being sick is not my intention. But I do think that as we enter life's third cycle, the best health insurance in the world is that we have made a strong response to the basic evolutionary directives of our birth chart. That far-reaching spiritual success boosts your immune response and helps keep your heart ticking and your blood pressure down.

But there is more to it, maybe something even deeper. Our very attitude toward mortality goes through a seismic shift at the second Saturn return. Here is an illustration: a doctor gives a thirty-eight-year-old woman bad medical news: she has six months left to live. She takes it hard. Who wouldn't, especially at that age, with—theoretically—so much life still ahead of us?

Move the exact same scenario three decades forward. The woman is now sixty-eight; she has lived well, following the evolutionary thread of her chart. Again, a doctor gives her six months to live. Again, naturally, the news hits her hard—*but not quite as hard as it would have thirty years earlier.* We all know what comes at the end of our physical life. As we move into the third cycle of life, we do not necessarily become morbid, constantly dwelling on death. But with a kind of fierce gentleness, death is whispering in our ears. We become more accepting of it, less afraid. We sense where we are in the ancient rhythm of life.

Something changes in us as we enter this third cycle of life; compared to younger people, even death loses some of its power to spook us. Let's not exaggerate that change, but let's not ignore it either. There is something deep, ancient, and wise inside of us all, something resident in every cell of your body, that knows and accepts the natural rhythms of life—that it is good to be born, and that, at some point, it is also good to die. As our madness diminishes, we sense that wisdom more clearly. We hear those angels calling us . . .

That is another one of the Elder's superpowers: *the emerging ability to laugh at death's feebleness.*

Talk about a solid foundation for happiness.

GRANDMA, WILL YOU TEACH ME HOW TO KNIT?

You know the scene: nine-year-old Gretchen is fascinated as a beautiful sweater emerges from grandma's balls of yarn. Inevitably, she asks grandma if she can try it herself.

Realistically speaking, trying to teach a nine-year-old how to knit comes with a 97.3% probability of total catastrophe. Grandma knows that—but she is happy to try anyway.

She also knows it is not really about knitting at all.

As the old teach the young, something truly magical is happening. Far more is being passed along than physical skills or information.

Grandpa, will you teach me how to fish? Little Justin, seven years old, is mesmerized by the spinning reels, rods, and colorful lures in grandpa's basement lair. Very likely, grandpa is going to wind up with tangled lines— and perhaps with a crying little boy who has managed to get a sharp hook poked into his finger—and everybody will be mad at grandpa about it.

But of course he eagerly agrees to teach Justin how to fish.

Grandpa knows, just like grandma, that it is not really about fishing at all.

That grandparents generally seem to have an *exaggerated* love for their grandchildren is a common observation. That is a beautiful thing, but here is our question: what is actually exaggerating that love? What is the nature of the inflating force? Of course there are naturally some exceptions— maybe grandpa is a real grump. But the pattern is generally quite unmistakable, to the point that it has become a cliché.

Because of its sweetness, along with all of the benign benefits it provides beleaguered parents, we tend not to look this particular gift horse too closely in the mouth. But let's do that—and I promise that careful scrutiny of the symbiosis of grandparents and grandchildren will not diminish its sweetness in the slightest.

The simple fact that grandparents generally love their grandchildren is not really our entry point here; that kind of family love arises naturally enough and does not require much explanation. Where we get to the heart of the matter is with the *exaggerated* quality of this love. On the surface, Gretchen and Justin are getting all the benefit. But might there be a flow in the other direction? Might those two children be feeding energy back into the mind-body-spirit systems of their grandparents?

Here is a way to understand that backflow.

* Much of the joy of life's third cycle derives from generosity.
* What we have created during the second cycle of life, we begin to give away in the third cycle. *And it makes us feel really happy to do that.*

Teach us to knit and fish—and who has the bigger smile, the grandparents or the grandkids? That act of generosity—*that act of passing something along to those whom we will soon leave behind*—is as beneficial to the elder as it is to the younger person who is actually receiving the gifts.

This is why grandma and grandpa can't seem to get enough of the grandkids. But the principle extends to much farther horizons. Many people have no children and thus no literal grandkids. No problem. *This symbiosis is not just about grandparents; it is about the ancient bond between true elders and everyone younger than themselves.*

A sixty-five-year-old businessman liquidates an asset. The taxman is salivating. Our businessman knows about a savvy offshore investment possibility, one that would beat the taxes and double his money in five years.

But his heart is just not in it. As he reflects, he comes to a decision: he is going to use that money to endow a scholarship in his own name at his *alma mater*. Sitting with the idea, he realizes that he feels really good about it. At this stage of the businessman's life, *generosity provides more joy than acquisition*. He is not a saint, nor does he need to be. But he is now in life's third Saturn cycle—which is much more than the cycle of the grandparent. And he is doing fine with it.

We might speculate a little further. The fact that our businessman is doing well with the third cycle of life very probably rests on the foundation of successful "dreaming" when he was young and subsequently his success at "making it all real" in the middle Saturn cycle. Maybe his money came from a business that he "dreamed up" when he was younger. Maybe that business paid him a lot more than money. Maybe he left a mark on his community. Maybe he married his secretary and lived happily ever after.

That is how it works. The youthful dream, if we are brave enough to follow its slender threads, brings us to a mid-life in which we don't hate Mondays. And then, in life's third cycle, we take joy in passing along something of what life has given us.

* A seventy-year-old master craftsman—a guitar-maker, let's say—has always been paranoid about people stealing his professional secrets. *But now he decides to take on an apprentice and teach him everything he knows.*
* A sixty-eight-year-old psychotherapist, wise and experienced, realizes that it is time for her to finally write the book she has been thinking about for twenty-five years. *She wants to gift the world with what she has learned before she packs her bags for another world entirely.*

In each of these vignettes, we see the highest expression of the third Saturn cycle: *generosity in action*. In each case, the elder is passing something along to those who will follow, each one defining the gift according to what he or she has *accumulated* over the years.

* The businessman has accumulated *money*, so that is what he gives away—and that is what gives him joy.
* The guitar-maker has accumulated *skill*—and he passes those skills on to his apprentice.
* The psychotherapist has accumulated *wisdom*—and here comes her book, soon to be available to one and all, even long after she is gone.

Meanwhile, years ago, grandma learned how to knit and grandpa learned how to fish. Perhaps Gretchen and Justin now actually learn those particular skills from them. There is real satisfaction in that. But of course so much more is going on here. An *understanding of life* is being passed along. So are family traditions and memories.

Who is happier, the kids or the grandparents?

That is probably not a question that we need to answer.

GETTING IT WRONG: THE CURMUDGEON

What if, after sixty years in this world, *we have nothing to give?* We blew the dreaming and we blew the "making it real." At best, we can only now serve as bad examples.

In this sad condition, we can see how the stilts are knocked out from underneath any possibility of real happiness in the third cycle of life. *No one wants what we are giving—in fact, they are probably afraid they will catch whatever soul-disease we have.* Anyone could understand the inherent sadness in that situation, but it becomes more tragic when we think of that grandparent-grandchild symbiosis. For people in Saturn's third cycle, a significant support for their sense of wellbeing lies in feeling appreciated and valued for what they can offer to those younger than themselves. If the younger ones "aren't buying," what happens? The old madnesses—sex, money, and power— are not delivering the way they used to deliver. Picasso once said: "One starts to get young at the age of sixty, and then it's too late." It doesn't really have to be that way, but sometimes it is.

If what I am saying is true, then one result would be *an epidemic of geriatric depression.* Just think of all of those failed elders, hearts still beating, but with nothing much left to live for—no basis for that life-sustaining generosity.

Quod erat demonstrandum, as our Latin buddies were once fond of saying.

Old age, as is commonly observed, is not for sissies. This point so powerfully demonstrates the fingerprints of the planet Saturn: psychologically and spiritually, we then get exactly what we deserve.

Of all the gifts an elder might possibly give, the one that most benefits both the elder and the recipient is the gift of wisdom. True enough—but remember our businessman, endowing his *alma mater* with funds for a scholarship? He made it onto our "good list" too.

We might easily imagine a scenario where an older person in fact has money to give, if not much else. With the right attitude, that transaction can be fine and meaningful, and a real support to a sense of engagement, aliveness, and purpose for that elder during life's third Saturn cycle. Let's honor the philanthropists of the world, in other words—and let's be careful not to shame anyone simply for making money.

But then another, darker vision looms: affluent wastrels and materialists in the family, all waiting impatiently for their inheritance, aiming death-vibes at grandma and grandpa. We have all seen family systems in which young jackals are circling what they hope to soon become a carcass—hardly an occasion of happiness for our curmudgeon, however prosperous he or she might be.

Being generous financially can be a real source of satisfaction for older people. But if *money is the only thing for which they are valued,* the situation speaks for itself.

SATURN AS THE GRANDFATHER OF THE EARTH FAMILY

Remember the "grand scheme" of the Earth signs that we introduced at the beginning of the book? In a nutshell, the Taurean "sense of smell" determines the nature of Capricorn's "mountain"—and before we can climb it, we need to acquire some Virgo skills and teachers.

Note how those core understandings of the interdependency of the three Earth signs underlie the three Saturn cycles as well. Each is the mirror of the other.

* Everything that we learned about the purpose of Taurus—the first Earth sign—earlier in these pages also applies perfectly to the first Saturn cycle: to know "which mountain to climb" requires the cultivation of an intuitive attunement to something trans-rational. Call that Taurus or call it youth; it is pretty much the same thing either way.

* We follow this same pattern unerringly as the second Saturn cycle unfolds—mid-life, with its distinctly Virgoan experiences of duty, skill, and responsibility.

* Then comes the third Saturn cycle with its very Capricornian reality of Elderhood.

THE THIRD SATURN RETURN

In our eighty-ninth year, Saturn once again returns to its starting point. Many of us live long enough nowadays to experience this once relatively-rare phenomenon.

What can it mean? In the historical past, certain individuals sometimes lived to ripe old ages, just as happens today. But the vast majority of people did not last that long—which means that, in terms of collective social mythology, the third Saturn return is still mostly *terra incognita*. Current generations are collectively mapping it in widespread fashion for the first time, even though others have dipped their toes into the territory in past aeons.

There are deep waters here—but the nature of the diving board is pretty obvious. By the time we are approaching ninety, not much life lies ahead—at least not in our present physical bodies.

Death is the true teacher here.

Fundamentally, at the third Saturn return, we directly face the *mystery of mortality*. Even if we are still strong and healthy, many of the peers whom we have loved and with whom we have shared our lives are now gone. If we are psychically sensitive, we probably feel their ghostly presence—we might even sense them "calling us to the other side," not necessarily in a spooky way, but only in the way that love always calls us.

It is not unusual that as we enter our nineties, we find ourselves living a somewhat ghost-like existence for physical reasons—half in this world, half in the next. It does not have to be that way, but it often is. Ask any wise nonagenarian about his or her greatest fear, and you are much more likely to hear the word "dementia" than the word "death."

We need to be careful in our thinking here, wary of the materialist delusions that pervade the modern worldview. After the third Saturn return, the veil that separates the worlds indeed often grows thin. Some people, in this fourth Saturn cycle of life, begin to drift between this dimension and the next one. Medicine has given scary names—dementia, Alzheimer's, senility—to these conditions.

Once we recognize that consciousness is not the same as the brain, all this becomes less frightening. The energy of the mind itself cannot be destroyed, but it can wander in realms far removed from this material world.

As with the previous cycles, in this fourth Saturn cycle, fresh wisdom and skills are arising: again, as with the previous Saturn returns, we now develop a new *superpower*. We begin to realize at a direct and visceral level that there is life beyond the physical body. We can "drift between this dimension and the next one" more intentionally and consciously—and still return to focus in this physical realm. Let's call that process *meditation*—and let's state the obvious: meditation is different from dementia. But let's make that distinction without falling into the trap of confusing the mind and the brain. Some of those "dementia patients" are also actually in a state of deep meditation. They too are transitioning into the next world, but just doing it a little more slowly than many of us.

Here, at this frontier, consciousness is now optimized for a new task. A new superpower is arising. Let's call it the *art of dying.* At this time, a kind of magnetic fascination with our impending journey begins to arise naturally in us.

For someone in the fourth Saturn cycle, that magnetic fascination is a great comfort; the fear of death loses most of its power. Something vast is beckoning us. But that sweet beckoning comes with a heavy price tag: it is almost impossible to explain it to anyone younger than ourselves.

And that means almost everyone

AFTERWORD

TELLING TALES . . .

*L*ooks bad for the good guys, but here comes the hero to save the day . . .
Have you ever heard that tale before? Easy question; humans have
been telling each other that same yarn since the beginning of our time
on earth. You find it thousands of years ago in *Beowulf* and in the epic of
Gilgamesh—and somewhat more recently you might have detected it in
Star Wars.

How's about *boy meets girl*? That tale has had a long run in the human
world too. (And please translate "boy meets girl" into whatever orientation
works for you.) Shakespeare's *Much Ado About Nothing* puts a happy, comic
spin on the familiar narrative, while his *Romeo and Juliet* shows the other
side of the coin, as does the film, *Titanic*.

The possible variants on boy meets girl are endless—what about the
movie, *Fatal Attraction*? The story can turn edgy, in other words. In the
classic romantic comedy, *Love, Actually*, we see its sweet face. In *When
Harry Met Sally*, we laugh until tears run down our cheeks.

What about Humphrey Bogart and Lauren Bacall in *To Have and
Have Not*? The sexual electricity they portrayed turned out to be the real
deal—and that erotic undercurrent is always part of the boy meets girl
narrative too.

With only a few totally trivial tweaks, we can turn the story into boy
meets boy. *Brokeback Mountain*, anyone?

Humans love this stuff.

Toss a question into any random crowd: *anyone in the mood for some boredom?* Tedium, anyone? A little endless repetition of the same old same old?

Of course there will be no takers. No one likes to be bored..

Or say we say.

But these stories that we love to tell and hear are always basically the same. And we have been telling them to each other since our species developed a larynx with working vocal cords. We never tire of them.

Reality check: anyone who feels like refuting my last few lines has a pretty obvious path forward: *wait a minute, those stories are in fact all very different from one another.* And that is true too: each one of them is wonderful in its own special fashion; each one makes a different point, illuminating our common humanity in a distinct and original way.

Fair enough—in the interests of world peace, the mediation committee has agreed on the final wording of the official communique: *these tales are all the same, only different.*

Meanwhile, a long time ago, in a galaxy far, far away . . . the galaxy we call "astrology" actually—exactly the same phenomenon we see unfolding in these stories is also happening with the planets and signs. "Looks bad for the good guys, but here comes the hero" is a *solar archetype*—and like any archetype, the story can manifest concretely in a virtually infinite number of ways.

We can say exactly the same thing about Virgo (*master and apprentice*) or Saturn (*the wise old wizard to the rescue*), or any of the other astrological symbols. They too represent *basic, coherent ideas that exist in some transcendent realm*, and which, as they come into actual worldly manifestation, can take many forms.

Our mediation committee agrees: the tales astrology tells are all "the same, only different."

Illustration: Capricorn, as we have learned earlier in these pages, is the sign of Great Works; people born under that sign—at least the ones who respond to it in a conscious way—are "fascinated by what is difficult." They devote their lives to manifesting a vision, no matter how hard it is to accomplish that goal or how many sacrifices it might require.

J.R.R. Tolkien was a Capricorn, and his Great Work was writing *The Lord of the Rings*—and, by the way, in that story, while it looked pretty bad at first for the good guys, along came Frodo Baggins, Gandalf, Aragorn and the rest of the gang to save the day.

Martin Luther King was a Capricorn too—and again we see a man faced with a very difficult mountain to climb. His mountain was, however, of a totally different nature than Tolkien's. Writing a thousand pages of luminous narrative is a noble expression of Capricorn energy—but the "orcs" that Rev. King faced were less fanciful. In the end, one of them actually got him.

What about Stephen Hawking, Johannes Kepler and Isaac Newton? All three were Capricorns—and all three accomplished great, difficult works, this time in the realm of science.

Are these biographies all the same story? Or are they all different? Probably the best answer is "yes."

No matter which Elemental family we are exploring, this is how astrology always works: *something that exists as an incomprehensibly vast field of potential in some transcendent, multidimensional realm faces the task of squeezing itself down to such small proportions that it can fit into a limited, time-bound, three-dimensional realm—the very realm that we call home.*

In that process of compression, nearly everything that could possibly exist within that vast archetypal field must be stripped away. Constrained by "the flesh"—that is to say, by hours, minutes, and three dimensions—there is only room for one thing to happen. All the other possibilities must hang back, ghost-like, in some subtle background quantum realm.

How many conceivable "boy-meets-girl" stories can there be? "Infinite" is a dangerous word to use, but it is tempting to invoke the term here. Suffice to say that humans have been "meeting each other," forming couples, for a very long time now, and the story has never been told in exactly the same way twice.

Here is an astrological translation of that observation: how many people in the history of the world have experienced either progressed Venus conjunct their Sun or the progressed Sun conjunct Venus? Either one of those aspects correlates rather reliably with important intimate encounters. *(Remembering that these two planets can never be more than 47° apart, so the answer to our question is "almost everyone.")*

The current best guess is that there have been something like one hundred billion of us on the earth since the beginning of human time. A hundred billion such stories, each one unique—and each one an expression of the same Venusian archetype.

Behind the world we see, there is another world, far vaster—and far closer in its nature to what we might call Ultimate Truth.

Those twenty-four words, by the way, provide a succinct definition of the term, "metaphysics". Long ago, the humans who truly put the "sapiens" in *homo sapiens* realized that we cannot explain life to ourselves very well while simultaneously maintaining the belief that the world that we see is all that exists.

"Metaphysics" literally means "beyond physics"—which is to say, beyond that which we conventionally take to be "reality." Ghosts, dreams, inexplicable coincidences, miracle cures, sudden insights, goosebumps in graveyards—it is not as if there is a lack of evidence for realms that lie beyond the reach of quantitative measurement.

Some people put a whole lot of faith in that famously greasy word, "reality." They tend to roll their eyes when they hear lines like my last ones, thinking that "beyond reality" there is simply nothing at all. These people are, in essence, the same ones who rolled their eyes at the first person who suggested that earth might be round rather than flat. They are the ones who laughed at Sigmund Freud when he posited the existence of the unconscious mind. They laughed at Albert Einstein when he wondered out loud if an hour might not always take an hour, or that one mile might not always be of the same length as other miles.

The truth is, physics is just a subset of metaphysics.

Local rules, that's all.

Over two millennia ago, Plato gave us the "allegory of the cave"—chained men see shadows projected onto the stone walls of the cavern. Since those shadows are all that they have ever seen, they believe that they are looking at reality.

But what is generating those shadows? What lies behind the appearances?

Once we began to sense as a species that there might be more to this universe than what we could actually see, hear, and smell, metaphysics was born. It is still a work in progress.

But right from the beginning, clues about its nature began to emerge in the form of repetitive, underlying *patterns* in our daily experience. Those are our stories.

Glug met Flug and one thing led to the next—but, wait a minute, *hadn't we heard that tale somewhere before?*

Things looked truly dismal for the Bazeebi tribe, but then along came Kaboobi the Great. But hey—didn't almost exactly that same thing happen when Great-Hearted Ranaboloni saved the Nazingas from the cruel tyranny of the N'galoofa people?

Why do the Bazeebis have the same myth as the Nazingas? Who stole it from who?

Legends and mythologies arose out of this archetypal, metaphysical background—and they are still emerging, and will always emerge. As a species, we remember these basic templates of experience and treasure them—and part of our stewardship of these legends and mythologies is to constantly re-create them. Thus did T*he Epic of Gilgamesh* become *Star Wars*.

More crucially, we can distill the specifics of each story into the elixir of wisdom. That is to say, slowly, by piecing together the clues we saw in this world, we began to map a world beyond this one.

Then, one day, long ago, some unsung genius remembered that blood-red Mars had just risen when "Kaboobi the Great" was born. A light bulb lit: perhaps the *Story-behind-all-the-stories* was encoded in the sky above us.

The idea made sense; when we think of a transcendent realm, it feels only natural to look up into the heavens. The metaphor could hardly be more obvious.

And astrology was born.

* We have the kaleidoscopic, chaotic, unpredictable diversity of daily life.
* Behind daily life, there are some basic strands of DNA—these fundamental story-patterns of Love and Heroism that we began to recognize. They are still very diverse—just not nearly as diverse and confusing as daily life.
* And behind and beyond those archetypal story-patterns, there was something far simpler and clearer—something that contained and transcended them all: planets dancing and weaving through the

night sky, telling these exact same stories, but now in the language
of the angels.
* We astrologers are the descendants of the men and women who
resolved to learn to speak and understand that mysterious tongue
that angels speak.

The great poet, Robert Bly, said it best: "Astrology is the great intellectual triumph of the mother civilization." We who practice this ancient
art do ourselves a good deed by remembering to occasionally stand back
from what we do, and just remember to say, "wow." In so doing, we refresh
and humble our own hearts, and we also honor the genius of our forgotten
ancestors—the original metaphysicians—who first figured out what was
really going on behind the appearances of this world. Like the chained humans in Plato's cave, they first figured out that what they were seeing was
only shadow-play. Then they looked up to the heavens and slowly began to
divine what was casting those shadows.

So far, in these few paragraphs, we've been storming heaven: starting
here on earth, with our individual stories and trying to use them as clues
about the higher realms. Turning all of this on its head, let's descend from
the heavens and come down to earth.

Planets form their mysterious patterns. Implicit in those patterns are
countless possible stories—or to say it another way, countless possibilities
regarding *how you might respond* to those planetary patterns.

All of those tales exist latently in the archetypal realm; anything that
can possibly exist here visibly on the theatrical stage of this world already
exists "up there" in the heavens.

*But out of those numberless possibilities, only one of them will actually
happen.*

I think of it like one of those six-page menus in a Chinese restaurant.
Potentially there are a hundred meals that you might choose to eat. But
soon the wait-person comes along and asks for your order. Out of all those
possibilities, only one of them is actually going to manifest on your plate.
What determines whether you will have the Kung Pao chicken or the Tofu
in Garlic Sauce? The answer does not come from the menu; it comes from
you. It is your life—and your meal.

That is exactly how astrology works. *Astrology is the menu itself, not the response you will make to it.*

Say that transiting Saturn is opposing your natal Venus. Along comes the cosmic waiter with the usual question: *so would you like the dumb choice or smart one?* Or something in between? And how spicy would you like it?

This is one reason why using astrology to try to predict what anyone will actually *do* is so futile. It is as if I were to hand you a menu, then expect you to use it to predict what the next customer to come through the door is actually going to order. You can't do that, of course. All we really know is that the customer will have to choose *something* from the menu. No one gets lasagna at a Chinese restaurant—and no one gets an all-expense-paid beach vacation out of a hard Saturn transit.

When it comes to specific predictions, we can only set some boundaries around the possibilities, in other words. Beyond that, everything else is some combination of guesswork, probabilities, and common sense.

Such is the power—and potentially, the dignity—of human freedom. I celebrate our ability to prove fatalistic astrologers wrong.

This volume of the Elements series has been a long meditation on the Earth family of astrological symbols. As you may recall, the title of the first chapter was "Making It Real." Those three simple words capture the underlying evolutionary purpose of these three signs and their attendant planets and houses. Each one of them plays a part in the endless process of converting visions and dreams into physical, biographical facts—which is to say, each one determines the *actual stories* we tell with our lives . . . stories that unerringly and honestly reveal the natures and true conditions of our souls.

In the last few pages, we have been talking about higher orders of reality. As one example, we invoked that archetypal "boy-meets-girl" realm out of which all intimate or romantic human narratives arise, whatever our gender orientation. To even conceive of that higher realm, we had to "look skyward"—which is to say, that we had to direct our awareness toward a higher octave of the universe, the place where all of those "movies" originate.

Then we realized that we are capable of looking even higher, beyond those archetypal stories of heroes and lovers, into an even simpler, higher, and purer realm where all the archetypes are stripped down to their bones. As astrologers, it is our privilege and our joy to contemplate that realm. That is our craft. That higher realm is the realm of the planets.

What if we look even higher? What lies beyond astrology?

No doubt there are good answers to that question too. All of them begin to sound like religion: beyond the realm of astrology, we encounter the Divine, God, Heaven, the *dharmakaya*, Cosmic Oneness, and so forth.

Close your eyes, empty your mind, and you can go there too. It is not so mysterious or alien. Just like Saturn, Venus, and Mercury, that transcendent realm is part of you. Ask the Earth signs: this monkey-body you inhabit is a terrific vehicle, but you are not quite that simple—or anywhere near that young.

In the layer-cake, hierarchical, structure that is the true nature of the universe, the Earth element is the one that lies closest to our own human neighborhood. In ascending order above us—and above the Earth element—we find the realms of Water, Fire, and then Air.

It would be a terrible error to imagine the Earth Family to be somehow inferior to the other three; that is not the point at all. As we saw back in chapter one, flesh is not worse than spirit—flesh is instead best understood as a *manifestation* of spirit. Flesh—or, more broadly, the Earth element—is simply how all of the more etheric, metaphysical layers of the cosmic layer cake make contact with our five senses.

The lowest note on the piano is not morally inferior to the highest note. The northern hemisphere is not more spiritually advanced than the southern hemisphere.

Were there no Earth element, we would therefore be cut off from divinity. It is our connection to the higher realms. Without it, there would be no road up and no road down—no road by which Divinity could descend, in other words. There would be no magic and no miracles. There would be nothing to feed and drive human imagination—hence, no art and no inspiration. Love would be a transaction of flesh alone. There would be no holy books, because they too, despite their flaws, are one way that the higher realms have left a trail of breadcrumbs for us to follow upward—homeward.

Spirit ascends—and spirit descends: two pathways, both as precious as breathing in and breathing out again.

Only a fool would fail to celebrate both of those sacred gifts.

The Book of Earth has been about spirit descending, about how "the Word becomes flesh", about the ancient sacrament of making our dreams come true —and putting our karma on the table where we can see it clearly and deal with it day by day and hour by hour.

In the next volume of this series, we will ascend to the realm of astrological symbolism that lies closest to "God, Heaven, the dharmakaya, and so forth . . ." We will soar into those lofty realms in *The Book of Air*—and maybe return to earth with a map or two.

See you then.

Steven Forrest
Borrego Springs, California
May 2019

LEARN ASTROLOGY WITH STEVEN FORREST

Interested in learning more about Steven's unique approach to astrology? For a listing of lectures and workshops that are available in a variety of audio and video formats, go to: **http://www.forrestastrology.com/store**.

Better yet, join the many successful students who have completed Steven's Astrological Apprenticeship Program, where he teaches both the specific techniques of interpretation and the style of presentation that have made him one of the most successful and influential astrologers in the world. Steven takes great joy in passing on the teachings and strategies that have worked for him over the years through his Apprenticeship Program.

The Apprenticeship Program presents students with a rare opportunity to learn astrology in a supportive environment of like-minded individuals, who together create a feeling of community and connection, leading to bonds that last throughout life. Some come to the program to train professionally, while others come for personal or spiritual enrichment.

Learn more at www.forrestastrology.com

Printed in Great Britain
by Amazon

48701927R00234